M000018896

BURIED
HOPE
or RISEN
SAVIOR?

EDITED BY CHARLES L. QUARLES

BURIED
HOPE
or RISEN
SAVIOR?

THE SEARCH FOR THE JESUS TOMB

ACADEMIC

NASHVILLE, TENNESSEE

Copyright © 2008
by Charles L. Quarles
All rights reserved

Printed in the United States of America

978-0-8054-4717-0

Published by B&H Publishing Group
Nashville, Tennessee

Dewey Decimal Classification: 232.97
Subject Heading: Apologetics/Jesus Christ—Resurrection

Translations of Scripture quotations are identified by acronym as
follows: HCSB are taken from the *Holman Christian Standard Bible*®
Copyright © 1999, 2000, 2002, 2004 by Holman Bible Publishers.
Used by permission. NASB, the *New American Standard Bible*, ©
the Lockman Foundation, 1960, 1962, 1963, 1968, 1971, 1972, 1973,
1975, 1977, 1995; used by permission. NIV, *The Holy Bible, New
International Version,* copyright © 1973, 1978, 1984 by International
Bible Society. RSV, the *Revised Standard Version of the Bible* copyright
1946, 1952, © 1971, 1973 by the National Council of the Churches
of Christ in the U.S.A. and used by permission. AMP, the Amplified®
Bible,⊠ Copyright © 1954, 1958, 1962, 1964, 1965, 1987 by The Lockman Foundation⊠. Used by permission (www.Lockman.org).

1 2 3 4 5 6 7 8 9 10 11 12 • 16 15 14 13 12 11 10 09 08
VP

CONTENTS

PREFACE

On the day the news broke that archaeologists had "discovered" the bones of Jesus in an ossuary in East Talpiot, a concerned Christian leader dropped by my office, looked at me across my desk, and asked, "What are we going to do?" My first reaction was, "What do you mean *we*?" I was already overwhelmed with deadlines on book projects. The last thing that I needed was another project.

Over the next few days I began to feel that maybe *we* had to do something after all. I encountered one Christian after another who was deeply troubled by the dramatic announcement. I obtained a copy of *The Jesus Family Tomb* on the day it was released and wrote a twelve-page response that was posted on my college Web site a few days before *The Lost Tomb of Jesus* documentary aired and then later on Darrell Bock's blog. I did so for two reasons. First, as a scholar I was disturbed that the public was being misled by absurd claims. Second, as a follower of Christ, I felt compelled to "contend earnestly for the faith" (Jude 3 NASB). A few days later one of my colleagues received an e-mail from a friend who had considered renouncing Christianity due to the claims of *The Lost Tomb of Jesus* documentary. After reading my article, he had seen the fallacies in the claims of the book, and his faith was renewed. Encouraged by his testimony, I began to think of producing a more extensive response that would be more widely read. When *The Jesus Family Tomb* book shot up to number 6 on the *New York Times* best-seller list a few weeks later, I knew that the claims had to be addressed.

I quickly realized that no single scholar possessed the wide range of expertise necessary to address the claims of *The Jesus Family Tomb*. I am a New Testament scholar who specializes in Gospel study and historical Jesus research, but I am not an archaeologist and certainly not a statistician. I began putting together a dream team of evangelical scholars including an archaeologist, a statistician, an expert on Jewish ossuaries, and New Testament and historical Jesus scholars so that each major claim of the hypothesis could be addressed by a true expert in that respective field. Richard Bauckham, Darrell Bock, William Dembski, Craig Evans, Gary Habermas, Mike Licona, Robert Marks, and Steven Ortiz committed to the project. The end result is *Buried Hope or Risen Savior? The Search for Jesus' Tomb*, the most comprehensive scholarly response to the Talpiot hypothesis to date.

This book could not have been produced without the assistance of many people. The president of Louisiana College, Joe W. Aguillard, saw the relevance of this project and released me from many of my administrative duties so that I could devote my time to building this team and editing these essays. This action entailed considerable personal sacrifice since a decreased administrative load for me meant an increased administrative load for him. Despite the extra burden that this project imposed on him, he has constantly encouraged me at every step of the project. I am continually baffled by his kind and Christlike spirit and deeply grateful for his ardent support of biblical scholarship. This book is appropriately dedicated to him.

Ray Clendenen, director of Academic Publishing at B&H, recognized the importance of the project and worked to hasten the approval process for the book so that the response could be timely. Throughout the project he has offered sound advice on a number of questions that have strengthened the book considerably. The editorial skills of Terry Wilder have immensely improved this volume and have doubtless spared the team from several embarrassing errors. My administrative assistant, Susan Middleton, worked tirelessly in contacting writers, distributing research materials, and proofing the book. Brandon Robin assisted me in gathering information about the Discovery Channel documentary and the Ted Koppel special. Terry Martin, director of the Richard W. Norton Memorial Library at Louisiana College, assisted by quickly acquiring rare works on ossuaries, the tombs of Jerusalem, and name frequencies. Jeff Griffin, director of libraries at New Orleans Baptist Theological Seminary, was immensely helpful in researching estimates of the Jewish population of Palestine in the ossuary period.

Finally, my wife Julie and my children Rachael, Hannah, and Joshua encouraged me with their love, support, and interest in this project. A gentle knock at my office door is normally a prelude to a warm smile, a hot cup of coffee, and a kind word that brightens my day after long hours at the computer spent on this and other projects. They wait patiently at the table while I type "just a few more words" before beginning supper. Julie carefully protects me from interruptions so I can concentrate on my work. They all make sure that I pause from time to time to laugh, relax, and "smell the roses." I thank God for a family that brings me so much happiness.

The title of this book reminds Christians of what is at stake with the claims of the Talpiot tomb hypothesis. If the Talpiot tomb is the tomb of Jesus of Nazareth, then Jesus is not our risen Savior. Our hope for divine forgiveness through Christ and future resurrection are nothing more than a "buried hope," a hope that died when Jesus breathed His last breath, a hope that was buried along with His bones in a sloppily inscribed ossuary in East Talpiot. Our outlook is as grim as that of the Emmaus disciples who had not yet recognized the risen Christ who walked beside them and lamented, "We *were hoping* that He was the One who was about to redeem Israel" (Luke 24:21). If Christ has not risen, this hope is now a thing of the past, and, as Paul wrote, "We should be pitied more than anyone" (1 Cor 15:19). For this reason, the subtitle of *The Jesus Family Tomb,* which claims that the Talpiot discovery, investigation, and evidence "could change history," is no exaggeration. If true, the claims of Jacobovici and Pellegrino would drastically change history by destroying one of the world's major religions, the very religion that formed the foundation of Western culture.

If its claims were convincing, *The Jesus Family Tomb* could constitute the death certificate of Christianity. But it won't. Jacobovici and Pellegrino are simply not qualified coroners. They are more like little children who scream "Mommy is dead!" because they see her lying down with her eyes closed even though she is really only napping. The arguments of Jacobovici and Pellegrino are filled with similar leaps in logic that bypass important evidence that a qualified coroner would never overlook. A close examination of all the evidence will lead those concerned by the children's screams to end the panicked 911 call abruptly: "Sorry. False alarm. The Christian faith is alive and well after all."

This book presents that necessary examination of the crucial evidence. It responds in detail to the most compelling arguments raised by the makers of the Discovery documentary and the authors of *The Jesus*

Family Tomb. It demonstrates that the evidence for Jesus' bodily resurrection is much, much stronger than the evidence for the interment of Jesus' bones in Talpiot. I believe that if you read this book with an open mind, you will conclude: Make no bones about it; the bones of Jesus of Nazareth were not interred in an ossuary in East Talpiot. He has risen!

Charles L. Quarles
Vice President for Integration of Faith and Learning
Professor of New Testament and Greek
Chair, Division of Christian Studies
Louisiana College
Pineville, Louisiana

INTRODUCTION

Charles L. Quarles

THE DRAMATIC ANNOUNCEMENT

On February 25, 2007, a newswire announced a press conference to be held in New York City at 11:00 AM on February 26 in which bone boxes believed to have belonged to Jesus of Nazareth and Mary Magdalene would be dramatically unveiled.[1] The press release advertised a documentary titled *The Lost Tomb of Jesus* that would air on Sunday, March 4, on the Discovery Channel. The documentary was produced by James Cameron, the award-winning director of the film *Titanic*, and was directed by Simcha Jacobovici, the popular host of the History Channel's *Naked Archaeologist*. The release also contained a brief mention of a book written by Jacobovici and Charles Pellegrino titled *The Jesus Family Tomb*, which would be released by HarperSanFrancisco on February 28.

The next day reporters from all over the world flocked to the main branch of the New York Public Library for the conference. Perhaps inspired by the Academy Awards from the night before, Oscar-winning filmmaker James Cameron and Emmy award-winning director Simcha Jacobovici put on a show that would make P. T. Barnum green with envy. Cameron began the session with an announcement of the remarkable discovery after which security guards lifted crushed black velvet sheets to unveil two ossuaries that dazzled viewers as they reflected the brilliant lights of the television cameras.[2]

1 http://www.prnewswire.com/cgi-bin/stories.pl?ACCT=104&STORY=/www/story/02–25–2007/0004533934 &EDATE

2 In fact the original discovery occurred nearly three decades earlier (1980) and had been published in several scholarly and popular resources. Furthermore, in 1996 the British

James Tabor, chair of the Department of Religious Studies at the University of North Carolina in Charlotte and author of *The Jesus Dynasty: The Hidden History of Jesus, His Royal Family, and the Birth of Christianity*, and Charles Pellegrino, coauthor of *The Jesus Family Tomb*, joined Cameron and Jacobovici in explaining the significance of the ossuaries. They argued that the original archaeological team that had excavated the tomb in Talpiot where the ten ossuaries were found dismissed the significance of the ossuary with the inscription "Jesus, son of Joseph" because of the popularity of the names Joseph and Jesus in Palestine in the ossuary period. The mistake of the original team was that they failed to consider the names in the other ossuary inscriptions in the group which were associated with Jesus in the New Testament Gospels. The ossuaries purportedly bear such inscriptions as "Jesus, son of Joseph," "Judah, son of Jesus," "Matthew," "Mary the master," "Mary," and "Jose" (a diminutive form of Joseph). Jacobovici argued that "Mary the master" was Mary Magdalene, the wife of Jesus, and that this point was confirmed by DNA analysis. "Jose" was a brother of Jesus mentioned in the Gospel of Mark. "Mary" was the mother of Jesus. The investigators also claimed that a new method called "patina fingerprinting" demonstrated that the controversial James ossuary bearing the inscription "James, son of Joseph, brother of Jesus" was stolen from the Talpiot tomb. Tabor compared the likelihood of finding this pool of names in a single tomb to the likelihood of finding the names George, John, Paul, and Ringo in closely connected tombs in Liverpool. Just as the pool of names in the Liverpool tomb would suggest that the men buried there were Beatles, the pool of names from the Talpiot tomb strongly suggested that this was the family tomb of Jesus.

The only dissenting voice from the platform during the press conference was that of Shimon Gibson, a senior fellow of the Albright Institute of Archaeological Research in Israel and a member of the original team responsible for the 1980 excavation of the Talpiot tomb. Gibson gave a detailed description of the archaeological find. He added that, although he was attempting to keep an open mind, he was skeptical about the claim that this tomb was the family tomb of Jesus of Nazareth.

filmmakers Ray Bruce and Chris Mann had produced a program similar to *The Lost Tomb of Jesus* for BBC/CTVC.

THE EARLY DEBATE

Even before the documentary aired or *The Jesus Family Tomb* book was released, there was a strong reaction to the claims made in the press conference. On the evening of the press conference, Larry King interviewed Simcha Jacobovici, James Cameron, James Tabor, Al Mohler Jr., president of the Southern Baptist Theological Seminary, and William Donohue, president of the Catholic League, on the subject of the lost tomb.[3] Jacobovici and Cameron admitted that they had not really made a new discovery. They had simply "connected the dots" or seen associations between the inscriptions on the ossuaries that had been previously overlooked. Jacobovici claimed that DNA analysis of residue left from the bones in the ossuaries belonging to Jesus and Mariamne proved that the persons interred in the ossuaries did not share the same mother. Since both persons were interred in the same family tomb, they were most likely husband and wife.

Ben Wedemann reported from the tomb site in Jerusalem. He stated that most Israeli archaeologists whom he had interviewed were highly skeptical of the claim that the Talpiot tomb was the tomb of Jesus. Among these scholars was Amos Kloner, the archaeologist who published the first detailed study of the Talpiot tomb. Al Mohler argued that the skepticism of the archaeological community should give the public pause about accepting the claims of the documentary. Jacobovoci insisted that some prominent archaeologists were open to the possibility that the Talpiot tomb was the tomb of the Jesus of the Gospels. As an example he mentioned Shimon Gibson, one of the original members of the excavation team and the same archaeologist who expressed his skepticism about the claims of the documentary earlier at the press conference.

Jacobovici argued that a proper understanding of the significance of the tomb required the integration of several fields, including both archaeology and statistics. He noted that archaeologists had assumed that the popularity of the names that appeared in the tomb was so great that the combination of names associated with Jesus of Nazareth was probably little more than an interesting coincidence. However, when he consulted statisticians, he found that the combination of names in the tomb was very unusual. He claimed that statisticians had calculated that the odds

---

3 Transcript of *Larry King Live,* "The Lost Tomb of Jesus," n.p. [cited 4 April 2007]. Online: http://transcripts.cnn.com/TRANSCRIPTS/0702/26/lkl.01.html.

were 2 million to 1 that the tomb belonged to Jesus of Nazareth. He cited Andrey Feuerverger, professor of statistics at the University of Toronto, as arriving at the most conservative estimate. He calculated that the odds were 600 to 1 in favor of identifying the tomb as that of the Jesus of the Gospels. Mohler acknowledged that the statistical argument was the most interesting argument raised by the team. He argued, however, that the DNA analysis was not helpful since a number of family relationships other than that of husband and wife were possible for two members of the same family who did not share the same mother.

Mohler also argued that certain features of the discovery did not fit with the identification of the Jesus of the ossuary with Jesus of Nazareth: "And then there are some rather really far-fetched claims. I mean, after all, you're talking about a poor, peasant family from Nazareth with an ancestral heritage in Bethlehem. There's no logical reason why their bones should end up in a middle class tomb in Jerusalem." Cameron replied, "But they were a religious movement with a very large followership. And they would have had the resources in later years to have a tomb at least as substantial as what we found."

Donohue particularly challenged Jacobovici on the claim that the James ossuary was the tenth ossuary missing from the Talpiot tomb collection. Donohue exclaimed:

> Fifteen experts in Israel looked at this and they said it was a monumental fraud. You have had guys from Tel Aviv University and from Harvard who say it's a fraud. You're quoted in today's *Newsweek* as saying you still believe it. How in the world could I have any credibility with you at this point?

Jacobovici replied that the jury was literally still out regarding the claims related to the James ossuary. This comment referred to the trial of Oded Golan, owner of the James ossuary, who was on trial for forgery. Donohue responded: "I'm simply saying that the Israel Antiquity Association voted 15–0 that it was a monumental fraud." In a brief sparring session with Cameron, Donohue argued that the 2 million dollar documentary *The Lost Tomb of Jesus* was actually "science fiction" similar to Cameron's upcoming film *Avatar*. When King asked Cameron if he actually believed that the claims of the documentary were true, Cameron replied, "So the short answer is, yes, provisionally, based on what we

4

know right now, I think that this is compelling. New evidence can come in tomorrow that refutes it. But right now, we are not there."

King probed the significance of the claims of *The Lost Tomb of Jesus* by asking Jacobovici, "Is this the end of the Easter bunny?" Jacobovici explained that he was not a theologian and was not qualified to evaluate the theological implications of the discovery. Mohler was less hesitant to share his opinion: "The one true thing that we have to affirm here is that if it ever could be proved that Jesus Christ did not rise from the dead, if the resurrection was a fraud, then Christianity falls."

THE INITIAL RESPONSE OF THE
ARCHAEOLOGICAL COMMUNITY

The February 26 edition of the *Jerusalem Post* quoted snippets of an interview with Amos Kloner, Jerusalem District archaeologist who led the original Talpiot excavation. Kloner dismissed the documentary's claims as "impossible" and "nonsense."[4]

On February 27, the *Jerusalem Post* published a transcription of the interview with Kloner.[5] When asked to evaluate the claims of the documentary, Kloner stated:

> It makes a great story for a TV film. But it's completely impossible. It's nonsense. There is no likelihood that Jesus and his relatives had a family tomb. They were a Galilee family with no ties in Jerusalem. The Talpiot tomb belonged to a middle class family from the 1st century CE.

When challenged with the unexpected confluence of names associated with Jesus of Nazareth, Kloner replied:

> The name "Jesus son of Joseph" has been found on three or four ossuaries. These are common names. There were huge headlines in the 1940s surrounding

---

4 *Jerusalem Post* staff, "Jesus, Magdalene and son in Talpiot tomb," n.p. [cited 4 April 2007]. Online: http://www.jpost.com/servlet/Satellite?pagename=JPost%2FJPArticle%2FShowFull&cid=1171894518254.
5 David Horovitz, "A Great Story but Nonsense," n.p. [cited 4 April 2007]. Online: http://www.jpost.com/servlet/Satellite?cid=1171894527185&pagename=JPost%2FJPArticle%2FShowFull.

another Jesus ossuary, cited as the first evidence of Christianity. There was another Jesus tomb. Months later it was dismissed. Give me scientific evidence, and I'll grapple with it. But this is manufactured.

Kloner strongly reacted to the claim that the tenth ossuary had disappeared from his care and was, in fact, the James ossuary:

> Nothing has disappeared. The 10th ossuary was on my list. The measurements were not the same (as the James ossuary). It was plain (without an inscription). We had no room under our roofs for all the ossuaries, so unmarked ones were sometimes kept in the courtyard (of the Rockefeller Museum).

Perhaps the most blistering criticisms of the project came from archaeologist Joe Zias, who was the curator for anthropology and archaeology at the Rockefeller Museum in Jerusalem from 1972 to 1997 and personally numbered the Talpiot ossuaries. He quipped: "Simcha has no credibility whatsoever. . . . He's pimping off the Bible. . . . Projects like these make a mockery of the archaeological profession."[6] Zias also posted a more extensive document on his personal Web site criticizing the program.[7]

Since most scholars felt that brief newspaper interviews did not afford the opportunity to provide the reasoned response that the claims in the press conference required, they expressed their objections to the claims through essays on Web sites or entries in respected blogs. Jodi Magness, the Kenan Distinguished Professor for Teaching Excellence in Early Judaism in the Department of Religious Studies at the University of North Carolina at Chapel Hill, published an essay titled "Has the Tomb of Jesus Been Discovered? A reasoned look at the evidence, instead of a media circus, yields an answer of NO!" on the Web site of the Archaeological Institute of America. She objected to introducing the public to these claims without first allowing scholars to examine and debate them. Magness wrote:

6 Lisa Miller and Joanna Chen, "Raiders of the Lost Tomb," *Newsweek*, 5 March 2007, 60–62, esp. 61.
7 Joe Zias, "Deconstructing the Second and Hopefully Last Coming of Simcha and the BAR Crowd," n.p. [cited June 24, 2007]. Online: http://www.joezias.com/tomb.html.

First let me point out that by making this announcement in the popular media, Jacobovici, Cameron, and
the others involved have chosen to circumvent the usual
academic process. Archaeology is a scientific discipline. New discoveries and interpretations typically
are presented in scientific venues such as professional
meetings or are published in peer-reviewed journals,
where they can be considered and discussed by other
specialists. By first making the announcement in the
popular media, those involved have precluded legiti-
mate and vital academic discourse. This is because it
is impossible to explain the many flaws of their claim
in a one-minute segment on TV or the radio, or in two
or three sentences in the newspaper, as I have been
asked to do repeatedly since the announcement was
made. The history and archaeology of Jerusalem in the
first century are far too complex to be boiled down to
a short sound bite, yet that is precisely what has happened here. This is a travesty to professional archaeologists and scholars of early Judaism and Christianity,
and it is a disservice to the public.[8]

Magness pointed out that archaeologists had known of the Talpiot
tomb since its discovery nearly three decades earlier. However, all but
a handful of scholars were confident that the Talpiot tomb was not the
tomb of Jesus of Nazareth. The Gospel accounts make clear that Jesus'
body disappeared from the rock-cut tomb owned by Joseph of Arimathea.
Magness argued that if the disciples of Jesus stole his body as early oppo-
nents of Christianity claimed, they would have buried Jesus in a trench
grave dug into the earth since Jesus' family could not have afforded even
a modest rock-cut tomb. Furthermore, if Jesus' family owned a rock-
cut tomb in Jerusalem, Jesus' body would have been interred there in
the first place rather than in the tomb of Joseph of Arimathea. Magness
argued that if Jesus' body were given a second burial by His disciples, as
Jacobovici claimed, the disciples would have dug a rectangular trench in

---

8 Jodi Magness, "Has the Tomb of Jesus Been Discovered? A reasoned look at the evidence, instead of a media circus, yields an answer of NO!" n.p. [cited 4 May 2007]. Online:
http://www.archaeological.org/ webinfo.php?page=10408.

the earth, placed Jesus' enshrouded body in the grave, and then marked the grave with a crude headstone. Magness insisted that ossuaries were associated only with rock-cut tombs, never with trench graves. Thus, one would not expect to find an ossuary of Jesus of Nazareth even if one dismissed the Gospel claims of Jesus' resurrection. Magness also argued that since Jesus' family had no known connections to Jerusalem, His body would likely have been buried in Galilee along with other family members rather than in Jerusalem. The archaeologist concluded:

> The identification of the Talpiyot tomb as the tomb of Jesus and his family contradicts the canonical Gospel accounts of the death and burial of Jesus and the earliest Christian traditions about Jesus. This claim is also inconsistent with all of the available information—historical and archaeological—about how Jews in the time of Jesus buried their dead, and specifically the evidence we have about poor, non-Judean families like that of Jesus. It is a sensationalistic claim without any scientific basis or support.[9]

THE LOST TOMB OF JESUS

The highly publicized documentary aired as scheduled on March 4. The film opened with a dramatic reenactment of Jesus' crucifixion and burial that did not even hint that Jesus' earliest disciples claimed that he had risen from the dead. It referred instead to the rumor preserved in Matthew that Jesus' body was removed from the tomb of Joseph and secretly reburied in an undisclosed location, a rumor that the narrator admitted was denied by the Gospels themselves.

9 Ibid. Magness received a Ph.D. in classical archaeology from the University of Pennsylvania and a B.A. in archaeology and history from the Hebrew University of Jerusalem. She has participated in numerous excavations in both Israel and Greece. She currently directs excavations in the Roman fort at Yotvata, Israel. Her publications include an award-winning book, *The Archaeology of Qumran and the Dead Sea Scrolls* (Grand Rapids: Eerdmans, 2002), and an article, "Ossuaries and the Burials of Jesus and James," *Journal of Biblical Literature* 124 (2005): 121–54. A revised version of her response to the claims of Jacobovici et al. appears in a special forum on the Web site of the Society for Biblical Literature: Jodi Magness, "Has the Tomb of Jesus Been Discovered?" n.p. [cited 4 April 2007]. Online: http://www.sbl-site.org/Article.aspx?ArticleId=640.

Introduction

The film recounted the accidental discovery of the Talpiot tomb in South Jerusalem by construction workers on March 28, 1980. Due to pressure from the construction company to complete the excavation as soon as possible, the team of archaeologists from the Department of Antiquities (now the Israel Antiquities Authority) had only three days for the excavation. The book *The Jesus Family Tomb* stressed that this excavation was "salvage archaeology" and strongly implied that the excavation was rushed, and inadequate, and that the discovery was not properly protected.[10] After excavation the ossuaries were catalogued and taken to the Rockefeller Museum. At the request of orthodox Jewish rabbis, the bones from the ossuaries were boxed for reburial.

The film next focused on the inscriptions on the Talpiot ossuaries. Tal Ilan stated that these words were not "monumental inscriptions" but were simply intended to enable the family members to identify whose remains were whose. Frank Moore Cross examined the most important inscription for the claims of the film, the inscription on ossuary 80.503. He described the inscription as "informal" and "messy" but added, "I have no real doubt that this is to be read Yeshua, and then Yeshua bar Yehosef, that is Jesus, son of Joseph."[11]

The film seemed to assume automatically that the ossuary belonged to Jesus of Nazareth. The narrator posed the question: "Does it [the discovery of Jesus' bone box] fit with Christian tradition? Does it challenge certain articles of faith?" The filmmakers turned to John Dominic Crossan, cofounder of the widely publicized Jesus Seminar. Crossan has claimed that Jesus' body was left unburied and was probably eaten by dogs.[12] Crossan stated: "If the bones of Jesus were to be found in an

10 Simcha Jacobovici and Charles Pellegrino, *The Jesus Family Tomb: The Discovery, the Investigation, and the Evidence That Could Change History* (San Francisco: HarperSanFrancisco, 2007), 3–7.

11 L. Y. Rahmani's *Catalogue of Jewish Ossuaries* placed a question mark behind his transcription "Yeshua" with a note: "The first name, preceded by a large cross-mark, is difficult to read, as the incisions are clumsily carved and badly scratched." See L. Y. Rahmani, *A Catalogue of Jewish Ossuaries in the Collections of the State of Israel* (Jerusalem: The Israel Antiquities Authority, 1994), no. 704. Similarly, the research of Amos Kloner, a member of the original excavation team, expressed his reservations about the name Yeshua by marking it with a question mark and noting, "The first name following the X mark is difficult to read. In contrast to other ossuaries in this tomb, the incisions are here superficial and cursorily carved." See Amos Kloner, "A Tomb with Inscribed Ossuaries in East Talpiyot, Jerusalem," *Atiquot* 29 (1996): 15–22, esp. 18.

12 John Dominic Crossan, *Historical Jesus: The Life of a Mediterranean Jewish Peasant* (New York: HarperCollins, 1991), 392; idem, *Jesus: A Revolutionary Biography* (San

ossuary in Jerusalem tomorrow and without doubt let's say they are definitely agreed to be the bones of Jesus, would that destroy Christian faith? It certainly would not destroy my Christian faith. I leave what happens to bodies up to God."

The narrator followed up Crossan's comment by promoting the idea that Jesus' resurrection and ascension were spiritual rather than physical in nature. He further claimed that the notion of a spiritual resurrection and ascension is consistent with Christian faith: "In fact, those who take a strictly historical approach to the Gospels would expect to find Jesus' remains in his family tomb." The segment concluded with an interview of James Tabor, author of the book *The Jesus Dynasty*, who ridiculed the historic Christian view of resurrection as a body magically disappearing and appearing in heaven.[13] He insisted that, if one wants to be "historical" and "realistic," this view could not be accepted.

The film then turned its attention to the other ossuary inscriptions from the Talpiot tomb. Na'ama Vilozny, assistant curator of the Israel Museum, claimed that the Mariah inscription on ossuary 80.505 was rare despite the fact that the name itself is the most common name for Palestinian Jewish women during the period: "One of the rare examples of that name on an ossuary in Israel." *The Jesus Family Tomb* further claims that the inscription is a Hebrew transliteration of a latinized form of the name Mary and that it was this latinized form by which Mary mother of Jesus was commonly known in the early church.[14]

The film discussed the inscription "Matia" or "Matthew" on ossuary 80.502. The narrator initially entertained the possibility that this might be the apostle Matthew, the author of the New Testament Gospel that bears the same name. However, since it would be highly unlikely for a disciple who had no familial relationship to Jesus to be buried in the family tomb, the filmmakers speculated that this Matthew was probably another member of Jesus' family. James Tabor claimed that Mary's genealogy in Luke

Francisco: HarperSanFrancisco, 1994), 123–26. Crossan is aware of some of the problems with this theory. See his *Who Killed Jesus? Exploring the Roots of Anti-Semitism in the Gospel Story of the Death of Jesus* (San Francisco: HarperSanFrancisco, 1995), 163–69.

13 James Tabor, *The Jesus Dynasty: The Hidden History of Jesus, His Royal Family, and the Birth of Christianity* (New York: Simon and Schuster, 2007).

14 Jacobovici and Pellegrino, *The Jesus Family Tomb*, 75. The authors admit that a similar inscription was found in the "Tomb of the Shroud" by James Tabor and Shimon Gibson. They claim that Mary, mother of Jesus, was distinguished from Mary Magdalene in the Acts of Philip and other apocryphal books by use of the latinized form of her name.

3 has "5, 6, 7 or 8 Matthews," so it should be expected that Jesus would have other family members named Matthew buried in his family tomb. Tabor then observed, "Every one of these names is Gospel-related."

In a discussion of the inscription on ossuary 80.504, the narrator of the film claimed that the specific spelling of the name "Jose" that appeared in Talpiot was found on no other ossuary inscriptions. Tabor added: "Jose [is a name that] you will never hear [in modern Hebrew] and you didn't hear it in the ancient world either." Tabor claimed that the only other known occurrence of the name was in Mark 6:3, which listed the names of Jesus' brothers.

In response, Amos Kloner, Frank Moore Cross, and David Mevorah, curator of the Israel Museum, insisted that the names of Talpiot are all common names. Mevorah adamantly insisted, "We find that these names are in many other places. So suggesting that this tomb was the tomb of the family of Jesus is a far-fetched suggestion. You need to be very careful with that."

Andrey Feuerverger, a professor of statistics at the University of Toronto, argued that Kloner, Cross, Mevorah, and most scholars failed to see significance in the pool of names at Talpiot because they examined the statistical probability of the occurrence of individual names. He rebutted that scholars must instead look at all of the names in unison. He argued that it was unlikely that so many names associated with Jesus of Nazareth would all appear in the same tomb unless the tomb belonged to Jesus of Nazareth: "It really is a possibility that this particular tomb site is in fact one of a NT family. It is a possibility that I think needs to be taken seriously."

The narrator explained that in order to take that possibility seriously, as Feuerverger suggested, scholars must look for more evidence either to confirm or falsify the Talpiot hypothesis. David Mevorah and Simcha Jacobovici were shown debating the likelihood that the Talpiot tomb is the tomb of Jesus of Nazareth. Jacobovici argued that it was inconsistent for Mevorah to claim that a particular ossuary belonged to Joseph Caiaphas, the high priest who supervised the proceedings that led to Jesus' crucifixion, and yet deny that the Jesus, son of Joseph from Talpiot, was Jesus of Nazareth. Mevorah countered that strong evidence supported the identification of the Joseph Caiaphas ossuary but that this evidence was lacking with regard to the Talpiot tomb. He admitted that though the identification of the Joseph Caiaphas of the ossuary with the high priest of the Gospels was highly probable, the identification is not certain. He stated: "We never know for 100 percent in archaeology."

The narrator immediately countered: "But the experts do seem 100-percent comfortable connecting some ossuaries directly to famous names in the Gospels as long as they steer clear of the Jesus family." He appealed to the Simon of Cyrene ossuary as an example of the certitude that many scholars have in identifying names inscribed on ossuaries with biblical figures. On the Simon ossuary, Tabor claimed to find a previously unpublished chevron identical to the symbol on the entrance to the Talpiot tomb. This discovery eventually led him and the research team to the conclusion that the chevron and circle were early Christian symbols. The presence of these symbols on the entrance to the Talpiot tomb was argued to confirm the theory that the tomb belonged to Jesus of Nazareth.

The film discussed in detail the inscription on ossuary 80.500 which the team translated, "Mary also known as Mara." After a description of Mary Magdalene, the film noted that Magdalene was a title of geographical origin indicating that Mary was from Magdala. The narrator claimed that people from Magdala spoke Greek as well as Aramaic. They observed that only this ossuary had a Greek inscription. Feuerverger claimed that if the person whose bones occupied this ossuary were indeed Mary Magdalene, "it [the hypothesis that the Talpiot tomb is the tomb of Jesus of Nazareth] would be statistically compelling."

Feuerverger calculated that 1 in 190 men in first-century Jerusalem was named "Jesus, son of Joseph." One in 20 men was named Jose, a diminutive of Joseph. One in 160 women was named Mariamne. One in 4 was named Maria. Feuerverger chose not to include Matthew in his calculation since it was not clear that Jesus of Nazareth had a family member by that name. He then divided his resulting probability by four to "compensate for unintended biases" and then again by 1,000, the number of all first-century tombs in Jerusalem. Feuerverger concluded that the chances were only 1 in 600 that the tomb belonged to someone other than Jesus of Nazareth *if* the name Mariamne could be definitively linked to Mary Magdalene.

At this point the film described the "real role" of Mary Magdalene in the original Jesus movement that was suppressed in later Christianity. Tal Ilan claimed, "Mary Magdalene was the real founder of Christianity." John Dominic Crossan insisted that "Mary Magdalene was a major apostle on par with Peter at the time of the New Testament." The narrator explained that the best portrayals of Mary Magdalene appeared in the *Gospel of Mary Magdalene* and *Acts of Philip*. However, these sources had been rejected (the film shows them being gathered and burned in a manner reminiscent of descriptions in Dan Brown's novel *The DaVinci Code*) by an increasingly patriarchal church. Although the *Acts of Philip* had been lost for centuries except for a few fragments, F. Bovon had discovered a 700-year-old manuscript of the *Acts of Philip*, a document originally written in the fourth century. The *Acts of Philip* described a woman named Mary who was a sister of Philip the evangelist and who served as a Christian missionary and apostle. Bovon claimed that this Mary was to be identified as Mary Magdalene. He further pointed out that she was called Mariamne in the *Acts of Philip*. The filmmakers claimed that the Mariamne of Talpiot was likely Mary Magdalene since (1) "Mara" in Aramaic meant "master" and this was an apt description of Mary's apostolic role; (2) the name Mariamne had "never been found before or since on any other ossuary"; and (3) The *Acts of Philip* stated that Mary Magdalene went to the Jordan Valley of Israel to die and be buried and that this clearly indicated that she was buried in Jerusalem.

The film claimed that the cross scratched on the Jesus ossuary was not a mere mason mark since it did not line up with a similar mark on the lid. Instead, the cross was a Christian symbol. The film questioned the consensus view, expressed in an interview with Jerome Murphy-O'Connor, that the cross was not established as a Christian symbol until the time of Constantine. Although the cross symbol that referred to Jesus' crucifixion might not have entered use until the fourth century, the cross might have served as a Christian symbol for other reasons. The final letter of the Hebrew alphabet, which bore the same form as a cross in first-century Hebrew script, had served as a mark securing divine protection for the righteous in Ezek 9:4 and was also prominent in the claim in Rev 22:13 that Jesus was the Alpha and Omega. This Greek translation preserved an original Aramaic statement in which Jesus claimed to be the *Aleph* and the *Tav*, the beginning and the end. Jacobovici concluded that the cross was indeed a Christian symbol.[15] In Jacobovici's view the presence of this Christian

15 See the more detailed discussion in Jacobovici and Pellegrino, *The Jesus Family Tomb*, 80–81, 196–98.

symbol on the ossuary of a "Jesus, son of Joseph" seemed to confirm that the one whose bones were interred in the ossuary was none other than Jesus of Nazareth.

The research team visited the necropolis excavated by Bagatti at *Dominus Flevit* that contains the ossuary of Simon bar Jonah, who is identified by some as the apostle Peter. The team claimed that the necropolis was part of a network of tombs belonging to the early Christian movement. The team members observed that one ossuary at *Dominus Flevit* had a symbol consisting of a dot under a gable. This confirmed for them their earlier suspicion that the symbol on the entrance to the Talpiot tomb was a Christian symbol.[16]

Steven Cox, a forensic scientist, collected samples of residue from the Jesus and Mariamne ossuaries for testing by the Thunder Bay Paleo-DNA lab. The narrator explained: "If these bone samples truly do belong to Mary Magdalene and Jesus of Nazareth, we would expect the tests to show that they are not genetically related. We would expect to find DNA representing two individuals with no familial ties. And that would be an extremely rare discovery in a family tomb unless the individuals were husband and wife." Unfortunately, the lab could not recover nuclear DNA from the samples. It was, however, able to recover, amplify, clone, and sequence the mitochondrial DNA. Comparisons of the Jesus and Mariamne DNA sequences highlighted several polymorphisms or variations between the sequences that demonstrated conclusively that this Jesus and Mariamne were not maternally related and were "most likely husband and wife."[17]

The researchers claimed that the highly debated James ossuary, which bears an inscription reading, "James, son of Joseph, brother of Jesus," is indeed authentic and is in fact a missing ossuary from the Tal-

---

16 Even more imaginative is the supposed connection between the mark that adorned the tomb entrance, a chevron with a circle inscribed beneath it, and the artwork of one of Leonardo Da Vinci's disciples, Pontormo. One could almost suspect that the fictional Harvard symbologist Robert Langdon served as a consultant for this research project. Such arguments strain credulity. When the researchers finally toss in the Knights Templar, their secret rituals, and the skull and crossbones of the Jolly Roger, one can be certain that the book belongs on the fiction aisle along with the latest Dan Brown thriller rather than beside serious works of history. See Jacobovici and Pellegrino, *The Jesus Family Tomb*, 124–34.

17 This claim involves a huge assumption. The DNA evidence is consistent with a number of other possible family relationships. For example, Mariamne could have been a half sister, sister-in-law, cousin, or aunt from the father's side, rather than the wife of the Jesus of the ossuary.

piot tomb. The researchers claimed that only 9 of the 10 ossuaries of Talpiot were actually delivered to the Rockefeller Museum. Tabor claimed
to have compared the dimensions of the James ossuary and the missing
but catalogued tenth ossuary and stated: "The dimensions of the ossuary
are the same!" He admitted that the Israel Antiquities Authority ruled
that the original inscription was "James, son of Joseph" and that the
words "brother of Jesus" were a later forgery. But he suggested that the
evidence supported the claim that the James ossuary was from the Tomb
of the Ten Ossuaries. He stated, "We are speculating but the time is right,
the name is right, and that I think would make it fairly clear that this is
the Jesus family." Feuerverger said that if the James ossuary were indeed
from Talpiot, the statistical argument identifying the tomb with that of
Jesus of Nazareth would be "an absolute slam dunk!"

The researchers submitted the James ossuary and Mariamne ossuary
to a test that they called "patina fingerprinting." They analyzed the chemical composition of the patina for the two ossuaries and compared these
to random samples. Of the ossuaries analyzed, the Mariamne ossuary
and the James ossuary had the most similar patina. Pelegrino exclaimed,
"The signature is the same! It matches!" In response to this new evidence, Feuerverger changed his more conservative probability from 1 in
600 to 1 in 30,000.

Finally, the film discussed ossuary 80.501. The inscription on the
ossuary reads, "Judah, son of Jesus." Based on the assumption that Jesus
was married to Mary Magdalene, the narrator claimed: "The NT doesn't
say that Jesus had a son. But perhaps in this instance, archaeology forces
us to throw a different light on the NT." The silence of the New Testament regarding the existence of a son of Jesus could be easily explained.
Since Jesus died a criminal's death, had claimed to be a king, and his
son would be born of this royal bloodline, Judas's existence would have
been kept a secret for his own protection from the Roman authorities.
The book and the film both speculate: "Perhaps the unnamed Beloved
Disciple referred to in the Book of John is actually the son of Jesus who
remains unnamed in the text to conceal the child's lineage." Although
John 19:6 has been traditionally interpreted as Jesus' words to Mary his
mother and the apostle John, the film suggested that Jesus was actually
addressing Mary Magdalene and Judas and cryptically urging Mary to

protect their son.[18] On the other hand, the narrator admitted that the presence of a son in the tomb might preclude the tomb from belonging to Jesus of Nazareth.

The film ended with officials from the IAA demanding that the research team reseal the Talpiot tomb that they had rediscovered underneath a concrete slab in the garden of an apartment complex. Frustrated, the team abandoned their exciting study of the actual tomb almost as quickly as it began. The last words of the narrator were provocative: "Who knows what secrets are still inside or for how long they will be kept hidden underneath the Talpiot apartments?"

THE IMMEDIATE SCHOLARLY REACTION

The program was immediately followed by another program hosted by Ted Koppel and titled: *Lost Tomb of Jesus: A Critical Look*. During the program, Koppel quizzed Simcha Jacobovici and James Tabor, who spoke in defense of the film, and two teams of scholars including archaeologists William Dever and Jonathan Reed, who were generally critical of the film.[19] Dever was the first scholar to open fire on the program:

> I think I'm open minded. I'm certainly not trying to defend the Christian tradition. I'm not a believer. As I've said to the press, I've no dog in this fight. I'm trying to be a good scholar and an honest historian and stick with the facts and not go beyond them. One of the problems that I have with this whole project is that it puts archaeology in a rather bad light. . . . For me it represents the worst kind of biblical archaeology even if its antibiblical because it seems to me that the conclusions are already drawn in the beginning. . . . I think that the argument goes far beyond any reasonable interpretation.

His comments were followed by an even more blistering critique from Professor Reed, who said, "It's [the film] what I call 'archaeoporn.'

---

18 See also Jacobovici and Pellegrino, *The Jesus Family Tomb*, 208–9.
19 William Dever retired in 2002 as professor of Near Eastern Archaeology at the University of Arizona. Jonathan Reed is professor of religion at the University of La Verne and coauthor of *Excavating Jesus: Beneath the Stones, Behind the Texts*.

It's very exciting, it's titillating. You want to watch it. But deep down you know it's wrong. . . . It's not the kind of thing that a long-lasting relationship is made up of and that's the relationship between science, archaeology, and the Bible."

Koppel observed that several of the experts who were interviewed in the program felt that their comments had been mishandled and that some were angered by the film. Koppel read a statement by Dr. Carney Matheson of the Lakehead University Paleo-DNA Laboratory in which he denied that the DNA evidence proved that the persons in the Jesus and Mariamne ossuaries were husband and wife as Jacobovici had claimed and noted that several other family relationships were possible.[20] Dever also felt that the program abused the testimony of several experts:

> It's a very clever film. I think it will be persua-
> sive to millions of people. . . . I noticed that many of
> the experts are quoted out of context. I can assure you
> that Frank Cross, who was my own teacher and who
> read the inscriptions for you and confirmed your read-
> ing, does not agree with you, and I noticed that he was
> carefully edited out just when he finished the reading,
> which was convenient for you.

Koppel read another statement by Robert Genna, director of the Suffolk County Crime Laboratory, which conducted the tests on the patina of the Mariamne ossuary and James ossuary that were used to claim that the two ossuaries originated in the same tomb. The statement included a serious disclaimer:

> The elemental composition of some of the
> samples we tested from the ossuaries are consistent
> with each other. But I would never say that they're
> a match. . . . No scientist would ever say defini-
> tively that one ossuary came from the same tomb as
> another. . . . We didn't do enough sampling to see if in
> fact there were other tombs that had similar elemental

20 Matheson elsewhere made an even stronger disclaimer. Mims quoted Matheson as saying: "The only conclusions we made was [sic] that these two sets were not maternally related. To me it sounds like absolutely nothing." See Christopher Mims, "Says Scholar Whose Work Was Used in the Upcoming Jesus Tomb Documentary: 'I think it's completely mishandled. I am angry,'" n.p. [cited 24 June 2007]. Online: http://blog.sciam.com/index. php?title=says_scholar_whose_work_was_used_in_the&more=1&c=1&tb=1&pb=1.

compositions. . . . The only samples that we can positively say are a "match" from a single source are fin-
gerprints and DNA.[21]

Participants also challenged the claim that the James ossuary originally belonged to the Talpiot collection. Amos Kloner was quoted as
insisting that the tenth ossuary was photographed, catalogued, and
unmarked. It could not be the James ossuary, which bore a clear inscription. Tabor suggested that Kloner missed the inscription. Reed denied
that an archaeologist of Kloner's competence would have overlooked
the inscription.

The conversation turned to a discussion of the significance of the
Mariamne inscription, which the program claimed was a reference to
Mary Magdalene. Andrey Feuerverger acknowledged that his calculation hinged in that pivotal identification: "I must work from the interpretations given to me and the strength of the calculations are [sic] based
on those assumptions. . . . If for some reason one were to read it as just
a regular form of the name Maria, in that case the calculation produced
is not as impressive, and the statistical significance would wash out
considerably."

Reed argued that it was unlikely that this Mariamne was Mary Magdalene. He pointed out that although Bovon claimed that the Mariamne
of the *Acts of Philip* was Mary Magdalene, no scholar held that Mary
Magdalene was called Mariamne at the time of her death. Tabor countered that Mary Magdalene was called Mariamne as early as the second
century in the writings of Hippolytus.[22] This made it possible that Mary
was known by that name in the first century as well.

At Koppel's invitation, Jacobovici offered these concluding remarks:
"I wanted the debate to begin and it has. I want all these fine scholars
to weigh in. . . . For 27 years it has been sitting in the shadows. No aca-

21 Another expert who was especially incensed over the way her statements were used
in the documentary was Tal Ilan, author of the *Lexicon of Jewish Names*, the source of
the information on name frequencies during the period of ossuary use in Palestine. See
Christopher Mims, "Says Scholar Whose Work Was Used in the Upcoming Jesus Tomb
Documentary: 'I think it's completely mishandled. I am angry,'" n.p. [cited June 24, 2007].
Online: http://blog.sciam.com/index.php?title=says_scholar_whose_work_
was_used_in_the&more=1&c=1&tb=1&pb=1.
22 The writings of Hippolytus actually date to the third century. See, for example, Allen
Brent, *Hippolytus and the Roman Church in the Third Century: Communities in Ten-
sion before the Emergence of a Monarch-Bishop*, Supplements to Vigiliae Christianae 31
(Leiden: E. J. Brill, 1995).

demics have weighed in. One sole article by Amos Kloner sixteen years after the discovery. This is actually making me so happy because I see far more serious people than me—these are academics—they're weighing in. This is great."

During the next segment of the program, Koppel interviewed Jacobovici and Tabor along with Father David O'Connell, Darrell Bock, and Judy Fentress-Williams.[23] Koppel first questioned O'Connell about the potential impact of the claims of the film on his faith. O'Connell argued that the issues were irrelevant. He was a believer in a faith handed down through many generations for two thousand years. When further questioned he stated that he was not convinced by the arguments of the documentary but that even if they were true they would not impact his faith.

Koppel asked Bock if the suggestion that Jesus did not bodily ascend were correct, would this be problematic for his faith. He replied: "It is absolutely problematic for the Christian faith. The Christian faith has declared a bodily resurrection on the third day which means that nothing was left behind." He cited 2 Maccabees 7 as proof that ancient Jews also affirmed a true bodily resurrection. He stated:

> I think what we see here in this special are people talking about Christianity who do not understand the theological subtleties of what it is that Christianity believes. So, on the one hand they think in good faith that we have brought forth evidence that Jesus had existed. We can still believe in a resurrection . . . but they don't understand that that resurrection is very different from what the Christian faith has taught throughout the centuries.

Koppel later commented that Bock seemed to be the only person on the panel who believed that a bodily resurrection was essential to the Christian faith: "So far, Professor Bock, you seem to be the only person who believes that this, were it to prove true . . . would be a real challenge to the Christian faith." Bock agreed:

> If Jesus' bones were left behind after a year then at the least, how should I say this, we have to tweak the

23 David O'Connell is president of Catholic University of America. Darrell Bock is research professor of New Testament at Dallas Theological Seminary. Judy Fentress-Williams is assistant professor of Old Testament at Virginia Theological Seminary.

message of the resurrection. And tweak it in a direction in which it says Jesus' spirit went up to heaven but don't think that it was His body that was raised, don't think it was the whole person that was raised. It was only part of the person. Part of what Christianity objects to in this idea of the spiritual resurrection only is this idea that we have split up the person that God has created. The recreation and the resurrection hope is that God renews the entirety of the person into eternal life and to only have a spirit go up to heaven is actually something that the church has opposed since the second century.

Tabor countered from 1 Corinthians 15 that the resurrection body was not flesh and bones and should be described as a spiritual rather than a material body. "He [Paul] says that there is a material body and a spiritual. I would go with Paul on that and really stick to the Scriptures." Bock countered by pointing to some of the specifics of Paul's discussion, particularly the illustration of the seed and the plant, and insisted: "It is a question of Paul describing this body taking on various forms. He uses the picture of the seed that becomes a plant. It is the same matter." Tabor replied, "That's helpful." Fentress-Williams commented that this was the kind of scholarly interaction that should have taken place before the film was produced.

SCHOLARLY REVIEW OF THE BOOK

One of the first reviews of *The Jesus Family Tomb* to appear in a scholarly journal was published by the *Review of Biblical Literature*, a publication of the Society of Biblical Literature, which is the largest association of biblical scholars in North America. The review, written by Jonathan Reed, contains some of the harshest criticisms of a book to appear in a scholarly review in recent decades.[24] Reed compared Jacobovici and Pellegrino's work to Umberto Eco's *Baudolino*, in which a group of men including a poet, a rabbi, two scientists, and a priest "pass

---

24 Jonathan Reed, review of S. Jacobovici and C. Pellegrino, *The Jesus Family Tomb*, *Review of Biblical Literature* (June 2007) [cited 26 June 2007]. Online: http://www.bookreviews.org/pdf/5934_6304.pdf.

themselves off as the twelve magi, sell fake relics to pay their expenses, and even fabricate a holy grail." Reed added, "It is a forgery they eventually treat as authentic as they are torn apart by deceit and murder." He then charged, "Unlike *Baudolino*, there is no murder in *The Jesus Family Tomb*, but there is plenty of deceit." Readers who do not commonly peruse reviews in scholarly journals should know that statements like this are rare in this venue. The harsh statement is a shocking alert that the book under examination is likely a product of pseudo-scholarship.

Reed identified five key links in the claims of the book. Of these, he accepted only one: the cluster of names generally fits Jesus' family. He, however, rejected the four other claims that are necessary to the hypothesis which argue that (1) Mariamne was Mary Magdalene, (2) the DNA evidence shows that Jesus and Mariamne were married, (3) the odds are 600 to 1 that this is Jesus' tomb, and (4) the patina fingerprinting makes the hypothesis, as Feuerverger claimed, "a statistical slam dunk." Reed argued, "If the evidence [is viewed] with each link having to bear the weight of the thesis, then the book remains utterly unconvincing. There are too many ifs."

Reed went on to demonstrate that the book distorted the research of F. Bovon who never claimed that Mary Magdalene was called Mariamne earlier than the fourth-century *Acts of Philip*. Reed quoted Bovon as reacting to the claims of Jacobovici and Pellegrino with the words: "The reconstructions of Jesus' marriage with Mary Magdalene and the birth of a child belong for me to science fiction." Reed also dismissed the claim that Magdala was a Greek-speaking city, which the book claims explains why only the Mariamne inscription was in Greek. Reed castigated the book's description of Magdala as a "description no archaeologist familiar with Galilee takes seriously."

Reed called the DNA analysis "both scientifically and morally questionable." It was scientifically questionable because samples were insufficient for the repeat testing necessary for peer review. It was morally questionable because the samples were taken without IAA permission, were illegal, and only served to antagonize Jewish religious authorities against archaeologists.

Reed argued that "the use of statistics borders on the absurd" because the calculations were based on skewed data. He calculated that probably close to four hundred men named Jesus had fathers named Joseph in the first century. The Talpiot tomb could have belonged to dozens of different Jesuses from the first century.

Reed charged that the inclusion of the James ossuary in the equation to increase the probability that the tomb belonged to Jesus of Nazareth "strains credulity." He also dismissed the claim that the symbol on the tomb entrance was an ancient Christian symbol and argued the pattern was a Jewish adaptation of a Roman theme.

Reed chided the authors for their inconsistent use of textual, particularly biblical, evidence in which they grab whatever fits their hypothesis and dismiss all else. He pointed out that Paul's apparent ignorance of Jesus' burial place in Jerusalem posed a real problem for the Talpiot hypothesis: "He knew Jerusalem and had many disputes with the Jerusalem church, but he did not have the faintest clue about this tomb. His and other early Christian's [sic] silence on a matter that would gut their central theological claim is inconceivable."

Although Reed admitted that he could not prove that the Talpiot tomb was not the tomb of Jesus of Nazareth, he felt "this book's attempt to make the case is an absolute failure." He concluded that it is "highly unlikely" that this tomb was the family tomb of the Jesus of the Gospels.

THE NEED FOR A THOUGHTFUL
AND EXTENSIVE RESPONSE

During the weeks following the airing of the documentary and release of the book, sales of *The Jesus Family Tomb* soared higher and higher. By the end of the second week of March, the book was number six on the *New York Times* best-seller list for hardback nonfiction. This significant public interest in the book demonstrated that Jacobovici's claims deserved the scholarly response that he had invited. This book is intended to offer that scholarly response.

The Lost Tomb of Jesus and *The Jesus Family Tomb* have raised a number of important questions such as:

- How have most archaeologists reacted to the Jesus family tomb hypothesis?
- Is the James ossuary an ossuary that was stolen from the East Talpiot tomb?

- Do the marks on the ossuaries or the symbol on the tomb entrance confirm that the tomb was associated with the early Jesus movement?
- How common were the names that appear in the ossuary inscriptions?
- What is the statistical probability that this tomb belonged to Jesus of Nazareth?
- How do the claims of Jacobovici and Pellegrino comport with the New Testament evidence regarding the events following Jesus' death?
- Can the claims of the documentary be reconciled with the Christian faith by claiming that Jesus' resurrection was merely spiritual?

Jacobovici is correct that scholars need to "weigh in" on these important questions. These questions and many others will be addressed in this book by an impressive group of scholars. This group consists of some of the most respected experts in the fields of archaeology, New Testament and historical Jesus research, apologetics, and probability analysis.

Steven Ortiz is associate professor of archaeology and biblical backgrounds at Southwestern Baptist Theological Seminary. He has over twenty years of field experience in biblical archaeology and has been a senior staff member on several archaeological field projects. He is currently the codirector and principal investigator at Tel Gezer. Ortiz's research focus is the Iron Age in the southern Levant. He specializes in the use of archeological methods and theory in the interpretation of the past and seeks to demonstrate how this enterprise can illuminate and reconstruct history relative to ancient Israel and the Hebrew Bible. Ortiz is currently writing a book titled *Intersections of Archaeology and Biblical Interpretation*. The authors of *The Jesus Family Tomb* and the producers of *The Lost Tomb of Jesus* have candidly admitted that they are not trained archaeologists. Ortiz will evaluate the Jesus family tomb hypothesis from the perspective of a trained and experienced archaeologist.

New Testament scholar **Craig Evans** is the author and editor of more than fifty books and hundreds of articles and reviews. He has written widely in the field of historical Jesus research. Professor Evans has given lectures at Cambridge, Durham, Oxford, Yale, and other universities, colleges, seminaries, and museums, such as the Field Museum in Chicago and the Canadian Museum of Civilization in Ottawa. He also regularly lectures and gives talks at popular conferences and retreats on the Bible, archaeology, Jesus, and the Dead Sea Scrolls. He has appeared in several History Channel and BBC documentaries and is a regular guest on *Dateline NBC*. Evans also served on the National Geographic Society's *Gospel of Judas* project. He invested intensive research in Jewish ossuaries for his recent book *Jesus and the Ossuaries.* Evans will introduce readers to the study of ossuaries and explain how they shed light on the study of the New Testament. He will examine the claim that the James ossuary was originally one of the ten ossuaries of East Talpiot and the theory that the symbols on the tomb entrance mark the tomb as a Christian site.

Richard Bauckham is a New Testament scholar and professor of New Testament studies at St. Mary's College, University of St. Andrews, Scotland. Bauckham is perhaps best known for his studies of the book of Revelation and for his commentaries on Jude and 2 Peter. In his book *God Crucified* (1999), Bauckham explored the riddle of how the radically monotheistic Jews who composed the earliest church could have come to call Jesus "Lord." In his recent book *Women of the Gospels*, he calculated the frequency of names and name forms of women mentioned in the Gospels. In his recent book *Jesus and the Eyewitnesses*, he used these name statistics to demonstrate the historical reliability of the Gospels. Bauckham will use his expertise in the frequencies of Jewish names in Palestine during the ossuary period to evaluate the Jesus family tomb hypothesis.

A mathematician and philosopher, **William A. Dembski** is research professor in philosophy at Southwestern Baptist Theological Seminary in Fort Worth. He is also a senior fellow with the Discovery Institute's Center for Science and Culture in Seattle as well as the executive director of the International Society for Complexity, Information, and Design. He has done postdoctoral work in mathematics at MIT, in physics at the University of Chicago, and in computer science at Princeton University. A graduate of the University of Illinois at Chicago where he earned a

BA in psychology, an MS in statistics, and a PhD in philosophy, he also received a doctorate in mathematics from the University of Chicago in 1988 and a master of divinity degree from Princeton Theological Seminary in 1996. Dembski has published articles in mathematics, philosophy, and theology journals and is the author/editor of more than ten books, most of which relate to the intelligent design of the universe. His work has been cited in numerous newspaper and magazine articles, including three front-page stories in the *New York Times* as well as the August 15, 2005 *Time* magazine cover story on intelligent design. He has appeared on the BBC, NPR (Diane Rehm, etc.), PBS (*Inside the Law* with Jack Ford; *Uncommon Knowledge* with Peter Robinson), CSPAN2, CNN, Fox News, ABC's *Nightline*, and the *Daily Show* with Jon Stewart.

Robert J. Marks II, PhD, is distinguished professor of electrical and computer engineering at Baylor University. He is fellow of both the Institute of Electrical and Electronic Engineers (IEEE) and The Optical Society of America. Marks is author of *The Handbook on Fourier Analysis and Its Applications* (Oxford University Press, 2008), *Introduction to Shannon Sampling and Interpolation Theory* (Springer Verlag, 1991), and is a coauthor of *Neural Smithing: Supervised Learning in Feedforward Artificial Neural Networks* (MIT Press, 1999). Marks was also a corecipient of a NASA Tech Brief Award for the paper "Minimum Power Broadcast Trees for Wireless Networks" and the Judith Stitt Award from the American Brachytherapy Society. He served 18 years as the faculty adviser for Campus Crusade for Christ at the University of Washington. Dembski and Marks combine their expertise in mathematics and computer technology to evaluate Feuerverger's arguments regarding the probability that the Talpiot tomb is the tomb of Jesus of Nazareth.

Gary Habermas is distinguished research professor and chairman of the Department of Philosophy and Theology at Liberty University. He is author or editor of 27 books that mainly concentrate on the topic of the resurrection of Jesus. His work defending the resurrection is often cited in the area of Christian apologetics. He has also specialized in cataloging and communicating trends among scholars in the field of historical Jesus and New Testament studies. Habermas will examine the claims of James Tabor about the burial of Jesus in light of the New Testament evidence.

Mike Licona is a New Testament historian and Christian apologist. He is the director of Apologetics and Interfaith Evangelism at the North American Mission Board (Southern Baptist Convention). Licona is the author of four books including *Paul Meets Muhammed,* which is a debate on the resurrection of Jesus between the apostle Paul and the prophet Muhammad, the award-winning *The Case for the Resurrection of Jesus,* which is a comprehensive self-study course, and *Cross Examined*, a legal novel defending the historicity of Jesus' resurrection. Licona will examine the claim that the apostle Paul taught that Jesus' resurrection body was an immaterial body that was composed of spirit, as claimed by both James Tabor and John Dominic Crossan.

Darrell Bock is research professor of New Testament Studies at Dallas Theological Seminary. He has earned international recognition as a Humboldt Scholar (Tübingen University in Germany) and for his work in Luke-Acts and in Jesus' examination before the Jews. He has been a *New York Times* best-selling author in nonfiction and is elder emeritus at Trinity Fellowship Church in Dallas. His works include the WUNT monograph *Blasphemy and Exaltation in Judaism and the Final Examination of Jesus*, and volumes on Luke and Acts in the *Baker Exegetical Commentary on the New Testament,* on Luke in the IVP New Testament Commentary Series and NIV Application Commentary, and on Mark in the Cornerstone Commentary. Bock is most known for his recent work, *Breaking the Da Vinci Code,* a response to the theological implications of the *The Da Vinci Code,* a book written by Dan Brown. His latest book is *The Missing Gospels.* Bock will conclude the book by summarizing the contributions of each preceding chapter, excluding this introduction. He also will analyze how information about Christianity is coming to the public in the digital age and discuss the implications of this new immediate access to information for the general public and for the Church.

Introduction

Although the essays in this book directly address the Talpiot hypothesis, most have a significance that will long outlive interest in the claims of Jacobovici and Tabor. For example, Evans shows the relevance of ossuary research for New Testament studies in general. Licona refutes the claim oft-repeated these days that Jesus' resurrection body was immaterial. Habermas marshals a battery of historical arguments for Jesus' bodily resurrection that are applicable to many recent challenges to the Christian faith.

The claims of *The Lost Tomb of Jesus* and *The Jesus Family Tomb* must not be casually brushed aside. Despite Larry King's humorous question in initial interviews at the early stage of this debate, far more is at stake here than the Easter bunny. The bodily resurrection of Jesus is absolutely crucial to the Christian faith. As the apostle Paul insisted to a congregation whose syncretism of Platonic dualism and Christianity led them to deny bodily resurrection:

> If there is no resurrection of the dead, then Christ has not been raised; and if Christ has not been raised, then our preaching is without foundation and so is your faith. In addition, we are found to be false witnesses about God, because we have testified about God that He raised up Christ—whom He did not raise up if in fact the dead are not raised. For if the dead are not raised, Christ has not been raised. And if Christ has not been raised, your faith is worthless; you are still in your sins. Therefore those who have fallen asleep in Christ have also perished. If we have placed our hope in Christ for this life only, we should be pitied more than anyone (1 Cor 15:13–19).

The contributors to this book are Christian scholars who are convinced that a reasonable evaluation of all the evidence supports the veracity of the claims of historic and biblical Christianity regarding Jesus' resurrection from the dead. We invite you to consider this evidence with us. We believe that when you do you will agree with us when we say, "Make no bones about it. The bones in the Jesus ossuary of Talpiot were not the bones of Jesus of Nazareth."

THE USE AND ABUSE OF
ARCHAEOLOGICAL INTERPRETATION
AND THE LOST TOMB OF JESUS

Steven M. Ortiz

INTRODUCTION

When the public debate surrounding the media attention to *The Lost Tomb of Jesus* arose, the most common question asked of me as an archaeologist was, "Is this the tomb of Jesus?" I responded "Yes!" because it is probable that a man named Jesus was buried in the tomb at Talpiot. Naturally the inquirer was taken aback because I am a professing evangelical Christian and this tomb does not support the accounts in the canonical Gospels regarding the death, burial, and resurrection of Jesus of Nazareth.

The next inquiry is, "Does the archaeology prove that this is the tomb of Jesus of Nazareth?" I reply, "Archaeological data alone cannot prove or disprove a proposition but can only support or critique propositions."

The person is usually frustrated at this time and will ask me if I believe that our Lord married, had children, died, and was buried with his family in this Talpiot tomb as the so-called documentary proposed. I then answer that the proposal is preposterous and certain to be rejected by the overwhelming majority of archaeologists and historians; without all the commotion in the media, it would hardly be worthy of a serious scholarly response.

This dialogue illustrates common misconceptions about the use of archaeology to "prove" or "disprove" the Bible. Unfortunately, I must respond to the outlandish claims espoused in *The Lost Tomb of Jesus*

28

because of the potential impact and influence this documentary will have on the general public. In particular, it is necessary to address the issues raised by this documentary because it distorts proper interpretation of the archaeological data.

Most public perceptions of an archaeologist follow the Hollywood model of Indiana Jones. He is an archaeologist with a dual personality of scholar in the classroom wearing a tweed coat during the academic semester, and then he becomes transformed into a whip-carrying swash-buckling hero who fights evil forces as he heads off on an adventure to find some lost object. It is humorous to those in the field of archaeology that whenever amateurs want to portray themselves as serious archae-ologists, who are responsible for some significant find, they portray themselves as a modern-day Indiana Jones. This is true whether they are looking for the lost ark of the covenant, Mount Sinai, Noah's ark, Paul's wrecked ship, the route of the exodus, or—now for the first time—the "real" location of the tomb of Jesus. The scripts for all of these amateur portrayals are similar and follow the same basic 10 points:

1. The prevailing hypothesis affirmed by the consensus of the schol-arly community is wrong.
2. The "discoverer" is not a trained archaeologist but is self-taught and knows the "true story" that all others have overlooked.
3. An expedition is planned for one season, and (lo and behold) at the first attempt they find exactly what they are looking for.
4. This is all documented while a camera crew happens to be filming the discovery.
5. The process is "detective work" that has been missed by the aca-demic community, and they (amateur archaeologists) are the ones who are able to unravel the mystery or solve the problem that has perplexed the experts.
6. No new data is presented, only a reworking of previously pub-lished data. A corollary is that not all of the data is consulted.
7. Upon the presentation of the discovery, the scholarly community scoffs at the find, and it is claimed that there is a secret conspiracy by those in power to suppress the information.
8. The amateurs sensationalize the "discovery" by claiming that it is so revolutionary that it will change our way of thinking and our lifestyle.

9. The old "discovery" is presented to the media as a "brand-new" discovery.
10. Usually a book or movie comes out within a week of the "new" discovery.

The presentation of *The Lost Tomb of Jesus* follows the above script. You could take the discovery of the tomb and replace it with the holy grail, the ark of the covenant, Mount Sinai, or any type of religious icon; and the script would be the same. The only thing separating this documentary from the typical Hollywood script is the absence of snake pits, rolling stones, a damsel in distress, and Nazis chasing the main character. While the above 10 points make an excellent movie script or docudrama, they are not reflective of the actual archaeological enterprise.

ARCHAEOLOGICAL METHODOLOGY: HOW DO ARCHAEOLOGISTS WORK?

If the above 10 points of the presentation of the Talpiot tomb are not representative of what archaeologists do, then the question needs to be asked, "How should they have researched the Talpiot tomb?" I will avoid a dense discussion of archaeological method and theory and instead illustrate the nature of archaeological inquiry by addressing each of the above 10 points related to the popularization of archaeology in the media and pop culture.

THE DISCIPLINE OF ARCHAEOLOGY

1. *The prevailing hypothesis affirmed by the consensus of the scholarly community is wrong.*
2. *The "discoverer" is not a trained archaeologist but is self-taught, and he knows the "true story" that all others have overlooked.*

Archaeology is an academic discipline with its own methods and theoretical base for the interpretation of the archaeological record. Most archaeologists go to school for several years in order to earn a PhD in archaeology or a related field and receive years of field training. Archaeology is not treasure hunting—digging holes and robbing tombs of special finds.[1] Granted, the basic unit of study of an archaeologist is the artifact, but it is not studied in isolation. An artifact is part of a larger cultural system. Archaeologists study artifacts in their cultural contexts, while treasure hunters focus on the artifact itself. The removal of an artifact from its archaeological context removes it from its historical and cultural context. This is why the antiquities market is so detrimental to archaeological research. Its presence encourages the looting of objects from archaeological sites without proper scientific investigation. While these objects are valuable and provide a wealth of information for reconstructing ancient society and addressing questions of social transformation, they lose a majority of their value when they are removed from the archaeological context without proper excavation.

Archaeology requires a systematic research design, knowledge of the historical context of the region and area of study, a theoretical basis for the reconstruction of ancient society based on the material correlates, and years of study of various artifacts and material culture. The archaeological enterprise consists of many specialists from auxiliary disciplines who aid the archaeologist in the interpretation and excavation of artifacts. While some artifacts have significant value in terms of information that is provided to the scholar (such as inscriptions), it is not the single artifact but the patterning of many artifacts within the archaeological record that is used to interpret the past. The Talpiot tomb is an example of an isolated discovery taken out of context to interpret a larger historical picture. No discussion or presentation by the producers occurred placing this tomb within the context of other tombs and the larger southern cemetery of the early Roman period; moreover, no serious attempt was made to interpret the artifacts of the tomb within their historical context.

Archaeological scholarship does not take place in a vacuum. The findings are published, and results are presented at academic meetings. Initial finds or interpretations should be presented before other archaeologists and historians and subject to peer review. While any academic discipline is political and there are power struggles and a tendency to preserve the status quo,[2] new ideas and interpretations are constantly

1 The history of archaeology did start with Western culture's fascination with other cultures and the past and the development of museums. Earlier excavations were, at their core, searches for unique objects to display in museums.
2 See T. S. Kuhn, *The Structure of Scientific Revolutions,* 3rd ed. (Chicago: University of Chicago, 1996) for a discussion of scholarly monopoly.

being presented and debated. The original excavators of the Talpiot tomb have published and presented their findings in major archaeological publications (the *Qadmoniyot* and *'Atiqot* journals of the Israel Antiquities Authority, formerly the Department of Antiquities), and several major works based on the archaeological excavations have been produced. Two notable examples are a major work on the Jewish ossuaries in the holdings of the IAA and a monograph on Jewish personal names.[3]

ARCHAEOLOGICAL EXCAVATIONS

3. *An expedition is planned for one season, and (lo and behold) at the first attempt they find exactly what they are looking for.*

4. *This is all documented while a camera crew happens to be filming the discovery.*

Archaeological excavations are labor-intensive enterprises. In the old days of "biblical archaeology," a scholar could almost begin an excavation merely with the permission of the landowner. In the early days of exploration, private donors and museums would fund excavations. Most of these were only focused on the collection of museum pieces for the public and were nothing more than treasure hunting. This contributed to the public's perception of archaeological research as archaeologists digging holes for goodies.

Archaeological excavations must be done within the context of broader research goals and strategies.[4] The granting of a license by the IAA is done only by an application that demonstrates professional competency by the director and his staff, support from an academic institute that has an archaeology department, and evidence for a budget that would support not only the field research but also publication and postseason analysis. Most archaeological excavations are multiyear projects involving a team of scholars who not only work during the excavation but also invest enormous amounts of time during the off-season in the lab.

At face value archaeological discoveries are usually chance finds. Rarely do archaeologists go to a site, mark an X on a spot, and determine

---

3 L. Y. Rahmani, *A Catalogue of Jewish Ossuaries in the Collections of the State of Israel* (Jerusalem: Israel Antiquities Authority, 1994); Tal Ilan, *Lexicon of Jewish Names in Late Antiquity, Part I: Palestine 330 BCE–200 CE* (Texts and Studies in Ancient Judaism 91; Tübingen: Mohr Siebeck, 2002).

4 The exceptions are salvage excavations of which the excavation of the Talpiot tomb is an example. This will be discussed below.

that they are going to find a specific artifact. Usually major finds are discovered as archaeologists are examining something else. This is not to say that archaeologists are blindly setting up a grid and haphazardly uncovering whatever is beneath the surface. They have a research design and methodology to explore a site. If they are investigating city planning, they will naturally set up a research design that looks at fortifications and various sections of an ancient city. Archaeological data are accumulated and analyzed over many field seasons. When this information is finally presented to the public, it is usually years after the initial investigation.

The Discovery Channel report of the Talpiot tomb was disingenuous because they recreated an "archaeological discovery" by attempting to "find" the tomb in the backyard of homeowners in the Talpiot neighborhood. In addition, the program implied that the producer and his crew were discovering the evidence for the first time—whether they were walking down the rows of shelves of the IAA storeroom facility or opening up the cement cap that was put over the tomb as a safety precaution to keep children from falling down the shaft. This is not to say that previously excavated finds should not be reevaluated. Archaeologists should always keep an open mind and constantly reevaluate old hypotheses and historical reconstructions as new evidence and finds continue to be discovered and studied.

There is value in recreating the event associated with the discovery for teaching, illustration, and even entertainment. The production of the film on the Talpiot tomb did not recreate the actual discovery or excavation but gave the impression that the crew was making a new discovery. In truth they were staging what amounted to a "rediscovery" of the archaeological data. The hoopla associated with the release of the documentary on the Talpiot tomb implied that there was a "new" discovery. Although some artistic license should be granted to the producers so they can present an entertaining story associated with the discovery, they did not use the original discovery as their story line. Instead, they created a new story line with themselves "discovering" the tomb. But the tomb did not need to be rediscovered because all the information had already been published and was easily available in the storehouses of the Israel Antiquities Authority.

POSTEXCAVATION RESEARCH

    5. The process is "detective work" that has been neglected by the academic community, and they (amateur archaeologists) are the ones who are able to unravel the mystery or solve the problem that has perplexed the experts.

    6. No new data is presented, only a reworking of previously published data. A corollary is that not all the data is consulted.

Archaeologists are constantly reevaluating their finds and conclusions in light of new excavations. Their work is subject to peer review. While there is a tendency to form a consensus within the scholarly community, there is also a belief that our reconstructions are always subject to reevaluation, especially as new data is uncovered. As stated earlier, the archaeological enterprise is analogous to a puzzle where we only have some of the pieces. We create or postulate a picture based on the limited number of puzzle pieces. As more pieces are added to the puzzle (e.g., new archaeological data), the picture becomes a bit clearer; and we are able to reconstruct a more accurate picture. Another analogy is crime scene investigation. As crime scene investigators analyze the data, new information is produced, and the reconstruction of the crime is reevaluated and modified accordingly.

The Talpiot tomb "discovery" was not new research or a new discovery. The data had already been published[5] and the excavations reported a decade before the Discovery docudrama, while the actual excavation was over 25 years earlier (March 1980).[6] Only two new analyses were performed on the existing data: the DNA tests on the bones in the ossuaries with the names Jesus and Miriam and the statistical analysis of the names.[7] Neither of these analyses provides any new evidence to debate. If they were important for a reconstruction of history or a better understanding of the archaeological record, the original researchers would have conducted the analysis. In addition, the data obtained from the tomb did not match the historical picture of Jesus of Nazareth, so the attempt

---

5 Rahmani, *A Catalogue of Jewish Ossuaries*; A. Kloner, "A Tomb with Inscribed Ossuaries in East Talpiyot, Jerusalem," *'Atiqot* 29 (1996): 15–22.

6 J. Gat, "East Talpiyot," *Hadashot Arkheologiyot* 76 (1981): 24–25 (Hebrew). This publication is the archaeological newsletter of the Israel Department of Antiquities and Museums.

7 I exclude the patina analysis on the Mariamne and James ossuaries for reasons that will become obvious later.

to connect the "Jesus son of Joseph" with the Jesus of the canonical Gospels was not seriously considered.

The Talpiot tomb is a family tomb containing the remains of some people who would have been related by blood and others who married into the family. All we know is that Jesus (ossuary 4) and Miriam (ossuary 1) are not blood related. We do not know if they were married. Miriam could have been married to Matityahu (Matthew) (ossuary 3), Yeshua (Jesus), Yehuda (Judas) the son of Jesus (ossuary 2), or perhaps even Joseph (if he is not the father of Jesus in ossuary 4). The original study by Amos Kloner estimates that the tomb represents three to four generations with an estimated 35 interments.[8]

The second "new" analysis is the statistical analysis of the names. This study will be discussed in another chapter. The original archaeologists, while aware of the historical context and issues connected with the historical Jesus, did not deem it unusual to have a family tomb with an individual named Jesus whose father was named Joseph. The six names of individuals mentioned on the ossuaries are the most common names found in the onomastic evidence[9] of the Hellenistic and Roman period.

The presentation of the Talpiot tomb onomastic evidence was disingenuous because the program quoted experts in the field of epigraphy, history, and archaeology (e.g., Drs. Cross, Ilan, Phann, and Kloner) and made it seem like they were in support of the major premise of *The Lost Tomb of Jesus* docudrama. In reality, none of these scholars hold to the hypothesis that the Jesus in the Talpiot tomb is the Jesus in the Gospel accounts. Noticeably missing from the presentation of the data is the fact that these are common names and any attempt to claim otherwise clearly distorts the larger onomastic evidence. The viewer is led to believe that it must be more than a coincidence that this tomb contains the names of Jesus and other New Testament personalities. This gives the impression that the archaeological community has either been hiding this information from the general public or was not clever enough to make the connection.

When the Talpiot tomb was first excavated, archaeologists recognized that there was nothing unusual about it in light of what was already known about Second Temple cemeteries, burial practices, or the histori-

8 Kloner, "East Talpiot," 21, 22.
9 Onomastic evidence refers to all names found in the archaeological and historical record.

cal Jesus. The names on the ossuaries and the tomb itself were consistent with what was already known about first-century Palestine. The data were not hidden or forgotten by scholars. They became part of larger synthetic studies of the archaeological data such as the study of Jewish ossuaries by Rahmani, onomastic data studied by Ilan, or Jewish cemeteries and burial customs of the Second Temple period by Kloner. New Testament scholars had access to the material and could have studied the results in light of historical Jesus research.

The producers made claims that they were only presenting evidence and allowing the public to make up their own minds. While this is a worthy endeavor on the surface, if this was intended to be a "new" analysis of data, then it behooves the producers to present all the evidence and allow viewers to make up their own minds.

ARCHAEOLOGICAL INTERPRETATIONS

7. *Upon the presentation of the discovery, the scholarly community scoffs at the find, and it is claimed that there is a secret conspiracy by those in power to suppress the information.*

8. *The amateurs sensationalize the "discovery" by claiming that it is so revolutionary that it will change our way of thinking and our lifestyle.*

The producers of *The Lost Tomb of Jesus* did not claim that there is a secret conspiracy of the scholarly community. This is the one point of the typical script that was not employed. It is common with most attempts to revise history. The most recent and noticeable occurrence was *The DaVinci Code*. This thriller and suspense novel claimed that "those in power"—in this instance, the Catholic Church—were keeping some secret from the public. Whereas the producers of *The Lost Tomb of Jesus* do not make this claim, it is only natural that the public would possibly gravitate toward this conclusion since this script is already part of the story line in popular revisions of history using archaeology. Though perhaps not the intent of the producers, there was much footage of the team walking down the aisles among hundreds of ossuaries in the bowels of a large storage facility.

The Talpiot tomb finds have not been hidden in some secret government storage facility. (I have been to this facility and although the IAA Beth Shemesh storage facility is hard to find within the city industrial

36

zone, it is not purposefully hidden.) Any professional (and apparently nonprofessional, since the film producers had easy access) can request a visit and inquire about research on any material culture items under the supervision of the IAA. The reason that the Talpiot tomb did not make waves in the archaeological community, in the past or present, is that it is a typical Second Temple tomb complex found in the suburbs of the modern city of Jerusalem. The inscriptions on the ossuaries contained common names, and the coincidence of the names with names associated with Jesus in the Gospel accounts did not surprise any archaeologist or historian of the first century AD.

The producers are presenting a completely new revision of the life and times of Jesus. Naturally if the claims are true, orthodox Christian belief in the death and resurrection of Jesus is wrong. Jesus did not die on the cross and rise from the dead. His followers did not see the resurrected Lord and radically alter their lives by preaching about the risen Lord throughout the Roman Empire and dying martyrs' deaths. Instead, Jesus was married to Mary Magdalene, had a son named Judas, lived in a village south of the city of Jerusalem (present-day Talpiot), and was buried in a family tomb. This historical reconstruction is based solely on a tomb containing ten ossuaries, six of them having common names of individuals. While any archaeological find that sheds light on the historical Jesus makes headlines, the initial find of this tomb years ago did not. The find was not considered newsworthy since the historical and cultural contexts of the biblical Jesus as well as the commonality of the names from the tomb make it doubtful that the names from the Talpiot tomb identify those interred there as individuals associated with Jesus in the biblical account. No radical revision of history could be made based on the evidence.

Unlike other sensational discoveries or claims by quasi-archaeological research, it appears that the initial proponents of *The Lost Tomb of Jesus* are stepping back from their claims. The scholarly reaction came from secular viewpoints and not necessarily conservative New Testament scholars. This leads us to the next topic—archaeology and public policy.

ARCHAEOLOGY AND THE PUBLIC

9. *The new "discovery" is presented to the media as a "brand-new" discovery.*
10. *Usually a book or movie comes out within a week of the "new" discovery.*

Archaeologists are no different from anyone else. They want their work to be recognized by the public. Most archaeologists invest years of their lives in research and exploration, and their work becomes a part of them. Every scholar considers his work valuable and something worthwhile that is making a contribution to society. Those who are reconstructing the past feel that an understanding of history is important for the humanities. There is a sense of responsibility in the way scholarship is conducted and presented to the community. There is a spectrum of what is considered ethical, and the scholarly community has checks and balances (usually referred to as peer review) to make sure that no one is presenting false claims or making interpretations that are not warranted by the data. Our knowledge has expanded to include many specialists in the scholarly enterprise. Archaeological fieldwork and research must be funded by public and private sources; hence, a natural relationship exists between the dissemination of information via the popular press and a sober presentation to the academic community. While archaeologists use the public media to inform about a major find or discovery, it is usually a tentative conclusion that must be verified by one's academic peers. When the archaeological discovery or new interpretation of previous data is not vetted among peers (those who know the data and can critique the argumentation and conclusions accurately), it becomes suspect.

The presentation of *The Lost Tomb of Jesus* circumvented the scholarly community. The supposed new research was not presented to specialists and scholars in the field. The public announcement coincided not with a scholarly symposium but with a new movie and book. The radical historical reconstruction proposed was nothing more than sensationalism designed to create interest among the media and public.

Immediately after the show and during the week between the media announcement and airing of the supposed documentary, many scholars stepped forward to dismiss the hypothesis of the producers. This was not because of some secret conspiracy or a desire to downplay attention to a nonspecialist. Scholars felt a responsibility to inform the public of the spurious nature of the hypothesis.

THE NATURE OF ARCHAEOLOGICAL INQUIRY

One of the issues of interpreting archaeological data is how to interpret the data as it relates to a reconstruction of ancient society. The portrayal of archaeology in the media and popular culture is that archaeology presents data to prove or disprove a hypothesis, similar to a "smoking gun" in a crime scene. Archaeology is not a science that proves or disproves an historical event based solely on a single archaeological find. In this case the Talpiot tomb by itself cannot prove or disprove that this is the tomb of Jesus Christ. Archaeology can only present data to assist in the plausibility of a historical reconstruction. A more apt analogy for the nature of archaeological work is not the Indiana Jones character but the Grissom character of the popular TV series *CSI*. He is a crime scene scientist who has evidence for an event (a crime) and has to reconstruct what happened. He gathers all the evidence that is found at the scene and pieces together the most plausible reconstruction of the crime based on the evidence. Archaeologists do the same. They gather all the data and develop a plausible historical reconstruction. One problem, however, is that the archaeological record does not represent the whole historical event. A lot of data is missing due to other variables (later disturbances of the site, robbing, erosion, etc.). Hence, archaeologists are assembling a puzzle with several of the pieces missing.

The archaeological evidence of the Talpiot tomb presented by James Cameron, Simcha Jacobovici, and James Tabor is generally accurate. The problem is that they are not looking at all of the data. Their reconstruction of the data is not historically plausible. This is why the scholarly community has not accepted the filmmakers' premise. Not one archaeologist has stepped forward to state that this is the tomb of Jesus of Nazareth of the Gospels and Christianity. In fact, the actual archaeologists state that *this is not the tomb of Jesus of Nazareth*. A flood of scholars is scoffing at the evidence presented in the "documentary of the Talpiot tomb."[10]

---

10 A one-hour discussion led by Ted Koppel after the documentary was the first sign that the scholarly community was not at all convinced by the hypothesis.

THE TALPIOT TOMB WITHIN ITS
ARCHAEOLOGICAL CONTEXT

What then can be said about the archaeology of the Talpiot tomb? In other words, if the producers decided to have a scholarly symposium to evaluate the Talpiot tomb hypothesis, what would be presented and what would we be able to say about the data? The first part of this chapter addressed the nature of the inquiry and presentation of the data, concluding that the documentary was nothing more than pop-archaeology—sensationalizing a find beyond its historical context. The documentary on the Talpiot tomb was nothing more than pseudo-science attempting to disclaim historical claims of the Christian faith by the discovery of a tomb with the name of Jesus. This next part of the chapter will discuss the Talpiot tomb in its archaeological context. That is to say, "How would the presentation look without the sensationalism?"

The Talpiot tomb is one of a hundred tombs excavated in the environs of Jerusalem. Even today the casual tourist hiking around the hills of Jerusalem will discover many exposed tombs. As the modern city of Jerusalem has expanded and several suburbs have been developed, it is common that many construction crews have come upon the necropolis of Jerusalem during the Hellenistic and Early Roman periods. The Jerusalem necropolis (ancient cemetery) stretches as far south as the Arab village of Sur Bahir and as far north as Mt. Scopus and Sanhedria. All suburbs and even most housing complexes have a tomb within the boundaries of the community. For the modern Jerusalemite, the discovery of another tomb is commonplace, part of the urban landscape of parks, apartment complexes, and parking lots. The modern visitor to Israel, particularly from the U.S., is struck by the comingling of modern buildings and ancient structures—as if each is vying for space in a limited area. This is especially evident in Jerusalem, where the ancient structures of history are considered sacred and become integrated into the city planning. What was once an obstacle to the city's expansion appears in the end to be central to the original design of the modern city. The Talpiot tomb is part of this larger mosaic of the ancient intertwined with the modern.

SALVAGE EXCAVATIONS

With the population expansion of the modern state of Israel and the many construction projects such as roads, businesses, and housing, many of these ancient tombs are discovered in the process of the expansion of the city. It is common that these tombs are found suddenly in the midst of major construction. It is also common that they are somewhat damaged in the process. The Israel Antiquities Authority (formerly the Department of Antiquities) is responsible for all archaeological sites of cultural and historical value. The IAA has several teams led by archaeologists who are available to conduct an excavation at a moment's notice. In addition, archaeologists who are responsible to protect and identify the archaeological heritage supervise several districts and subdistricts. These district archaeologists oversee excavations in their assigned area, help the police stop any illegal activity such as antiquities smuggling and/or robbing, and serve as liaisons between the state and the various communities and businesses that have property containing cultural and historical heritage.

Although salvage excavations, as the name implies, usually salvage the cultural remains of an archaeological site, they are conducted using proper excavation methodology and techniques. Usually someone reports to the Israel Antiquities Authority or police when there is an archaeological site that might get damaged or destroyed. An inspector is quickly dispatched to determine if any action needs to be taken. Construction work immediately stops as plans are quickly negotiated to coordinate the construction work and the salvage excavation. The excavation is conducted by archaeologists and workers of the IAA and is normally funded by the construction company or property owner. Due to time constraints the excavation is usually intense. Although the excavations are completed rapidly, the work is not done haphazardly.

The excavation of the Talpiot tomb was done under these conditions, but it was done properly with staff that were trained and experienced in salvage work. The report was published, and all data and finds were cataloged and stored in the facilities of the Israel Antiquities Authority where they are available for any scholar to review. In fact, the producers of the documentary apparently had complete access to the data and were also granted permission to perform tests on the artifacts (e.g., two of the ossuaries). Any questions or concerns as to so-called "missing or misplaced" artifacts or substandard work because it was a salvage excavation should not be entertained.

CEMETERIES OF JUDEA AND JERUSALEM

Several cemeteries have been found throughout the land of Israel. The necropolis of the ancient city was found in the extramural suburbs of the city. The cemetery of ancient Jerusalem has been well studied.[11] As stated earlier, our knowledge of the necropolises of Jerusalem has been greatly increased with the unification of Jerusalem in 1967 and the subsequent population growth as evidenced by the many new neighborhoods that have been built. Archaeologists have defined some patterns of Second Temple cemeteries of the ancient city of Jerusalem. By the time of the New Testament, all burials (except the tombs of the earlier Judean kings) were outside the city. The cemeteries of Jerusalem formed a five-kilometer belt around the city. The cemeteries were mainly located in three zones: the north (modern neighborhoods of Mount Scopus, Giv'at ha-Mivtar, French Hill, and Ramot Eshkol); the east (Mount of Olives and the village of Silwan); and the south (Peace Forest and North Talpiot). Since the winds blew from the west, few tombs were located there. About 40 percent were found in the northern zone, 16 percent in the eastern zone, 32 percent in the southern zone, and only 12 percent in the western zone.[12]

The cemeteries contain rock-cut tombs hewn into the sides of hills surrounding the city. To date, about 800 tombs have been surveyed or excavated.[13] The individual tombs in the cemeteries were randomly distributed. There was no central plan or systematic placement. Apparently the rock formation and the topography determined where the tomb would be located. Most were cut into the soft nari stone common on the slopes of the Mount of Olives east of the city; others were cut into the harder *melekh* or *qa'qulah* rock found in the north, west, and south.

11 G. Barkay, *Ketef Hinnom: A Treasure Facing Jerusalem's Walls* (Jerusalem: Israel Museum, 1986); L. Y. Rahmani, "Ancient Jerusalem's Funerary Customs and Tombs: Part One–Part Four," *Biblical Archaeologist* (1981): 43–53; 109–19; 171–77; 229–35; David Ussishkin, *The Village of Silwan: The Necropolis from the Period of the Judean Kingdom* (Jerusalem: Israel Antiquities Authority, 1993).

12 Data comes from John J. Rousseau and Rami Arav, "Jerusalem, Tombs" in *Jesus and His World: An Archaeological and Cultural Dictionary* (Minneapolis: Fortress, 1995), 167.

13 Hillel Geva, "Tombs-Jerusalem," *The New Encyclopedia of Archaeological Excavations in the Holy Land,* ed. Ephraim Stern et al. (Jerusalem: Carta, 1993), 747–56, esp. 747.

BURIAL TOMBS

Rock-hewn burial chambers originated during the Iron Age (Old Testament times). Natural caves were originally used, and this evolved into the elaborate hewing of multiple chambered tombs. Most of the tombs of Jerusalem dating to the Herodian period are small and simple.

There are several characteristic features of most Jerusalem tombs of the Second Temple period. Over half of the tombs had an open-air, rock-cut forecourt that served as an entryway. The more elaborate tombs had benches in the forecourt. The entrance to the tomb was cut into the back wall of the forecourt. This wall was usually hewn to form a smooth wall with a doorway that was typically less than a meter in height. Entrance to the tomb required a person to stoop or crouch down to enter the actual tomb chamber.

Most popular images of tombs dating to the New Testament consist of a tomb closed by a circular rolling stone. This is the description that we have of Jesus' tomb (which would have been Joseph of Arimathea's tomb) in the canonical Gospel accounts. Although this can be granted in the case of a rich man's tomb, based on the archaeological record, this type of tomb enclosure seal was very rare. It is found in only a few cases.[14] These types of rolling stones weighed several hundred pounds.[15] The most common type of tomb entrance seal would have been a square-shaped stone that was cut to fit the square entrance of the tomb. These stones look like square-shaped mushrooms that formed a plug that was inserted into the opening.

The inside of the tomb consisted of a square or rectangular-shaped room lined with benches. This was the burial chamber that was hewn into the rock. This is similar to earlier Iron Age tombs. What is unique and characteristic of tombs dating to the New Testament era (Second Temple period) is that most tombs contain long burial niches (loculi, *kokhim* [Hebrew]) where the bodies would be interred. These loculi were cut at right angles to the back and side walls of the burial chamber. They were about two feet wide by two feet in height and were dug back for about six feet. Loculi were found in over half of all the burial chambers, and the number of loculi in each burial chamber varied from a few to a

14 The most famous tomb is the "Tomb of Herod's Family" located on the western slope of the Hinnom Valley, near the King David Hotel.
15 Geva notes that they weigh "a few hundred kilograms." See his "Tombs-Jerusalem," 748.

few do. The loculi were hewn into the walls, usually at the same level, so that upon entering the burial chamber an individual would see these burial niches lining the chamber.

There were many variations in the basic Second Temple tomb. The tombs of the affluent were hewn with smooth-dressed walls and well-measured, rectangular rooms. In addition, there was no set pattern for the placement of the tombs. Sometimes an additional burial chamber was dug into one of the walls. Some tombs dug into other nearby tombs and created some unique variations and connections between adjoining tombs. The majority did not have benches. Some of the burial chambers contained repositories for bones. Some of the loculi were double in size, and some of the tombs had loculi on multiple levels. Some of the loculi had stone slabs that sealed the individual loculi as well as the stone that sealed the outside of the burial chamber. A later development was the arcosolium. About 100 of the tombs around Jerusalem contained an arcosolium. This was a burial niche cut parallel into the wall creating a bench or shelf for the body. This only allowed space for one individual along a wall rather than the two or three loculi that could have been hewn. The arcosolium was about six feet in length and about three feet from the floor. Sometimes the ceiling of the arcolosium was shaped with an arch.

A class of tombs in the Jerusalem area stands out because they are elaborate edifices. There are about 25 of these tombs. The most famous are the tombs in the Kidron Valley (the so-called "Tomb of Absalom" and "Tomb of Zechariah") that are striking landmarks viewed by most tourists who travel along the southeastern corner of the Old City. Other well-known tombs are the Tombs of the Sanhedrin, Cave of Jehoshaphat, Tomb of Queen Helene, Tomb of Bene Hezir, Tomb of Jason, Tomb of Nicanor, and the Cave of Umm el–'Amed. These are tombs with elaborate facades and several architectural decorations carved into the rock. Some of these include capitals and friezes in the Doric and Ionic styles, as well as pyramids and concave cornices from Egyptian architectural influence. The entrances and tombs were decorated with floral motifs, fruit, and geometric patterns and frames. While these were atypical, it does show that in the world of the dead, there was a variation in the abode based on wealth, similar to the world of the living.

Most of these rock-cut tombs belonged to the middle and upper classes of society. The poor and lower classes would have been buried directly in the ground. Unfortunately most of these burials do not survive in the archaeological record. The best example of in-ground interment is the cemetery of Qumran. Here we have examples of simple interments of the Second Temple period. The family of Jesus—that is, from his father Joseph—would have probably interred their family in the ground. If Joseph did have a rock-cut family tomb, it would have been up in Nazareth where Joseph was from, not in Jerusalem. We know from the Gospel accounts that Jesus was temporarily buried in the tomb of a rich man, Joseph of Arimathea. It apparently was one of these tombs with a rolling stone.

OSSUARIES

One of the unique features of Second Temple Jewish culture is the use of ossuaries. This practice was unique to the Jerusalem region.[16] Ossuaries are small stone coffins or burial boxes used for the secondary burial of bones (*ossilegium*). Over 2,000 of these ossuaries have been discovered.[17] Ossuaries are carved out of soft limestone, although there is a subclass that is carved out of hard limestone. Their average size is 45–70 cm long, 25–30 cm wide, and 25–40 cm high. They are rectangular in shape. Some have short legs raising them up a few inches. All have lids that are flat, rounded, or gabled. The lids usually fit into grooves on the box. Occasionally the ossuaries were painted red or yellow.

Decorations, Marks, Inscriptions. Most of the ossuaries were decorated by carving the soft stone. Most of the decoration was done on the long sides of the box. Favorite motifs were floral and geometric designs. The most common was a stylized rosette with six or more petals. Rahmani identifies the ossuaries as part of the larger stone vessel industry that boomed during the first century AD. The technique of decorative carving is known as *Kerbschnitt* (chip-carving). In addition, there are many marks such as crosses, Xs, lines, and such. These are notations that serve as markers to line up the lid on top of the ossuary. Many of these

16 Ossuaries have been found in tombs in the Jericho region, Shephelah, and in Galilee; the majority of distribution is solely in Jerusalem.
17 This number only represents those that have been excavated and/or recorded from museum and private collections. There are probably hundreds more in private collections or the collections of illicit antiquities trading.

ossuaries have inscriptions in Greek, Aramaic, and Hebrew either carved in the stone or written directly on the sides.

Origin of Ossilegium. The ossuaries were introduced during the Herodian era (first century BC) and became ubiquitous during the first century AD. It appears this burial practice began to disappear after the destruction of Jerusalem in AD 70. Some sporadic use continued into the second and third centuries AD.

Three prevailing views seek to explain this burial practice. Eric Meyers first offered that the practice of *ossilegium* (bone-gathering) is the continuation of the practice of secondary burial from the Iron Age (Old Testament) period.[18] A second view is that the use of ossuaries is connected with the belief in individual, physical resurrection from the dead which was becoming a standard and popular belief within the Pharisaic community.[19] A third view is that this practice comes from a Roman practice adopted by Herod the Great. The Romans used urns and small stone boxes for their secondary burials after the bodies of the deceased were cremated. The ashes were placed in containers. This view notes that the practice originated concurrently in Jerusalem society at the time that Herod was introducing and adopting several Roman practices. At this point it is clear that no single variable was the cause for this practice, but that the confluence of burial customs and beliefs during the Second Temple period created the environment for the widespread use of ossuaries in the Jerusalem region.

East Talpiot Jesus Tomb

The Jesus tomb of East Talpiot was a typical tomb of the Second Temple period and was the object of a typical salvage excavation by a team from the Israel Antiquities Authority (it was called the Department of Antiquities and Museums when the excavations took place). The tomb was exposed during construction in the neighborhood of East Talpiot in the spring of 1980. A brief summary excavation report appeared the following year in the Hebrew language publication of *Hadishot Arkheologiyot.* An English excavation report of the tomb was published in

18 Eric Meyers, *Jewish Ossuaries, Reburial and Rebirth* (Rome: Biblical Institute Press, 1971).

19 Levi Yizhaq Rahmani, "Ossuaries and *Ossilegium* (Bone-Gathering) in the Late Second Temple Period," in *Ancient Jerusalem Revealed,* ed. Hillel Geva (Jerusalem:Israel Exploration Society, 1994), 191–205.

1996 in *'Atiqot*, a bilingual journal of the Israel Antiquities Authority. The ossuaries and their inscriptions were published in earlier auxiliary reports, most notably the large monograph of Jewish ossuaries in the collection of the State of Israel (under the care of the storerooms of the IAA or in public museums such as the Israel Museum or the Rockefeller Museum).

The East Talpiot tomb consisted of a square-shaped burial chamber with an outer court that had a roofed antechamber. The dimensions of the outside courtyard are unknown, but the width was nearly 14 feet. The antechamber averaged 7 feet in length and width. The entrance to the tomb chamber had a decorated façade. It was decorated in relief by a pointed gable over a circle and an incomplete rosette. The main chamber is 7½ feet by 7½ feet and about 5 feet in height. There are no benches but there were six *kokhim* (shelves) from 4 to 5½ feet in length with an average width of 1½ feet. In addition to the *kokhim*, there were two *acrosolium* about 5 feet in length. The tomb was disturbed in antiquity as broken ossuary lids and broken and powdered bones were found throughout the tomb. Ten ossuaries were found in the tomb. Half of these were decorated, and six were inscribed (five in Hebrew and one in Greek). One ossuary contained a mason's mark. C. Evans and R. Bauckham will present in detail the discussion of the ossuaries and their inscriptions in chapters 2 and 3.

Amos Kloner, one of the prominent outspoken critics of *The Lost Tomb of Jesus* docudrama, presented the principal archaeological analysis of the East Talpiot burial. He originally concluded that the burial cave was used for three or four generations and probably dated to the Second Temple period (ca. from the end of the first century BC to the beginning of the first century AD).

SUMMARY

The archaeological evidence for burial practices matches the historical accounts of Jewish burial customs and beliefs, specifically the use of secondary burials. Secondary burial was common during the Old Testament period and continued into the New Testament era. The main difference is the transition from the use of a repository where all the bones were collected in a single location to the use of ossuaries. The corpse of a family member was placed in a *kokh* or on a shelf. About a year later, after the decomposition of the flesh of the corpse, the individual bones were collected and placed in an ossuary.

The East Talpiot tomb was a typical first-century AD burial tomb that was one of hundreds of tombs excavated throughout the modern suburbs of Jerusalem. The excavation of the tomb was done properly, and the results have been available to the academic community and the general public for decades. Contrary to the docudrama, nothing was mishandled in the excavation or publication. The tomb and inscriptions were known to the academic community, and no one proposed that the Jesus in the Talpiot tomb should be associated with the Jesus found in the Gospel accounts. There is no evidence or tradition of this tomb being recognized as the tomb of Jesus of Nazareth nor as a sacred site by the early Christian community in Jerusalem.

HISTORICAL RECONSTRUCTION BASED ON THE ARCHAEOLOGICAL DATA

Most of our knowledge of burial practices during the time of Jesus (Second Temple period) comes from literary sources as well as archaeology. There are several major studies addressing burials of Jerusalem, as well as specific studies addressing ossuaries.[20] Several popular overviews have also been published. This knowledge is widely shared in the archaeological community, and hence most scholars reacted negatively to the pop-archaeology of *The Lost Tomb of Jesus* documentary. The Talpiot Jesus tomb is a typical Second Temple Jerusalem tomb. There are no unique or outstanding features. The original excavators published the data and made it available to the scholarly community. The discovery did not cause a ripple, nor did archaeologists believe that they had a unique find that could be associated with the historical figure of Jesus Christ. In addition, no scholar secretly hid the findings or downplayed the implica-

20 Amos Kloner, "Burial Caves and Ossuaries from the Second Temple Period on Mount Scopus," in *Jews and Judaism in the Second Temple, Mishnaic and Talmudic Periods: Studies in Honor of Shmuel Safrai,* ed. Il Gavni, A. Oppenheimer, M. Stern (Jerusalem: Yad Izhak Ben-Zvi, 1993), 75–106 (Hebrew); David Ussishkin, *The Village of Silwan: The Necropolis from the Period of the Judean Kingdom* (Jerusalem: Israel Antiquities Authority, 1993); P. Figueras, *Decorated Jewish Ossuaries,* DMOA 20 (Leiden: Brill, 1983); E. M. Meyers, *Jewish Ossuaries: Reburial and Rebirth,* BibOr 24 (Rome: Pontifical Biblical Institute Press, 1971); L. Y. Rahmani, *A Catalogue of Jewish Ossuaries in the Collections of the State of Israel* (Jerusalem: The Israel Antiquities Authority, 1994).

tions. Naturally for the novice or uninitiated the discovery of this tomb would appear to be a phenomenal find because it has the names of Jesus and Joseph, along with other names found in the New Testament (e.g., Mary/Miriam, Matthew, James).

The names found in the tomb did not raise further investigation by the scholarly community because most are aware that these were common names in first-century Palestine (see discussion by Bauckham). In addition, what is known about the historical Jesus does not match the archaeological data from the Talpiot tomb (see discussion by Habermas).

WHICH JESUS IS IN THE TOMB? JESUS OF NAZARETH OR JESUS OF TALPIOT?

All that the archaeological data can tell us is that the Talpiot tomb contained a person whose name was Jesus. In another chapter the *Lexicon of Jewish Names* will be discussed, demonstrating that Jesus was a common name. The identity of the Jesus in the Talpiot tomb highlights one of the key issues concerning the use of archaeological data to reconstruct the past. The archaeological record is mute. It must be interpreted. It is difficult without inscriptional or textual data to associate a historical figure with artifactual data.

Archaeologists must interpret the archaeological record in light of historical sources. In the case of the tomb of Jesus, our most pertinent historical sources are the Gospel accounts and later writings of the early church. One of the glaring gaps in the supposed documentary is that they did not present any opposing viewpoint or at least address the traditional site of the tomb of Jesus. As the producer Simcha Jacobovici has stated in many press conferences before and after the airing of the documentary, he wants the public to examine the evidence. If the documentary was actually concerned with the accurate location of the tomb of Jesus, they would have presented a comprehensive documentary of all the evidence and various proposals for the tomb of Jesus. Instead they chose to sensationalize the Talpiot tomb. Any archaeological investigation must first analyze all the archaeological data, then coalesce that data with the historical data, and finally, present a reconstruction of the past. The producers of *The Lost Tomb of Jesus* docudrama start with the assumption that this is the tomb of Jesus and then selectively choose the data they need to support their premise.

While the Talpiot tomb is not the tomb of Jesus of Nazareth, archae-ologists have found the actual tomb of Jesus. As previously mentioned, the Discovery Channel documentary did not present all the evidence and proposals for the tomb of Jesus. If the data had been presented, it would be clear that the tomb at the Church of the Holy Sepulchre in the heart of the modern-day Old City of Jerusalem is the most likely candidate for the tomb of Jesus of Nazareth. This is the tomb that Christians have identified for nearly 2,000 years as the tomb where their Lord and Savior was buried and resurrected.[21]

21 The garden tomb is a recent location put forth for the tomb of Jesus. It was originally proposed in the nineteenth century and probably is the main location that Protestants pro-pose. While Christian tourists have popularized this location, most biblical scholars and archaeologists do not support this view.

THE EAST TALPIOT TOMB IN CONTEXT

Craig A. Evans

Befort assessing the claims recently set forth that the East Talpiot of south Jerusalem may have been the tomb of Jesus of Nazareth and His family, it will be helpful to review Jewish burial practices. It will also be helpful to review how these practices came into play in the life and teaching of Jesus. After establishing a proper context, aspects of the East Talpiot tomb hypothesis will be critically reviewed.

In late antiquity most Jews who owned tombs (whether hewn or natural caves) practiced secondary burial. This was especially the case in the Herodian period.[1] Most who owned such tombs were affluent or upper class. The majority of Jews did not own tombs or burial caves but buried their deceased family members in trench graves and therefore did not practice secondary burial.[2]

Jewish secondary burial is called *ossilegium*, or the gathering and reburial of the bones of the deceased.[3] Primary burial normally took

---

1 Dating from 30 BC to AD 70. It is conjectured that a great increase in population in and around Jerusalem, in combination with the presence of thousands of stonecutters, encouraged widespread usage of ossuaries. Most ossuaries in and around Jerusalem are made of limestone; some are made of clay or wood.

2 See M. Avi-Yonah, *Oriental Art in Roman Palestine,* Studi Semitici 5 (Rome: Università di Roma-Centro di Studi Semitici, 1961), 25–27; V. Tzaferis, "Jewish Tombs at and Near Giv'at ha-Mivtar, Jerusalem," *IEJ* 20 (1970): 18–32. The men of Qumran buried their dead in trench graves, though in ways that were distinctive from typical Jewish practice. On this, see R. Hachlili, "Burial Practices at Qumran," *RevQ* 16 (1993): 247–64.

3 For studies and introductory treatments, see E. M. Meyers, *Jewish Ossuaries: Reburial and Rebirth,* BibOr 24 (Rome: Pontifical Biblical Institute Press, 1971); N. A. Silberman, "Ossuary: A Box for Bones," *BAR* 17/3 (1991): 73–74; L. Y. Rahmani, "Ossuaries and *Ossilegium* (Bone-Gathering) in the Late Second Temple Period," in H. Geva, ed., *Ancient Jerusalem Revealed* (Jerusalem: Israel Exploration Society, 1994), 191–205; S. Fine, "A

---

place on the day of death (unless death occurred at night or at end of day, in which case the body remained in the house and was buried in the morning). The body was washed, perfumed, wrapped, and then placed in the family tomb (or in a cemetery outside the village). Mourning at graveside (or in tomb[4]) perdured for seven days. Mourning consisted of hymns, prayers, weeping, and music. One year later the bones were gathered and placed in an ossuary (or bone pit), perhaps with the deceased's name inscribed: "Hanin, son of Eliezer."[5] The bodies of executed persons were normally not permitted burial in the family tomb until the flesh had decomposed. These practices will be treated in greater detail in the discussion that follows.

JEWISH OSSILEGIUM AND JESUS

Many of the traditions associated with Jewish burial practices, including *ossilegium*, are presupposed or reflected in the life, teaching, and activities of Jesus of Nazareth.[6] Knowledge of these practices is necessary if aspects of His teaching and activity are to be properly understood.

In the New Testament Gospels we sometimes read of funerals. In the story of the widow of Nain, whose son had died, we should assume that death occurred either the very day of the event described or the night before: "As he drew near to the gate of the city, behold, a man who had died was being carried out, the only son of his mother, and she was a widow; and a large crowd from the city was with her" (Luke 7:12 RSV). We are to imagine that as Jesus approached the gate of the city (in order to enter it), He encountered the funeral procession exiting the city on its

Note on Ossuary Burial and the Resurrection of the Dead in First-Century Jerusalem," *JJS* 51 (2000): 69–76; M. Aviam and D. Syon, "Jewish Ossilegium in Galilee," in L. V. Rutgers, ed., *What Athens Has to Do with Jerusalem: Essays on Classical, Jewish, and Early Christian Art and Archaeology in Honor of Gideon Foerster,* Interdisciplinary Studies in Ancient Culture and Religion 1 (Leuven: Peeters, 2002), 151–85.

4 One can see sections of tomb floors that have been carved more deeply, thus allowing mourners to stand while praying, in the Jewish fashion. This is seen, for example, in the tomb on the Mount of Olives, at *Dominus Flevit*.

5 For a recent and comprehensive treatment of Jewish burial traditions, see R. Hachlili, *Jewish Funerary Customs, Practices, and Rites in the Second Temple Period,* JSJSup 94 (Leiden: Brill, 2005). No study of Jewish ossuaries is possible without reference to L. Y. Rahmani, *A Catalogue of Jewish Ossuaries in the Collections of the State of Israel* (Jerusalem: The Israel Antiquities Authority, 1994).

6 These are explored in C. A. Evans, *Jesus and the Ossuaries: What Jewish Burial Practices Reveal about the Beginning of Christianity* (Waco: Baylor University Press, 2003).

way to the cemetery. We find another example of Jesus coming upon a funeral in process: "And when Jesus came to the ruler's house, and saw the flute players, and the crowd making a tumult" (Matt 9:23 RSV). The ruler's child had died, and the mourning—including music and public lamentation—had gotten under way, even before the arrival of the desperate father.

Primary funerals last seven days. Josephus stated this explicitly: "Now Archelaus continued to mourn for seven days out of respect for his father— the custom of the country prescribes this number of days—and then, after feasting the crowds and making an end of mourning, he went up to the temple" (Josephus, *Ant.* 17.8.4 §200). The custom grew out of biblical precedent, as seen in Joseph's mourning for Jacob ("he made a mourning for his father seven days"; Gen 50:6–10 AMP) and the mourning for King Saul and his sons ("they took away the body of Saul and the bodies of his sons, and . . . buried their bones under the oak in Jabesh, and fasted seven days"; 1 Chr 10:12 NASB; cp. 1 Sam 31:13). When we are told that Lazarus, the brother of Mary and Martha, had been dead four days, we should understand that the week of mourning was about half spent (more on this story below).

Secondary burial takes place about one year after death (*b. Qiddushin* 31b "twelve months"). During this time the flesh has decomposed, and the bones may be gathered and placed in an ossuary.[7] Mourning at the time of secondary burial is only for one day.[8] Sometimes the bones were anointed with oil or wine.[9] It was believed, moreover, that the decomposition of the flesh atoned for what sins may have remained.[10]

---

7 "When the flesh had wasted away they gathered together the bones and buried them in their own place" (*m. Sanh.* 6:6). "My son, bury me at first in a niche. In the course of time, collect my bones and put them in an ossuary but do not gather them with your own hands" (*Semahot* 12.9; cf. *Semahot* 3.2; 12.7; *y. Moʿed Qatan* 1.5). "The bones may not be gathered until the flesh has wasted away; once it has, the features are no longer recognizable in the skeleton" (*Semahot* 12.7 [attributed to Rabbi Aqiba, a late first-, early second-century sage]). The limestone on which Jerusalem is situated and from which most ossuaries were made facilitated rapid decay.

8 "Mourning must be observed for only one day" (*Semahot* 12.1).

9 "The bones may be sprinkled with wine and oil" (*Semahot* 12.9). Some authorities dispute the usefulness of sprinkling with wine (because it evaporates). There is archaeological evidence for this practice, as seen in the discovery of oil juglets and wine amphorae. For discussion and photographs, see Hachlili, *Jewish Funerary Customs, Practices, and Rites*, 378–79, 383–85 + pls. X–3, X–4 (for examples of ungentaria), X–5, and X–6.

10 "(On the day of ossilegium) the son mourned, but the following day he was glad, because his forebears rested from judgment" (*y. Moʿed Qatan* 1.5; cf. *b. Rosh Hashanah*

It is probable that the man who responded to Jesus' summons to discipleship with the request "Lord, let me first go and bury my father" (Matt 8:21 = Luke 9:59 RSV) was referring to secondary burial. That is, his father was not aged or lying on his deathbed; rather, his father had already died and the anniversary of secondary burial was approaching. When this important filial responsibility is discharged, the man will be available to follow Jesus. But Jesus retorted: "Let the dead bury their own dead" (Matt 8:22 = Luke 9:60a). Jesus has not told the would-be disciple to neglect an aged or suffering parent; He has urged him to leave the dead in the family tomb to attend to secondary burial.[11] It is far more urgent that the man proclaim the rule of God (see Luke 9:60b) than be diverted by secondary burial.

Jewish burial traditions are seen in the story of Lazarus and his grieving sisters Mary and Martha (John 11). When Jesus was told that Lazarus "has been dead four days!" (John 11:39 RSV), His Jewish contemporaries would have assumed that all hope was lost. According to tradition: "For three days (after death) the soul hovers over the body, intending to re-enter it, but as soon as it sees its appearance change (on the fourth day), it departs" (*Lev. Rab.* 18.1 [on Lev 15:1–2]).[12] Because Lazarus has been dead four days, his soul had departed; resuscitation was no longer possible. Accordingly, the raising of Lazarus, on the fourth day of his death, would have astounded everyone.

Excavation of tombs in Palestine and the anthropological and medical study of the skeletal remains found within them have provided important information regarding health and longevity of the Jewish people in the time of Jesus. Skeletal remains suggest that as many as one quarter of the population on any given day was in need of medical help; often only one-third of the skeletons found in tombs are of adults.[13] Jesus' reputation as a successful healer guaranteed that people would try to touch Him

17a; *b. Sanh.* 47b "the decay of the flesh is also necessary for forgiveness").

11 This is rightly argued by B. R. McCane, "'Let the Dead Bury Their Own Dead': Secondary Burial and Matt 8:21–22," *HTR* 83 (1990): 31–43.

12 "The full intensity of mourning lasts up to the third day because the appearance of the face is still recognizable" (*Qoh. Rab.* 12:6 §1).

13 J. Zias ("Anthropological Analysis of Human Skeletal Remains," in G. Avni and Z. Greenhut, in collaboration with others, *The Akeldama Tombs: Three Burial Caves in the Kidron Valley, Jerusalem,* Israel Antiquities Authority Reports 1 [Jerusalem: Israel Antiquities Authority, 1996], 117–21) remarks: "However, the mortality profile . . . is in accordance with that of tombs from the Roman period. . . . Collectively 48% of the deceased failed to reach adulthood. This is normative and indicates that the relative wealth of the

(see Mark 5:28; 6:56; 8:22; 10:13). This then explains why when "such a very large crowd gathered . . . He got into a boat" (Mark 4:1 NASB). In order to teach unmolested, Jesus found it necessary to create around Himself a moat.

On one occasion Jesus rebuked some of the religious teachers for criticizing His disciples for eating with unwashed hands (Mark 7:1–13). Jesus referred to the tradition of dedicating something to sacred use: "You say, 'If a man tells his father or his mother, What you would have gained from me is Corban' (that is, given to God)—then you no longer permit him to do anything for his father or mother, thus making void the word of God through your tradition which you hand on" (Mark 7:11–13 RSV). This word *corban*, meaning sacred gift, is found inscribed on an ossuary: "Everything that a man will find to his profit in this ossuary (is) an offering to God *[corban]* from the one within it." The use of the word *corban* in this inscription parallels exactly the tradition to which Jesus made reference.[14]

Observation of the monumental tombs, especially those that run along the Kidron Valley,[15] clarifies Jesus' scathing remarks against His critics: "You are like whitewashed tombs"; and "You build the tombs of the prophets!" (Matt 23:27,29 RSV). At the approach of major festivals, these tombs were whitewashed, and sometimes the inscriptions were highlighted with bright colors.[16] Jesus' graphic comparisons would have readily conjured up familiar images in the minds of His hearers.

There is a striking point of comparison with Simon Peter and one of the many ossuary inscriptions that bear the name Simon. On the end of the ossuary, the inscription reads: "Simon, builder of the temple."[17]

families buried here, manifested by tomb architecture and the ossuaries, did not confer any significant health advantages" (118).

14 For discussion of this inscription, see J. A. Fitzmyer, "The Aramaic Qorban Inscription from Jebel Hallet Et-Turi and Mk 7:11/Mt 15:5," *JBL* 78 (1959): 60–65; repr. Fitzmyer, *Essays on the Semitic Background of the New Testament* (London: Chapman, 1971; repr. SBLSBS 5; Missoula: Scholars, 1974), 93–100.

15 These include the Tomb of Jehoshaphat, the Tomb (or Pillar) of Absalom, the Tomb of the Sons of Hezir, and the Tomb of Zechariah.

16 For discussion of these monumental tombs, see Hachlili, *Jewish Funerary Customs, Practices, and Rites*, 29–43. Traces of red paint can still be found in part of the inscription on the Tomb of the Sons of Hezir (again see Hachlili, *Jewish Funerary Customs, Practices, and Rites*, 168).

17 Rahmani, *A Catalogue of Jewish Ossuaries*, 124 (no. 200). The inscription appears twice—once in Hebrew and once in Aramaic. See also Mas no. 561: "Simo *[sic]* the builder."

We immediately think of Matt 16:18, where Jesus told Simon, whom he nicknamed "Peter": "I will build My church." It is not suggested here that either Jesus or the Matthean evangelist alluded to the person mentioned in the ossuary inscription. Rather, it may well be that the occupational description, "builder of the temple," served a quasi-religious function. Simon and many others were builders of the temple of Jerusalem, a building project that commenced before Jesus was born and which finally concluded some 30 years after His death. Building the temple, therefore, was a constant throughout His lifetime. Perhaps mimicking this way of speaking, as reflected in the Simon ossuary inscription, Jesus declared that His Simon Peter will become the "builder" of Jesus' church, something parallel to and perhaps over against the temple.

One should also mention the remarkable ossuary found at *Dominus Flevit* and identified by Bellarmino Bagatti, which seems to read *Shimon bar Yonah* ("Simon, son of Jonah").[18] One thinks of the beatitude that Jesus pronounced on Simon Peter: "Blessed are you, Simon son of Jonah [*bar Yonah*]" (Matt 16:17 NIV). If Bagatti's reading is correct—and it is disputed—then we may be in possession of fragments of Peter's ossuary.[19]

In the death, burial, and resurrection of Jesus Jewish burial traditions have much to teach us. We find many interesting points of contact:

"She has anointed my body beforehand" (Mark 14:8 RSV). When Jesus interpreted the generous anointing of Himself by the unnamed woman as an anointing of His "body beforehand," He hinted at His anticipation of a criminal's death, where anointing might be omitted (for perfume, see Josephus, *Ant.* 15.3.4 §61; for spices, see ibid., *Ant.* 17.8.3 §196–99). Jesus' hasty burial as an executed criminal explains why the women visited His tomb early Sunday, bearing with them spices (Mark 16:1). It has already been mentioned that juglets and perfume bottles have been found in Jewish tombs that date to the time of Jesus.[20]

18 B. Bagatti, "Scoperta di un cimitero giudeo-cristiano al 'Dominus Flevit'," *Studii Biblici Franciscani Liber Annuus* 3 (1952–53), 149–84, esp. 162. Some of the ossuary fragments of *Dominus Flevit* bear the Greek letters *chi-rho*, signifying *Christos* ("Christ," or "Messiah").

19 For more on this ossuary and its inscription, see B. Bagatti and J. T. Milik, *Gli scavi del "Dominus Flevit' (Monte Oliveto—Gerusalemme): Parte I. La necropoli del periodo romano* (Jerusalem: Francescani, 1958), 83 + pls. 75 and 81. Milik reads more cautiously: "Simon, son of . . . " He is not sure that the second name is *Yonah*.

20 See n. 9 above.

"Then those who had seized Jesus led him to Caiaphas the high priest, where the scribes and the elders had gathered" (Matt 26:57 RSV; see Mark 14:53 RSV, "All the chief priests and the elders and the scribes were assembled"). The family tomb and ossuary of Caiaphas the high priest may have been found, in Peace Forest, not far from East Talpiot. One inscription reads: "Joseph, son of Caiaphas."[21] Josephus mentions this priest: "the high priest Joseph called Caiaphas" (*Ant.* 18.4.3 §95). It is amazing to think that this beautifully ornamented ossuary may have contained the skeletal remains of the man who condemned Jesus and delivered Him to the Roman governor.[22] Ossuaries belonging to or mentioning the names of other Jewish high priests have also been recovered.[23]

"And they bound Jesus and led him away and delivered him to Pilate" (Mark 15:1 RSV). The name of the governor has been found inscribed on a stone at Caesarea Maritima, the official residence of the governor of Judea. The inscription reads: "Pontius Pilate, Prefect of Judea, dedicates the Tiberieum of the (?)."[24] The inscription gives Pilate's rank as *praefectus*, not *procurator*, as stated mistakenly in Cornelius Tacitus, the Roman historian: "Christus . . . suffered the death penalty during the reign of Tiberius, by sentence of the procurator Pontius Pilate" (*Annals* 15.44).

"Having scourged Jesus, he delivered him to be crucified" (Mark 15:15 RSV). Roman scourging was severe and was standard procedure in cases of crucifixion (cf. *Digesta* 48.19.8.3). Josephus tells us of another Jesus, one son of Ananias, who in AD 62 began proclaiming the downfall of Jerusalem and the destruction of the temple: "The magistrates brought him (Jesus ben Ananias) before the Roman governor; there, although flayed to the bone with scourges, he neither sued for mercy nor shed a

21 For discussion and photographs, see R. Reich, "Caiaphas Name Inscribed on Bone Boxes," *BAR* 18/5 (1992): 38–44, 76; idem, "Ossuary Inscriptions from the 'Caiaphas' Tomb," *'Atiqot* 21 (1992): 72–77.
22 A few scholars have expressed reservations about the Caiaphas identification. See W. Horbury, "The 'Caiaphas' Ossuaries and Joseph Caiaphas," *PEQ* 126 (1994): 32–48.
23 They are reviewed in Evans, *Jesus and the Ossuaries*, 108–12. They include Theophilus, Ananias, Qatros, Boethus, and Yoezer (or Joazar). See also Hachlili, *Jewish Funerary Customs, Practices, and Rites*, 262–73.
24 Originally published by A. Frova, "L'iscrizione di Ponzio Pilato a Cesarea," *Rendiconti dell'Istituto Lombardo* 95 (1961): 419–34 + fig. 3. See now G. Alföldy, "Pontius Pilatus und das Tiberieum von Caesarea Maritima," *Scripta Classica Israelica* 18 (1999): 85–108. Alfödy thinks the Tiberium was a building related in some way to the harbor facilities at Caesarea Maritima, which underwent refurbishing during the administration of Pilate.

tear" (*J.W.* 6.5.3 §303–4). The phrase "flayed to the bone with scourges" translates literally the Greek text.

"And they led him out to crucify him" (Mark 15:20 RSV). Jesus was crucified in a public place outside the walls of Jerusalem. Public crucifixion was meant to terrify, as one Roman explained: "Whenever we crucify the condemned, the most crowded roads are chosen, where the most people can see and be moved by this terror. For penalties relate not so much to retribution as to their exemplary effect" (Ps.–Quintilian, *Declamations* 274). Similarly, Josephus explains that General Titus's "main reason for not stopping the crucifixions (during the siege of Jerusalem) was the hope that the spectacle might perhaps induce the Jews to surrender" (*J.W.* 5.11.1 §450–51).[25] The people whom Titus crucified were not taken down before nightfall, and they were not buried. Denial of burial, to the Jewish mind, was almost as horrible as death itself.

"And they compelled a passer-by, Simon of Cyrene, who was coming in from the country, the father of Alexander and Rufus, to carry his cross" (Mark 15:21 RSV). According to Plautus, the condemned man carried the crossbeam of his cross (the *patibulum*) through the city to the place of crucifixion (*Carbonaria* 2; *Miles gloriosus* 2.4.6–7 §359–60); so also Plutarch: "Every wrongdoer who goes to execution carries out his own cross" (*Moralia* 554A-B). Likewise, Jesus of Nazareth carried the *patibulum*, or at least tried to. Unable to carry the cross the distance, a bystander—one Simon of Cyrene, the father of Alexander and Rufus, was compelled to assist him (Mark 15:21). Amazingly enough, we may actually have the ossuary of Alexander, son of Simon of Cyrene. On the front and back sides of the ossuary appears the Greek inscription "Alexander, son of Simon." On the lid of the ossuary appears the Greek "of Alexander" and the Hebrew "Alexander the Cyrene."[26]

"And they crucified him" (Mark 15:24 RSV). An ossuary containing the skeletal remains of one Yehohanan, crucified during the administration of Pontius Pilate, was found in 1968 in Jerusalem in the district *Givʿat ha-Mivtar* (ossuary no. 4. in Tomb I). Quite surprisingly, an iron spike that had pierced the right heal was still in place. Evidently those

25 For more on crucifixion in Roman late antiquity, see M. Hengel, *Crucifixion: In the Ancient World and the Folly of the Message of the Cross* (London: SCM Press; Philadelphia: Fortress, 1977).
26 For discussion and photographs, see N. Avigad, "A Depository of Inscribed Ossuaries in the Kidron Valley," *IEJ* 12 (1962): 1–12 + plates 1–4.

who took down the body of Yehohanan had been unable to extract the spike.[27] Discovery of the skeletal remains of a victim of crucifixion demonstrates that Pilate (as well as other Roman officials) did indeed permit the proper burial, according to Jewish customs, of executed criminals.[28] *"Pilate . . . granted the body to Joseph . . . and [he] laid him in a tomb"* (Mark 15:42–46 RSV). Jewish law did not permit the burial of executed criminals in places of honor (by which is usually meant one's family tomb). We see this expressed in various allusions to Jewish law and custom: "They used not to bury (the executed criminal) in the burying-place of his fathers, but two burying-places were kept in readiness by the court, one for them that were beheaded or strangled, and one for them that were stoned or burnt" (m. *Sanh.* 6:5); "When the flesh had wasted away they gathered together the bones and buried them in their own place" (*m. Sanh.* 6:6); "Neither a corpse nor the bones of a corpse may be transferred from a wretched place to an honored place, nor, needless to say, from an honored placed to a wretched place; but if to the family tomb, even from an honored place to a wretched place, it is permitted" (*Semahot* 13.7). One text specifically refers to crucifixion: "If one's (relative) has been crucified in his city, one should not continue to reside there. . . . Until when is one so forbidden? Until the flesh is completely decomposed and the identity unrecognizable from the bones."[29] Because the Jewish Council (or Sanhedrin) surrendered Jesus to the Roman authorities for execution, it was incumbent upon it to arrange for proper burial (as in *m. Sanh.* 6:5 cited above). Jesus was not buried *honorably*, but He was buried *properly*. This task fell to Joseph of Arimathea, a member of the Council.

There is no evidence that Roman authorities, during peacetime, denied burial to criminals. Besides the aforementioned evidence of the

27 For discussion and photographs, see J. Naveh, "The Ossuary Inscriptions from Givʿat ha-Mivtar, Jerusalem," *IEJ* 20 (1970): 33–37; Y. Yadin, "Epigraphy and Crucifixion," *IEJ* 23 (1973): 18–22 + plate; J. Zias and J. H. Charlesworth, "Crucifixion: Archaeology, Jesus, and the Dead Sea Scrolls," in J. H. Charlesworth, ed., *Jesus and the Dead Sea Scrolls,* ABRL (New York: Doubleday, 1992), 273–89 + plates (following p. 184). On the use of nails in crucifixion, see J. W. Hewitt, "The Use of Nails in the Crucifixion," *HTR* 25 (1932): 29–45. Nails and spikes have been found in tombs, probably having been used to incise names on ossuaries and on the walls of the tombs.

28 Skeletal remains of other persons evidently executed but properly buried have been recovered. For more on this, see C. A. Evans, "Jewish Burial Traditions and the Resurrection of Jesus," *JSHJ* 3 (2005): 233–48, esp. 244.

29 See Meyers, *Ossuaries,* 73–74 (n. 7), 90 (+ n. 63), for support of an early date of the tradition in the minor tractate *Semahot.*

crucified Yehohanan, whose body was properly buried, we have literary evidence that the Romans respected Jewish sensitivities in this regard. The primary motivation for burying the dead before nightfall was to avoid defiling the land, as commanded in Scripture (see Deut 21:22–23). Both Philo and Josephus claim that the Romans honored Jewish law and customs (Philo, *Leg. ad Gaium* 300; *Flaccus* 83; Josephus, *Ag. Ap.* 2.73). Even Roman law allowed the bodies of the crucified to be taken down and be buried (*Digesta* 48.24.1, 3).[30]

"Mary Magdalene and Mary the mother of Jesus saw where he was laid" (Mark 15:47 RSV). It was necessary for Jesus' family and friends to observe the place where the body of Jesus was placed, for it was not placed in a tomb that belonged to His family or otherwise was under their control. The reburial of the bones of Yehohanan, the man who also had been crucified under the authority of Pontius Pilate, demonstrates that the Jewish people knew how to note and remember the place of primary burial. The family and friends of Jesus anticipated recovering His skeletal remains, perhaps one year later, so that they "may be transferred from a wretched place to an honored place," as the law allowed (see *Semahot* 13.7; *m. Sanh.* 6:6).[31]

"And when the Sabbath was past, . . . [they] brought spices, so that they might go and anoint him" (Mark 16:1 RSV). The women intended to mourn for Jesus privately; spices and perfumes were therefore necessary. Mourning privately (because of the criminality of the deceased) is addressed in Jewish law: "They used not to make [open] lamentation . . . for mourning has place in the heart alone" (*m. Sanh.* 6:6). On the tradition of perfuming the deceased, see Josephus, who says that Herod "provided a very fine tomb and a great quantity of perfumes" for his son Aristobulus, whom Herod had arranged to be

---

30 For these reasons and others the novel proposal that the body of Jesus was not buried but either was left hanging on the cross or was cast into a ditch where it was eaten by animals must be rejected without reservation. For this proposal, see J. D. Crossan, *Who Killed Jesus? Exposing the Roots of Anti-Semitism in the Gospel Story of the Death of Jesus* (San Francisco: HarperCollins, 1995).

31 Judging by Caesar's inscription found in the vicinity of Nazareth (and its original provenance is uncertain), unauthorized transfer of human remains was a serious offence. See *SEG* VIII no. 13, which is discussed by, among others, B. M. Metzger, "The Nazareth Inscription Once Again," in *New Testament Studies: Philological, Versional, and Patristic,* NTTS 10 (Leiden: Brill, 1980), 75–92. The inscription reads in part: "If someone has transferred them to another place, to the dishonor of those buried there . . . I command a trial take place."

murdered (*Ant.* 15.3.4 §61). In the case of Herod's funeral, Josephus tells us that several hundred servants carried spices to the Herodium, the place where burial took place (*Ant.* 17.8.3 §196–99). In the case of Jesus, the women intended to perfume His body and spread fragrant aroma in the tomb. Because Jesus had been executed as a criminal, *public* lamentation would not be permitted, but *private* mourning was allowed.

"Who will roll away the stone . . . ?" (Mark 16:3 RSV). Matthew says a guard was posted to prevent violation of the laws that forbade either public lamentation or removal of the body to a place of honor (Matt 27:65–66). The women knew that there would be reluctance to assist them in rolling back the stone that covered the opening of Jesus' tomb. Study of the skeletal remains from this period of time indicates that the average woman was under five feet tall and weighed less than 100 pounds. The average man was five feet four inches and weighed 135 pounds. Sealing stones weighed hundreds of pounds. Even round stones, which were designed to be rolled aside, would have been very difficult to move. The Markan evangelist, moreover, comments that the stone was very large (Mark 16:4). Accordingly, the women wonder where they might find assistance.

"They saw that the stone was rolled back" (Mark 16:4 RSV). The statement that the "stone was rolled back" implies a round stone over the entrance to the tomb. In Jewish Palestine of late antiquity, 80 percent of the doors of tombs were square; only 20 percent were round.[32] Discovery of the opened and empty tomb would have dismayed the women, especially Mary, the mother of Jesus. For this would mean that the body of Jesus had been relocated. Sunday was the third day of death; if Jesus' body were not found *that day*, then it probably would never be identified. As noted above, it was believed that on the fourth day the soul departed and the face of the corpse was no longer recognizable. *Resurrection of an individual was not expected.*

---

32 See H. Geva, "Tombs," in E. Stern, ed., *The New Encyclopedia of Archaeological Excavations in the Holy Land* (4 vols.; Jerusalem: The Israel Exploration Society, 1993), 2:747–49. Geva remarks: "The opening was thoroughly sealed with a square stone, set in a depressed frame that was cut to fit. In only a few caves was there a circular rolling stone, weighing a few hundred kilograms, that could be moved in a fixed track between two rock-cut or artificially built walls" (747–48). Two of the best-known Jerusalem tombs with circular sealing stones and grooved tracks are the Tomb of the Family of Herod and the Garden Tomb (a.k.a. Gordon's Tomb).

PROBLEMS WITH THE EAST TALPIOT
TOMB HYPOTHESIS

There are several problems with the hypothesis that the East Talpiot tomb excavated by Yosef Gat and Amos Kloner in 1980[33] is none other than the tomb of Jesus of Nazareth and His family. To reach this conclusion Simcha Yacobovici and Charles Pellegrino made a series of claims,[34] most of which have serious problems. The present chapter treats three of these problems: (1) The claim that the X-mark at the beginning of the inscription, "Yeshua, son of Yehosef," signifies a cross and as such is a Christian symbol. There also are difficulties with the incision of the name Yeshua. (2) The claim that the gable and circle above the tomb's entrance is a Jewish-Christian symbol. (3) The claim that the James ossuary, which was brought to public attention in 2002, is the tenth, so-called "missing" ossuary of the East Talpiot tomb. All three of these claims are highly problematic and almost certainly false.

CLAIM I: THE X-MARK ON THE "YESHUA, SON OF YEHOSEF" OSSUARY

The inventory number of the unadorned ossuary bearing the inscription "Yeshua, son of Yehosef" is 80.503.[35] To the right of the inscription (that is, at the beginning of the inscription, remembering that Hebrew and Aramaic read from right to left) incised on one end of this ossuary one observes an X-mark. Because a few Christian marks have been found on ossuaries in and around Jerusalem (such as the *chi-rho* symbol mentioned above), it is theoretically possible that the X-mark on the East Talpiot tomb ossuary is a Christian mark. Indeed, a few archaeologists and scholars have argued that some of the X-marks on ossuaries

---

33 The tomb was accidentally uncovered in March 1980 during construction on Dov Gruner Street in the Jerusalem neighborhood of East Talpiot. A brief report of the discovery and excavation was published the following year. See Y. Gat, "East Talpiot," *Hadashot Arkheologiyot* [= *Archaeological News*] 76 (1981): 24–25 (Hebrew). Not long after publication head archaeologist Gat died, leaving it to Kloner to publish the fuller report (in English). See A. Kloner, "A Tomb with Inscribed Ossuaries in East Talpiyot, Jerusalem," *'Atiqot* 29 (1996): 15–22 (with sketches by S. Gibson).

34 See S. Jacobovici and C. Pellegrino, *The Jesus Family Tomb: The Discovery, the Investigation, and the Evidence That Could Change History* (San Francisco: HarperCollins, 2007). The release of this book coincided with a television documentary that aired on Discovery Channel and other cable outlets. Neither author is an archaeologist, historian, or biblical scholar.

35 It appears in Rahmani, *Catalogue of Jewish Ossuaries*, 223, as no. 704.

are Christian symbols of the cross,[36] an interpretation that others have vigorously challenged.[37]

It is far more probable that the X-mark on ossuary 80.503 is the mark of the stone mason who made the ossuary or the mark of the person who incised the inscription. The typical function of the X-mark was to align the lid with the ossuary. This function is clearly seen in several ossuaries.[38]

One more issue needs to be raised concerning ossuary 80.503. The name Yeshua in the inscription is barely discernible. However, after comparison with three other ossuary inscriptions, where the name Yeshua occurs,[39] as well as taking into account ossuary 80.501 of the East Talpiot tomb, whose inscription reads "Yehudah, son of Yeshua,"[40] it should be acknowledged that Yeshua is probably the correct reading of ossuary 80.503. But the matter remains complicated, for some epigraphers believe the name Yeshua may have been incised over another name, perhaps Yudan (as S. Pfann details in a forthcoming work). If so, this is quite unusual and raises yet more unanswered questions. The inscription of ossuary 80.503 needs further study.

---

36 As first suggested by pioneer archaeologist Charles S. Clermont-Ganneau. His suggestion has been defended and developed further in Bagatti and Milik, *Gli scavi del "Dominus Flevit' (Monte Oliveto—Gerusalemme): Parte I. La necropoli del periodo romano*, 63–69; J. Daniélou, *Primitive Christian Symbols* (Baltimore: Helicon, 1964), 139–45.

37 The suggestion that some of these marks are Christian has been challenged by C. H. Kraeling, "Christian Burial Urns?" *BA* 9 (1946): 16–20. E. R. Goodenough agrees with Kraeling, concluding that the X-marks and +–marks have nothing to do with Christianity. See also G. E. Wright, "New Information Regarding the Supposed 'Christian' Ossuaries," *BA* 9 (1946): 43; E. R. Goodenough, *Jewish Symbols in the Greco-Roman Period*, vols. 1–3, Bollingen Series 37 (New York: Pantheon Books, 1953), 1:130–31 (for discussion); and 3: figs. 227, 228, and 229 (for photographs); R. H. Smith, "The Cross Marks on Jewish Ossuaries," *PEQ* 106 (1974): 53–66. Smith sensibly concludes that the "crude cross marks on ossuaries are non-religious in nature" (66). He wonders, moreover, why Christians would incise crude cross signs that cannot be distinguished from marks "placed there as guides for the matching of lids to receptacles" (65).

38 See P. Figueras, *Decorated Jewish Ossuaries,* Documenta et Monumenta Orientis Antiqui 20 (Leiden: Brill, 1983), plate 8, for examples of the stone mason's mark. Nos. 468, 577, 638 are clear examples of X-marks; nos. 568 and 638 are clear examples of X-marks and other types of marks that indicate proper alignment of lid with ossuary. See also Rahmani, *Catalogue of Jewish Ossuaries*, 166 (no. 392 + pl. 56).

39 See Rahmani, *Catalogue of Jewish Ossuaries*, 77 (no. 9), 108 (no. 121), and 113 (no. 140). Of the three the last comes closest to the form of the name in ossuary 80.503.

40 See Rahmani, *Catalogue of Jewish Ossuaries*, 223 (no. 702).

CLAIM 2: THE GABLE AND CIRCLE ABOVE THE TOMB'S ENTRANCE IS A JEWISH-CHRISTIAN SYMBOL

Perhaps the most demonstrably false claim in the East Talpiot tomb hypothesis is the claim that the pointed gable and circle over the tomb's entrance is an early Jewish-Christian symbol. The gable over a circle (or rosette)[41] is not mysterious, and it is not Christian. It is Jewish and it is pre-Christian.

The pointed gable over a circle or rosette is seen in other tombs and ossuaries, some of which predate the Christian era and none of which is believed to have anything to do with Jesus and His movement. We see this artistic design in the outer and inner façades of the so-called "Sanhedrin Tombs" in Jerusalem. Over the inner entrance of this tomb complex one can see the pointed gable over a rosette, comprised of acanthus leaves. A gable is also found over the outer entrance but without a rosette.[42] This pattern is seen in the Hinnom Valley Tomb, the Tomb of Jehoshaphat, and the so-called Grape Tomb.[43]

In his *Jewish Symbols in the Greco-Roman Period* Erwin Goodenough provided several photographs and facsimiles that depict the gable and circle/rosette. Among these items are ossuaries, a tomb façade, a coin (struck by Philip, tetrarch of Gaulanitis in the time of Jesus), and epitaph art.[44] One of the more common features is the Torah ark (which contains Scripture scrolls), over which the pointed gable and circle appear. Goodenough remarked that "the box with Moses, and all the arks of the synagogue, shows a form extremely old, one chiefly associated with

41 Jacobovici and Pellegrino (*The Jesus Family Tomb*, 11–12, 128–30) misleadingly refer to the gable as a chevron or inverted V and create the impression that there is something mysterious about the circle/rosette beneath the gable.

42 See J. J. Rothschild, "The Tombs of Sanhedria," *PEQ* 84 (1952): 23–28; 86 (1954): 16–22; N. Avigad, "Sanhedrin Tombs," in Stern, ed., *The New Encyclopedia of Archaeological Excavations in the Holy Land*, 2:752 (with photograph).

43 Hachlili, *Jewish Funerary Customs, Practices, and Rites*, pl. IV–2 (of Tomb of Jehoshaphat; with pointed gable over circular vine and cluster), 45, fig. II–12 (the Hinnom Valley Tomb); 46–49 + fig. II–14; p. 139 + fig. IV–7 (the "Grape Tomb" and the Tomb of Jehoshaphat). See also Goodenough, *Jewish Symbols in the Greco-Roman Period*, 3: fig. 23 (the Sanhedrin Tombs); fig. 24 (the "Grape Tomb"). For discussion of the "Grape Tomb," see Goodenough, *Jewish Symbols in the Greco-Roman Period*, 1:80.

44 Goodenough, *Jewish Symbols in the Greco-Roman Period*, 3: figs. 142 and 143, 239 (ossuaries), 508 (tomb façade); 676 (coin struck by Philip, tetrarch of Gaulanitis); 707 and 710 (epitaph art: Torah arks with gable and circle); for commentary on fig. 710, see 2:6, "I should judge that the circle within the gable would have been a wreath or rosette in a larger drawing."

tombstones. . . . It is customary to call this object a temple, but it may well have been a chest which, like the Ark, brought the divine presence." He comments further, with reference to another example of a Torah ark: "The design was almost certainly affected, or made to seem pertinent, by the great stone Temple of Herod."[45]

In his study of the Jews of ancient Rome, Harry Leon provided an image of an epitaph, at the bottom of which is a Torah ark containing six Scripture scrolls. Over the ark is a pointed gable.[46] Excavations of the Jewish tombs of Beth Shearim in Galilee have uncovered the same artistic motifs. Again we find a Torah ark, at the top of which is the gable above a circle (or rosette), painted on a sealing stone. Benjamin Mazar commented: "The subject portrayed on this sealing-stone is one of the most common in ancient Jewish art; it occurs in synagogues in Palestine and abroad, in catacombs, on tombstones, on gold glass from Rome, etc. In all of these instances we frequently find representations of the Holy Ark ('hekhal') or an Ark between two Menorahs."[47]

It has already been mentioned that the symbol of pointed gable over circle or rosette appears on coins minted by Philip the tetrarch, son of Herod the Great. The symbol is also found on Hasmonean coins from an earlier period and, with some variation, on Bar Kokhba coins of a later period. The rosette over a temple façade is a standard feature in Bar Kokhba's coins.[48]

The gable and circle/rosette pattern is found on several ossuaries, with the circle or rosette on the end of the ossuary, over which rests the

45 E. R. Goodenough, *Jewish Symbols in the Greco-Roman Period: Abridged Edition,* ed. Jacob Neusner (Princeton: Princeton University Press, 1988). For Torah arks, adorned with pointed gables (beneath which appear rosettes or similar patterns), see figs. 9, 38, and 47. The first quotation above is taken from p. 205 and is in reference to fig. 47. The second quotation above is taken from p. 197 and is in reference to fig. 38.

46 H. J. Leon, *The Jews of Ancient Rome,* The Morris Loeb series (Philadelphia: Jewish Publication Society of America, 1960; rev., with Introduction by C. Osiek; Peabody: Hendrickson, 1995), pl. xx, fig. 34, with transcription and translation on p. 325.

47 B. Mazar, *Beth She'arim: Report on the Excavations During 1936–1940.* Volume I: *Catacombs 1–4* (New Brunswick: Rutgers University Press, 1973), 110–13. See figs. 1 and 2 on p. 113. These images depict exactly what Mazar describes. See also N. Avigad, *Beth She'arim: The Excavations 1953–1958.* Volume III: *Catacombs 12–23* (New Brunswick: Rutgers University Press, 1976), pl. XLIV.1, which depicts a pointed gable over an elaborate rosette or halfshell; for discussion, see p. 145; and Figueras, *Decorated Jewish Ossuaries,* 28–29, for discussion of rosettes/circles.

48 L. Mildenberg, *The Coinage of the Bar Kokhba War* (Typos: Monographien zur antiken Numismatik 6; Franfurt am Main: Sauerländer, 1984), 32 (fig. 1). For other figures (by way of comparison) see 34 (figs. 2 and 3), 35 (fig. 4), 41 (fig. 10).

gabled lid, or on the end of the lid itself, thus forming the very pattern seen over the entrance to the East Talpiot tomb.[49] An ossuary found on Mount Scopus is particularly relevant, for it depicts monumental façades, with temple motifs, on all four sides.[50] Both ends and one side present pointed gables over entrances. Beneath two of these pointed gables (on one end of the ossuary and on the less finished side of the ossuary) is a circle, in a pattern quite like what we see over the entrance to the East Talpiot tomb.[51]

And finally, depictions of the Torah ark, complete with gable and circle (or rosette) are found in synagogue art. Striking examples are found in the art adorning the walls of the Dura Europos Synagogue, where the designs are in reference to the Jerusalem temple.[52]

The evidence is overwhelming. The pointed gable and circle over the entrance to the East Talpiot tomb is Jewish and has nothing to do with Jesus and early Christians. The symbol is probably in reference to the temple. Given the fact that aristocratic and high priestly families were buried in the greater Talpiot area and the fact that every single name in the East Talpiot tomb is Hasmonean,[53] it is probable that this tomb belonged to a wealthy, aristocratic Jerusalem family with ties to the temple. Indeed, some of the members of the family buried in the East Talpiot tomb may have been ruling priests. The suggestion that the gable

49 See Rahmani, *Catalogue of Jewish Ossuaries*, 143–44 (no. 282 + pl. 40), 146 (no. 294 + pl. 42), 166 (no. 392 + pl. 56), 169–40 (no. 408 + pl. 59), 184–85 (no. 482 + pl. 72), and 262–63 (no. 893 + pl. 134); Hachlili, *Jewish Funerary Customs, Practices, and Rites*, pl. III–3 (of a wooden coffin found at Nahal David; end of gabled lid presents a rosette).

50 A. Kloner, "An Ossuary from Jerusalem Ornamented with Monumental Facades," in Geva, ed., *Ancient Jerusalem Revealed*, 235–38. We are concerned with Ossuary 14 found in Chamber E (now catalogued as 74.1508). The excavation was carried out in May and June 1974. See also Rahmani, *Catalogue of Jewish Ossuaries*, 184–85 (no. 482 + pl. 72).

51 See Kloner, "An Ossuary from Jerusalem Ornamented with Monumental Facades," 236, figure on the lower left of the page (end of the ossuary) and lower right of page (less finished side of the ossuary, to the right). Some of the artistic motifs parallel those found in some of the Akeldama tombs, which may have belonged to high priestly families (including High Priest Annas, mentioned in John 18). See Avni and Greenhut, *The Akeldama Tombs*, color pl. 4 and pp. 26–29, depicting Cave 3, Chamber C.

52 See J. Gutman, *The Dura-Europos Synagogue: A Re-evaluation (1932–1992)*, USF Studies in the History of Judaism 25 (Atlanta: Scholars Press, 1992), 149. On the west wall, north half, one can see several examples of the pointed gable over a rosette (p. 215 [fig. 5]).

53 On the popularity of Hasmonean names, especially among the upper class, see the discussion in T. Ilan, *Lexicon of Jewish Names in Late Antiquity. Part I: Palestine 330 BCE–200 CE*, TSAJ 91 (Tübingen: Mohr Siebeck, 2002), 6–8.

and circle constituted an early Christian symbol has no foundation and ignores a mountain of contrary evidence.

CLAIM 3: THE JAMES OSSUARY AS THE TENTH, "MISSING" OSSUARY

In October 2002 Andre Lemaire and Hershel Shanks announced the discovery of an ossuary bearing the inscription "James, son of Joseph, brother of Jesus."[54] Controversy immediately ensued, with allegations that part or all of the inscription is modern. In June 2003 the Israel Antiquities Authority issued a report concluding that some of the inscription is a forgery. The owner of the ossuary has been charged and the matter has gone to trial.[55]

According to the hypothesis that the East Talpiot tomb is the tomb of Jesus and His family, the James ossuary is the tenth ossuary, which, advocates of this hypothesis maintain, has gone "missing." They point out that ten ossuaries were reported,[56] yet only nine are warehoused.[57] It is asserted that the missing East Talpiot ossuary, the one catalogued as 80.509, is in fact the James ossuary.

This claim, however, is utterly gratuitous and contradicts the published accounts of archaeologists Yosef Gat and Amos Kloner. Kloner described the ossuary as "plain," lacking adornment and an inscription. In the wake of the recent controversy, he has publicly stated that the tenth ossuary is not the James ossuary.[58] Moreover, the dimensions of the

54 A. Lemaire, "Burial Box of James the Brother of Jesus," *BAR* 28/6 (2002): 24–33, 70; H. Shanks and B. Witherington, *The Brother of Jesus: The Dramatic Story and Meaning of the First Archaeological Link to Jesus and His Family* (San Francisco: HarperCollins, 2003).

55 The IAA report has itself come under attack, particularly that portion dealing with the geochemical properties of the ossuary and its inscription. The IAA report claims that the patina is inauthentic and recent. However, the scientific explanation of the composition and application of the alleged false patina has been widely criticized by geochemists. Moreover, the false patina is not present in the high quality, close-up photographs taken by the Royal Ontario Museum (Toronto, Ontario, Canada) in the fall of 2002, *months before* the IAA took possession of the ossuary. If the false patina was not present in the fall of 2002, how did it make its appearance in 2003? This troubling development has given rise to suspicions that the IAA itself may have had something to do with the false patina.

56 The ten are reported in Kloner, "A Tomb with Inscribed Ossuaries in East Talpiyot, Jerusalem," 17–21.

57 Their inventory numbers are 80.500–509. See also Rahmani, *Catalogue of Jewish Ossuaries*, 222–24 (nos. 701–709). Rahmani omits 80.509 (the tenth ossuary).

58 Amos Kloner, David Mevorah (curator, Israel Museum), and others have stated that plain ossuaries (i.e., ossuaries that are uninscribed and unadorned) are sometimes not stored in the museum warehouse but are placed outside. Accordingly, there is nothing mysterious about not finding ossuary 80.509 on a shelf in the warehouse.

tenth ossuary do not exactly match the dimensions of the James ossuary. Kloner reported the tenth ossuary as 60 cm in length, 26 cm wide, and 30 cm deep.[59] The James ossuary, however, is some 50 cm in length (at the base), lengthening to about 56 cm at the top, some 30 cm wide at one end and 26 cm wide at the other end, and about 30 cm deep. Admittedly, the width and depth of the two ossuaries approximate one another, but there is a significant discrepancy in their respective lengths.

There is also a serious chronological problem with the argument that these ossuaries are one and the same. The East Talpiot tomb was discovered in 1980. There is dated photographic evidence that the James ossuary was in circulation years earlier.[60]

When all of the relevant facts are taken into account—not least the published report of archaeologist Amos Kloner, along with his current statements—the proposal that the tenth ossuary of the East Talpiot tomb (i.e., ossuary 80.509) is the James ossuary should be dismissed.

CONCLUSION

There are many problems with the proposal that the East Talpiot tomb was the tomb of Jesus of Nazareth and His family. This chapter has briefly reviewed Jewish burial traditions, with special attention given the practice of *ossilegium*, and has refuted three specific claims made in support of the East Talpiot tomb hypothesis. The other chapters in this book will refute other erroneous claims offered in support of this improbable hypothesis.

---

59 Kloner, "A Tomb with Inscribed Ossuaries in East Talpiyot, Jerusalem," 21.
60 The photographic evidence has been presented in court. See the report by Amiram Barkat in Haaretz.com (posted 9 February 2007). The 1976 photograph of the ossuary shows all five words of the Aramaic inscription.

THE NAMES ON THE OSSUARIES

Richard Bauckham

S ix of the ten ossuaries found in the Talpiot tomb are inscribed with names. Jacobovici and Pellegrino's case for identifying the tomb with that of the family of Jesus depends on identifying these names with those of Jesus, known members of His family, and others presumed by Jacobovici and Pellegrino to have been members of His family.

NAMES ON OSSUARIES

We begin with some general remarks about names on ossuaries. By no means are all ossuaries inscribed. Of the 897 ossuaries in L. Y. Rahmani's catalogue of the ossuaries in the collections of the state of Israel, some 233 are inscribed, but Rahmani is careful to point out that this high proportion (about 25%) is misleading, since many undecorated and uninscribed ossuaries were discarded by excavators or excluded from the catalogue. The real proportion of inscribed ossuaries to others must have been much lower.[1] In many tombs that have been excavated, the ossuaries included only a small proportion of inscribed ones or none at all. But the fact that a majority of those in the Talpiot tomb were inscribed is not

---

1 L. Y. Rahmani, *A Catalogue of Jewish Ossuaries in the Collections of the State of Israel* (Jerusalem: Israel Antiquities Authority/Israel Academy of Sciences and Humanities, 1994), 11.

unparalleled.[2] Rahmani observes, "There is no discernible rule governing the proportion of inscribed ossuaries."[3]

Though some inscriptions are in ink or charcoal, most, like those in the Talpiot tomb, were incised with a chisel or nail. They are not integrated into the decorations of the decorated ossuaries and are "carelessly executed, clumsily spaced, and, often, contain spelling mistakes . . . even in cases of renowned families, including those of high-priestly rank."[4] They were usually made by relatives of the dead and often in the darkness of the tombs. It is not surprising that some of the inscriptions on the ossuaries from the Talpiot tomb are very difficult to read.

The inscriptions are not like those on modern tombstones, set in a public place and intended to identify and describe the dead for anyone reading them. They would not normally have been seen by anyone except members of the family that used the tomb. In view of the fact that so many ossuaries are uninscribed, it is not easy to understand why some were inscribed. In the case of the uninscribed ossuaries, would the family remember whose bones they contained without having to label the ossuary, or was it not necessary to remember? When bones were placed in an ossuary, was there a ritual that could include the inscribing of names?[5] Or were the inscriptions meant to identify the dead so that close relatives of theirs could later be interred in the same ossuary?[6] This would not account for the fact that some inscriptions include not only a name or a name with close relationship indicated (usually "son of . . . ," "daughter of . . . ," or "wife of . . .") but also some minimal details of the dead such as their profession or their place of origin. Those who made the inscriptions must have thought it appropriate to honor the dead by recording such details,[7] but they are rare. We probably cannot conclude anything from the fact that no such details appear on the ossuaries from the Talpiot tomb, though some details such as "from Galilee" would certainly have helped the case for identifying the tomb as that of Jesus' family.

---

2 See the data in Rahmani, *A Catalogue*, 304–7.
3 Ibid., 11.
4 Ibid., 11–12.
5 Rachel Hachlili, *Jewish Funerary Customs, Practices and Rites in the Second Temple Period*, JSJSup 94 (Leiden: Brill, 2005), 163.
6 Ibid., 172.
7 Ibid., 171–72.

THE NAMES OF THE RELATIVES OF JESUS

Before discussing the identities of the people buried in the Talpiot tomb, we need to note carefully what is securely known, from all our early sources, about members of the family of Jesus (see table 1 at the end of this chapter).[8] We know, of course, that Jesus' mother was called Mary (Mariam or Maria), while her husband, treated in the sources as Jesus' legal, if not biological, father, was Joseph (see Luke 2:33,48; John 1:45; 6:42). From the Gospels we know that Jesus had four brothers and at least two sisters.[9] Of these the eldest was probably James, who became, with Peter and Paul, one of the three most important leaders in the early Christian movement, head of the Jerusalem church, put to death by the Jewish authorities in AD 62. Another brother of Jesus was the Judas to whom the New Testament letter of Jude is attributed. Not all scholars regard the attribution as authentic, but, even if it is not, the use of the name of this brother of Jesus testifies to his importance in the early church. The other two brothers were called Joses and Simon. Mark 6:3 gives the list as James, Joses, Judas, Simon, while Matt 13:55 has James, Joseph, Simon and Judas. Joses is a short form of Joseph, and we can easily understand why a son of Joseph would often be known by the short form Joses[10] in order to distinguish him from his father, much as in a modern Western family James and Jim might be used for father and son. Jesus' sisters are not named in our earliest sources. Later traditions, which may or may not be correct, give them the names Mary and Salome.[11]

The precise family relationship between Jesus and these brothers and sisters has been a matter of controversy in Christian history.[12] From the New Testament references we would doubtless most readily suppose them to have been children of Joseph and Mary, born after Jesus. But from the mid-second century we have evidence that they were regarded

8 For a full account and discussion of the evidence, see Richard Bauckham, *Jude and the Relatives of Jesus in the Early Church* (Edinburgh: T & T Clark, 1990), chapters 1–2.
9 In Greek "all his sisters" (Matt 13:56) need not indicate more than two.
10 Matthew prefers Joseph to Joses also in the case of another individual whom Mark calls Joses: Matt 27:56; Mark 15:40,47.
11 Bauckham, *Jude and the Relatives,* 37–44.
12 The three views are outlined and discussed in Bauckham, *Jude and the Relatives,* 19–32. For some support for the second view, see also Richard Bauckham, "The Brothers and Sisters of Jesus: An Epiphanian Response to John P. Meier," *CBQ* 56 (1994): 686–700.

as children of Joseph by a previous marriage. This became the traditional view in the eastern Orthodox tradition. It is not inconsistent with the evidence of the New Testament. The third possibility, which became the official view of the western Catholic tradition, is that they were not children of Joseph or Mary but first cousins of Jesus. This view was first put forward by Jerome in the fourth century and is the least likely to be historically correct. There is more to be said for the second view than modern scholars usually allow, but fortunately for our present purposes the matter can be left open. Even proponents of the third view hold that these "brothers" and "sisters" of Jesus formed a family unit with Mary and Jesus at the time of Jesus' ministry.

A few more members of the family are known from Hegesippus, a second-century Christian author who reports Palestinian Jewish Christian traditions. According to Hegesippus, two grandsons of Jesus' brother Judas (Jude), named James and Zoker, were leaders in the Christian movement in Palestine around the end of the first century.[13] These are the only descendants of Jesus' brothers that we know of. Also from Hegesippus we know that Joseph had a brother called Clopas, and the name is so unusual we can be confident that he is the same person as the Clopas whose wife Mary was with Jesus' mother Mary at the cross, according to John 19:25, and probably also the Cleopas to whom the risen Jesus appeared on the road to Emmaus (Luke 24:18).[14] Hegesippus mentions him because his son Simon or Simeon (the names are equivalent) became leader of the Jerusalem church after the death of James and continued in that role until he was martyred early in the second century.[15]

ONOMASTIC RESOURCES

For the study of names (onomastics) in first-century Jewish Palestine, we now have rich resources. We know the names of about three thousand Palestinian Jews who lived in the period 330 BC to AD 200. Their names have been preserved not only in the literary sources but also plentifully in documentary and epigraphic sources. We know the names of many people about whom we know only a little else, often

13 Bauckham, *Jude and the Relatives,* 94–106.
14 Ibid., 15–18; Richard Bauckham, *Gospel Women: Studies of the Named Women in the Gospels* (Grand Rapids: Eerdmans, 2002), chapter 6.
15 Bauckham, *Jude and the Relatives,* 79–94.

their relationship to another person and where and roughly when they lived. Since 2002 we have had this information readily available in an invaluable database, the *Lexicon of Jewish Names in Late Antiquity: Part I: Palestine 330 BCE—200 CE*,[16] compiled by the Israeli scholar Tal Ilan. The sources include the works of the Jewish historian Josephus, the New Testament, the texts from the Judean desert and from Masada, the earliest (Tannaitic) rabbinic sources, and, of course, the inscriptions on ossuaries from the Jerusalem area. For study of the names on ossuaries and in the Gospels, the period of five centuries covered by the *Lexicon* may seem too broad, since the Gospels were written in the late first century AD about characters who lived the first half of that century, while the ossuary inscriptions almost all belong to the century up to the fall of Jerusalem in 70 AD. However, it seems that in many respects naming practices remained fairly constant throughout the five centuries covered by the *Lexicon*. Moreover, in fact a large proportion of the data in the *Lexicon* actually comes from the first century AD and the early second century AD (up to 135), just because the sources for this shorter period are much more plentiful than for the other parts of the whole period. For our purposes it seems wise to use all the comparative data we have available and not to limit ourselves solely to the names on ossuaries, as some comments on the Talpiot tomb have done.

The statistics about the relative frequency of various names that I shall use in this chapter are based on my own calculations based on the data in Ilan's *Lexicon*.[17] I differ from her in a few respects relating to the criteria by which figures for the frequency of names should be calculated and occasionally in judgments about specific evidence. The resulting differences in our figures for the frequency of the most common names are very small.

For our present purposes the most relevant conclusions we can draw from the onomastic data concern the relative frequency of various names and also of various forms of the same names. An important feature of the data is that there are a small number of very common names[18] and a large number of very uncommon ones. Of course, the larger totals are

16 TSAJ 91 (Tübingen: Mohr Siebeck, 2002).

17 For a fuller explanation of how I have employed the data, see Richard Bauckham, *Jesus and the Eyewitnesses: The Gospels as Eyewitness Testimony* (Grand Rapids: Eerdmans, 2006), 68–71.

18 For reasons why the common names were popular, see Bauckham, *Jesus and the Eyewitnesses*, 74–78.

statistically more significant than the smaller ones. We can be pretty sure that Simon (243 occurrences) and Joseph (218 occurrences) were the most popular male names, but we cannot really be sure that, say, Hillel (11 occurrences) was more popular than Zebedee (5 occurrences). But in the case of the names on the ossuaries from the Talpiot tomb we are in luck because they are all among the most common names, as are the names of Jesus and His close family (parents and siblings).[19] Moreover, the accuracy of the calculations of relative popularity among the most common names can be checked by observing the breakdown of the total figures for certain identifiable sources of the data: the New Testament, Josephus, ossuaries, and the texts from the Judean desert. (These four sources complement one another in being of different kinds: literary, epigraphic, and documentary.) These can be seen in table 2, where I have listed, with the relevant statistics, the eleven most popular male names (those with 40 or more occurrences) and the four most popular female names (those with 20 or more occurrences).[20] It is striking how far the relative popularity of these most common names in the four specific sources come close to the relative popularity in the overall figures for these names. It is not surprising that there are some anomalies (such as only one Eleazar [Lazarus] in the New Testament, even though the total data show it to be the third most popular male name), since the figures for each of the four specific sources are rather small. But the general pattern should strengthen our confidence in the reasonable accuracy of the relative popularity of the names that is indicated by the total figures for each.

From the data in table 2 at the end of this chapter we may gain an initial impression of the popularity of the names represented on the ossuaries in the Talpiot tomb, along with those known to have been borne by Jesus and His relatives (excluding the two grandsons of Jude, who lived too late to be relevant). We can tabulate the results thus:

---

19 Clopas, the name of His uncle, is rare.
20 There are far more named men than named women, since women frequently appear without names in the sources, even on their own ossuaries.

Names in order of Popularity	Occurrences in Talpiot tomb	Occurrences in family of Jesus
Male		
1 Simon/Simeon		2
2 Joseph/Joses	2	2
3 Eleazar/Lazarus		
4 Judas (Yehuda)	1	1
5 John (Yohanan)		
6 Jesus (Yeshua')	1	1
7 Ananias		
8 Jonathan		
9 Matthew/Matthias	1	
10 Manaen (Menahem)		
11 James (Jacob)		1
Female		
1 Mary	2	2
2 Salome		
3 Shelamzion		
4 Martha	1?	

It is striking that the matches between the two categories (names that occur in both cases) are confined to some of the most common names of all: the second, fourth, and sixth most popular male names, and the most common female name. However, there are further factors to consider: specific forms of some of the names and the way persons are related to one another. These factors could reduce or increase the degree of correspondence between the two sets of names.

THE NAMES ON THE OSSUARIES

In Rahmani's catalogue the Talpiot ossuaries that have inscriptions are numbered 701–6. One (701) is in Greek script, the others in Jewish script, and in most cases the language of the latter can be identified as Aramaic. These are Rahmani's readings of the six inscriptions:[21]

			English New Testament forms of the names
701	Μαριαμηνου (η) Μαρα (*Mariamēnou ē Mara*)	Mariamenon [who is] Mara	
702	יהודה בר ישוע (*yhwdh br yšwᶜ*)	Yehuda bar Yeshuaᶜ	Judas son of Jesus
703	מתיה (*mtyh*)	Matia	Matthias (Matthew)
704	ישוע בר יהוסף (*yšwᶜ br yhwsp*)	Yeshuaᶜ (?) bar Yehosef	Jesus (?) son of Joseph
705	יוסה (*ywsh*)	Yose	Joses
706	מריה (*mryh*)	Maria	Mary

The first word on ossuary 704 is difficult to read, but Yeshuaᶜ is the only plausible suggestion and has been generally accepted. The most problematic inscription is that on ossuary 701. Jacobovici and Pellegrino accept Rahmani's reading, but since the Discovery film was launched, a different reading has been proposed. This reading is also of special importance for Jacobovici and Pellegrino's identification of the tomb as that of the family of Jesus. We shall therefore leave the discussion of the inscription on 701 to last.

If we leave aside 701 for the time being, there are six names (counting Yehosef and Yose as forms of the same name). The database enables us to calculate the following figures for the five male names:

---

21 Rahmani, *A Catalogue,* 222–24.

Rank	Name	Total occurrences	Percentage of total for all male names
2	Joseph/Joses	218	8.3%
4	Judas	164	6.2%
6	Jesus	99	3.4%
9	Matthew	62	2.4%

The sixth name, Mary, is the only female name on ossuaries 702–6. It was the most popular of female names, with 70 occurrences, and was borne by a staggering 21.4 percent of all the women in the database. The names on the ossuaries were clearly among the most popular Jewish names at the time.

We shall discuss each inscription in turn.

702 Yehuda bar Yeshuaᶜ

Jacobovici and Pellegrino claim that this is the name of a son of Jesus of Nazareth, and go on to speculate that he is the anonymous "disciple Jesus loved" in the Gospel of John and the anonymous young man who fled naked from Gethsemane according to Mark 14:51.[22] Of course, the identification can be made only on the basis of the argument that the tomb is that of Jesus' family; it cannot further that argument. It could actually count against that argument. How likely is it, we might ask, that Jesus had a son of whom there is no trace in any of our ancient sources? Why is he not mentioned among those relatives of Jesus (James, Jesus' other brothers,[23] His cousin Simon, and the grandsons of His brother Judas) who took leading roles in the early Christian movement in Jewish Palestine? One would have thought he would have qualified for such a role. The wider issue of whether Jesus was married is clearly also relevant and will be discussed at the end of this chapter. The name Yeshuaᶜ will be discussed below in the context of inscription 704.

---

22 Simcha Jacobovici and Charles Pellegrino, *The Jesus Family Tomb: The Discovery, the Investigation, and the Evidence That Could Change History* (New York: HarperCollins, 2007), 207–9.
23 1 Cor 9:5.

703 Matia

This is a short form of the popular name Mattathias (מתתיה [*mttyh*], Ματταθίας, the ninth most common Jewish male name. Various short forms were in fact much more widely used than the full form of the name (which occurs only 14 times among the 62 occurrences of the name in all forms). Among the short forms the most common in Hebrew (12 times) is the form used here on the ossuary (מתיה [*mttyh*]). A Greek version of this occurs once in the New Testament, as the name of the apostle Matthias who was chosen to replace Judas Iscariot among the Twelve (Acts 1:23: Μαθθίας [Maththias]).[24] The name of the apostle Matthew, the tax collector, is a different short form: Μαθθαῖος (Maththaios; three times in our database), representing the Hebrew short form Mattai (three times in our database: מתי [*mty*] or מתתי [*mtty*]). So, on grounds of the form of the name alone, the man in the ossuary is not very likely to be the apostle Matthew, though he could be the apostle Matthias. But, despite their association with Jesus, there is no known reason why either should have been buried in the tomb of Jesus' family. Family tombs were for family members, not friends or disciples.

Jacobovici and Pellegrino admit that this inscription "did not explicitly match any known family member" but nevertheless speculate that the apostle Matthias could have been a relative of Jesus: "That would explain his sudden elevation to the status of disciple."[25] Even as a speculation this is unlikely. The qualification to replace Judas as one of the Twelve was that such a man must have been a close disciple of Jesus from the beginning of His ministry to the end. Two such men were proposed, Matthias and Joseph Barsabbas, and Matthias was chosen by lot (Acts 1:21–26). For Matthias to have been a disciple who accompanied Jesus' throughout His ministry is sufficient to explain his nomination. To support the likelihood that Jesus would have had a relative called Matthew, Jacobovici and Pellegrino also claim that "Mary's grandfather was called Matthew, so it is entirely possible that, for example, a first cousin called Matthew, after the grandfather, might be buried in the family tomb."[26] This remark depends on the assumption that the genealogy

24 This spelling is unique, but Ματθίας (Matthias) occurs 13 times in the database.
25 Jacobovici and Pellegrino, *The Jesus Family Tomb,* 78. Of course, Matthias had been a "disciple" throughout Jesus' ministry (Acts 1:21–22). His elevation was to be one of the Twelve.
26 Jacobovici and Pellegrino, *The Jesus Family Tomb,* 78.

of Jesus in Luke 3:23–38 is not, as the Gospel presents it, the genealogy of Joseph but that of Mary, a view taken, not by "many scholars" as Jacobovici and Pellegrino claim, but by very few.[27] Be that as it may, the name of Jesus' great-grandfather according to Luke 3:24 was Matthat ~~(Ματθάτ), another of the short forms of Mattathias (its Hebrew form מתת~~ [*mtt*] occurs six times in our database). This is not an obstacle to supposing that another family member named after him could be called Matia/Matthias. Different forms of the same name could well be used within a family. But we are in the realm of completely baseless speculation. Of course, it is "entirely possible" that there was a member of the family of Jesus called Matia/Matthias. Since the name was in any case so common, we need not even refer to the genealogy to think it "entirely possible" that a member of the family of Jesus was called Matia/Matthias. It is also entirely possible that there were members of the family of Jesus called Eleazar, John, Ananias, and Jonathan, but there is no evidence for any of these possibilities.

704 Yeshua‹ (?) bar Yehosef

As noted above, the first word of this inscription is scribbled in an almost illegible way, and Rahmani's reading of it as Yeshua‹ certainly cannot be regarded as certain, but it has been generally accepted, and we shall go with it here.[28] Of this name, James Tabor, who is, to my knowledge, the only established scholar who supports the identification of the Talpiot tomb as that of the family of Jesus, writes:

27 These few are mentioned in Raymond E. Brown, *The Birth of the Messiah* (expanded edition; New York: Doubleday, 1993), 89 n. 65, 588–89; and add James D. Tabor, *The Jesus Dynasty* (New York: Simon & Schuster, 2006), 51–53. Tabor, *The Jesus Dynasty,* 55–56, followed by Jacobovici and Pellegrino, *The Jesus Family Tomb,* 78, claims that Matta-thias/Matthew was a priestly name. Some prominent bearers of the name were priests, but the evidence does not require the conclusion that it was exclusively used by priests. It is unlikely that there were many, if any, exclusively priestly names in this period. A (probably fictional) individual named Mattathias in the list of the Septuagint translators (*Letter of Aristeas* 47) is said to be a member of "the second tribe" of Israel, which is unlikely to be Levi.

28 Stephen Pfann has suggested reading Hanun or Hanin, but against this possibility the letter *sin* or *shin* (שׁ) seems clear. Steve Caruso (http://www.aramaicdesigns.com/?title=The_Lost_Tomb_of-Jesus, 3/4/2007) calls it "a textbook form." Caruso raises the possibility that the X mark in front of the word might actually be the first letter of the word, an *aleph* (א), but finds no known name that would fit this reading. It seems to me possible that we should read (אישׁוע) (’yšw‹) and understand it as an eccentric spelling of Yeshua‹, comparable with איסי (’ysy) for יוסי (ywsy or "Yose": Ilan, *Lexicon,* 151 no. 54).

It is known, of course, but to say it is common is incorrect. If you take all the forms of the name Joshua known to us from inscriptions and literary sources as compiled by Tal Ilan . . . one finds 100 examples of the name out of a total of 2,538 male names, which is 3.9%. The specific shortened nickname "Yeshua" is less common than that. For example, on the 214 inscribed ossuaries in the Israeli State Collections, besides the Talpiot tomb (which has two ossuaries with the name), there are only three other examples of this name (Rahmani # 9, 121, 140). . . . In fact, depending on how one understands such terms, I would like to say the name is known but relatively uncommon.[29]

My own calculations using Ilan's data differ only slightly: the name Joshua/Jesus, in all forms, occurs 99 times[30] and constitutes 3.4 percent of a total of 2,625 instances of male names.[31]

But we must also consider the frequency of the various forms of the name (see table 3). In asserting that the short form Yeshuaʿ, which, incidentally, is not a nickname[32] but simply a contracted form of Yehoshuaʿ, is "relatively uncommon," Tabor has chosen not to give a breakdown of Ilan's data but to limit his data to the ossuary inscriptions in Rahmani's catalog. This gives a somewhat misleading impression.

Of the 99 persons bearing the name in Ilan's list (excluding fictitious persons), there are several of whom more than one different form of the name is used in the sources. The full evidence for the forms of the name therefore in fact constitutes 111 instances. Of these 62 are in Jewish script (Hebrew or Aramaic). There are 17 occurrences of the full name

---

29 James D. Tabor, *The Jesus Dynasty Blog*: http://jesusdynasty.com/blog/2007/04/29/the-talpiot-tomb-separating-truth-from-fiction/.

30 I differ from Ilan in thinking the Yeshuaʿ of 4Q551, her no. 98, is probably a fictional character.

31 I am not sure how Tabor gets the figure 2,538. Ilan, *Lexicon*, 55 (table 2) calculates 2,509. My figure is larger because, whereas she counts persons, I count occurrences of a name. Where an individual bore two genuine and genuinely different names (as distinct from nicknames created *ad hoc* or family names, and from two forms of the same name) I have counted both names. This way of calculating is more useful for the purpose of gauging the relative popularity of names. See further Bauckham, *Jesus and the Eyewitnesses*, 69.

32 For true nicknames, which were common, see Hachlili, *Jewish Funerary Customs*, 205–13.

Yehoshuaᶜ (יהושע [*yhwš*ᶜ], once יהושוע [*yhwšw*ᶜ], once יישוע [*yyšw*ᶜ]), 44 of the short form Yeshuaᶜ (ישוע [*yšw*ᶜ], once ישועה [*yšw*ᶜ*h*], once ישועא [*yšw*ᶜᵃ], once שוע [*šw*ᶜ]), and one of the very short Yeshu (ישו [*yšw*]).³³ This shows that the form Yeshuaᶜ was much the most popular. However, we should also note that 13 occurrences of the full form Yehoshuaᶜ, while referring to persons in our period, occur in rabbinic literature (Mishna, Tosefta, and the Talmuds),³⁴ while the remaining two are on incantation bowls (these are the eccentric spellings יהושע [*yhwš*ᶜ] and יישוע [*yyšw*ᶜ]).³⁵ These cases may well not be good evidence of the *form* of the name used in our period. As Tal Ilan comments, "The use of יהושע [*yhwš*ᶜ] in the later literary sources may be seen as a return to the traditional Old Testament pre-exilic spelling."³⁶ It seems very likely that almost everyone bearing the name in our period used the short Hebrew form Yeshuaᶜ.

The distinction between the longer and shorter forms does not exist in Greek. The Greek Iēsous (Ἰησοῦς) was used to represent both Yehoshuaᶜ and Yeshuaᶜ. There are 48 instances of Iēsous (Ἰησοῦς and several eccentric spellings), and one of a more phonetic rendering of Yeshuaᶜ (Ἰεσουα [Iesoua]). We may reasonably guess that most, if not all, of the persons so called would have called themselves Yeshuaᶜ in Hebrew.

In fact (unless the contested ossuary of "James son of Joseph the brother of Jesus" proves genuine), we have no contemporary evidence of the Hebrew/Aramaic form of the name of Jesus of Nazareth. Later rabbinic literature calls him both Yeshuaᶜ and, most often, Yeshu. Although the occurrence of the latter on one ossuary (Rahmani 9) shows that it was not invented by the rabbis as a way of avoiding pronouncing the real name of Jesus of Nazareth,³⁷ it may still be that their use of it was a deliberate attempt to distinguish him from rabbis bearing the biblical name Yehoshuaᶜ. We cannot tell whether it preserves a usage going back to the time of Jesus Himself. But the general evidence of the usage of

---

33 This form occurs on an ossuary (Rahmani no. 9, Ilan no. 43) which also has the form ישוע (*yšw*ᶜ) for the same person.

34 These are Ilan's nos. 19–22, 24–34.

35 Ilan no. 23. Ilan gives only the two forms found on incantation bowls, but the same person appears in rabbinic literature as יהושע (yhwšᶜ).

36 Ilan, *Lexicon*, 129.

37 Cf. Gustav Dalman, *Jesus—Jeshua*, tran. Paul P. Levertoff (London: SPCK, 1929) 6; Rahmani, *A Catalogue*, 77. The *Toledot Yeshu* gives the name a derogatory interpretation, but this is a later development.

the name makes it virtually certain that Jesus of Nazareth was normally called by the short Hebrew/Aramaic form Yeshua'.

It is curious, but doubtless coincidental, that the ossuary (Rahmani 9) that provides the sole instance of the short form Yeshu in our period is the same one that also calls the same person Yeshua' bar Yehosef, just as on the Talpiot ossuary. It is true that we do not know the provenance of that ossuary, but its genuineness has not been doubted, and so there seems to be no great significance in the fact, noted by Tabor, that "the Talpiot tomb ossuary [is] the single provenanced example [of 'Jesus son of Joseph'] from the period."[38] The coincidence of the two names Yeshua' and Yehosef in the same relationship in these two ossuary inscriptions and in the case of Jesus of Nazareth would be more noteworthy if we knew the fathers of more of the individuals called Yeshua'/Yehoshua' in Ilan's list. In fact, we know the father's name in less than half of these cases (44 out of 99, including these two ossuaries and Jesus of Nazareth).

Ossuary 704 tells us of a man bearing the sixth most common Jewish male name (Joshua/Jesus, 99 occurrences) who was the son of a man bearing the second most common male name (Joseph/Joses, 218 occurrences). As an indication of how common such a combination of common names might be, we can look at some similar cases. In Ilan's list of 99 individuals called Joshua/Jesus, five had a father also called Joshua/Jesus, and two a father called Judas/Judah.[39] The third most common Jewish male name is Eleazar. Of the 166 individuals in Ilan's list of people bearing this name, seven had fathers called Simon, five had fathers called Judas/Judah, and four had fathers called Joseph/Joses.[40] The fourth most common name is Judas/Judah. Of the 164 individuals of this name in Ilan's list, four had fathers called Joseph, four had fathers called John/Yohanan, four had fathers called Judas/Judah, and three had fathers called Simon.[41] The fifth most common male name is John/Yohanan. Of

38 Tabor, *The Jesus Dynasty Blog*: http://jesusdynasty.com/blog/2007/04/29/the-talpiot-tomb-separating-truth-from-fiction/. Ilan, *Lexicon*, 131 n. 94, claims that "other examples [besides Rahmani no. 9, her no. 43] of ישוע בן יהוסף [yšw' bn yhwsp] are found even within this list," but this seems to be a mistake. The only other example in her list is no. 51, the Talpiot tomb ossuary.

39 In Ilan's list these are 37, 54, 55, 73, 78 (son of Joshua/Jesus); 47, 92 (son of Judas/Judah).

40 In Ilan's list these are 10, 34, 101, 130, 136, 160, 177 (son of Simon); 41, 48, 62, 133, 146 (sons of Judas/Judah); 36, 51, 116, 158 (sons of Joseph).

41 In Ilan's list, these are 20, 59, 122, 151 (sons of Joseph); 56, 85, 96, 107 (son of John); 13, 82, 134, 158 (son of Judas); 6, 19, 142 (sons of Simon).

the 122 individuals in Ilan's list of persons bearing this name, five had fathers called Joseph, three had fathers called Joshua/Jesus, and two had fathers called Simon.[42] The seventh most common name is Ananias/Hananiah. Of the 82 individuals of this name in Ilan's list, five had fathers called Simon.[43] The eighth most common name is Jonathan. Of the 71 Jonathans in Ilan's list, three had fathers called Joseph. In the light of this data, it would not be in the least surprising to find three different individuals called Joshua/Jesus son of Joseph among those known to us who bore the name Joshua/Jesus.

705 Yose

On this name we begin by again quoting James Tabor:

> It is the case that the name Joseph in its various forms (Yehosef, Yosi, Ioseph, Iosepos) is relatively common. After Shimon, it is the second most common male Jewish name of the period. . . . However, the specific nickname Yose in Aramaic (Yod, Wav, Samech, Heh) is extremely rare. It is found only once on an ossuary, namely the one from the Talpiot tomb with only two other examples known (a papyri [*sic*] and an inscription). The name in Greek (Iose or Ioses) is equally rare with only five examples given by Tal Ilan outside the N.T. gospels. In contrast, the nickname, Yosi is quite common with dozens of examples listed by Tal Ilan.[44]

Again, this account of the matter is rather misleading. The details of the name usage are set out in table 4. יוסה (*ywsh*), יסה (*ysh*), and יוסי (*ywsy*) are simply alternative spellings of the same short form of the name: Yose.[45] The first is an Aramaic spelling (and the second a defective version of it) since in Aramaic the final *he* (ה), as well as the final

---

42 In Ilan's list these are 39, 52, 94, 100, 103 (son of Joseph); 33, 58, 99 (son of Joshua); 77, 110 (son of Simon).
43 In Ilan's list these are 43, 51, 56, 79, 80.
44 Tabor, *The Jesus Dynasty Blog*: http://jesusdynasty.com/blog/2007/04/29/the-talpiot-tomb-separating-truth-from-fiction/ p. 4.
45 See Ilan, *Lexicon*, 157 n. 3. יסה (*ysh*; Ilan no. 89) is a defective spelling (see Ilan, *Lexicon*, 30 §2.7.1) and is Ilan's own reading of an ossuary inscription (see Ilan, *Lexicon*, 163 n. 232).

yod (ʾ), can stand for a final long *e* sound, whereas in Hebrew only the *yod* can do so.[46] The spelling with the final *yod* (יוסי [*ywsy*]) was almost certainly pronounced, not as Yosi but as Yose.[47] Since the pronunciation was the same for all three spellings, there is no reason to think that the name of any individual would always be written with one of these spellings. Most people rarely, if ever, wrote their own name, while in ossuary inscriptions and most of our other evidence the names were not written by the person to whom they refer but by others, who would use whatever spelling came to mind on that occasion. It would be misleading to say that the person to whom the ossuary inscription refers was named יוסה (*ywsh*) rather than יוסי (*ywsy*). He bore the common short form of the name Joseph, which accounts for 34 of the 156 occurrences of forms of the name Joseph in Jewish script in Ilan's list.

In Greek this short form of the name is rarer and does not seem to have any consistent spelling.[48] Among the Greek forms of the name Joseph, *Iōsēpos* (Ἰωσηπος) is overwhelmingly dominant, accounting for 47 of the 69 occurrences in Ilan's list. It looks as though individuals who might have used a short form in Aramaic/Hebrew preferred this full form in Greek; or it was preferred by those who wrote down their names or who, like Josephus, wrote about them (14 instances of Ἰωσηπος are in Josephus, and it is also common in papyri).

Could the same individual have been known by both full and short forms of his name? This seems very likely, as in the case of other names with common abbreviated forms. Ilan cites the evidence of the Babylonian Talmud, which uses full and abbreviated forms for the same individuals.[49] We should also note that both the individuals named Joses (probably Ἰωσης [*Iōsēs*],[50] though only the genitive form Ἰωσητος [*Iōsētos*] occurs in the text) in Mark's Gospel—Jesus' brother (Mark 6:3) and another man, evidently a disciple of Jesus (Mark 15:47)—are called

---

46 Tabor as reported in Jacobovici and Pellegrino, *The Jesus Family Tomb*, 64–65, there made the mistake of reading יוסה (*ywsh*) as Yosa but avoids this in his blog discussion.

47 The Greek transliterations Ἰωση (*Iōsē*), Ἰοσε (*Iose*) and Ἰωσε (*Iōse*) (Ilan nos. 28?, 113, 115, 127) seem to be evidence of this, but in any case we should expect the short *e* in the final syllable of the full name Yosef or Yehosef to become a long *e* in the abbreviated form, not a long *i*.

48 The forms Ἰωσιος (*Iōsios*) and Ἰωσιας (*Iōsias*) are attempts to give the name a more typically Greek form.

49 Ilan, *Lexicon*, 159 n. 96.

50 Ilan, however, supposes Ἰωση (*Iōsē*; no. 28).

Joseph (Ἰωσηφ) by Matthew (13:55; 27:56).[51] Perhaps the short form seemed too colloquial to Matthew. In any case, since Jesus' brother Joses was doubtless named after his father Joseph, it must have been proper to call him Joseph even though Joses was the more commonly used form (helpfully distinguishing him from his father).

Since therefore the same person could properly be called by both full and short forms of the name, it is possible that the Yose of the inscription on ossuary 705 of the Talpiot tomb is the same person as the Yehosef, father of Yeshua῾, named on ossuary 704. Jacobovici and Pellegrino treat them as two persons, identifying the former with Jesus' brother Joses and the second with Jesus' father Joseph. This distinction is necessary for their case since it would be particularly unlikely to find Joseph the father of Jesus of Nazareth buried in a family tomb near Jerusalem rather than in Nazareth (assuming, as most do, that Joseph died before the period of Jesus' ministry). However, as far as the evidence of the inscriptions themselves go, we could be dealing with two persons or with one. There is no way of deciding the matter.

706 Maria

Of this inscription, Jacobovici and Pellegrino write:

> Ossuary number 80/505 was inscribed with the name Maria, a Latin version of the biblical Miriam, written in Hebrew letters. This was extremely unusual. Shimon [Gibson] would recall that when he first saw the name, it was possible to believe that here lay a Jewish woman who just happened to have been known to many Gentiles and Jews by the Latin version of her Hebrew name, Mary.[52]

A footnote here reads: "To date, out of thousands of ossuaries that have been found, only eight others bear the name Maria in Hebrew letters." Later in the book they repeat the claim that Maria is a Latinized version of the Hebrew name Miriam, continuing: "Anyone who has listened to 'Ave Maria'—the haunting Catholic liturgy [sic] in praise of the mother

---

51 These are nos. 27 and 28 in Ilan's list, but she notes the short form only in the case of 28.

52 Jacobovici and Pellegrino, *The Jesus Family Tomb*, 16.

of Jesus—knows that in Church tradition the Mother of the Lord is referred to in one way and one way only: Maria."[53]

The idea seems to be that the origin of this constant usage in the Catholic tradition lies in the fact that Mary the mother of Jesus was called Maria in her lifetime, and the inscription on the ossuary, alleged to be hers, reflects that usage. They do not explain why this form of the name was used of her in her lifetime. Do they mean that because she was already perceived, in the Christian movement, as a universal figure, she was already given an appropriately Latin name? One obvious objection to such an idea is that this understanding of the significance of Latin is anachronistic. The universal language of the time was Greek, so much so that it was the official language of the Christian community in Rome until at least the middle of the second century. That community's literature was written in Greek. There is little, if any, Christian literature composed in Latin from before the third century.[54]

In any case it is unlikely that the name Maria (מריה [*mryh*]) on this ossuary is a Latin formation. It is true that there was a Latin name Maria, the feminine form of the male name Marius,[55] but this is probably not the source of the use of the name Maria by Palestinian Jewish women of our period.[56] Rather, it was a matter of creating an appropriately Greek form of the Hebrew name Mariam. In this period the Hebrew name of Moses' sister, which the Massoretes later vocalized as Miriam, was pronounced Mariam. One option for writing the name in Greek was simply to transliterate it as Μαριάμ (Mariam). But from the evidence collected by Ilan (see table 5) it can be seen that this was a minority choice. Of 42 occurrences of the name in Greek script, only five take that form. The reason is that Mariam in Greek looks barbaric. The only consonants that end Greek words are ν (n), ρ (r) and ς (s). A word ending in μ (m) looks barbaric. To make the name look more Greek there were two options. The most popular was to add a long "e" and create the form Mariame

53 Ibid., 202.
54 Fifth Ezra may be an exception. Cf. Jean Daniélou, *The Origins of Latin Christianity*, tr. David Smith and John Austin Baker (London; Darton, Longman & Todd/Philadelphia: Westminster, 1977), xiii–xvi.
55 See François Bovon, "Mary Magdalene in the *Acts of Philip*," in F. Stanley Jones, ed., *Which Mary? The Marys of Early Christian Tradition*, SBL Symposium Series 19 (Atlanta: SBL, 2002), 75–89, here 77–78.
56 For the use of Maria by Jews in the diaspora, see Bovon, "Mary Magdalene," 76–77; David Noy, Alexander Panayotov, and Hanswulf Bloedhorn, eds., *Inscriptiones Judaicae Orientis*, vol. 1: *Eastern Europe*, TSAJ 101 (Tübingen: Mohr Siebeck, 2004), 109.

or Mariamme. Many Greek female names end in a long "e." Of the 42 occurrences, 22 use this form (including two eccentric spellings). The other option was to drop the final *m* and create the form Maria, of which there are instances in Greek in Ilan's list. It is not impossible that people who used this form were aware of the Latin name Maria and assimilated the Hebrew to the Latin name,[57] but there were other female Greek names that ended in –*ia*. Among properly Greek names actually used by Palestinian Jewish women we find Carpia, Cyria, Lydia, and Lysia.[58] So the Jewish use of Maria may have originated simply from conforming the Hebrew name to that Greek pattern. The coincidence with the Latin name Maria may be no more than a coincidence.

The use of the Greek form Maria had a somewhat curious result. This form of the name was transliterated back into Hebrew and became another Hebrew form of the name besides Mariam. We find 9 occurrences of this Hebrew Maria (מריה [*mryh*]) among the 37 occurrences of the name in Jewish script in Ilan's list, including the inscription on ossuary 706 from the Talpiot tomb. This retrojection of a hellenized form of a name back into Hebrew is unusual, but there are many examples of the transliteration of Greek names into Jewish script, and presumably this happened in the case of Maria because the Greek form Maria was used so frequently. We should not forget that nearly a quarter of all Palestinian Jewish women were called by one of the forms of the name Mary. Perhaps in Aramaic-speaking contexts it was useful to have another version of the name besides Mariam, and Maria could have functioned as a short form of the name in the same way that Yose did for Yosef/Yehosef. As in the latter case, the same woman could be called both Mariam and Maria: there is a clear case, with both forms in Jewish script, in Ilan's list (no. 61).

So there turns out to be nothing exceptional about the name Maria (מריה [*mryh*]) on ossuary 706. Jacobovici and Pellegrino have to try hard to make it sound exceptional: "To date, out of thousands of ossuaries that have been found, only eight others bear the name Maria in Hebrew letters."[59] Rahmani's catalogue of ossuaries in the collections of the state of Israel catalogs 897 ossuaries. I do not know how many there are in other collections, but there are not "thousands." But most ossuaries are

---

57 Cf. Ilan, *Lexicon*, 245 n. 14.
58 See Ilan, *Lexicon*, 320–22.
59 Jacobovici and Pellegrino, *The Jesus Family Tomb,* 16n.

not inscribed, so the relevant figure is that of inscribed ossuaries. Only 233 in Rahmani's catalog are inscribed, and the name Maria in Jewish script occurs on three of them. The other six are included in Ilan's list, where Maria in Hebrew characters accounts for 9 occurrences out of 37 occurrences of forms of the name in Jewish script. This proportion (25%) indicates a rather common usage. But we should also notice that the name in Greek script provides another 13 occurrences. This makes 22 occurrences out of the total of 79 occurrences of the name Mary in all forms, a proportion of 27.8 percent. What is entirely clear is that the use of the form מריה [*mryh*] needs no special explanation. In its onomastic context it is unremarkable.

Finally, we should note the forms of the name used for Mary the mother of Jesus (see table 6). In the New Testament both Mariam and Maria are used, but the former is more common. It is prominent espe-cially in Luke's birth and infancy narratives, where Luke is deliberately evoking a traditional Palestinian Jewish setting. Matthew, on the other hand, prefers Maria. What we have are the preferences of these two writ-ers. It would be hazardous to try to determine by which form of her name the mother of Jesus was commonly called in her own circle or in the ear-liest Christian movement, but, on the other hand, we have no basis here for thinking that Maria was the normative form, as Jacobovici and Pel-legrino seem to suppose. In early Christian literature in Greek, some of the early Fathers call her Maria (Ignatius, Justin, Irenaeus, Hippolytus); but most of the Greek Fathers, from Origen onwards, use Mariam.[60] The familiarity of the form Maria in the Western Catholic Christian tradition, by which Jacobovici and Pellegrino seem so impressed, derives from the Latin Fathers and the Latin versions of the New Testament. Of course, it was natural for anyone writing in Latin to use the form Maria.

701 Mariamenou (he) Mara or Mariame kai Mara

The inscription on ossuary 701 is crucial to Jacobovici and Pellegri-no's case because it is their interpretation of this inscription that is the

---

60 Stephen J. Shoemaker, "A Case of Mistaken Identity? Naming the Gnostic Mary," in Jones, ed., *Which Mary?*, 5–30, here 12. There seems to be only one Christian work in Greek that uses Mariamme for the mother of Jesus: the Bodmer papyrus of the mid-second century Protevangelium of James (Shoemaker, "A Case," 14–15). Since Mariam(m)e is the form used in Josephus for the princesses of the Herodian family, perhaps this usage relates to the Protevangelium's depiction of Mary's family as aristocratic.

major new argument they have to add to the claims already made about the Talpiot tomb in Ray Bruce's and Chris Mann's television documentary shown on BBC television in the UK in 1995. It is not without significance that between 1995 and the making of the Discovery Channel film the entirely baseless speculation that Jesus married Mary Magdalene became immensely well-known from Dan Brown's novel *The Da Vinci Code,* as well as its source on these matters: Baigent, Leigh, and Lincoln's pseudo-historical work *Holy Blood, Holy Grail.*[61] Otherwise it may never have occurred, even to Jacobovici and Pellegrino, that an ossuary containing the bones of Mary Magdalene had any place in a tomb used by the family of Jesus.[62]

Jacobovici and Pellegrino followed the reading of the inscription given by Rahmani in his catalog in 1994, which was also followed by Kloner in his excavation report published in 1996.[63] As interpreted by Rahmani, the inscription consists of two words written in close succession without a gap—*Mariamēnou Mara* (Μαριαμηνου Μαρα)—but with a vertical stroke between the two words. He interpreted this as the Greek letter *eta* (η). The first word he took to be a genitive (meaning that the ossuary belonged to this person) of Mariamenon, a neuter form because it is a diminutive. Mariamenon would be a diminutive of Mariamēnē (Μαριαμηνη), a form of the name Mary which Rahmani found attested only in an inscription from the third century in the Jewish catacomb at Beth She'arim, where it is spelled Μαριαμενη (*Mariamenē*). He found a similar diminutive, *Mariamnou* (Μαριαμνου), also in the genitive, on ossuary 108 in his catalogue. He understood this diminutive form to derive from *Mariamnē* (Μαριαμνη), which he saw as a contraction of *Mariamēnē* (Μαριαμηνη).

Rahmani understood Mara to be a second name of Mariamenon. A common Greek formula for referring to both names of a person who

61 Michael Baigent, Richard Leigh and Henry Lincoln, *Holy Blood, Holy Grail* (London: Jonathan Cape, 1982).

62 For their uncritical attitude to the claims made in *The Da Vinci Code* and *Holy Blood, Holy Grail,* see Jacobovici and Pellegrino, *The Jesus Family Tomb,* 207: 'There is also no question that various secret societies have subscribed to this belief [that Jesus had a wife and child] for centuries, if not millennia.' On the contrary, the supposed evidence for this has been indubitably exposed as fraudulent. In 1993 Pierre Plantard admitted to a judge, under oath, that he had invented the whole story of the Priory of Sion and forged the documents purporting to derive from it.

63 Amos Kloner, "A Tomb with Inscribed Ossuaries in East Talpiyot, Jerusalem," *'Atiqot* 29 (1996): 15–22, here 17.

used two is: X who is (ὁ καὶ [*ho kai*] or ἡ καὶ [*hē kai*]) Y.[64] It is used for example, in Acts 13:9, where Luke introduces Paul as "Saul who is also called Paul" (Σαῦλος ὁ καὶ Παῦλος). The formula is sometimes abbreviated to just the relative pronoun, which in the inscription would be the stroke Rahmani read as ἡ (*hē*). Thus the inscription means "of Mariamenon who is also called Mara." The second name Mara seems to be attested as a short form of Martha, since ossuary 468 in Rahmani's catalog carries the two names Mara and Martha (in different places) and Rahmani understands these to be two names for the same woman.

There are considerable problems with this reading of the inscription, as we shall see. But first we should note what Jacobovici and Pellegrino do with Rahmani's reading. First, they repeatedly say that the name on the ossuary is Mariamne.[65] It is not. According to Rahmani, it is the diminutive Mariamenon, formed from Mariamene. Mariamne, according to Rahmani, would be a contracted form of Mariamene. Second, they take Mara to be not a name but a title and translate the inscription as: "(This is the ossuary) of Mariamne, also known as the Master." James Tabor is cited as having provided this translation.[66] Presumably, the supposition is that Mara represents the Aramaic word *mar* (מר: "lord," "master") in the determined state, which in Aramaic is equivalent to the definite article in English or Hebrew (מרא [*mrʾ*]: "the lord," "the master"). Jacobovici and Pellegrino do not explain why this masculine term should be used of this woman they claim is Mary Magdalene. Since they associate the term with the representation of Mary Magdalene as an apostle in the *Acts of Philip*,[67] they perhaps suppose that this was a generally male role which this woman was exceptionally given. It is not clear why "master" should be considered equivalent to "apostle."

Tabor's more recent discussion apparently takes *mara* to be a feminine term. He writes:

---

64 Gregory H. R. Horsley, "Names, Double," in ABD 4.1011–7, here 1012–13.

65 E.g. Jacobovici and Pellegrino, *The Jesus Family Tomb*, 43–45. On p. 76 they say, incorrectly, that the name as actually written is "Mariamnu," and explain that, "The nu was a diminutive of the more familiar 'Mariamme.'"

66 Jacobovici and Pellegrino, *The Jesus Family Tomb*, 76.

67 Ibid., 76: In the *Acts of Philip* "she is described as an apostle or 'master.'" In the *Acts of Philip* Mariamne is not called "apostle" in the singular but is included in a group (Philip, Bartholomew, Mariamne) that is collectively known as "the apostles" (8:16, 21; 13:1–2:4).

Mara is a Greek form of the Aramaic, mar/mara, which is lady or mistress, here in the absolute. The emphatic would be mart(h)a. Since we have no suitable word in English for the feminine of "master" (i.e., "mistress" is misleading), one has to go to something like "honorable lady."[68]

This is misleading. The form *mara* (מרא [*mrʾ*] or מרה [*mrh*]) could be either the feminine absolute or the masculine determined (emphatic). The meaning could be either "a mistress" or "the master." For "the mistress" one would need the feminine determined (emphatic) state: *marta* (מרתא). The absolute could not be used as a title, and so the only way *mara* (מרא) can be construed as a title is to retain the masculine sense that Jacobovici and Pellegrino gave it in their book. But there is another problem with taking the word to be a title. The Greek formula for recording a second name (ἡ καὶ [hē kai]: "who is also") is only used to introduce a second true name, not an epithet or a title. If Rahmani was right to take the stroke to represent this formula, as Jacobovici, Pellegrino, and Tabor suppose, he was also right to understand Mara as a name.[69]

However, there are several problems with Rahmani's own reading and interpretation of the inscription. (1) No parallels have been cited for a single stroke representing the Greek letter eta (η). (2) In standard Greek grammar the relative pronoun and the second name should agree in inflection with the first name, i.e., they too should be in the genitive case: either ἧς Μαρας (*hēs Maras*) or (in neuter gender agreeing with Μαριαμηνου [*Mariamēnou*]) οὗ Μαρας (*hou Maras*). (3) It seems the stroke is not part of the inscription but an unrelated scratch. Stephen Pfann and Steve Cox, reporting an examination of the ossuary, write: "The mysterious 'stroke' that stands before MARA has a gently rounded trough, similar to other inadvertent marks on the ossuary's surface. The shape of this trough eliminates it as having been made by either tool utilized for the inscription."[70] On the other hand, Tabor, on the basis of his

---

68 James D. Tabor, http://jesusdynasty.com/blog/03/14/2007/ p. 2.
69 Mara is used as an honorific title on ossuaries. Rahmani no. 327 has the inscription: "Yehosef the master (מרה [*mrh*]) son of Benaya son of Yehuda." But this Aramaic inscription simply places the title after the name and has it, appropriately, in the masculine determined state.
70 The View from Jerusalem blog, http://www.uhl.ac/blog/?cat=, 6/5/2007: "Preliminary Autopsy of CJO 701 (80.500) MARIAME KAI MARA."

own inspection of the inscription, remains convinced that the stroke is part of the inscription, not a random scratch.[71] (4) Rahmani's understanding of Mariamēnou (Μαριαμηνου) as a diminutive is problematic, since the normal Greek diminutive ending would be –ion, not –on.[72] (5) When a Palestinian Jew bore two names, they were either a Semitic and a Greek or Latin name or a common Semitic name and a distinctive nickname or family name. There do not seem to be authentic cases of two Semitic names.[73] A possible solution to the difficulty this creates for reading the inscription as "of Mariamenon who is also Mara" could be to suppose that Mara is here used as an abbreviated form of Mariamenon.

We might have to live with some of these problems, ascribing them to the errors of the scribe who wrote the inscription, but for the fact that Stephen Pfann has proposed a different reading of the inscription: Μαρι-αμη και Μαρα (*Mariamē kai Mara*), meaning "Mariame and Mara." He detects two different scribal hands, responsible for "Mariame" and "and Mara" respectively. The first is a documentary, the second a cursive hand. He also maintains that the second part of the inscription was written with an instrument similar to that of the first but with a sharper point. As we have already noticed, he discounts Rahmani's "stroke" as a scratch unconnected with the inscription. He also reads as και (*kai*) the three letters Rahmani took to be νου (the last three letters of Mariam-enou).[74] The implication he draws is that the inscription records the presence of the bones of two women in the ossuary. Mariame was interred first; later the second woman, named Mara, was also placed in the ossuary. (It is common for the ossuaries to contain the bones of more than one person, and sometimes "and" [και; *kai*] is used to connect the names in the inscriptions.)

---

71 James D. Tabor, http://jesusdynasty.com/blog/2007/04/29/the-talpiot-tomb-separating-truth-from-fiction/ p.4.

72 These points are explained in more detail in Stephen F. Pfann, "Mary Magdalene Is Now Missing: A Corrected Reading of Ossuaries CJO 701 and CJO 108": http://www.uhl.ac/MariameAndMartha, 9/5/07, pp. 2–4.

73 Bauckham, *Jesus and the Eyewitnesses*, 108–10. The inscription on ossuary Rahmani no. 552, which Rahmani understands as referring to a woman called both Little Salo and Mariame, could refer to two women, and the same is true of the two names Mariam and Yohana on ossuary Rahmani no. 31.

74 Pfann, "Mary Magdalene Is Now Missing"; cf, also "The View from Jerusalem" blog, http://www.uhl.ac/blog/?cat=, 6/5/2007: "Preliminary Autopsy of CJO 701 (80.500) MAR-IAME KAI MARA."

It seems that Emile Puech and Tal Ilan, both scholars of considerable expertise in epigraphy, independently came up with the same or a similar revised reading.[75] It has been generally accepted. I am not an epigrapher, but so far as I can judge, Pfann's reading is convincing. It disposes neatly of the serious problems in Rahmani's reading and interpretation. But James Tabor is unconvinced and, although Rahmani's opinion of Pfann's reading does not appear to be known, Tabor reports that Leah Di Segni, whom Rahmani consulted on his readings of the inscriptions and who confirmed his reading of 701 at that time, still holds to it.[76]

Partly for this reason I will give further attention to the name Mariamenon. It is a key point in Jacobovici and Pellegrino's case, since they claim that it is an unusual form of the name Mariam that can be shown to have been the form used by Mary Magdalene. Rahmani, as we have noticed, found a similar diminutive, Mariamnon, on ossuary 108 in his catalog. This ossuary has the dead person's name inscribed in Greek no less than four times, three times as *Mariamē* (Μαριαμη), but once, according to Rahmani's reading, as *Mariamnou* (Μαριαμνου), which Rahmani understands as the genitive case of a diminutive formed from *Mariamnē* (Μαριαμνη). As in the case of ossuary 701, there is a problem here in that we should expect the Greek diminutive ending to be *–ion*, not *–on*. An additional problem is that it is somewhat odd that this name, alone of the four, is in the genitive case. But Pfann has plausibly proposed a different reading of this inscription, reading this one, like the other three on the ossuary, as *Mariamē* (Μαριαμη).[77] If he is correct, then nothing like the name Mariamne is attested before the third century, when, as we have noted, *Mariamenē* (Μαριαμενη) occurs in the Jewish catacomb at Beth She'arim.[78] Also in the third century the name Mariamne appears for the first time in Christian sources referring to Mary Magdalene.

Before examining forms of the name used in various sources for Mary Magdalene, we must complete our study of the ossuary inscription by returning to the name Mara. It is not common. Ilan lists only nine

75 Ilan proposed: Μαριαμ η και Μαρα (*Mariam ē kai Mara*), "Mariam who is also Mara."

76 James D. Tabor, http://jesusdynasty.com/blog/2007/04/29/the-talpiot-tomb-separating-truth-from-fiction/ p. 4.

77 Pfann, "Mary Magdalene Is Now Missing," 8–9.

78 M. Schwabe and B. Lifshitz, *Beth She'arim II: The Greek Inscriptions* (New Brunswick, NJ: Rutgers University Press, 1974), 4–5 (no. 8). A nearby Hebrew inscription, Miriam (מירים [*myrym*]), may refer to the same woman.

instances.[79] In two of these cases the name (מרה [mrh], Μαρα [Mara]) clearly belongs to males.[80] In these cases we clearly have the Aramaic word for "master," appropriately in the determined state, used as a male name. But in another case the name seems to be female. This is ossuary 468 in Rahmani's catalog, which has two inscriptions in different places: Mara (מרה [mrh]) and Martha (מרתא [mrtʾ]). They could be alternative names for the same woman,[81] and this is the strongest basis for the claim that Mara was used as a short form of the Aramaic female name Martha. But could the names not belong to two women interred in the same ossuary, or to a man called Mara and his wife Martha?[82] The other occurrences of Mara in Ilan's list she has arbitrarily classified as female and states this clearly.[83] There are also a variety of forms (מרא [mrʾ], Μαρα [Mara], Μαρες [Mares], Μαρι [Mari], Μαρ [Mar]). The last two seem best understood as male names, Mari meaning "my master," and Mar being an abbreviated form of the same.[84] The evidence is ambiguous for the interpretation of Rahmani no. 701. The person interred with Mariame could, as has been suggested, be a close female relative, but could also be her husband.[85] This throws even more doubt on the claim that the ossuary is that of Mary Magdalene alleged to be the wife of Jesus.

THE NAMES OF MARY MAGDALENE

Jacobovici and Pellegrino claim that the name Mariamne, which they allege to be the name on ossuary 701 from the Talpiot tomb, was the real name of Mary Magdalene, for which the evidence is that she is so called in the *Acts of Philip*.[86] This alleged use on the ossuary of a form of

---

79 One is in the Addendum (Ilan, *Lexicon*, 450) and has been missed by others writing about Rahmani no. 701.

80 Ilan, *Lexicon*, 392, 450.

81 According to Ilan, *Lexicon*, 423, the inscription "states categorically that מרה [mrh] is also called מרתא [mrtʾ]." That does not seem to me to be the case.

82 Jewish names that could be used as either male or female are rare.

83 Ilan, *Lexicon*, 423.

84 See Ilan, *Lexicon*, 53 (7.6.5.1).

85 For the burial of a husband and a wife in the same ossuary, see Hachlili, *Jewish Funerary Customs,* 304, 312, 317.

86 Jacobovici and Pellegrino, *The Jesus Family Tomb*, 204–7. They do not always distinguish properly between Mariamme (a quite common Greek form of the name Mariam) and Mariamne (the distinctive form which is attested almost exclusively in the *Acts of Philip*). But it is clear that they do attach importance to the *n* in Rahmani's reading of the name as Mariamenou.

the name Mariam that is also attested as that of Mary Magdalene seems to be the clinching argument in their case:

> From the beginning we focused on this particular ossuary because it seemed to be the key to the whole story. Everything depended on this unique artifact.[87]

We need to look carefully at the way Mary Magdalene is named in early Christian literature. The four Gospels in the New Testament are unquestionably our earliest Greek sources for this.[88] In table 6 it can be seen that in these she is only ever named Mariam or Maria. The variant readings make it difficult to tell in every case which is the more original reading. Evidently scribes themselves preferred one or another version of the name and sometimes changed the form in the manuscript they were copying. But if we accept the readings in the Nestle-Aland Greek text, edition 27, Mary Magdalene is almost always called Maria. The two exceptions are interesting. In John 20:11 Mary Magdalene encounters the risen Jesus near to the empty tomb. She does not recognize Him until He speaks her name, "Mariam," in presumably the way He had used to do. The form used here is Mariam, and it is used again in the next reference to her, which is the last in the Gospel (20:18). The writer may well have thought it appropriate, since Jesus would have been speaking Aramaic, to give the form of the name that Jesus Himself would have used.[89]

Be that as it may, there is no instance of the form Mariam(m)e in the New Testament, with reference either to Mary Magdalene or to any other Mary. This form appears in only eight Christian texts extant in Greek from before the seventh century.[90] Three of these refer to the wife of King Herod (who is always known as Mariame or Mariamme, as in Josephus). One refers to Mary the mother of Jesus (*Protevangelium of James*, Bodmer papyrus). The remaining four refer to Mary Magdalene.

Origen, the third-century Christian theologian, cites the second-century pagan critic of Christianity, Celsus, referring to various Christian sects whose alleged leaders or founders were women: "[Celsus]

---

87 Jacobovici and Pellegrino, *The Jesus Family Tomb,* 204.

88 Some scholars consider the *Gospel of Thomas* earlier than some of the canonical Gospels. We have its references to Mary Magdalene only in Coptic and so cannot be sure of the form of the name in the original Greek, but the Coptic form is Mariham. In the extant text of the *Gospel of Peter* (12:50), Mary Magdalene is called Μαριαμ (Mariam).

89 Compare Jesus' address to Peter as "Simon son of John" in John 21:15,16,17.

90 Shoemaker, "A Case," 13.

knows also of Marcellians who follow Marcellina, and Harpocratians who follow Salome, and others who follow Mariamme [Μαριάμμης (*Mariammēs*)], and others who follow Martha (C. Cels. 5:62)."[91]

The followers of Mariamme were evidently one of the Gnostic groups (using the term in the broad sense) of the second century. These may well have been the group who used the *Gospel of Mary*, of which we have a Greek fragment in which Mary Magdalene is called *Mariammē* (Μαριάμμη).[92]

Hippolytus, in his *Refutation of All Heresies* (written between 228 and 233), says that a Gnostic group known as the Naassenes claimed to have a secret teaching that James the brother of Jesus had transmitted to Mary (5.7.1; 10.9.3). What is especially notable is that here the manuscript evidence is divided between the two forms *Mariammē* (Μαριάμμη) and *Mariamnē* (Μαριάμνη). Both readings are found at the two occurrences of the name in 5.7.1, but in 10.9.3, where the name occurs once, there is manuscript support only for Mariamnē.[93] The last of the four texts that refer to Mary Magdalene as *Mariammē* is the apocryphal *Acts of Philip* (from the late fourth or early fifth century), but there, while there is some manuscript evidence for Mariammē,[94] the textual tradition is strongly in favour of Mariamnē. These variant readings in the manuscript tradition of Hippolytus and the dominant usage in the manuscripts of the *Acts of Philip* seem to be the only evidence we have for the form *Mariamnē*. It looks as though this is a variant or deformation of the form *Mariammē* that arose in Christian usage at a time and place when the name was not actually in use and so was unfamiliar.[95] Whether this form should be connected with the isolated example of *Mariamenē* (Μαριαμενη) in a

---

91 Translation from Henry Chadwick, *Origen: Contra Celsum*, 2nd ed. (Cambridge: Cambridge University Press, 1965), 312.

92 The Greek text is quoted, with the parallel Coptic version (which has Mariham), in Silke Petersen, *"Zerstört die Werke der Weiblichkeit!" Maria Magdalena, Salome und andere Jüngerinnen Jesu in christlich-gnostichen Schriften,* Nag Hammadi and Manichaean Studies 48 (Leiden: Brill, 1999), 140.

93 I am dependent on Wendland's edition: *Hippolytus Werke*, vol. 3: *Refutatio Omnium Haeresium*, ed. Paul Wendland, GCS (Leipzig: Hinrichs, 1916) 78–79, 268.

94 Bovon, "Mary Magdalene," 80, says that the name is "spelled sometimes Μαριάμμη in one or two of the manuscripts, particularly the oldest one, P," but I cannot find these readings in the apparatus of the edition: François Bovon, Bertrand Bourvier, and Frédéric Amsler, *Acta Philippi*, vol. 1: *Textus*, CCSA 11 (Turnhout: Brepols, 1999).

95 Mariam(m)e is found in none of the five volumes of Peter Marshall Fraser and Elaine Matthews, eds., *A Lexicon of Greek Personal Names* (Oxford: Oxford University Press, 1987–2005).

third-century inscription from the Jewish cemetery at Beth She'arim, to which we referred in discussing the inscription on Talpiot ossuary 701, remains uncertain.

The evidence thus suggests that the form *Mariammē* (Μαριάμμη) was used of Mary Magdalene only in some Gnostic Christian circles in the second and third centuries. Most of the Gnostic literature we possess is extant only in Coptic translations where it is difficult to tell what the underlying Greek form was. In one such work, the *Sophia of Jesus Christ* (CG III,4), the form Mariamme (Marihamme) does appear in the Coptic (98:10; 114:9), and there is one instance of this form in the Coptic of the *Pistis Sophia* (3:133).[96] It also appears in the *Manichaean Psalm Book* in Coptic.[97] Often the Coptic texts use the form Mariham or Mariam. We probably cannot know whether the underlying Greek in these cases had Μαριαμ (*Mariam*) or Μαριαμμη (*Mariammē*),[98] though the fact that in the case of the *Gospel of Mary* we have in parallel the Greek Μαριαμμη (*Mariammē*) and the Coptic Mariham certainly suggests that the latter may well represent Μαριαμμη (*Mariammē*) in the Greek quite frequently. On the other hand, the *Great Questions of Mary*, a Gnostic work of which we have a report, though not an actual quotation, in Greek from Epiphanius, uses Maria (Μαρία).[99]

There has been some discussion about the identity of the figure(s) of Mary in the Gnostic literature.[100] It has been suggested that some of the references that have been generally assumed to be to Mary Magdalene (such as in the *Gospel of Mary* and the *Great Questions of Mary*) are rather to the mother of Jesus, or that the two figures have sometimes

---

96 Shoemaker, "A Case," 9 n. 12. Elsewhere in this work the forms *Maria* and *Mariham* both occur. For the frequency, see Ann Graham Brock, "Setting the Record Straight—the Politics of Identification: Mary Magdalene and Mary the Mother in *Pistis Sophia*," in Jones, ed., *Which Mary?*, 43–52, here 45.

97 See Antti Marjanen, *The Woman Jesus Loved: Mary Magdalene in the Nag Hammadi Library and Related Documents* (Nag Hammadi and Manichaean Studies 40; Leiden: Brill, 1996), chapter 10.

98 Marjanen, *The Woman,* 63–64, is unhelpful in not distinguishing the usage of Mariham and Marihamme in the Coptic texts.

99 Epiphanius, *Pan.* 26.8.1–9.5. See the text and translation in Marjanen, *The Woman,* 191–94.

100 See especially the essays in Jones, ed., *Which Mary?*; also Esther A. de Boer, *The Gospel of Mary: Beyond a Gnostic and a Biblical Mary Magdalene* (London: T. & T. Clark, 2004), 16–18.

been fused,[101] just as Mary Magdalene was widely identified with Mary the sister of Martha of Bethany. We cannot resolve all these issues here, but it still seems most probable that the Gnostic Mary was principally a development of the figure known in earlier texts and traditions as Mary Magdalene, even if some identification or confusion with other Marys has also taken place in these texts, which are often only vaguely concerned with historical reference. To what extent the prominent and authoritative role that Mary Magdalene plays in some of these Gnostic works preserves genuinely early traditions about her[102] is also a difficult issue that we can leave aside here since we are primarily concerned with the forms of her name. There is no reason to assume that a tradition of early origin that reaches us only in late texts will preserve an early usage in the form of the name Mary that it uses.

For Jacobovici and Pellegrino, the key witness to the original and authentic form of Mary Magdalene's name is the *Acts of Philip*, [103] one of the many apocryphal acts of apostles that were written from the second century onwards. It was one of the later works in this genre, dating from the late fourth or early fifth century[104] (Jacobovici and Pellegrino never mention the date of the work!), and the complete text has only recently become available in the magnificent edition, with French translation and extensive commentary, by François Bovon, Bertrand Bourvier, and Frédéric Amsler.[105] It is, indeed, a fascinating work, which depicts Mariamne, the sister of the apostle Philip, playing the part of an apostle alongside her brother and the apostle Bartholomew.[106] Although the depiction of this Mary as sister of Philip is a creative development, unattested in any earlier source, she is apparently identified with both Mary Magdalene

101 On this see also Ann Graham Brock, *Mary Magdalene, the First Apostle: The Struggle for Authority,* HTS 51 (Cambridge: Massachusetts: Harvard University Press, 2003), chapter 7.

102 For example, de Boer, *The Gospel of Mary,* argues that the *Gospel of Mary*, which she denies is Gnostic, preserves early traditions independent of the New Testament Gospels.

103 Jacobovici and Pellegrino, *The Jesus Family Tomb,* chapter 6.

104 Frédéric Amsler, *Acta Philippi,* vol. 2: *Commentarius,* CCSA 12 (Turnhout: Brepols, 1999), 438, dates different parts of the work to dates between the mid-fourth and mid-fifth centuries. The material about Mariamne belongs to the earliest of these parts.

105 François Bovon, Bertrand Bourvier, and Frédéric Amsler, *Acta Philippi,* vol. 1: *Textus,* CCSA 11 (Turnhout: Brepols, 1999); Frédéric Amsler, *Acta Philippi,* vol. 2: *Commentarius,* CCSA 12 (Turnhout: Brepols, 1999). Jacobovici and Pellegrino, *The Jesus Family Tomb,* 95–96, say that in June 2000 Bovon and Bourvier published the first complete translation, in French, but this is mistaken.

106 Bovon, "Mary Magdalene."

and Mary of Bethany (who were often identified in early Christian literature)[107] and also acquires some aspects of the figure of Mary the mother
of Jesus in patristic literature.[108]

Jacobovici and Pellegrino regard the *Acts of Philip* as providing "a
~~much more complete version of Mary Magdalene than the Gospels"~~[109]
and apparently mean this in the sense of a historically reliable account:

> The Acts of Philip provided very important infor-
> mation to be weighed against the Talpiot tomb. First,
> it provided a name for the mother of Jesus: Maria, and
> one for Mary Magdalene: Mariamne; second, it pro-
> vided a status for Mariamne—she was an apostle, a
> teacher, or, to use the Aramaic, a "Mara"; third, she
> moved in Greek circles; and fourth, her bones were
> buried in Israel.[110]

However, Jacobovici and Pellegrino have no scholarly support whatsoever for supposing that the *Acts of Philip* preserve anything worth knowing about the historical Mary Magdalene, not even her name.[111] François
Bovon, interviewed about the *Acts of Philip* in both the film and the
book, quickly thereafter made clear that he did not at all support their
use of the *Acts of Philip*:

> I do not believe that Mariamne is the real name of
> Mary Magdalene. . . . [The portrayal of Mariamne in
> the Acts of Philip] fits very well with the portrayal of
> Mary of Magdala in the Manichean Psalms, the Gos-
> pel of Mary, and Pistis Sophia. My interest is not his-
> torical, but on the level of literary traditions.[112]

107 See, for example, the early second-century *Epistle of the Apostles (Epistula Apostolo-
rum)*, where three women visit the tomb, share the meeting with the risen Christ that John
20 narrates of Mary Magdalene, and report to the apostles. There is confusion about the
names of the three in the two versions (Coptic and Ethiopic), but it looks likely that the
original referred to two of them as Martha and Mary Magdalene, assuming the latter to be
Martha's sister Mary. Cf. also Marjanen, *The Woman*, 132 n. 43.
108 Bovon, "Mary Magdalene," 87–88. This does not mean that she is identified with the
mother of Jesus, who is mentioned in 6.13, 16, as Μαρία (Maria).
109 Jacobovici and Pellegrino, *The Jesus Family Tomb*, 96.
110 Ibid., 102.
111 James Tabor does not seem to have supported this aspect of their case.
112 François Bovon, "The Tomb of Jesus": http://sbl-site.org/Article.aspx?ArticleId=656,
27/03/07.

With regard to the forms of the name Mary, we must say, first, that there is no justification at all for connecting *Mariamēnon* (Μαριαμη-νον), which is Rahmani's reading of the name on the Talpiot ossuary 701, with *Mariamnē* (Μαριάμνη), as used in the *Acts of Philip.* We have no evidence at all that Mary Magdalene was ever called either *Mariamēnon* or *Mariamēnē* (Μαριαμηνη), the hypothetical form of the name of which Mariamenon is alleged to be a diminutive. While Mari-amne might conceivably be a contraction of Mariamene, the history of its use makes it much more likely that it is a variation of Mariamme that occurred only in a few Christian works no earlier than the third century. Jacobovici and Pellegrino's mistake was to make a connection between the name on a first-century ossuary and the name used in a work of the late fourth century without investigating the intervening three centuries of onomastic history.

However, when we do investigate that history, we find strong evidence for the use of the form *Mariamme* for Mary Magdalene in Gnostic circles from the mid-second century onwards. Might we, therefore, be justified in connecting this evidence with Pfann's reading of the name on the Talpiot ossuary 701 as Mariame? Might the Gnostic literature preserve the form of Mary's name that was used during her lifetime and that therefore supports the identification of Talpiot ossuary 701 as her ossuary?

First, we should recall that there are 22 occurrences of Mariame (or 23 if we include the woman named on Talpiot ossuary 701) in Ilan's list of 79 occurrences of some form of the name in Hebrew or Greek script, or 42 (43) of those in Greek script. Half of those Jewish women for whom we have a Greek form of the name Mary attested were called Mariame. Second, the forms *Maria* and *Mariam*, especially the latter, are exclusively the forms used with reference to Mary Magdalene in Greek Christian literature up to the mid-second century (including not only the canonical Gospels but also *Gos. Pet.* 12:50).[113] While there is no obvious explanation for the Gnostic use of the form *Mariamme,* the evidence strongly suggests that it was a later development.

---

113 The extant fragments in Greek of other noncanonical Gospels prior to the *Gospel of Mary* do not mention Mary Magdalene.

DID JESUS MARRY MARY MAGDALENE?

We have already noticed that Jacobovici and Pellegrino erroneously take for granted that there are old traditions to the effect that Jesus married Mary Magdalene. They do not use the evidence of the Talpiot tomb to argue for this but use the prior presumption that Jesus married Mary Magdalene to interpret the inscriptions on the ossuaries and actually to prove that the tomb is that of Jesus' family. Mary Magdalene, of course, could not be expected to be found in a tomb of Jesus' family unless she was related to the family by marriage. Even an extra-marital sexual liaison with Jesus would not entitle her to a place in such a tomb, and so we are dealing with the claim that Jesus was actually married to her. On this presumption rest Jacobovici and Pellegrino's claims about the inscriptions on ossuaries 702 (Yehuda bar Yeshuaᶜ) and 701. So some discussion of this issue is required here.

I know of no suggestion prior to the twentieth century to the effect that Jesus married Mary Magdalene. The silence of the early sources (including all the noncanonical Gospels and even the *Acts of Philip*!) is deafening. Admittedly, if Jesus married but was then widowed or divorced before the beginning of His public ministry the sources might never have had occasion to say so, but the claim we are considering is that His wife was the best known woman in the earliest Christian movement, His disciple Mary Magdalene.

It is true that the *Gospel of Philip* and the *Gospel of Mary* both say that Jesus loved Mary more than other women (*Gos. Mary* 10:2–3) and more than the male disciples (*Gos. Mary* 8:14–15; *Gos. Phil.* 63:34–35; 64:2), but it should be evident that the reference is not to erotic love but to a high degree of the sort of love with which Jesus loved all the disciples. This is why the male disciples are irked by Jesus' preference for Mary. The *Gospel of Philip* adds to the statement that Jesus loved her more than all the disciples the additional statement that He used to "kiss her [often] on her [mouth]" (63:35–36), while elsewhere it makes the claim, made famous by its quotation in *The Da Vinci Code*, that Mary Magdalene was called the "companion" of Jesus (59:8–9). If these statements do carry some kind of erotic or marital significance, then in their context in the *Gospel of Philip* they must be read according to that work's use of marital terms to designate spiritual relationships (76:6–9; 81:34–82:26). Mary Magdalene would be Jesus' spiritual consort, prototype of the spiritual partnerships with their heavenly counterparts that the *Gospel's* readers can enter. The *Gospel* is no more interested in sexual union in the case of Jesus and Mary than in the case of its readers.

As to Jesus' kissing Mary, the text is unfortunately fragmentary, and we can only guess where He kissed her, but in the ancient world kissing, even a man kissing a woman and even on the mouth, was by no means necessarily erotic. Again, since the disciples' reaction to the fact that Jesus kissed Mary is to be offended and to ask why He loved her more than all of them (63:37–64:2), it is clear that the kiss is a mark of privilege, not of sexual love. The significance is as in the *Second Apocalypse of James*, also a Gnostic text, where Jesus kisses James on the mouth as a mark of the privilege of being selected by Jesus as the recipient of secret revelations (56:14–57:5).[114]

Arguments that Jesus must have been married regularly assert that it was unheard of for Jewish men to remain unmarried, and more especially, that Jesus as a Jewish rabbi would have been obliged to marry and raise children. The fact is, we have no idea how many Jewish men in first-century Palestine remained single: there is simply no evidence on the matter. The idea that the commandment to "be fruitful and multiply" in Genesis 1:28 is a law that imposes an obligation on every adult Jewish man to marry and procreate is attested no earlier than the Mishnah at the beginning of the third century. The Mishnah does report a debate between the houses of Hillel and Shammai as to whether a son and a daughter or only two sons adequately fulfill the commandment (*m. Yebam.* 6:6), and so the interpretation of the Genesis commandment as a binding law may go back to the Pharisees in the time of Jesus.[115] But the contrast between the more lenient Hillel and the stricter Shammai is such a commonplace of rabbinic literature that we can hardly be sure it is authentic in this case. In any case, Jesus was neither a Pharisee nor a rabbi learned in the traditions of the Pharisees but a charismatic teacher and miracle worker. The practice of religious celibacy was by no means unknown in first-century Jewish Palestine. The Essenes—or at least the

---

114 There is a full discussion of Jesus' relationship to Mary in the *Gospel of Philip* in Marjanen, *The Woman*, chapter 7.

115 On the whole question of Genesis 1:28 as a law in rabbinic literature, see Jeremy Cohen, *"Be Fertile and Increase, Fill the Earth and Master It": The Ancient and Medieval Career of a Biblical Text* (Ithaca, NY: Cornell University Press, 1989), chapter 3.

stricter category of them—were well-known for it (Josephus, *B.J.* 2.120; *A.J.* 18.21; Philo, *Hypoth.* 11.14–17; Pliny the Elder, *Nat.* 5.73).

It is hard to prove a negative such as that Jesus did not marry, but there is one rather compelling argument that is too often neglected. A saying of Jesus found only in Matthew's Gospel (19.12) speaks of three classes of eunuchs: those born such, those made eunuchs by others, and "eunuchs who have made themselves eunuchs for the sake of the kingdom of heaven" (NASB). The last category must refer to men who adopt a celibate lifestyle for the sake of service of the kingdom. Jesus says that this is not a teaching that all can adopt but that those who can should. If the saying is authentic, we can hardly imagine that Jesus did not Himself belong to the category of "eunuchs who have made themselves eunuchs for the sake of the kingdom of heaven." The saying both requires us to envisage Jesus as celibate and explains why He was.

Finally, we must mention the DNA evidence that Jacobovici and Pellegrino claim shows that the Yeshuaᶜ bar Yehosef and the Mariamenon of the Talpiot tomb ossuaries must have been husband and wife. We should remember that ossuaries often contained the bones of more than one individual, as well as the fact that the most probable reading of the inscription on ossuary 701 indicates that this ossuary certainly did. The bone fragments from each ossuary that were tested belonged to only one of the individuals interred in each ossuary, so that we cannot know whether they belonged specifically to Yeshuaᶜ and Mariamenon/Mariame. But, even supposing that they did, the DNA tests proved only that these two people were not children of the same mother. Jacobovici and Pellegrino's habit of presupposing their conclusions in their arguments is illustrated by their extraordinary statement: "The only reason two unrelated individuals, male and female, would appear together in a *family* tomb in first-century Jerusalem is if they were husband and wife."[116]

They could, of course, have been children of the same father by different mothers. Especially in a society where women not infrequently died in childbirth, it was common for men to marry more than once and have children by more than one wife. But there are many other possibilities. Mariamenon/Mariame (if the DNA sample is hers) could have been married to any other male member of the same family: Yehosef, Yose, Matia, or any of the many others whose bones undoubtedly lay in

---

116 Jacobovici and Pellegrino, *The Jesus Family Tomb,* 207.

the tomb without an inscription to record them.[117] She could have been related to Yeshua' as a cousin on his or her paternal side. In short, the DNA tests prove next to nothing about two individuals whom we cannot even be sure were Yeshua' and Mariamenon/Mariame.

CONCLUSION

The following are the main conclusions we have reached with regard to the names in the ossuary inscriptions from the Talpiot tomb and their possible identification with members of the family of Jesus:

1. There is no reason to think a person called Matia (cp. ossuary 703) belonged to the family of Jesus.
2. In the light of parallel examples, it is not at all unlikely that the Yeshua' bar Yehosef of ossuary 704 (and 702) was a different individual from Jesus of Nazareth.
3. Yose (ossuary 705), as a short form of the name Yehosef, was not unusual.
4. Yose (ossuary 705) could have been the same person as Yehosef (ossuary 704).
5. Maria (ossuary 706) was a common form of the name Mary among first-century Jews, both in Greek and in Hebrew.
6. There is no reason to think that the mother of Jesus was known as Maria rather than Mariam.
7. The inscription on ossuary 701 should probably be read as "Mariame and Mara" (with "and Mara" as a later addition).
8. Mara is here a name, not a title, and may refer to a man (perhaps Mariame's husband) or to a woman.
9. In Christian literature up to the middle of the second century, Mary Magdalene is always called either Maria or Mariam, never Mariamme or Mariamne.
10. Only in some Christian Gnostic circles in the second and third centuries was Mary Magdalene known as Mariamme.
11. The form Mariamne, found only in Hippolytus (early third century) and the *Acts of Philip* (late fourth century), is probably not

---

117 For the number of people who would have been interred in the tomb, see Kloner, "A Tomb," 22 n.2.

connected with Mariamenon (even if this is the correct reading of ossuary 701), but is a late Christian variation of Mariamme.

12. We cannot be sure that the samples from ossuaries 701 and 704 that were DNA tested were of Mariamenon/Mariame and Yeshuaʿ, rather than of other individuals interred in the same ossuaries.

13. The DNA results are compatible with a wide variety of family relationships between the persons tested.

14. Jesus of Nazareth was almost certainly celibate, and so the Yeshuaʿ of ossuary 702 (Yehuda bar Yeshuaʿ) is unlikely to be He.

Table 1
The Relatives of Jesus

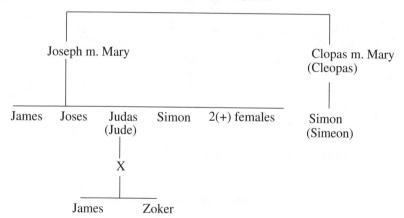

Table 2

The most popular male names among Palestinian Jews (40 or more occurrences), 330 BCE–200 CE

Rank	Name as in English NT	English form used by Ilan	Total valid	Total in Gospels and Acts	Total in Josephus	Total on ossuaries	Total in Judean Desert texts
1	Simon/ Simon	Simon	243	8	29	59	72
2	Joseph/ Joses	Joseph	218	6	21	45	78
3	Lazarus	Eleazar	166	1	20	29	52
4	Judas	Judah	164	5	14	44	35
5	John	Yohanan	122	5	13	25	40
6	Jesus	Joshua	99	2	14	22	38
7	Ananias	Hananiah	82	2	10	18	13
8	Jonathan	Jonathan	71	(1)	14	14	21
9	Matthew/ Matthias	Mattathias	62	2	12	17	15
10	Manaen	Menahem	42	1	2	4	23
11	James	Jacob	40	5	4	5	10

Total occurrences of all male names: 2,625

The most popular female names among Palestinian Jews (20 or more occurrences), 330 BCE–200 CE

Rank	Name as in English NT	English form used by Ilan	Total valid	Total in Gospels and Acts	Total in Josephus	Total on ossuaries	Total in Judean Desert texts
1	Mary	Mariam	70	6	7	42	9
2	Salome	Salome	58	1	3	41	8
3		Shelamzion	24		1	19	3
4	Martha	Martha	20	1		17	

Total occurrences of all female names: 328
Total occurrences of all names, male and female: 2,953

Table 3
The Joshuas in Ilan's *Lexicon*

(Ilan lists 103 persons under "Joshua," but I have omitted two she considers fictitious and another I consider fictitious. In the case of ten persons for whom two or three forms of the name are attested, I have counted both or all forms, so that my list is of 111 occurrences of the name.)

In Hebrew/Aramaic script

יהושע	Yehoshua‘	15
יהושוע	Yehoshua‘	1
ייׁשוע	Yeshua‘	1
יׁשוע	Yeshua‘	41
יׁשועה	Yeshua‘	1
יׁשועא	Yeshua‘	1
ׁשוע	[Ye]shua‘	1
יׁשו	Yeshu	1

In Greek script

Ἰεσουα	Iesoua	1
Ἰησους	Iesous	38
Ἰεσους	Iesous	2
Βαριησους	Bar-Iesous	1
Ἰησιου (gen.)	Iesiou	1
Ἰησουου (gen.)	Iesouou	4
Ἰασσουου (gen.)	Iassouou	2

Table 4

The Josephs in Ilan's *Lexicon*

(Ilan lists 231 persons under "Joseph," but I have omitted the ten she considers fictitious, and, in the case of five persons for whom two forms of the name are attested, I have counted both forms, so that my list is of 226 occurrences of the name.)

In Hebrew/Aramaic script

יוסף	Yosef	21
יהסף, יהוסף, יהוספ	Yehosef	93
יוסי	Yose (spelling with *yod*)	30
יסה, יוסה	Yose (spelling with *he*)	4
יהוסה	Yehose	2
איסי, אסי	'Ise	6

In Greek script

Ἰωσηφ	Joseph	9
Ἰωσηπ	Josep	3
Ἰωσηπος	Josepos	47
Ἰωσιπος	Josipos	1
Ἰωσης	Joses	2
Ἰωση, Ἰωσε, Ἰοσε	Jose	4
Ἰωσιος	Josios	1
Ἰωσιας	Josias	1
Ἰος	Jos	1

In Latin script

Iosepu		1

Table 5
The Marys in Ilan's *Lexicon*

(Ilan lists 80 persons under "Mariam," but I have omitted the six she considers fictitious, and, in the case of four persons for whom two forms of the name are attested, I have included both. One of these is Mary the mother of Jesus, for whom Ilan gives only the form *Maria* [Μαρια], but who is also frequently called *Mariam* [Μαριαμ] in the New Testament. Another is the Mariame of Rahmani ossuary no. 108, for whom Ilan gives only that form [Μαριαμη] but who is also called *Mariamnon* [Μαριαμνον] on her ossuary, according to Rahmani. Thus my list is of 79 occurrences of the name. I have retained Rahmani's readings of Mariamenon on ossuary no. 701 and Mariamnon on ossuary no. 108 for the purposes of this table, but both have been reread by Stephen Pfann as Mariame, and I think his readings are probably correct. In that case we should drop Mariamnon from the list entirely and, instead of Mariamenon, add one more Mariame to the total, making 21.)

In Hebrew/Aramaic script

מרים, מרימ	Mariam	27
מריה	Maria	9
מרימא	Mariama	1

In Greek script

Μαριαμ	Mariam	5
Μαριαμη	Mariame	20
Μαριεαμη	Marieame	1
Μαραμη	Marame	1
Μαρια	Maria	13
Μαριαμηνον	Mariamenon	1
Μαριαμνον	Mariamnon	1

Table 6
The Marys in the New Testament

The readings are those of Nestle-Aland 27.

* = variant reading.

Mary the mother of Jesus

Μαριαμ (nom.)	Matt 13:55; Luke 1:27,34,38,39,46,56; 2:19
(voc.)	Luke 1:30
(acc.)	Matt 1:20*; Luke 2:16,34
(dat.)	Luke 2:5; Acts 1:14

Μαρια (nom.)	Luke 2:19*
Μαριαν (acc.)	Matt 1:20
Μαριας (gen.)	Matt 1:16,18; 2:11; Mark 6:3; Luke 1:41

Mary Magdalene

Μαριαμ	Matt 27:56*, 61*; 28:1*; Mark 15:40*; John 19:25*; 20:1*,11*,16,18
Μαρια	Matt 27:56, 61; 28:1; Mark 15:40,47; 16:1; Luke 8:1; 24:10; John 19:25; 20:1,11

Mary the mother of James and Joses

Μαρια	Matt 27:56, 61; 28:1; Mark 15:40,47; 16:1; Luke 24:10

Mary the wife of Clopas

Μαρια	John 19:25

Mary of Bethany

Μαριαμ (nom.)	Luke 10:39, 42; John 11:2,20,32; 12:3
(acc.)	John 11:19,28,31,45

Μαρια (nom.)	Luke 10:39*, 42*; John 11:2*,20*,32*; 12:3*
Μαριαν (acc.)	John 11:19*,28*,31*,45*
Μαριας (gen.)	John 11:1

Mary the mother of John Mark

Μαριας (gen.)   Acts 12:12

Mary of Rome

Μαριαμ (acc.)   Rom 16:6*

Μαριαν (acc.)   Rom 16:6

THE JESUS TOMB MATH

William A. Dembski and Robert J. Marks II
www.jesustombmath.org

AN IMPROBABLE CHALLENGE

Probability and statistics lie at the heart of the startling claim by James Cameron, Simcha Jacobovici, and others that the Talpiot tomb, discovered 25 years ago outside Jerusalem, is the tomb of the New Testament Jesus. Specifically, proponents of this view have put forward a number—1 in 600—as the probability that the Talpiot tomb could be other than the tomb of Jesus. Thus conversely, it is supposed to be highly probable—with probability 599 in 600—that this is Jesus' tomb. Thus, one is informed on *The Jesus Family Tomb* Web site: "After listening to filmmaker Simcha Jacobovici explain the so-called 'Jesus equation,' you'll realize just how *unlikely* it is that this *isn't*, in fact, his tomb."[1]

Readers of Simcha Jacobovici and Charles Pellegrino's *The Jesus Family Tomb: The Discovery, the Investigation, and the Evidence That Could Change History* and viewers of Discovery Channel's documentary *The Lost Tomb of Jesus* are given the impression that to deny that the Talpiot tomb is the tomb of Jesus is to renounce the rigors of mathematical thinking and to embrace irrationality. Thus Jacobovici writes: "At the end of the day, if I were a betting man and you let me be the house, and you could assure me that each time a player spun my wheel the odds were 600 to 1 in my favor, I would not hesitate to play."[2]

---

1 See http://www.jesusfamilytomb.com/evidence/probability.html (last accessed 15 June 2007).
2 Simcha Jacobovici and Charles Pellegrino, *The Jesus Family Tomb: The Discovery, the Investigation, and the Evidence That Could Change History* (San Francisco: Harper, 2007), 115.

Accordingly, to reject the claim that the Talpiot tomb belongs to the New Testament Jesus is like stirring at random a pot containing 599 white balls and 1 black ball and then betting that the selected ball should be black, clearly, the smart money is on white. But where does this 1 in 600 probability come from? And how are we to interpret it? Because probabilities can be difficult to assign and even more difficult to interpret, Simcha Jacobovici, the driving force behind the recent effort to make the Talpiot tomb the greatest archeological find in history, therefore enlisted a professional statistician to perform the relevant probability calculations and then to interpret them: University of Toronto statistician Andrey Feuerverger.

In this paper we examine both the logic by which Feuerverger came to his improbability of 1 in 600 and then the logic by which Jacobovici and others concluded that the Talpiot tomb must in all likelihood be Jesus' tomb. Although Feuerverger's approach contains some valid insights, it also commits some fatal oversights. In cleaning up Feuerverger's math, we find that the improbabilities are not nearly as bad as he makes out. Indeed, we find that a significant number of families in Palestine at the time of Jesus were likely to have the pattern of names found in the Talpiot tomb.

A corrected version of Feuerverger's model using reasonable estimates of the probabilities for the New Testament names found in the Talpiot tomb shows that there were likely to be as many 154 Jewish families living in Palestine at the time with the pattern of names found in the Talpiot tomb. On *The Jesus Family Tomb* people's reckoning, this would yield a probability of 153 in 154 that the Talpiot tomb is *not* the tomb of Jesus. And even if we go with *The Jesus Family Tomb* people's smaller probability estimates for the New Testament names found in the Talpiot tomb, a Bayesian analysis that takes into account additional evidence not considered by Feuerverger increases this probability close to one.

In consequence, Jacobovici and others have no rational basis for identifying the Talpiot tomb with that of Jesus. In fact, the most reasonable inference—leaving aside any presuppositions about the infallibility of the Bible or the truth of Christianity—is that this most probably is *not* Jesus' tomb.

REALITY CHECK

As professionals in the mathematical and engineering sciences, we had misgivings about *The Jesus Family Tomb* story from the start. Investigator bias is always a danger in analyzing data. People, and we include ourselves here, are notorious for wanting to see their wishes fulfilled. For this reason, science imposes constraints on researchers so that their biases do not cloud their conclusions. These constraints take the form of prescribed methods for properly conducting research. In other words, they prescribe ways scientists are supposed to conduct their research to keep them out of trouble.

Take the testing of new drugs as an example. Such studies are supposed to be double-blind, meaning that neither the subject receiving the new experimental drug nor the experimenter administering it and judging its effectiveness is supposed to know whether the actual drug or a placebo was administered. Only then can the drug's effectiveness be evaluated fairly. Otherwise, the patient or experimenter or both, having prior expectations about the drug's effectiveness, may rate the patient's performance in line with those expectations rather than objectively. Ideally, if proper research methods are employed, it should be possible for any outside observer to look at the data and come to roughly the same conclusion.

With *The Jesus Family Tomb* people, however, we are dealing with no such controls. Here we have a group of people who stand to profit (and indeed have already profited) from sensationalizing the Talpiot tomb as the tomb of Jesus. Moreover, they are eager to state and advertise their conclusions before the hard work of properly analyzing the data is done. Andrey Feuerverger, on whose probability calculations their case rests, admits that this work has yet to be properly done and vetted. On his academic Web site, addressed to "Dear Statistical Colleagues," he writes: "A detailed paper is being prepared and hopefully will undergo timely peer review; if successful in the refereeing process it will be made available."[3] Such an admission hardly inspires confidence given the extravagant claims being made on the basis of Feuerverger's work. Not only has the rigorous statistical work not been properly vetted; it is still in the process of preparation.

---

3 See http://fisher.utstat.toronto.edu/andrey/OfficeHrs.txt (last accessed 18 June 2007).

WHY EVEN THINK THAT THIS MIGHT BE JESUS' TOMB?

A Christian who believes that Jesus rose from the dead and therefore has no remains to place in a tomb would naturally dismiss *The Jesus Family Tomb* story out of hand. But why should anyone without such a prior faith commitment accept the Talpiot tomb as the final resting place of Jesus? The Talpiot tomb contains 10 ossuaries, or chests with bones. Such tombs with ossuaries were common in Palestine during about a 100–year window, beginning the middle of the first century BC and ending abruptly with the fall of Jerusalem in AD 70.

In the Talpiot tomb, four ossuaries have no names inscribed on them, and two have names with no obvious connection to Jesus' family: Matya (a variant of Matthew) and Yehuda bar Yeshua (Judah son of Jesus). Indeed, the Matthew of the New Testament, also known as Levi, is never portrayed as part of Jesus' family. Moreover, the New Testament gives no indication that Jesus was married, much less had a son. Accordingly, *The Jesus Family Tomb* people assign no statistical weight to these two names.

That leaves four ossuaries with names corresponding to Jesus' circle of family and friends as given in the New Testament. Of these, the following three were inscribed in the Hebrew script: Yeshua bar Yehosef (Jesus son of Joseph), Marya (a variant of Mary that leaves off the traditional "m" ending of the Hebrew Miriam or Mariam), and Yose (a short form of Joseph, used in Mark 6:3 to refer to one of Jesus' brothers). The other name, inscribed in Greek, is Mariamne (a Greek variant of Mary, transliterated this way by *The Jesus Family Tomb* people [4]). The first three names can indisputably be placed in Jesus' family. *The Jesus Family Tomb* people regard the fourth as signifying Mary Magdalene, whom, on the basis of certain apocryphal writings, they think to be the wife of Jesus. According to them, these four names are so specific as to leave no option but that this is the tomb of the New Testament Jesus.

To see what's at stake, Simcha Jacobovici asks us to imagine a large football stadium containing the inhabitants of Jerusalem at the time of Jesus (Jacobovici estimates that there were 80,000 people living in Jerusalem at the time). He then imagines asking those present in the sta-

---

4 Actually, the genitive of this name (transliterated "Mariamenou") appears in the tomb on an ossuary, and it is combined with another appellation, "e Mara." *The Jesus Family Tomb* people refer to it inaccurately as "Mariamne." For the sake of argument, we won't quibble with this usage.

dium to play what may be called a "specification game." Jacobovici's specification game is similar to the "game of 20 questions," in which one has up to 20 questions to narrow a field of possibilities to identify some unknown item of interest.

In Jacobovici's specification game, we imagine the stadium announcer running through the names in the Talpiot tomb that correspond to known names in Jesus' circle of family and friends. The announcer starts by asking all persons named Yeshua bar Yehosef (Jesus son of Joseph) to stand. Next he asks those with a mother named Marya to continue standing and the rest to sit down. Next he asks only those with a brother named Yose to continue standing. Finally, he asks those with a wife named Mariamne to remain standing. As each name is given, it further specifies, and therefore narrows, the number of people in the stadium with the given pattern of family names.

In general, when describing an object, one may *underspecify*, *uniquely specify*, or *overspecify* it. In underspecifying it, one identifies a class of objects that contains the object in question but also contains other objects. For instance, the description "American presidents" underspecifies Bill Clinton since the class of objects it identifies contains other presidents as well. On the other hand, the description "the 42nd American president" uniquely specifies Bill Clinton since it identifies him and only him. Finally, the description "the 42nd American president whom Congress did not impeach" is overly specific since no object answers to it.

According to Jacobovici, with only 80,000 people in the stadium, at most one person would likely be left standing at the end of the game, namely, the New Testament Jesus. The pattern of names given by the announcer is therefore supposed to uniquely specify Jesus. Jacobovici's point is that just as this specification of names would uniquely identify someone in the stadium, so would finding them in a tomb of ossuaries.[5]

Jacobovici's specification game could, given enough of the right names, uniquely specify the family of the New Testament Jesus. Suppose, for instance, we found a tomb whose ossuaries included the following inscriptions (note that the last four are the names of Jesus' brothers as given in Mark 6:3):

5 See the video short at http://www.jesusfamilytomb.com/evidence/probability/jesus_equation.html (last accessed 25 June 2007).

- Jesus son of Joseph and Mary
- Joseph the father of Jesus
- Mary the mother of Jesus
- Mary of Magdala
- James the brother of Jesus and son of Joseph
- Joses the brother of Jesus and son of Joseph
- Juda the brother of Jesus and son of Joseph
- Simon the brother of Jesus and son of Joseph

In this case the pattern of inscriptions would uniquely specify the family of the New Testament Jesus. Indeed, unless the tomb inscriptions were deliberately faked, it would be inescapable that here was the family tomb of the New Testament Jesus.

On the other hand, if we had a tomb whose only inscription was "Jesus the brother of Simon," it would be a stretch to claim that here was the family tomb of the New Testament Jesus. Jesus and Simon were exceedingly common names in New Testament times (Simon was the most common of all the Jewish men's names at the time, accounting for more than 10 percent). Thus, there would have been many men in Jerusalem, to say nothing of ancient Palestine, named Jesus with a brother named Simon. In Jacobovici's football stadium analogy, if we asked only those persons named Jesus with a brother named Simon to stand, lots of persons in the stadium would be standing. The inscription "Jesus the brother of Simon," would therefore underspecify the family of the New Testament Jesus.

The pattern of names in the Talpiot tomb clearly provides more specificity than "Jesus the brother of Simon" but less specificity than the combination of eight names given above. The key question before us is whether the pattern of names in the Talpiot tomb underspecifies or uniquely specifies the family of the New Testament Jesus. Jacobovici and his colleagues claim that it uniquely specifies the family of Jesus. To make their case, they put forward what they call "the Jesus equation." We turn to that equation next.

THE JESUS EQUATION

Even though *The Jesus Family Tomb* people frequently refer to "the Jesus equation," in fact they do not write out an actual equation. What they do is take various probabilities and correction factors and then multiply them together to form the probability that the pattern of names "found in the Talpiot tomb could have belonged to a different family than the one described in the New Testament."[6] Implicit in this calculation, however, is an equation that is easy to reconstruct. Accordingly, if they had written out "the Jesus equation," it would look as follows:

$$p = p_1 \times p_2 \times p_3 \times p_4 \times c_1 \times c_2 \times c_3$$

Here p is the purported 1–in–600 probability that the Talpiot tomb could by chance be other than the tomb of Jesus, p_1 to p_4 are probabilities associated with names found in the Talpiot tomb, and c_1 to c_3 are correction factors that adjust these raw probabilities.

To determine the probabilities p_1 to p_4, Andrey Feuerverger, the lead statistician for *The Jesus Family Tomb* people, starts with the names mentioned in the Talpiot tomb that correspond to New Testament names known or suspected to belong to Jesus' family. These are Yeshua bar Yehosef, Mariamne, Marya, and Yose. Next they determine the relative frequencies of these names in light of Tal Ilan's *Lexicon of Jewish Names in Late Antiquity*.[7] Ilan lists all the occurrences of Jewish names that archeologists and historians have discovered and can place around the time of the New Testament. The relative frequencies are as follows:

> Yeshua: 103/2,509
> Yehosef: 231/2,509
> Mariamne: 1/317
> Marya: 26/317
> Yose: 9/2,509

Note that all the denominators here are either 2,509 or 317. That's because in Ilan's lexicon, only a total of 2,509 men and 317 women are listed. Note also that all of these names are either very common or variants of very common names. Among male names, Yeshua (Jesus) has a frequency of 4 percent. Yehosef (Joseph) has a frequency of 9 percent. Yose is a variant of Yehosef. The most common male name is Simon/

6 Christopher Mims, "Should You Accept the 600–to-One Odds That the Talpiot Tomb Belonged to Jesus?" *Scientific American* 296 (March 2007): available online at http://sciam.com/article.cfm?articleID =14A3C2E6–E7F2–99DF–37A9AEC98FB0702A (last accessed June 27, 2007).
7 Tal Ilan, *Lexicon of Jewish Names in Late Antiquity: Palestine 330 BCE—200 CE*, Texts & Studies in Ancient Judaism 91 (Tübingen: Mohr Siebeck, 2002).

Simeon, with a frequency of around 10 percent. Mariamne and Marya are variants of Mary. In Ilan's lexicon, variants of Mary account for a total of 80 out of the 317 female names. That's more than 25 percent.

Feuerverger treats these relative frequencies as probabilities, making the following adjustments: to get the relative frequency for the compound name Yeshua bar Yehosef (Jesus son of Joseph), he multiplies 103/2509 by 231/2509. Moreover, because Mariamne's name appears in the Talpiot tomb with the further designation "e Mara" and because Yose admits a variant, he multiplies the relative frequencies next to Mariamne and Yose by a "combinatorial factor" of two. This yields the following probabilities:[8]

Yeshua bar Yehosef: $103/2,509 \times 231/2,509 = p_1$
Mariamne: $2 \times 1/317 = p_2$
Marya: $26/317 = p_3$
Yose: $2 \times 9/2,509 = p_4$

Because how one person is named is thought not to affect how another person is named, Feuerverger treats these probabilities as independent, which means that the joint probability of these names is the product of the individual probabilities (see appendix A.6).[9] He therefore multiplies these probabilities together, yielding the probability

$$q = p_1 \times p_2 \times p_3 \times p_4$$

which is approximately 1 in 71,000,000.

Next, Feuerverger multiplies this number by three correction factors:

- Correction for number of four–name clusters as "surprising" as this one: $c_1 = 30$

---

8 These numbers are taken from what, at the time of this writing, is the most exact statement of the Jesus equation as given by Andrey Feuerverger in his paper addressed to the statistical community: http://fisher.utstat.toronto.edu/andrey/OfficeHrs.txt (last accessed 28 June 2007).

9 Within families, names are not probabilistically independent—sons, for instance, may be more likely to be named after fathers; moreover, sons of the same father are unlikely to receive the same name (George Foreman naming all his sons George is the exception). But across families, independence seems a reasonable assumption. And even within families, this assumption seems approximately true. In any case, we do not dispute this assumption. The problems with the Jesus equation go much deeper.

- Correction for names missing from Talpiot tomb expected to be there if this truly were the tomb of the New Testament Jesus: $c_2 = 4$
- Correction for the number of tombs that might have displayed this cluster of names: $c_3 = 1,000$

The motivation for these correction factors is as follows:

Regarding c_1

Imagine that you are playing poker and win the game by drawing a royal flush in the suit of spades. Someone exclaims, "What an incredible hand. The odds against getting it by chance are 1 in 2,598,960. You must have been cheating!" In response, you point out that the odds really aren't quite that drastically small. Yes, getting a royal flush in the suit of spades has that precise probability, but there are also royal flushes in the suits of clubs, diamonds, and hearts. Presumably, your interlocutor, who accused you of cheating for getting a royal flush in the suit of spades, would also have accused you of cheating if you had gotten a royal flush in any of these other suits, each of these hands being as "surprising" as the one you got. But in that case, the relevant probability is not that of getting a royal flush in one particular suit but rather of getting a royal flush in any suit. Accordingly, one needs to multiply this 1–in–2,598,960 improbability by 4, which serves as a correction factor that raises this probability to 1 in 649,740.

Similarly, Feuerverger multiplies his 1 in 71,000,000 improbability ($= q$) by a correction factor of $c_1 = 30$ to take into account all the other four–name clusters that match up as surprisingly with the family of the New Testament Jesus. Consider, for instance, what would have happened if the Talpiot tomb included, as before, the names Yeshua bar Yehosef, Marya, and Mariamne but then substituted Yaakov bar Yehosef (James son of Joseph) for Yose. This new pattern of names would constitute as surprising a matchup with the family of the New Testament Jesus as the pattern of names actually discovered. Just as different ways of obtaining a royal flush need to be factored into assessing the improbability of a royal flush, so different patterns of names that are to the same degree characteristic of the family of the New Testament Jesus as the one actually discovered need to be factored into any assessment of whether the pattern of names actually discovered is unlikely to have occurred by chance. Given Feuerverger's correction factor to adjust for "surprising-ness," his improbability of 1 in 71,000,000 now comes down to 1 in 2,400,000 ($= q \times c_1$), a number that appears prominently in *The Jesus Family Tomb* literature.

Regarding c_2

Imagine that you are a detective trying to uncover a husband-and-wife blackmailing team. You don't have photos of the pair, but you have detailed physical descriptions as well as extensive dossiers that describe their personal habits. In particular, you have it on good authority that they are virtually inseparable. In your investigation you find a man who matches the physical description of the husband to a tee. But, as you track his movements, you never see him with a woman who could in any way be construed as a consort. If all you knew about the suspect was that he closely matched the physical description of the criminal in question, you would think it highly probable that you've got the right man. But when you factor in the absence of a woman who is known to be constantly together with the criminal, you are no longer so sure that you've got the right man. Now the probability of having the wrong man goes up.

Likewise, with the Talpiot tomb, not only are certain New Testament names conspicuous by their presence, but others are conspicuous by their absence. Jesus the son of Joseph has to be there. But what about James the son of Joseph, the brother of Jesus (Mark 6:3)? In his letter to the Galatians (regarded by many scholars as the earliest writing in the New Testament—c. AD 49), Paul refers to James as a "pillar" of the church (Gal 2:9). According to the book of Acts, James was an important leader in the Jerusalem church. As a prominent member of Jesus' family who was also active in Jerusalem (and thus near the Talpiot tomb), why does he not merit an ossuary displaying his name in that tomb if it is indeed the family tomb of the New Testament Jesus? In 2002, an ossuary was discovered that bears just such an inscription (i.e., "James son of Joseph, brother of Jesus"). But its provenance is uncertain, and it is widely sus-pected to be a forgery. And although the *The Jesus Family Tomb* people have suggested that the "James ossuary" originally belonged to the Tal-piot tomb,[10] their chief statistician Andrey Feuerverger takes the absence

10 See http://www.jesusfamilytomb.com/the_tomb/james_ossuary.html (last accessed 30 June 2007) as well as an analysis of the patina on the James ossuary that is supposed to

of James's name (and that of others in Jesus' family, such as Joseph himself and Judah the brother of Jesus, both of whom are absent from the tomb) as reason to attenuate the probability that the Talpiot tomb belongs to Jesus' family. Feuerverger therefore multiplies the probability of 1 in 2,400,000 (= $q \times c_1$) by $c_2 = 4$, yielding a probability of 1 in 600,000 (= $q \times c_1 \times c_2$) "in favor of the tomb belonging to the family of Jesus of Nazareth."[11]

Regarding c_3

Imagine that your daughter comes up to you claiming that she just tossed 10 heads in a row with a penny. That's a remarkable repetition of heads, you think. You examine the penny, and it appears to be a fair coin (i.e., a rigid homogeneous flat, rather than warped, disk with distinguishable sides). Moreover, when you question your daughter, she assures you that she really gave the coin a good jolt each time; these were not phony flips. Yet before you accept that this succession of heads was a remarkable coincidence (the improbability of tossing a coin 10 times and getting 10 heads in a row is about 1 in 1,000, and therefore is more extreme than the 1 in 600 put forward by *The Jesus Family Tomb* people), you have one more question for your daughter: how many times did she toss the coin before coming to you and reporting this remarkable succession of heads? As it turns out, she was tossing the coin all afternoon. You do a quick calculation and determine that she tossed the coin 2,000 or 3,000 times. With that many tosses, it becomes highly likely that she would witness a run of 10 heads. When she finally did, she reported it to you.

At issue in this example is what statisticians call *the file-drawer effect*. The file-drawer effect refers to events that end up in a "file drawer" unreported before an event of interest finally is reported. The file drawer acts as a trash can that relegates to oblivion results we would rather ignore and forget. Thus, in determining whether and to what extent an event is improbable, we need to factor in what ended up in the file drawer. Specifically, we need to factor in how many opportunities there were for the event in question to happen (such opportunities are called *probabilistic resources*—see appendix A.9). Only then does it become clear whether an event is truly improbable. To fail to factor in what's in the file drawer

have the same spectral signature between pages 110 and 111 in Jacobovici and Pellegrino, *Jesus Family Tomb*.

11 Jacobovici and Pellegrino, *Jesus Family Tomb*, 114.

is to commit *the file-drawer fallacy*. Thus, in the case of the Talpiot tomb, it is not enough merely to consider how improbable it was for the pattern of names observed there to occur by chance. That same pattern of names could also have occurred in other tombs. Feuerverger therefore introduced the correction factor $c_3 = 1,000$ as "the maximum number of tombs that might have once existed in Jerusalem, dating to the first century."[12] By multiplying the probability of 1 in 600,000 ($= q \times c_1 \times c_2$) by c_3, Feuerverger obtained a probability of 1 in 600 ($= q \times c_1 \times c_2 \times c_3$).

Here, then, is how *The Jesus Family Tomb* people arrived at their improbability of 1 in 600. Since $q = p_1 \times p_2 \times p_3 \times p_4$, the Jesus equation may therefore be rewritten as

$$\frac{1}{600} = p_1 \times p_2 \times p_3 \times p_4 \times c_1 \times c_2 \times c_3$$

where $p_1 = 103/2,509 \times 231/2,509$ (the Yeshua-bar-Yehosef probability), $p_2 = 2 \times 1/317$ (the Mariamne probability), $p_3 = 26/317$ (the Marya probability), $p_4 = 2 \times 9/2,509$ (the Yose probability), $c_1 = 30$ (correcting for equally surprising patterns of names), $c_2 = 4$ (correcting for absence of expected names), $c_3 = 1,000$ (correcting for the chance of seeing the same pattern of names in other tombs).

Can this equation statistically justify that the Talpiot tomb is the family tomb of the New Testament Jesus? There are too many problems with this equation for it to accomplish this task. We turn to these problems next.

PROBLEMS WITH THE JESUS EQUATION

INCORRECT CALCULATION OF BASIC PROBABILITIES

Let E denote the event of a Jewish person around the time of Jesus being named Joseph and F the event of a Jewish person around the time of Jesus being named Mary. Based on Tal Ilan's *Lexicon of Jewish Names in Late Antiquity*, *The Jesus Family Tomb* people assigned a probability of $231/2,509$ to E and a probability of $80/317$ to F. But this assignment is incorrect. These probabilities are conditional on the gender of the person named (out of the 2,509 men's names in the lexicon, 231 were some

12 Ibid.

variant of Joseph; out of the 317 women's names, 80 were some variant of Mary). Since E denotes the naming of a male and F the naming of a female, $\mathbf{P}(E) = \mathbf{P}(E \ \& \ \text{Person-Named-Is-Male}) = \mathbf{P}(E \mid \text{Person-Named-Is-Male}) \times \mathbf{P}(\text{Person-Named-Is-Male}) = 231/2,509 \times 1/2$ and $\mathbf{P}(F) = \mathbf{P}(F \ \& \ \text{Person-Named-Is-Female}) = \mathbf{P}(F \mid \text{Person-Named-Is-Female}) \times \mathbf{P}(\text{Person-Named-Is-Female}) = 80/317 \times 1/2$. (For the relevant math see appendices A.4 and A.5.)

Note that the probability of one-half here corresponds to the roughly equal proportion of males and females (i.e., $\mathbf{P}(\text{Person-Named-Is-Male}) = \mathbf{P}(\text{Person-Named-Is-Female} = 1/2)$. Note also that $\mathbf{P}(E \mid \text{Person-Named-Is-Male})$ and not $\mathbf{P}(E)$ is the probability that is properly assigned $231/2,509$ and likewise $\mathbf{P}(F \mid \text{Person-Named-Is-Female})$ and not $\mathbf{P}(F)$ is the probability that is properly assigned $80/317$. In consequence, to legitimately multiply the probabilities in the Jesus equation, each of them must first be multiplied by a factor of one-half (or else by the probability of the relevant gender if it differs from one-half). Otherwise, multiplying these probabilities is like combining apples and oranges. This additional factor of one-half for each of the probabilities in the Jesus equation seems, at first blush, to intensify the statistical challenge posed by *The Jesus Family Tomb* people, rendering it even more improbable that the Talpiot tomb could by chance be other than the tomb of Jesus. Other things being equal, that would be the case. But other things are not equal, as we show next.

FALLACY OF OVERSPECIFICATION

In the New Testament, written in Greek, Mary the mother of Jesus and Mary Magdalene are always referred to with the most common Greek forms of the name Mary: Μαρία and Μαριάμ (i.e., Maria and Mariam).[13] To find less common variants of the name in the Talpiot tomb and then use the probabilities of these less common variants to calculate the probability of the pattern of New Testament names in the tomb is to commit a fallacy of overspecification, narrowing the range of the target in question more than is warranted. To see what's at stake in this fallacy, imagine that you reside in Chicago, a city of approximately 3 million.

---

13 In fact, all the Marys in the New Testament are referred to with the most common Greek form of that name: in addition to Mary the mother of Jesus and Mary Magdalene, there is Mary the mother of James and Joses, Mary the wife of Cleophas, and Mary the sister of Lazarus and Martha.

As you're riding the subway one day, you overhear two people raving about a certain Susan Smith, who they claim is the best masseuse in Chicago. Your neck is killing you, and you think, *Wouldn't it be nice if I could meet this woman sometime and have her give my neck a massage.* A week later you're flying from Chicago to New York and seated next to you is a woman. Attached to her carry-on bag is an address label. As you glance at it, you notice that it reads "Suzanne Smythe, Chicago, Illinois."

Those two chaps on the subway never spelled the name, and for all you know there could be hundreds of Susan Smiths (with the usual spelling) in the Chicago area. But "Suzanne Smythe" is an unusual spelling. You think it's unlikely that there are any others in the Chicago area. Just to make sure, you ask this person about the spelling of her name and its pronunciation. She admits that it is an unusual spelling (she's the only one in the phone book) and notes that it is pronounced just the same as "Susan Smith." At this point, do you reason that because the spelling of this name is so improbable, the person seated next to you must be the masseuse described by the two subway riders on whom you were eavesdropping? Without further information, do you ask, "Hey, how about giving me a massage?" Of course not. And yet that is essentially what *The Jesus Family Tomb* people are doing when they use the improbability of variant spellings of Mary to claim that the Talpiot tomb is the family tomb of the New Testament Jesus.

To know whether the Suzanne Smythe you met on the plane is the masseuse described on the subway, you need additional relevant information. If you learn that she is a masseuse, that will be reason (though not conclusive reason) to think that she is the same person as described on the subway. If you learn that the names of her friends correspond to those described by the chaps on the subway, that will also be reason (though not conclusive reason) to think she is the same person. Now *The Jesus Family Tomb* people claim to have such additional information. In our analogy, overhearing the subway talkers describe Susan Smith is like reading the New Testament account of Mary Magdalene. Coming across an ossuary with the name Mariamne is like bumping into Suzanne Smythe on the airplane. But *The Jesus Family Tomb* people would add, the analogy now becomes imperfect because there's additional evidence that Mary Magdalene was referred to as Mariamne, and this strongly suggests that the Mariamne in the Talpiot tomb is indeed Mary Magdalene.

But what is this evidence? Principally it derives from a fourth-century apocryphal book known as the *Acts of Philip*, which refers to a Mariamne who is the sister of Philip. This book describes Mariamne and Philip's missionary journeys after Jesus ascends to heaven. The book gives no indication that this Mariamne is Mary Magdalene, much less that she was married to Jesus.[14] For a text suggesting that Jesus was married to Mary Magdalene, the closest one can find is the apocryphal *Gospel of Philip*, which depicts Mary Magdalene as Jesus' favorite disciple but gives no indication that they were married. Moreover, in that text, she is referred to as Mary, not as Mariamne.[15] In any case, François Bovon, the leading authority on the *Acts of Philip*, writes:

> As I was interviewed for the Discovery Channel's program *The Lost Tomb of Jesus,* I would like to express my opinion here. . . . Having watched the film, in listening to it, I hear two voices, a kind of *double discours.* On one hand there is the wish to open a scholarly discussion; on the other there is the wish to push a personal agenda. I must say that the reconstructions of Jesus' marriage with Mary Magdalene and the birth of a child belong for me to science fiction. . . . I do not believe that Mariamne is the real name of Mary of Magdalene. Mariamne is, besides Maria or Mariam, a possible Greek equivalent, attested by Josephus, Origen, and the *Acts of Philip*, for the Semitic Myriam.[16]

Return to our Susan Smith analogy: imagine you heard about a wonder-masseuse with a name that sounds like Susan Smith on the Chicago subway (which corresponds to reading about Mary Magadalene in the New Testament) and then sat next to Suzanne Smythe on an airplane, learning only the spelling of the name (which corresponds to finding the ossuary inscribed "Mariamne" in the Talpiot tomb). On reading a

14 For the *Acts of Philip*, go here: http://www.newadvent.org/fathers/0818.htm (last accessed 3 July 2007).
15 For the *Gospel of Philip*, go here: http://www.gnosis.org/naghamm/gop.html (last accessed 3 July 2007).
16 François Bovon, "The Tomb of Jesus," statement to the Society of Biblical Literature Forum.

vast literature in which a wonder-masseuse from Chicago is consistently referred to as "Susan Smith" (which corresponds to reading the vast literature of church fathers and New Testament apocrypha that consistently refers to Mary Magdalene as "Mary"), you find that a few passages in this vast literature refer to a "Suzanne Smythe," though it's not at all clear from these passages that this is the Chicago masseuse (which corresponds to the reference to Mariamne in the *Acts of Philip*). In that case there's no more reason to think that the Suzanne Smythe you met on the airplane is the wonder-masseuse from Chicago than to think that the bones of the Mariamne found in the Talpiot tomb are those of Mary Magdalene. Here, Suzanne Smythe is no more characteristic of the Chicago's wonder-masseuse than Susan Smith; likewise, Mariamne is no more characteristic of the New Testament woman from Magdala than Mary.

It follows that in assessing the probability that chance could produce the pattern of New Testament names found in the Talpiot tomb, the relevant probability for Mariamne is not the low probability of that particular name but the high probability of the generic form of Mary. Exactly the same reasoning applies to the other Mary in that tomb, referred to by *The Jesus Family Tomb* people as Marya and thought by them to be the mother of Jesus. The probability associated with her name needs likewise to be the high probability of the generic form of Mary.

That leaves the names Yeshua bar Yehosef and Yose. The probability that *The Jesus Family Tomb* people associate with Yeshua bar Yehosef seems right, save for the factor of one-half by which the name needs to be made conditional on this person being male (see the previous subsection). As for the probability they associate with Yose, it, as with the two Marys, is too small. A case can be made that *The Jesus Family Tomb* people were guilty of a fallacy of overspecification here as well since Yose is just a short form of Joseph, and even though a brother of Jesus is referred to as Yose in Mark 6:3, that same brother is referred to by the unshortened form of Joseph in Matthew 13:55. But since Yose is distinguished from another Joseph in the Talpiot tomb (namely, the father of Jesus), a case can also be made that the pattern of New Testament names in the Talpiot specifies Yose and not merely the generic Joseph. If we do that, we get a probability for Yose that is less than that for a generic Joseph. Even so, we don't get a probability as small as the one calculated by *The Jesus Family Tomb* people. The problem is that there were several written variants of Yose that sound alike (compare Cathy with Kathy and Kathie). In a largely oral culture in which spelling was often up for grabs (there were no dictionaries or spell-checkers), these alternate spellings must be factored into any specification of Yose. Richard Bauckham counts 34 such instances in Tal Ilan's lexicon, up from the nine used by *The Jesus Family Tomb* people.[17]

Given the considerations adduced in this and the last subsection, we submit that the basic probabilities associated with the New Testament names found in the Talpiot tomb need to be recalculated as follows (note the factors of one-half per subsection 5.1):

$$p_1 = 1/2 \times 103/2{,}509 \times 231/2{,}509 \approx .00189 \text{ (Yeshua bar Yehosef)}$$
$$p_2 = 1/2 \times 80/317 \approx .126 \text{ (Mariamne and Marya both treated as Mary)}$$
$$p_3 = 1/2 \times 34/2{,}509 \approx .00678 \text{ (Yose)}$$

UNJUSTIFIED CORRECTION FACTORS

Correction factor c_1 (= 30; see section 4) takes into account patterns of New Testament names as surprising as the one discovered at the Talpiot tomb that would likewise have implicated the family of the New Testament Jesus. Conversely, correction factor c_2 (= 4; see section 4) takes into account the absence of certain New Testament names from the Talpiot tomb that would have been expected to be there if this really were the family tomb of the New Testament Jesus. Both these factors, considered on general statistical grounds, seem relevant to assessing the probability that the Talpiot tomb could by chance have matched up to the degree that it did with names in Jesus' family. Note, however, that the principles of statistical rationality underlying these correction factors are different and would need to be mixed carefully. With the correction factor c_1, the mode of probabilistic reasoning is Fisherian (i.e., finding a suitable rejection region for testing the statistical significance of a hypothesis—see appendix A.8). With the correction factor c_2, the mode of probabilistic reasoning is Bayesian (i.e., updating one's probability in light of supporting or countervailing evidence—see appendix A.10). *The Jesus Family Tomb* people never make clear how these approaches can be mixed, nor do they offer any argument or justification for how the actual

17 See the chapter in the present volume by Richard Bauckham on "The Names on the Ossuaries."

numbers they assigned to these correction factors were calculated. Perhaps Andrey Feuerverger will produce such a justification in the paper he is preparing for peer review. But for now the actual numbers assigned to these correction factors appear taken out of a hat.

WRONG REFERENCE POPULATION

Unlike correction factors c_1 and c_2, *The Jesus Family Tomb* people do offer a justification for how they arrived at the number they assigned to the correction factor c_3. This number, set at 1,000, estimates "the maximum number of tombs that might have once existed in Jerusalem, dating to the first century."[18] This correction factor, as we pointed out in section 4, attempts to circumvent a file-drawer fallacy in which one calculates the probability that the pattern of New Testament names discovered in the Talpiot tomb could by chance have occurred *just there*. The problem with tying such a probability calculation to a single tomb is that it fails to take into account the opportunities for this same pattern of names to occur in other tombs from that time and in that locale. Any of these other tombs might also have been a "Jesus family tomb." Given enough tombs, it becomes extremely likely that not just one but numerous tombs would display this pattern of New Testament names. By disregarding these other tombs and thus placing them, as it were, in a file drawer, one fails to assess the true probability of witnessing this pattern of names by chance. Accordingly, the probability we assign to the Talpiot tomb belonging to the New Testament Jesus must factor in these additional tombs.

We have just summarized Andrey Feuerverger's justification for setting c_3 equal to 1,000. In thereby attempting to circumvent a file-drawer fallacy, he rightly underscored an important statistical principle, namely, the need to factor in the opportunities for an event to occur (known formally as its *probabilistic resources*—see appendix A.8) in assessing whether the event may rightly be regarded as improbable. Unfortunately, though aware of the principle's importance, Feuerverger also misapplied it, focusing too narrowly on the actual number of tombs near Jerusalem. There are two problems with this: (1) In determining whether some family or other around Jerusalem might by chance exhibit some pattern of names, what's crucial is how many such families there were and not how many of them could additionally have afforded a tomb with ossuaries.

18 Jacobovici and Pellegrino, *Jesus Family Tomb*, 114.

The correction factor c_3 therefore should not have been set to the maximum number of actual tombs in the Jerusalem area around the time of Jesus but to the total number of relevant families in the area—regardless of whether they had the financial resources to own a tomb. Most families in the time of Jesus were too poor to afford such tombs. In particular, because Joseph, Jesus' legal father, was a carpenter and because carpentry was not a lucrative profession, Jesus' family seems not to have been an ideal candidate for having a family tomb. Accordingly, what's crucial in assessing the probability that the Talpiot tomb was the family tomb of Jesus is not the actual number of family tombs but the actual number of families living at that time and in that area. (2) The second problem is that Feuerverger focuses unduly on Jerusalem and its immediate surroundings. Yes, the Talpiot tomb is just a few miles from Jerusalem and, yes, Jesus' brother James was active in Jerusalem. If we knew nothing else, we might therefore think it likely that James should be buried in the immediate vicinity of Jerusalem (though the evidence is against his having an ossuary in the Talpiot tomb). But we know a lot more. We know that Jesus and His family throughout His life was based 65 miles north of Jerusalem in the town of Nazareth. In fact He is often called "Jesus of Nazareth." Moreover, Magdala, the town from which Mary Magdalene hails, is 15 miles still further north. Thus the number of families in the immediate vicinity of Jerusalem in the period of ossuary use underestimates the number of relevant families to deciding whether the Talpiot tomb is, on probabilistic grounds, the tomb of Jesus.[19] In calculating this number of families, we need to consider a radius of at least 80 miles around Jerusalem. In other words, we need to consider all Jewish families living in ancient Palestine during the time that ossuaries were popular.

How many such families lived in Palestine during that time? To answer this question, let's start with a simpler question: How many Jewish people as such lived in Palestine during the period of ossuary use? A conservative lower-bound estimate is 500,000 on the number of Jewish people living in Palestine at any one point in time during that period.[20] Moreover, the

19 As a gauge on the number of families near Jerusalem during that time, *The Jesus Family Tomb* people estimate that "only 80,000 males lived in Jerusalem during the time period of ossuary use." Ibid., 77.

20 "Knowledge of the number of clergy is not without importance in estimating the size of the Palestinian population at the time of Jesus. . . . The priests and Levites, with women and children, would number about 50,000 to 60,000. The priests and Levites returning

period of ossuary use spans 100 years.[21] Given that the average lifespan during that period was well under 50 years, a conservative lower-bound estimate on the number of Jewish people living in Palestine during that entire period is twice 500,000, or 1,000,000. Given an average of 10 people per family, as in the Talpiot tomb, that would leave 100,000 families as the right reference population for any probability calculations used to infer that the Talpiot tomb is the final resting place of Jesus.

THE NEW AND IMPROVED JESUS EQUATION

In the previous section we analyzed the problems with Andrey Feuerverger's Jesus equation. This analysis now suggests a new and improved Jesus equation. Given an arbitrary family of size n and given k distinct names, if in the wider population the first name has probability p_1, the second p_2, and so on through k, then the probability p that this family will by chance have at least m_1 family members with the first name, at least m_2 with the second, and so on through k, where each m_i ($1 \; i \leq k$) is at least 1, is governed by the multinomial distribution and has the following value:[22]

$$
p = \sum_{\substack{n_1+n_2+\cdots+n_k+n_{k+1}=n \\ n_1 \geq m_1, \ldots, \, n_k \geq m_k, \, n_{k+1} \geq 0}} \frac{n!}{n_1! n_2! \cdots n_k! n_{k+1}!} \; p_1^{n_1} p_2^{n_2} \cdots p_k^{n_k} \cdots p_{k+1}^{n_{k+1}}
$$

from exile with Joshua and Zerrubbabel made up about one-tenth of the entire community (Ezra 2.36–42, cp. 2.64; Neh. 7.39–45, 66), a generally credible proportion. Thus, Palestine in the time of Jesus had a Jewish population of 10 x 50,000 (or 60,000), about 500,000 or 600,000. In my opinion, this is a more likely number than the million often assumed." Quoted from Joachim Jeremias, *Jerusalem in the Time of Jesus: An Investigation into Economic and Social Conditions during the New Testament Period* (Philadelphia: Fortress, 1969), 205. A more recent estimate likewise sets the number at 500,000: "By the first century the Jewish population of Palestine had grown massively, perhaps to as much as 500,000. . . . The size of the population of ancient Palestine cannot be determined, but 500,000 is a plausible figure for the population of the Palestinian interior." Quoted from Seth Schwartz, *Imperialism and Jewish Society, 200 B.C.E. to 640 C.E.* (Princeton: Princeton University Press, 2001), 11, 41.

21 "For about a hundred years, from 30 BCE to 70 CE, people in the Jerusalem area practiced a specific form of 'secondary burial' involving small limestone ossuaries." Quoted from *The Jesus Family Tomb* Web site: http://www.jesusfamilytomb.com/essential_facts/ossuaries.html (last accessed 6 July 2007).

22 See William Feller, *An Introduction to Probability Theory and Its Applications*, vol. 1, 3rd ed. (New York: Wiley, 1968), 167–69.

This, then, is the new and improved Jesus equation. Even though it looks complicated, summing over these multinomial terms on the right to evaluate p is standard fare in introductory probability and statistics courses. The calculation is tedious but conceptually straightforward. Note that p_{k+1} is the probability that none of the k names in question are selected at random; hence $p_{k+1} = 1 - (p_1 + p_2 + \cdots + p_k)$. Note also that all the probabilities p_i ($1 \le i \le k+1$) are strictly positive (i.e., none of them is a zero probability). Note lastly that factorials in this equation (e.g., $n! = 1 \times 2 \times \cdots \times n$) take into account combinatorial possibilities that were mistakenly ignored the original Jesus equation. These combinatorial terms make the probability that the Talpiot tomb by chance acquired its pattern of New Testament names much larger than the 1 in 600 value computed by *The Jesus Family Tomb* people.

Two additional numbers, derived from p, are going to be crucial in assessing whether probabilities support the hypothesis that the Talpiot tomb is the final resting place of Jesus. To calculate these numbers, we first need an estimate for the number of Jewish people living in ancient Palestine while ossuaries were in use. Let us call this number N. As we saw in subsection 5.4, a conservative estimate for this number is 1 million. By contrast, *The Jesus Family Tomb* people were in fact willing to countenance 5 million as an estimate for N.[23] In the sequel we therefore take N to be 1 million. With N in hand, the fraction N/n estimates the number of families of size n during that time. Granted, this estimate is somewhat rough in that it treats families as having the same size and as constituting nonoverlapping units, which strictly speaking they do not. But, this assumption seems unproblematic since variability of family size and overlap among families will tend to push up the number of families and therefore the opportunities for families to exhibit the pattern of New Testament names found in the Talpiot tomb. In any case, given N and N/n, we now define the following two numbers:

---

23 Andrey Feuerverger assumes that there were "five million Jews who lived during that era." See Christopher Mims, "Should You Accept the 600–to-One Odds That the Talpiot Tomb Belonged to Jesus?" *Scientific American* 296 (March 2007): available online at http://sciam.com/article.cfm?articleID =14A3C2E6–E7F2–99DF–37A9AEC98FB0702A (last accessed 27 June 2007).

$$p^* = 1 - (1 - p)^{N/n}$$
$$M = (N/n) \times p$$

p^* is the probability that at least one out of N/n families exhibits the pattern of names in question if the probability that a single family exhibits that pattern of names is p. The underlying assumption here is that naming across different families is probabilistically independent (i.e., how one family names its children does not affect the probabilities of how other families name their children). Accordingly, the probability that no family of size n has this pattern of names is $(1 - p)^{N/n}$ (here $1 - p$ is the probability that a particular family of size n does not have that pattern of names, which then, by the independence assumption, gets multiplied by itself N/n times). It follows in turn that the complementary event (i.e., that at least one family of size n has this pattern of names) is therefore $1 - (1 - p)^{N/n}$.[24] Note that the independence assumption seems approximately true, especially since most families have contact with only a few other families and thus cannot name their children by consciously copying how most other families, with whom they are not in contact, name their children. Note that p^* corresponds to the p-value calculated by *The Jesus Family Tomb* people's Jesus equation, gauging the likelihood that the Talpiot tomb is the last resting place of the New Testament Jesus.

As for M, it gives the expected number of Jesus families (i.e., families with the pattern of New Testament names observed in the Talpiot tomb) living in Palestine during the period of ossuary use. To see that $M = (N/n) \times p$ does indeed give the expected number of Jesus families, treat each Jewish family living in Palestine during that period as a Bernoulli trial (i.e., as a binary, success-failure trial) with probability p of successfully obtaining the pattern of names observed in the Talpiot tomb. Then the number of families exhibiting this pattern follows a binomial distribution with probability p of success on any individual trial and with total number of trials N/n.[25] *The Jesus Family Tomb* people suggest that any reasonable way of calculating the expected number of Jesus families will never yield a number greater than one. But they are mistaken, as we see next by calculating p, p^*, and M for four instructive cases:

---

24 See Feller, *Introduction to Probability*, 148.
25 These results about binomial distributions may be found in any introductory probability or statistics text. See, for instance, Feller, *Introduction to Probability*, 147–50, 223.

Case 1

$n = 10$; $N = 1,000,000$; m1 = m2 = m3 = m4 = 1
p1 = 1/2 x 103/2,509 x 231/2,509 (Yeshua bar Yehosef)
p2 = 1/2 x 2 x 1/317 (Mariamne)
p3 = 1/2 x 26/317 (Marya)
p4 = 1/2 x 2 x 9/2,509 (Yose)

$p = 1.9154 \times 10^{-6}$; $p^* = .1743$; $M = .1915$

Case 2

$n = 20$; $N = 1,000,000$; $m_1 = m_2 = m_3 = m_4 = 1$
$p_1 = 1/2$ x $103/2,509$ x $231/2,509$ (Yeshua bar Yehosef)
$p_2 = 1/2$ x 2 x $1/317$ (Mariamne)
$p_3 = 1/2$ x $26/317$ (Marya)
$p_4 = 1/2$ x 2 x $9/2,509$ (Yose)

$p = 3.5229 \times 10^{-5}$; $p^* = .8282$; $M = 1.7615$

Case 3

$n = 10$; $N = 1,000,000$; $m_1 = m_3 = 1$; $m_2 = 2$
$p_1 = 1/2$ x $103/2,509$ x $231/2,509 \approx .00189$ (Yeshua bar Yehosef)
$p_2 = 1/2$ x $80/317 \approx .126$ (Mariamne and Marya both treated as Mary)
$p_3 = 1/2$ x $34/2,509 \approx .00678$ (Yose)

$p = 2.9960 \times 10^{-4}$; $p^* = 1 - 9.6959 \times 10^{-14} \approx 1$; $M = 30$

Case 4

$n = 20$; $N = 1,000,000$; $m_1 = m_3 = 1$; $m_2 = 2$
$p_1 = 1/2$ x $103/2,509$ x $231/2,509 \approx .00189$ (Yeshua bar Yehosef)
$p_2 = 1/2$ x $80/317 \approx .126$ (Mariamne and Marya both treated as Mary)
$p_3 = 1/2$ x $34/2,509 \approx .00678$ (Yose)

$p = 3.0838 \times 10^{-3}$; $p^* = 1 - 8.5639 \times 10^{-68} \approx 1$; $M = 154$

In cases 1 and 3, we equate family size n with 10. This seems a low-end estimate of family size. From the New Testament we know that Jesus had Joseph and Mary as legal parents, four brothers, and at least two sisters (see Mark 6). That makes at least nine family members right there in but two generations, excluding spouses. In the Talpiot tomb, which may span three or more generations, we find 10 ossuaries, and some of them may contain the bones of more than one person. Indeed, given the size of families back then and the naturalness of including three generations (grandparents, parents, and children) in a family unit, equating family size n with 20 seems more in keeping with the average size of families back then. Hence, the value of n in cases 2 and 4.

N, the number of Jews living in Palestine during the period of ossuary use, is set conservatively at 1 million and is constant in all four cases. As we noted in subsection 5.4, this reference class for the tomb probabilities is more appropriate than estimates for the population size of Jerusalem since Jesus and His family were based 65 miles north of Jerusalem in Nazareth and around the Sea of Galilee. In cases 1 and 2, we go with the probability of individual names as assigned by *The Jesus Family Tomb* people (see the probabilities section 4, though these have to be multiplied additionally by a factor of one-half to take into account gender differences—see subsection 5.1). This takes the probabilities of Mariamne, Marya, and Yose way down. In cases 3 and 4, by contrast, we go with the more realistic estimates of probabilities for these names as given and justified in subsection 5.2 (this collapses Mariamne and Marya into a generic Mary).

In cases and 1 and 2, p^* is the number of interest and corresponds to the probability of at least one Jewish family in Palestine while ossuaries were in use having the pattern of New Testament names observed in the Talpiot tomb. As such, it corresponds to the p-value calculated by Andrey Feuerverger and used to assess the probability that this could be Jesus' family tomb. But even though we use the same probabilities for individual Jewish names as used by *The Jesus Family Tomb* people, we don't get anywhere near as "impressive" results as they did. In place of 1 in 600 for this pattern of names occurring by chance as in the original Jesus equation, with the new and improved Jesus equation, we find that for family size $n = 10$ the probability rises to better than 1 in 6 (.1743) and for $n = 20$ the probability rises even more dramatically to better than

4 in 5 (.8282).[26] No statistical theory regards these numbers as remarkable or even statistically significant.

In cases 3 and 4, *M* is the number of interest and corresponds to the number of Jewish families of a given size *n* we could expect to see exhibit the pattern of New Testament names found in the Talpiot tomb. Given realistic naming probabilities, we find that for small families of size 10 we would expect to see 30 of them exhibit the Talpiot pattern of New Testament names and for medium families of size 20 we would expect to see 154 of them exhibit this pattern of names. Even in case 2, taking family size at 20, we are more likely to see two rather than one family with the more restrictive name set and lowered probabilities promoted by *The Jesus Family Tomb* people.

Bottom line: when the math is done correctly, probabilities that might be cited in evidence for the Talpiot tomb being the final resting place of the New Testament Jesus are not impressive and would not even achieve a minimal level of significance as gauged by conventional statistical theory.

ELIMINATING REASONABLE DOUBT

To an outsider coming to this debate over probabilities connected with the pattern of New Testament names found in the Talpiot tomb, it may seem that *The Jesus Family Tomb* people still have a point. Granted, the probabilities are not nearly as bad as they make out (see the previous section). But by going with their numbers, it would seem that at most one or two Jewish families around the time of Jesus might have exhibited this pattern of names. And by going with our numbers, it would seem that at least 30 Jewish families around the time of Jesus would have

26 That these probabilities should be, relatively speaking, so large may seem startling to the uninitiated, but come about because of the way combinatorial factors can increase seemingly small probabilities. If, for instance, you walk into a room with 252 other people, you have an even chance of finding someone with the same birthday as yours. If, on the other hand, you walk into a room with 22 other people, you have an even chance of finding some pair of people in the room that share a birthday. This is known as the birthday paradox, and the much larger probability of some pair of people in a group sharing a birthday rather than somebody in the group matching a fixed birthday results from the former probability factoring in all the combinatorial ways of matching different people. In a room with 23 people (cp. the group of 22 other people plus yourself), there are 253 (cp. the group of 252 other people plus yourself) ways to match up people. For the birthday paradox, see Feller, *Introduction to Probability*, 33.

exhibited this pattern of names. An outsider with no stake in this debate might therefore conclude that a handful (say five or so) of Jewish families around the time of Jesus are likely to have exhibited this pattern of names. But in that case it would seem that the Talpiot tomb might still have a good shot at being the family tomb of the New Testament Jesus. To be sure, the probabilities would suggest that this is not Jesus' tomb. But, at the same time, they would leave a reasonable doubt that it is.

We want in this section to close off this loophole. To do so, we employ a consequence of Bayes's theorem (see appendices A.9 and A.10). Bayes's theorem may be thought of as a way to update probabilities in light of additional information or evidence. The probabilities we assign are always subject to change in light of additional information or evidence. To illustrate this fact about probabilities, take the case of someone we'll call George. For the last five years George has religiously worked out at the health club Mondays, Wednesdays, and Fridays at 7:00 p.m. He hasn't missed a workout for five years. Today is Monday. What is the probability that George will work out today at 7:00 p.m.? Given the information just presented, you would rightly assign a high probability to this event. But suppose next you learn that George has just been in a terrible car accident and is on life support. What is the probability that George will be working out tonight? Given this additional information, the probability goes way down. But suppose next you learn that George's buddies can't stand to see their friend miss a workout and so are planning to sneak into the hospital and remove George, taking him to the health club and putting him on the workout machines, forcing his shattered body to go through exercise motions. Now the probability goes up. By adding still further information, the probability can continue to go down and up.

To see how this updating of probability works in the case of the Talpiot tomb, let J denote the hypothesis that this tomb is the final resting place of the New Testament Jesus and let $\sim J$ denote the negation of this hypothesis (see appendix A.4). Then, if the expected number of Jesus families, denoted by M, is at least two, one can rationalize assigning a probability of $1/M$ to J and $(M-1)/M$ to $\sim J$, in other words, $P(J) = 1/M$ and $P(\sim J) = (M-1)/M$. Moreover, if M is not even 1, one can rationalize assigning a probability of p^* to $\sim J$ and $1 - p^*$ to J, in other words, $P(J) = 1 - p^*$ and $P(\sim J) = p^*$. Given that p^* corresponds to the p-value calculated by *The Jesus Family Tomb* people, this is in fact how said people interpret **P(J)** and **P(~J)**.[27]

Suppose now we go with the worst-case probabilistic scenario from the vantage of those who think, as we do, that ~**J** rather than **J** is true—in other words, we go with case 1 in section 6. Here **P(~J)** = .1743, or approximately one in six, thus making **P(J)** approximately five in six. If you were a betting man, it would seem that you should therefore bet that the Talpiot tomb is in fact the final resting place of Jesus even if it doesn't make the grade that statisticians would regard as significant. And even if these numbers were reversed (i.e., **P(J)** equals one in six and **P(~J)** equals five in six), one would still, if one had no other information, be in one's rights to suspect that the Talpiot tomb might indeed be the final resting place of Jesus. But there is other information, and its inclusion radically revises the probabilities **P(J)** and **P(~J)**, even in the worst-case scenario where **P(~J)** = .1743.

The point is that we know a lot about Jesus that undercuts the probability of His being buried in the Talpiot tomb. Consider the following items of information:

- The New Testament evidence that Jesus and His family were of modest means and therefore would be unlikely to be able to afford a tomb.

- The fact that Jesus and His family hailed from Nazareth, which was 65 miles north of Jerusalem, and that His supposed wife, as conjectured by the "Jesus Family Tomb" people (i.e., Mary Magdalene), was from the town of Magdala even further north of Jerusalem.

- The uniform witness of the best attested historical sources that Jesus was unmarried, to say nothing of His not being married to Mary Magdalene.

- The widespread perception shortly after Jesus' crucifixion that He had been resurrected (Paul, writing in Galatians, which both liberal and conservative scholars date around AD 50, demonstrates a clearly developed understanding of Jesus' resurrection). Regardless of whether Jesus actually did resurrect, the

27 "After listening to filmmaker Simcha Jacobovici explain the so-called 'Jesus equation,' you'll realize just how *unlikely* it is that this *isn't*, in fact, his tomb." In our terminology, P(J) is large and P(~J) is small. Quoted from http://www.jesusfamilytomb.com/evidence/probability.html (last accessed 15 June 2007).

perception early on among His followers that He did and the interest of His followers in denying that there was any tomb that housed His bones would have tended to preclude any tomb that purported to hold His remains.

Let us now denote the conjunction of these items of information by E. In consequence of Bayes's theorem, we can now update the probabilities $P(J)$ and $P(\sim J)$ as follows. Because we have this additional information E in hand, we would like to form $P(J \mid E)$ and $P(\sim J \mid E)$, but to do so, we must go through Bayes's theorem. As long as $P(J)$ and $P(\sim J)$ fail to take into account E, $P(J)$ is about five times as large as $P(\sim J)$. To compare these two quantities, Bayesian probabilists often form their ratio: $P(\sim J)/P(J)$. Because this fraction is about 1/5, the preponderance of probability here favors J. Yet by Bayes's theorem, this ratio, when updated by E to form $P(\sim J \mid E)/P(J \mid E)$, results from multiplying $P(\sim J)/P(J)$ by the factor $P(E \mid \sim J)/P(E \mid J)$ (see appendix A.10). In other words,

$$\frac{P(\sim J \mid E)}{P(J \mid E)} = \frac{P(E \mid \sim J)}{P(E \mid J)} \times \frac{P(\sim J)}{P(J)}$$

Even though $P(\sim J)/P(J)$ is about 1/5, there's every reason to think that $P(E \mid \sim J)/P(E \mid J)$ is huge and will swamp the previous factor, thereby rendering $P(\sim J \mid E)/P(J \mid E)$ huge. To see this consider that the items of information in E are well attested and, on the hypothesis that the Talpiot tomb is not the final resting place of Jesus, have probability close to 1. This is because the probability of E is unaffected if the Talpiot tomb is just another tomb unrelated to Jesus' family. On the other hand, if the Talpiot tomb is indeed the final resting place of Jesus, E becomes highly unlikely, taking $P(E \mid J)$ close to zero. Indeed, E is deeply inconsistent with J. Accordingly, the ratio $P(E \mid \sim J)/P(E \mid J)$ skyrockets, and the same happens to $P(\sim J \mid E)/P(J \mid E)$, urging that $\sim J$ is far better attested than J. Thus, even though J, simply in light of the pattern of New Testament names found in the Talpiot tomb, may be the preferred hypothesis, once E is factored in, $\sim J$ becomes strongly preferred. Note that we've taken the worst-case scenario. More realistic numbers suggest that $\sim J$ is to be preferred over J simply in light of the Talpiot, leaving aside independent evidence (i.e., E) against this being the tomb of the New Testament Jesus, which then, as in the worst-case scenario, eliminates reasonable doubt about this still possibly being Jesus' final resting place.

If the preceding discussion seems hand-waving, welcome to the world of Bayesian probability. Often Bayesian arguments are more qualitative than strictly quantitative, suggesting ways that probabilities may radically change in light of novel information and evidence rather than providing precise calculations with well-defined numbers. It will therefore help to have an instance in mind where the calculations are precise and the numbers well-defined. Suppose you are confronted with a white ball that you've just chosen at random from one of two urns. The urn on the left contains a million black balls and one white ball whereas the urn on the right contains a million white balls and one black ball. In determining from which urn you drew your ball, someone besides yourself rolled a die and gave you the left urn if it came up one through five and the right urn if it came up six. As with **J** and **~J** in the worst case scenario (case 1 of section 6), it is more likely, with odds of five to one, that the die roll came up between one and five rather than that it came up six. Without additional information you would therefore think that the die roll came up other than six. But because a white ball was selected, and white balls are so much more likely to be chosen at random from the right urn than from the left urn, in fact it is far more likely that the die roll came up six than that it came up between one and five.

This line of reasoning can be made precise. Indeed, the probabilities in this example can be calculated exactly. Let L and R denote respectively whether the left urn or the right urn was sampled (which depends respectively on whether a die roll came up between one and five or came up six). Let B and W denote respectively whether in the process of sampling a black or white ball was selected. Then

$$\mathbf{P}(L) = 5/6$$
$$\mathbf{P}(R) = 1/6$$
$$\mathbf{P}(L \mid W) = 1/200{,}001$$
$$\mathbf{P}(R \mid W) = 200{,}000/200{,}001$$

The last two probabilities here follow from Bayes's theorem (see appendix A.9). Thus, even though L (like **J**) is improbable in the absence of additional information, R (like **~J**) becomes overwhelmingly probable given that additional information. That additional information removes all reasonable doubt that the Talpiot tomb might, after all, be the family tomb of the New Testament Jesus. The statistical evidence rules decisively against this hypothesis.

CONCLUSION

The mathematics needed to determine the probability that the Talpiot tomb could by chance have exhibited the pattern of New Testament names found inscribed on its ossuaries was entirely elementary, something a bright undergraduate with a semester of probability theory could in principle have figured out. Yet Andrey Feuerverger, acting as the statistical expert for *The Jesus Family Tomb* people, failed to figure it out. His math was not only wrong but also inadequately developed, leaving crucial elements unjustified (e.g., his first two correction factors). In consequence, the use that *The Jesus Family Tomb* people made of his work was irresponsible. They confidently proclaimed that the Talpiot tomb was the final resting place of the New Testament Jesus when a correct, detailed, properly vetted treatment of the underlying mathematics remained to be done. We believe we have provided such a treatment in this paper. Despite bending over backwards to concede to *The Jesus Family Tomb* people all the small probabilities they ever wanted, our numbers still indicate that nothing statistically significant is going on inside the Talpiot tomb and that, in fact, the relevant statistics strongly suggest that this is *not* Jesus' final resting place. But don't take our word for it. Run the numbers yourself by visiting our Web site at www.jesustombmath.org.

APPENDIX A: A PRIMER ON PROBABILITY

1. DISTINCTION BETWEEN OUTCOMES AND EVENTS

Probabilities are numbers between zero and one that are assigned to *events* (and by extension to objects, patterns, information, and even hypotheses). Events always occur with respect to a reference class of possibilities. Consider a die with faces one through six. The reference class of possibilities in this case can be represented by the set $\{1, 2, 3, 4, 5, 6\}$. Any subset of this reference class then represents an event. For instance, the event E_{odd}, namely, "an odd number was tossed," corresponds to $\{1, 3, 5\}$. Such an event is said to occur if any one of its outcomes occurs—in other words, if either a one is tossed or a three or a five. An *outcome* is any particular thing that could happen. Outcomes can therefore be represented as singleton sets, which are sets with only one element. Thus, the outcomes associated with $E_{odd} = \{1, 3, 5\}$ are $E_1 = \{1\}$, $E_3 = \{3\}$, and $E_5 = \{5\}$. Outcomes are sometimes also called *elementary events*. Events include not only outcomes but also *composite events* such as E_{odd}, which includes more than one outcome.

2. THE AXIOMS OF PROBABILITY

Probabilities obey the following axioms: (1) The impossible event (i.e., an event that entails a physical or logical impossibility) is represented by the empty set and has probability zero. (2) The necessary event (i.e., an event that is guaranteed to happen) is represented by the entire reference class of possibilities and has probability one (e.g., with the die example, $E_{nec} = \{1, 2, 3, 4, 5, 6\}$ has probability one). Events that are mutually exclusive have probabilities that sum together. Thus, in the previous example, $\mathbf{P}(E_{odd}) = \mathbf{P}(E_1) + \mathbf{P}(E_3) + \mathbf{P}(E_5)$ (i.e., $\mathbf{P}(\{1, 3, 5\}) = \mathbf{P}(\{1\}) + \mathbf{P}(\{3\}) + \mathbf{P}(\{5\})$). Important: mutually exclusive and exhaustive events always sum to one.

3. INTERPRETATION OF PROBABILITY

Probabilities are interpreted in three principal ways: (1) Frequentist approach—probability is a relative frequency (i.e., the number of occurrences of an event divided by the number of observed opportunities for the event to occur; relative frequencies are also called empirical probabilities). (2) Theoretical approach—probability derives from properties of the system generating the events (e.g., dies are rigid, homogeneous cubes whose symmetry confers probability 1/6 on each face; quantum mechanical systems have probabilities derived from eigenvalues associated with the eigenstates of an observable). (3) Degree of belief—probability measures strength of belief that an event will occur. *The Jesus Family Tomb* people focus mainly on the first of these interpretations.

4. CONJUNCTION, DISJUNCTION, AND NEGATION

Events can form new events via conjunction, disjunction, and negation. $E \,\&\, F$ is the conjunction (or intersection, also written $E \cap F$) of E and F and denotes the event such that both E and F occur. $E \lor F$ is the disjunction (or union, also written $E \cup F$) of E and F and denotes the event such that either E or F or both occur. $\sim\!E$ is the negation (or

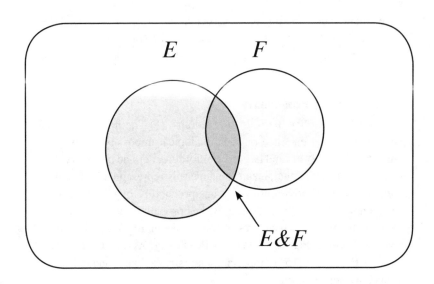

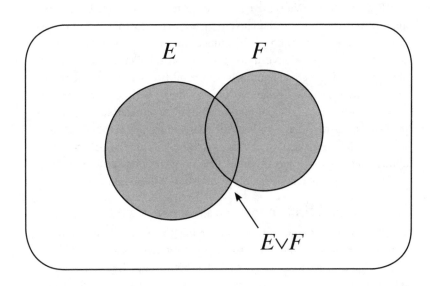

144

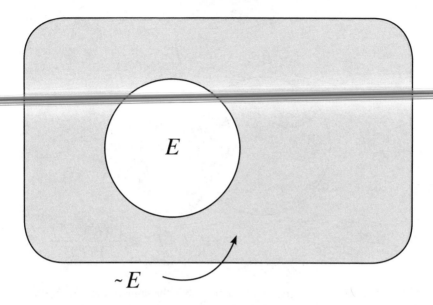

$\sim E$

complement, also written E^c) of E and denotes the event that excludes E's occurrence.

5. CONDITIONAL PROBABILITY

Suppose event F is known to have occurred, and we then ask what is the probability of E. In that case the reference class of possibilities contracts to F, and the probability of E is no longer simply $\mathbf{P}(E)$ (i.e., the probability of E within the original reference class) but the probability of that portion of E that resides within the new reference class F. This probability is called the conditional probability of E given F and is written $\mathbf{P}(E|F)$. This probability is defined as

$$\mathbf{P}(E \mid F) = \frac{\mathbf{P}(E \& F)}{\mathbf{P}(F)}$$

Graphically, this probability can be represented as follows:

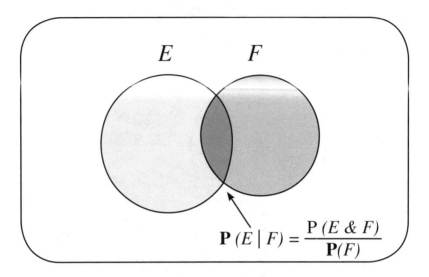

$$\mathbf{P}(E \mid F) = \frac{P(E \,\&\, F)}{\mathbf{P}(F)}$$

In assessing whether the Talpiot tomb is the tomb of the New Testament Jesus, it is critical to determine how many Jewish families in ancient Palestine might have had the pattern of names associated with Jesus' family as found in that tomb. Those families constitute the reference class (i.e., F) in light of which the discovery of the pattern of names in the Talpiot tomb (i.e., E) needs to be assessed. That assessment is carried out in section 6 and indicates that considerably more than one such family exhibited that pattern of names.

6. PROBABILISTIC INDEPENDENCE

As we have seen, for mutually exclusive events probabilities add. Specifically, the probability of a disjunction of mutually exclusive events is the sum of the probabilities of the disjuncts. Thus, if E_1, $E_2, \ldots, E_n$ are mutually exclusive, $\mathbf{P}(E_1 \vee E_2 \vee \cdots \vee E_n) = \mathbf{P}(E_1) + \mathbf{P}(E_2) + \cdots + \mathbf{P}(E_n)$. Does a corresponding relationship hold for conjunction? For $E_1, E_2, \ldots, E_n$ arbitrary events such that no conjunction of them has zero probability, it follows from the definition of conditional probability that

$$\mathbf{P}(E_1 \,\&\, E_2 \,\&\, \cdots \,\&\, E_n) = \mathbf{P}(E_1) \times \mathbf{P}(E_2 \mid E_1) \times \mathbf{P}(E_3 \mid E_1 \,\&\, E_2) \times \cdots \\ \times \mathbf{P}(E_n \mid E_1 \,\&\, E_2 \,\&\, \cdots \,\&\, E_{n-1})$$

To see this in the case of E_1 and E_2, note that

$$\mathbf{P}(E_1 \,\&\, E_2) = 1 \times \mathbf{P}\,(E_1 \,\&\, E_2)$$
$$= [\mathbf{P}(E_1)/\,\mathbf{P}(E_1)] \times \mathbf{P}(E_1 \,\&\, E_2)$$
$$= \mathbf{P}(E_1) \times [\mathbf{P}\,(E_1 \,\&\, E_2)\,/\,\mathbf{P}(E_1)]$$
$$= \mathbf{P}(E_1) \times \mathbf{P}(E_2|\, E_1)$$

If, now, $\mathbf{P}(E_2|\, E_1) = \mathbf{P}(E_2)$, it follows that

$$\mathbf{P}(E_1 \,\&\, E_2) = \mathbf{P}(E_1) \times \mathbf{P}(E_2)$$

In that case we say that E_1 and E_2 are probabilistically (or stochastically) independent. In general, we say that events $E_1, E_2, \ldots, E_n$ are independent if for all distinct events taken from this class, i.e., E_{i_1}, $E_{i_2}, \ldots, E_{i_k}$, $1 \le k \le n$,

$$\mathbf{P}(E_{i_1} \,\&\, E_{i_2} \,\&\, \cdots \,\&\, E_{i_k}) = \mathbf{P}(E_{i_1}) \times \mathbf{P}(E_{i_2}) \times \cdots \times \mathbf{P}(E_{i_k}).$$

Events are probabilistically independent if they derive from causally independent processes. The converse, however, is not true—events can be probabilistically independent without being causally independent.

7. Equiprobability and Uniform Probability

In many situations individual outcomes (elementary events) each have the same probability. In that case, if there are N possible outcomes, each outcome has probability $1/N$. Equiprobability in this sense is a special case of uniform probability in which isomorphic events under some equivalence relation have identical probability (see my 1990 article on uniform probability at http://www.designinference.com/documents/2004.12.Uniform_Probability.pdf).

8. The Fisherian Approach to Statistical Inferences

In Ronald Fisher's approach to hypothesis testing, one is justified in rejecting a chance hypothesis (e.g., the hypothesis that the New Testament names found in the Talpiot tomb are likely to have occurred by chance) provided that a sample falls within a prespecified *rejection region* (also known as a *critical region*).[28] For example, suppose one's chance hypothesis is that a coin is fair. To test whether the coin is biased in favor of heads, and thus not fair, one can set a rejection region of 10 heads in a row and then flip the coin 10 times. In Fisher's approach, if the coin lands 10 heads in a row, then one is justified in rejecting the chance hypothesis.

Fisher's approach to hypothesis testing is the one most widely used in the applied statistics literature and the first one taught in introductory statistics courses. It was also the one used by *The Jesus Family Tomb* people. Nevertheless, in its original formulation, Fisher's approach is problematic: for a rejection region to warrant rejecting a chance hypothesis, the rejection region must have a small enough probability. *The Jesus Family Tomb* people, for instance, thought 1 in 600 was small enough. But why?

Given a chance hypothesis and a rejection region, how small does the probability of the rejection region have to be so that if a sample falls within it, then the chance hypothesis can legitimately be rejected? Fisher never answered this question. The problem here is to justify what is called a *significance level* such that whenever the sample falls within the rejection region and the probability of the rejection region given the chance hypothesis is less than the significance level, then the chance hypothesis can be legitimately rejected.

More formally, the problem is to justify a significance level α (always a positive real number less than one) such that whenever the sample (an event we will call E) falls within the rejection region (call it T) and the probability of the rejection region given the chance hypothesis (call it H) is less than α (i.e., $P(T|H) < \alpha$), then the chance hypothesis H can be rejected as the explanation of the sample. In the applied statistics literature, it is common to see significance levels of .05 and .01. The problem to date has been that any such proposed significance levels have seemed arbitrary, lacking "a rational foundation."[29]

---

28 For a brief summary of Fisher's views on tests of significance and null hypotheses, see Ronald A. Fisher, *The Design of Experiments* (New York: Hafner, 1935), 13–17.

29 Colin Howson and Peter Urbach, *Scientific Reasoning: The Bayesian Approach*, 2nd ed. (LaSalle, IL: Open Court, 1993), 178. For a similar criticism see Ian Hacking, *Logic of Statistical Inference* (Cambridge: Cambridge University Press, 1965), 81–83.

In *The Design Inference*, one of us (WmAD) shows that significance levels cannot be set in isolation but must always be set in relation to the probabilistic resources relevant to an event's occurrence.[30] In the context of Fisherian significance testing, probabilistic resources refer to the number of opportunities for an event to occur. The more opportunities there are for an event to occur, the more possibilities there are for it to land in the rejection region. And this in turn means that there is a greater likelihood that the chance hypothesis under consideration will be rejected. It follows that a seemingly improbable event can become probable once enough probabilistic resources are factored in. In the case of the Talpiot tomb, the relevant probabilistic resources are the number of Jews living in Palestine around the time of Jesus—the greater this number, the more likely that the pattern of New Testament names found in that tomb could have arisen by chance.

9. BAYES'S THEOREM

Given an event E and chance hypotheses $H_1, H_2, \ldots, H_n$ that are mutually exclusive and exhaustive, the probability of any one of these hypotheses H_i given E is

$$P(H_i \mid E) = \frac{P(E \mid H_i)\, P(H_i)}{P(E)}$$

This is the simple form of Bayes's theorem (named after Thomas Bayes). Since $H_1, H_2, \ldots, H_n$ are mutually exclusive and exhaustive, it follows that the denominator here can be rewritten as

$$
\begin{aligned}
P(E) &= P([E \,\&\, H_1] \vee [E \,\&\, H_2] \vee \cdots \vee [E \,\&\, H_n]) \\
&= P(E \,\&\, H_1) + P(E \,\&\, H_2) + \cdots + P(E \,\&\, H_n) \\
&= P(E|H_1)P(H_1) + P(E|H_2)\,P(H_2) + \cdots + P(E|H_n)\,P(H_n)
\end{aligned}
$$

These equalities follow simply from unpacking the axioms of probability and the definition of conditional probability. Substituting this last expression for the denominator in the simple form of Bayes's theorem now yields the standard form of Bayes's theorem:

---

30 William A. Dembski, *The Design Inference: Eliminating Chance through Small Probabilities* (Cambridge: Cambridge University Press, 1998), chap. 6.

$$P(H_i \mid E) = \frac{P(E \mid H_i)P(H_i)}{P(E \mid H_1)P(H_1) + P(E \mid H_2)P(H_2) + \cdots + P(E \mid H_n)P(H_n)}$$

10. THE BAYESIAN APPROACH TO STATISTICAL INFERENCES

In Bayesian statistical inference, one considers an event E and two competing hypotheses H_1 and H_2. Think of H_1 as the hypothesis that the Talpiot tomb belonged to the New Testament Jesus and H_2 as the hypothesis that the pattern of New Testament names in the Talpiot tomb occurred by chance. Moreover, think of the event E as evidence for either of these hypotheses. To decide whether the evidence E better supports either H_1 or H_2 therefore amounts to comparing the probabilities $P(H_1|E)$ and $P(H_2|E)$ and determining which is bigger. These probabilities are known as *posterior probabilities* and measure the probability of a hypothesis given the event/evidence/data E.

Posterior probabilities cannot be calculated directly but must rather be calculated on the basis of Bayes's theorem. Using the simple form of Bayes's theorem, we find that the posterior probability $P(H_i|E)$ ($i = 1$ or 2) is expressed in terms of $P(E|H_i)$, known as the *likelihood* of H_i given E, and $P(H_i)$, known as the *prior probability* of H_i. Often prior probabilities cannot be calculated directly. Moreover, in calculating the posterior probability, we still need to compute the denominator in the simple form of Bayes's theorem, namely, $P(E)$.

Fortunately, this last term does not need to be calculated. Because the aim is to determine which of these hypotheses is better supported by the evidence E, it is enough to form the ratio of posterior probabilities

$$\frac{P(H_1 \mid E)}{P(H_2 \mid E)}$$

and determine whether it is greater than or less than 1. If this ratio is greater than 1, it supports the hypothesis in the numerator (H_1, which we are treating as the "Talpiot equals Jesus tomb" hypothesis). If it is less than 1, it supports the hypothesis in the denominator (H_2, which we are treating as the "Talpiot names occurred by chance" hypothesis).

This ratio, using the simple form of Bayes's theorem, can now be rewritten as follows (note that the denominator in Bayes's theorem simply cancels out):

$$\frac{P(H_1 \mid E)}{P(H_2 \mid E)} = \frac{P(E \mid H_1)}{P(E \mid H_2)} \times \frac{P(H_1)}{P(H_2)}$$

The first factor on the right side of the equation is known as the *likelihood ratio*; the second is the ratio of priors, which measures our relative degree of belief in these two hypotheses before E entered the picture. Since the ratio on the left side of this equation represents the relative degree of belief in these two hypotheses once E is taken into account, this equation shows that updating our prior relative degree of belief in these hypotheses (i.e., before the evidence E was factored in) is simply a matter of multiplying the ratio of prior probabilities times the likelihood ratio.

In this way, the likelihood ratio, i.e.,

$$\frac{P(E \mid H_1)}{P(E \mid H_2)}$$

is said to measure the strength of evidence that E provides for H_1 in relation to H_2. Thus, since we are treating H_1 as the "Talpiot equals Jesus tomb" hypothesis and H_2 as the "Talpiot names occurred by chance" hypothesis, if this ratio is bigger than 1, E favors the former hypothesis and supports that the New Testament Jesus really was buried in the Talpiot tomb. On the other hand, if this ratio is less than 1, it favors the latter hypothesis and therefore supports that someone else is buried there.

THE RESURRECTION OF JESUS
AND THE TALPIOT TOMB

Gary R. Habermas

T
he authors in this volume argue that severe problems beset the Talpiot tomb hypothesis. Rarely is this more apparent than when this proposal purports to address the known data regarding the early church's claims that Jesus' burial tomb was empty and that He later appeared to His disciples in a resurrected body. In this chapter, we will compare the Talpiot hypothesis to the accredited information that contemporary research has confirmed on these topics.

A WORD ABOUT METHODOLOGY

In addressing this topic, it must be emphasized that there will be no effort to argue that the Talpiot hypothesis is mistaken simply because it disagrees with the New Testament, Christian tradition, or with orthodox Christian beliefs. This approach has appeared occasionally in the recent dialogue but is the wrong tact for those who wish to evaluate the strength of the claims themselves.

Conversely, we will rely almost exclusively on the established information that the vast majority of scholars who study this topic take to be historical. Whenever such scholarly agreement is present concerning particular historical data, it is usually because strong reasons exist to establish such a consensus. This is especially intriguing when specialists of different theological persuasions still share similar views on historical issues that are crucial to the Christian faith.[1]

The critiques that are perhaps the most difficult for the Talpiot hypothesis appear to be those that are drawn from generally accredited information that is approved by a scholarly consensus, precisely due to the strength of the data. If these strongest and best-established historical facts make it difficult to accept the Talpiot theme, then this will be a weighty hurdle, indeed. In the space of this essay, I will be unable to reconstruct the actual details of how this historical consensus is established. However, I have done so elsewhere in a great amount of detail.[2]

JAMES TABOR'S HYPOTHESIS

James Tabor[3] is one of a small number of scholars to champion the possibility that the Talpiot tomb is the actual burial chamber that stored the reburied bones of Jesus of Nazareth. In the process Tabor attempted to develop a plausible scenario that explains what happened to Jesus' body while still remaining at least partially within the bounds of the Gospel accounts.

Following the testimony of our earliest New Testament accounts, Tabor stated, "I have to agree with evangelical apologists that Paul knows an 'empty tomb' tradition. I cannot see how his language can make any

---

1 It is crucial to distinguish that scholars often agree about particular facts while still disagreeing about either additional specifics or their applications.

2 For just a few examples of this approach as applied to the resurrection of Jesus, see Gary R. Habermas, *The Risen Jesus and Future Hope* (Lanham, MD: Rowman and Littlefield, 2003); Habermas, "Experiences of the Risen Jesus: The Foundational Historical Issue in the Early Proclamation of the Resurrection," *Dialog: A Journal of Theology* 45 (2006): 288–97; Habermas, "Resurrection Research from 1975 to the Present: What Are Critical Scholars Saying?" *Journal for the Study of the Historical Jesus* 3 (2005): 135–53; Habermas, *The Historical Jesus: Ancient Evidence for the Life of Christ* (Joplin, MO: College Press, 1996); Habermas and Michael R. Licona, *The Case for the Resurrection of Jesus* (Grand Rapids: Kregel Publications, 2004).

3 For the record, I want to state clearly that James Tabor and I are good friends. For instance, almost a full year before the Talpiot story made the news, we visited for a few hours, discussing some of his research, including the possibility mentioned in his book below that DNA testing might be performed on the Talpiot ossuaries (although nothing had been done at that time). I mention this so that my critique will not be construed in any way other than what it is: a hearty disagreement with the thesis of a scholar whom I respect, who still remains a good friend.

sense otherwise."[4] Both Mark and John present a hasty burial due to the approaching Sabbath. But Tabor added, "This initial burial of Jesus was by definition a *temporary* and emergency move, based on necessity, until something more permanent could be worked out or arranged."[5]

Beyond this, details of the initial, temporary tomb are "unfortunately a matter about which historians can say little." Still, we "must assume that the corpse was taken and reburied, perhaps as soon as the Sabbath was over." That Joseph of Arimathea performed this task would be likely, "given that the tomb near the crucifixion site was never intended as a permanent place for Jesus' corpse."[6]

What about the general scenario that the vast majority of scholars follow regarding the early creedal material found in Paul's undoubted epistles and elsewhere, along with any early preaching traditions in Acts? And what of Paul's well-accredited accounts of his two trips to Jerusalem to ascertain the nature of the gospel message as it was preached by the other apostles, chiefly Peter, James the brother of Jesus, and John (Gal 1:18–2:10)? Tabor thinks that we can know little during this time frame (up until Paul's writings in the 50s) and referred to Paul's claim that the other apostles accepted his gospel message as "a myth of origins."[7] But Tabor explained that his primary purpose behind his reconstruction of the events is "to make the simple point" that "we would expect that first tomb to be empty within twenty-four hours. And I think we can safely assume that it was."[8]

In fairness to Tabor, he did not simply develop this scenario as the Talpiot thesis emerged in early 2007. A year earlier he had published a discussion of these and other matters, being one of the first historical Jesus scholars to mention in some detail the discovery of the Talpiot tomb. He was clear that any potential DNA testing could never prove that the tomb belonged to Jesus' family.[9]

---

4 James D. Tabor, "Two Burials of Jesus of Nazareth and the Talpiot Yeshua Tomb," *Society of Biblical Literature Forum*, April 2007, 1–2 [http://www.sbl-site.org/Article. aspx?ArticleId=651].
5 Tabor, "Two Burials," 2 (his emphasis).
6 Ibid.
7 Ibid.
8 Ibid.
9 James D. Tabor, *The Jesus Dynasty: The Hidden History of Jesus, His Royal Family, and the Birth of Christianity* (NY: Simon & Schuster, 2006), 22–33, esp. 26–27.

Although he seems to have grown more convinced of the Talpiot thesis since his earlier book was published, he maintains that the scenario is "possible, even likely, though not conclusively proven."[10] Sometimes Tabor states his view more simply by saying that this opinion should not be dismissed out of hand.[11]

Tabor also seems to have taken a different angle on a few other matters, too. For instance, in the 2006 volume, Tabor apparently thought that the Maria who was buried in that tomb might be the wife of the man named Yeshua.[12] Further, he still favored a Galilean burial for Jesus, as pronounced by a sixteenth-century Kabbalistic rabbi, Isaac ben Luria, rather than a Talpiot interment in the Jerusalem area.[13] He originally thought that the best candidates for moving Jesus' body on the first Sabbath were Jesus' mother Mary, the other women, and the family members,[14] rather than Joseph of Arimathea.

HISTORIOGRAPHY AND THE USE OF THE GOSPELS AND PAUL

I will now formulate a response to Tabor's version of the Talpiot hypothesis[15] that specifically challenges its ability to provide an alternative account for the accredited scholarly data that we have regarding the New Testament claims that certain alleged events happened after Jesus' crucifixion. My concerns are grouped under three main headings: the best historiographical use of the Gospels and Paul, Tabor's response to Jesus' burial and the empty tomb, and Tabor's response to the appearances of the risen Jesus. I hold that not only does the Talpiot hypothesis fare poorly in its overall attempt to establish this tomb as the burial place for Jesus' family[16] but that, at each of these three critical junctures, it

10 Tabor, e-mail, 17 March 2007; also, e-mail, 28 February 2007.
11 Tabor, "Two Burials," 4; e-mail, 28 February 2007.
12 Tabor, *Jesus Dynasty*, 24–25.
13 Ibid., 238–40; personal discussion with Tabor in Charlotte, NC, on 6 June 2006.
14 Ibid., 234–35.
15 However, it is not as if there are many scholarly attempts to defend this full thesis that needs to be addressed. To date Tabor's defense of the specific details is not only the *best* formulation, but basically the *only* one from a scholar.
16 The overall thesis is the purview of the rest of this volume. Also, I have written a brief book on the Talpiot tomb hypothesis titled *The Secret of the Talpiot Tomb: Unravelling the Mystery of the Jesus Family Tomb* (Nashville: B&H Publishing Group, 2007).

especially misses the mark by a wide margin. I will add a few additional thoughts on the empty tomb and the resurrection appearances of Jesus.

As Tabor appropriately reminds us,[17] all historical data must be interpreted. Crucial historical events do not stand on their own, with their meaning written into them. Rather, historians and other scholars must study the data to arrive at the clearest understanding possible. Hence, we must organize the available data. Differences will emerge here. No one is unbiased or always chooses the best routes on every single issue. But generally, the preferred solutions are those that account best for the known data with as little contrary remainder as possible. As a result, some interpretations provide better accounts than do others with regard to the known facts, as nearly as they can be ascertained. Furthermore, historians must choose which explanations to subordinate to other material, and so on.

But sometimes this subordination appears to be positioned too far in one direction or the other. When Tabor repeatedly seems to use the New Testament when it favors his viewpoint while parting from it when it does not support his view, even though there are good scholarly reasons for affirming the authenticity of the New Testament material, this provides cause for concern. Yet I am afraid that this tendency manifests itself too often.

For example, Tabor follows the broad outline of the Gospel accounts when they depict the crucifixion of Jesus.[18] Likewise, he appreciates the Gospel reports that point to a hasty burial in a rock tomb due to the approaching Sabbath, even though burial in a trench grave was the most common mode of Jewish burial in Jesus' day. Tabor also espouses the empty tomb, found in all four Gospels and implied by Paul, whom all, including Tabor, agree is our earliest and most reliable source.

But when it comes to Mark's testimony that the women returned on Sunday morning in order to anoint Jesus' dead body (16:1–2), Tabor begins to sidestep the Gospel accounts. Although there is a total lack of Gospel (or any other) testimony that either Joseph of Arimathea or Jesus' family sought to move the body elsewhere, Tabor lists the *temporary* burial of Jesus' body as a solid fact, one that is not only expected[19] but

17 Tabor, *The Jesus Dynasty*, 233–34, 305, 316–17.
18 Ibid., 228–30.
19 Tabor, "Two Burials," 2.

is also "indisputable."[20] But on what *evidence* are these seemingly bare assertions based? No evidence from the New Testament, Jewish burial practices, or other ancient reports supports these points or his claim that Jesus' body was transferred to another tomb. However, these assertions line up nicely with the Talpiot tomb burial.

Tabor surprisingly favors John's account, where Mary Magdalene presumes that the gardener moved Jesus' body.[21] This is rather astounding since there is no multiple attestation of John's report, and John is generally treated as the least reliable Gospel. But once again, this idea favors his thesis.

Directly after stating what he thinks *can* be said from the texts with some assurance, Tabor argues, "What happened next . . . is unfortunately a matter about which historians can say little, given the theological nature of our sources and their relatively late apologetic character."[22] Without disparaging his motives,[23] it does appear that what Tabor needs to support his thesis can be conveniently gleaned from the Gospels and Pauline literature. However, in some places where the sources provide strong arguments against the thesis, the sources suddenly become problematic.

And this is not the only place where this happens in the development of his thesis. As indicated earlier, Tabor dismisses the widely held view affirmed by the majority of scholars that Paul checked out his gospel message with the chief apostles, James the brother of Jesus, Peter, and later John, and received their affirmation (Gal 1:18–2:10). Tabor calls this a "myth of origins."[24] Elsewhere, he develops this idea in greater detail, affirming that earliest Christianity followed a distinctly Jewish brand of theology led by James, along with Jesus' mother and family. In the views of earliest Christianity, Jesus was apparently thought to be neither deity nor raised from the dead. This movement "of ethical and spiritual values" bore "no trace of Paul's gospel."[25]

20 Tabor, *The Jesus Dynasty*, 228.
21 Ibid., 234–35.
22 Tabor, "Two Burials," 2.
23 I mean this literally because often I have seen James Tabor kindly attribute the best reading to his opponent, compliment the views of others with whom he disagrees, and graciously consider the possibility of other positions (for example, see *The Jesus Dynasty*, 317). But as I have also said above, all of us speak from our own perspectives and viewpoints.
24 Tabor, "Two Burials," 2.
25 Tabor, *The Jesus Dynasty*, 310–12; cp. 244–47, 307, 315.

Yet many powerful reasons favor Paul's gospel stance as being basically identical to the earliest Christian message.[26] For example, the pre-Pauline creedal tradition that Paul received and then passed down in 1 Cor 15:3–8, including the death, burial, and resurrection appearances of Jesus, dates from the early to mid–30s AD. Few conclusions are better established in the critical literature. Further, it can be shown to be the original Christian proclamation.

This creed(s) *predates by one or more decades* not only Paul's writings but also the letter of James, the Q material, and the *Didache*, which are Tabor's favorite sources. Why should we favor these last texts that are both significantly later than the content of this early creed and of much more questionable provenance?[27] The material in 1 Cor 15:3–7 is more strongly supported on all counts: a much earlier date, probable authorship, strong pedigree, and scholarly approval.

Additionally, most scholars conclude that Paul received this material or at least its general content from the apostle Peter and James the brother of Jesus during Paul's first visit to Jerusalem (Gal 1:18–20). Most scholars also concur that during Paul's second trip to Jerusalem (Gal 2:1–10) he subjected his gospel message to the apostolic scrutiny not only of Peter and James but also of John, lest he be mistaken (2:2). However, the most influential leaders in the early church added nothing to Paul's gospel presentation (2:6) and welcomed his witness to its truth (2:9). Paul likewise attests that he knew the details of their apostolic message about the death, burial, and resurrection appearances of Jesus and that they all taught the same thing (1 Cor 15:11–15).

These data are so well attested and affirmed by contemporary critical scholars that it is difficult to understand how a critique could dislodge these central conclusions. Perhaps Paul is too self-serving in Gal 1:18–2:10 by saying that the other apostles agreed with him. If so, then why are his two trips to Jerusalem preceded immediately by a passage

---

26 For this argument, see Habermas, "Experiences of the Risen Jesus," 288–97; Habermas, "Resurrection Research from 1975 to the Present," 141–43. For many more details, see Habermas, *The Risen Jesus and Future Hope*, especially chapter 1.

27 There is much scholarly debate about both the author and date of the letter of James, which nonetheless affirms the deity of Jesus (1:1; 2:1). The existence as well as the authorship and content of the Q sayings document have never been questioned as much as recently. Besides, Q denies neither the deity of Jesus nor His resurrection. The *Didache* has no known author and is probably much later than the other sources.

that declares his independence since he was taught directly by Jesus? Why should he go at all to the chief apostles for confirmation?[28]

Furthermore, if Paul were so self-serving, why should he acknowledge that having labored in vain was even a possibility (2:2)? Moreover, why does he turn immediately to record an argument between himself and Peter over the issue of Jewish fellowship with Gentiles (Gal 2:11–21)? If the response is that telling his account of Peter's error elevated himself at Peter's expense, this still militates against and risks the unanimity that was the central point that Paul had just finished recording in 2:6,9.

In order to sidestep the force of Gal 1:18–2:10 one must somehow challenge Paul's credibility. Yet Paul is both the earliest and most accredited source that we have in the early church as is attested by the vast majority of contemporary critical scholars. What source that contradicts Paul is both earlier and more reliable?

Tabor states that "many" scholars have questioned Paul here.[29] Although I do not doubt that he could produce a few names of scholars who take his position, the issue, of course, will not be decided by a "head count." Still, it may be true, as is often thought, that the preponderance of scholarly opinion often renders particular positions more credible, due *not* to the sheer numbers themselves but to the *reasons* on which these positions are taken. If this is the case, then Tabor's stance against Paul's witness to the major beliefs of the earliest church is not likely to succeed. This is the area in which I have specialized over my entire career. I have even kept a tally of scholarly opinion regarding these issues over the last 30 years, and it shows that texts like 1 Cor 15:3–8 and Gal 1:18–2:10 are well accredited, being accepted by the vast majority of scholars.

After speaking of the consensus scholarly view that Paul received this material in Jerusalem from a reliable source, Richard Bauckham contended in a recent work that in 1 Cor 15:11, Paul "asserts the unanimity between himself and the other apostles on the key matters he has

---

28 Victor Furnish is probably correct that, in Galatians 1, Paul is distinguishing between the *content* of the gospel message, being given to him by Jesus during the resurrection appearance to him, and the human, testimonial *confirmation* of the message by those others who also saw Jesus' appearances (Furnish, *Jesus according to Paul* [New York.: Cambridge University Press, 1993], 29; cf. 65).
29 Tabor, "Two Burials," 2.

just rehearsed (v. 11). This unanimity existed *because* he had received the tradition in question from the Jerusalem apostles."[30]

Reginald Fuller remarked on the pre-Pauline creedal tradition in 1 Corinthians 15: "The importance of Paul's statement can hardly be overestimated." It presents a clear example of the earliest Christian claims, as witnessed by the eyewitnesses who experienced these events.[31] Even Jewish New Testament scholar Pinchas Lapide listed eight reasons for holding that this creedal text is early and predates Paul. He concluded that this tradition "may be considered as a statement of eyewitnesses."[32] In spite of being agnostic on the issue of the resurrection, Wedderburn says that the statements preserved here "are the foundations of the church."[33]

Can this text be cross-examined? Years ago German historian Hans von Campenhausen attested: "This account meets all the demands of historical reliability that could possibly be made of such a text."[34] Much more recently, Howard Clark Kee was even more specific: the early traditions recorded by Paul "can be critically examined and compared with other testimony from eyewitnesses of Jesus, just as one would evaluate evidence in a modern court or academic setting."[35] Even skeptical scholars regularly think that Paul was in the right place at the right time, where he met with the right witnesses to have received this testimony concerning the early Christian gospel. Accordingly, this material is usually dated in the early to mid–30s AD.[36]

30 Richard Bauckham, *Jesus and the Eyewitnesses: The Gospels as Eyewitness Testimony* (Grand Rapids: Eerdmans, 2006), 266 (Baukham's emphasis). For further confirmation of this scholarly consensus and Paul's knowledge that the other apostles agreed with him on the nature of the resurrection appearances, Bauckham cites several works, including those by A. Eriksson, Martin Hengel and A. M. Schwemer (endnotes 7, 8).
31 Reginald H. Fuller, *The Formation of the Resurrection Narratives,* 2nd ed. (New York: Macmillan, 1980), 43–44; cf. 170.
32 Pinchas Lapide, *The Resurrection of Jesus: A Jewish Perspective* (Minneapolis: Augsburg, 1983), 97–99.
33 A. J. M. Wedderburn, *Beyond Resurrection* (Peabody, MA: Hendrickson, 1999), 116.
34 Hans von Campenhausen, "The Events of Easter and the Empty Tomb," *Tradition and Life in the Church* (Philadelphia: Fortress, 1968), 44.
35 Howard Clark Kee, *What Can We Know about Jesus?* (Cambridge: Cambridge University Press, 1990), 1–2.
36 Robert W. Funk and the Jesus Seminar, *The Acts of Jesus: The Search for the Authentic Deeds of Jesus* (San Francisco.: Harper Collins, 1998), 453–55; Gerd Lüdemann, *The Resurrection of Jesus,* trans. John Bowden (Minneapolis: Fortress, 1994), 38; Wedderburn, *Beyond Resurrection,* 111, 274, note 265; Michael Goulder, "The Baseless Fabric of a Vision," in Gavin D'Costa, ed., *Resurrection Reconsidered* (Oxford: Oneworld, 1996), 48; Thomas Sheehan, *The First Coming: How the Kingdom of God Became Christianity* (New York: Random House, 1986), 118; cp. 110–12, 135; Michael Grant, *Saint Paul* (Glasgow:

Likewise, the majority of scholars who consider the possible sources of the tradition that Paul preserves here think that Paul received this material from Peter and James the brother of Jesus in his first trip to Jerusalem (Gal 1:18–20). This gospel message was later confirmed during Paul's second trip during which he consulted with these same apostles, plus John (Gal 2:1–10).

For instance, A. M. Hunter speaks for many in favoring the great antiquity and apostolic origin of the creed because of the presence of Semitisms in the creed which seem to indicate that it originated in Palestine and because the names of the apostles Peter and James both surface in 1 Corinthians 15 and in Galatians 1. Accordingly, the tradition recorded by Paul is *"open to testing."*[37] Other scholars agree with this and affirm that Paul checked out his message with the other apostles and received their confirmation.[38]

For reasons like these, C. H. Dodd concluded: "Thus Paul's preaching represents a special stream of Christian tradition which was derived from the main stream at a point very near to its source." Therefore, anyone who wants to "maintain that the primitive Christian Gospel was fundamentally different from that which we have found in Paul must bear the burden of proof."[39] Since Paul is our earliest and most critically attested source, his testimony is difficult to set aside. Paul was indeed at the right place and the right time, gathered the crucial evidence from

William Collins Sons, 1976), 104; G. A. Wells, *Did Jesus Exist?* (London: Pemberton, 1986), 30; Jack Kent, *The Psychological Origins of the Resurrection Myth* (London: Open Gate, 1999), 16–17.

37 A. M. Hunter, *Jesus: Lord and Saviour* (Grand Rapids: Eerdmans, 1976), 100 (Hunter's emphasis).

38 Even Gerd Lüdemann takes a similar view in *What Really Happened to Jesus* (Louisville: Westminster John Knox, 1995), 12–13. See also Martin Hengel, *The Atonement: The Origins of the Doctrine in the New Testament* (Philadelphia: Fortress, 1981), 37–39; Bauckham, *Jesus and the Eyewitnesses,* 264–71; Hans Dieter Betz, *Galatians: A Commentary on Paul's Letter to the Churches in Galatia* (Philadelphia: Fortress, 1979), 76; William Farmer, "Peter and Paul, and the Tradition Concerning 'The Lord's Supper' in 1 Cor. 11:23–25," *Criswell Theological Review* 2 (1987): 122–30; cp. 135–38 regarding the Petrine nature of this tradition. Compare the views of John Alsup, *The Post-Resurrection Appearance Stories of the Gospel Tradition: A History-of-Tradition Analysis with Text-Synopsis,* Calwer Theologische Monographien 5 (Stuttgart: Calwer Verlag, 1975), 55; Joseph Fitzmyer, "The Ascension of Christ and Pentecost," *Theological Studies* 45 (1984): 409–440; Furnish, *Jesus according to Paul,* 29, 65; Grant Osborne, *The Resurrection Narratives: A Redactional Study* (Grand Rapids: Baker, 1984), 222.

39 C. H. Dodd, *The Apostolic Preaching and Its Developments* (Grand Rapids: Baker, 1980), 16.

the proper persons, and passed it on to his readers. The reasons for this are sufficient to convince the majority of contemporary critical scholars concerning the early apostolic agreement on the nature of the Christian gospel data.

On the other hand, Tabor's reasons for dismissing Paul's claims regarding Jesus' resurrection are not strong enough to offset the position. Tabor seems to dismiss Paul's testimony for the same reason that he rejected elements of the Gospel accounts that oppose the Talpiot hypothesis: it creates havoc for his position. In fact, the pre-Pauline creed in 1 Cor 15:3–8 connected with Gal 1:18–2:10 presents a formidable roadblock against his hypothesis. As long as these data stand, the earliest gospel of the death, burial, and resurrection appearances of Jesus also stands. This was the central message not only of Paul but also of James the brother of Jesus, Peter, John, and the other apostles.

THE EMPTY TOMB OF JESUS AND
THE TALPIOT RESPONSE

All our ancient sources, whether by friend or foe, agree that Jesus' burial tomb was found empty shortly afterwards. Every Gospel reports that the women who visited Jesus' tomb discovered that it was open and empty. Reportedly, even the Jewish authorities thought that the tomb was empty.[40] Our earliest source (1 Cor 15:4) states that Jesus rose from the dead just three days after the crucifixion.

Surprisingly, the scholarly literature lists more than 20 reasons for the historicity of the empty tomb. Most frequently championed is the unanimous agreement that women were the initial witnesses. In the patriarchal culture of Palestine in the first century AD, women were unlikely to be asked to provide important testimony. Although there were exceptions, there was generally an inverse relation between the magnitude of the subject and whether women would be allowed to testify in court.

Why are the women enumerated by each Gospel as the initial witnesses to the empty tomb unless they actually were the first witnesses? Moreover, why would we be told also that Jesus' male disciples reacted

---

40 Matthew 28:11–15; Justin Martyr, *Dialogue with Trypho*, 108; Tertullian, *On Spectacles*, 30. The *Toledoth Jesu*, although very late, also presents a similar account (Habermas, *The Historical Jesus*, 205–6; cp. Paul L. Maier, *In the Fullness of Time: A Historian Looks at Christmas, Easter, and the Early Church* (San Francisco: Harper Collins, 1991), 200–2.

to the report by belittling the women and accusing them of spreading tales—basically gossip (see Luke 24:11)? Here we have two examples of the principle of embarrassment since it is unlikely that the New Testament authors would humiliate their heroes without good reasons.

Several strange items are operating here. If the authors wanted the greatest impact in evidencing the crucial report of the empty tomb and are as uncritical as some contemporary scholars think, why not simply invent the story that the men found the empty tomb? Their testimony would certainly be received more readily. Even if female testimony was utilized, by all means avoid criticizing the later leaders of the church, the male disciples. After all, it is counterproductive to make the early church leaders, who were taught by Jesus, look so badly mistaken. This is a horrible way to establish a case for the empty tomb unless the Evangelists were committed to reporting the events precisely as they occurred.

Another major reason establishing the empty tomb is that the city of Jerusalem would presumably be the last location for this claim to have originated if it were not so. As both the birthplace of the Church as well as the stronghold of its many enemies, it was risky business to proclaim a message that could almost immediately be checked out. An afternoon walk by either foe or friend could either verify or falsify the claim. If the tomb were not empty, it could easily have been disproven.

One objection is that the Gospel accounts do not begin to surface until about 35 or 40 years after the events. But this objection overlooks more than one crucial point. For instance, the predominant Jewish notion of afterlife at this time is clearly that of *bodily* resurrection.[41] How could the disciples have gotten away with proclaiming Jesus' resurrection appearances if the stone still remained in place, blocking His tomb? Anyone who went further and opened the tomb would disprove the entire enterprise in one easy step.

Just one other consideration favoring an empty tomb will be mentioned. Ancient historian Paul Maier points out, "Many facts from antiquity rest on just one ancient source, while two or three sources in agreement generally render the fact unimpeachable."[42] Yet the empty tomb is

41 For many details on the Jewish view, see especially N. T. Wright, *The Resurrection of the Son of God* (Minneapolis: Fortress, 2003), chaps. 3–5; Robert Gundry, *Sōma in Biblical Theology with Emphasis on Pauline Anthropology* (Cambridge: Cambridge University Press, 1976), especially chap. 13.
42 Maier, *In the Fullness of Time*, 197.

taught or implied in three to six independent sources, both in the Gospels and elsewhere.[43] By ancient standards, as Maier reminds us, this is simply excellent attestation. Due to these and many other reasons, most critical scholars hold that Jesus' burial tomb was discovered to be empty shortly afterwards. This is the best explanation of our data.[44]

How does the Talpiot hypothesis account for this information? As we have seen, Tabor holds that Jesus of Nazareth died by crucifixion and was buried hastily in a tomb, according to the general outline in the Gospels. Very quickly, perhaps even immediately after the initial Sabbath, the body was probably moved to the Talpiot tomb, either by Joseph of Arimathea or by family members. After perhaps a year, when His flesh would have rotted, Jesus' bones would have been reburied in the ossuary that bears His name.

Tabor's thesis has nothing to do with someone "stealing" Jesus' dead body. The body was simply transferred to the Talpiot tomb in an orderly fashion, with the bones being placed in the ossuary a little later.[45]

But this scenario appears bizarre, one that would seem never to have been imagined unless one were trying specifically to coalesce the burial story preserved in the Gospels with the assumptions of the Talpiot tomb hypothesis. It fails to make the best sense of the known data regarding Jesus' burial.

To begin, why would Joseph or Jesus' family members rebury His body just 24 hours or so after the original interment? Granted, we must concede that the body was buried hastily due to the oncoming Sabbath. But what was wrong with the initial tomb? Contrary to Tabor, a *hasty* burial is far from a *temporary* burial. Further, not a single ancient source supports such a move.

Even if it could be established that the body was moved so quickly, what is the advantage of placing it in the same sort of tomb that Jesus' body had already occupied? At the outset, we made the methodological

---

43 Besides the three to four sources that scholars think lie behind the Gospel texts, there is also the potential early creedal statement in Acts 13:29–30,35–37, along with the implications of Paul's early creedal report in 1 Cor 15:3–5. This does not count the attestations by Justin Martyr and Tertullian, which are too late to provide the sort of evidence we need, but are still worth mentioning.

44 See Gary R. Habermas, "The Empty Tomb of Jesus: Recent Critical Arguments," forthcoming.

45 Tabor, "Two Burials," 1–2; *The Jesus Dynasty*, 22–31, except that Tabor did not initially say that the Talpiot tomb was the location of the reburial.

point that we need to work with the best explanation of our data, in keeping with the wide recognition of scholars, unless we have *strong reasons* for doing otherwise. But we have *no* good reasons to hold that Jesus' body was reburied perhaps a day after His death, but prior to the third burial in the ossuary, unless the chief goal is to get Jesus' bones into the Talpiot tomb. But, simply said, no data establishes this scenario.

There is another relevant issue here. Biblical archaeologist Jodi Magness concluded that the best explanations of the available data are that Jesus was raised from the dead or that Jesus' body was reburied in a trench grave, which was the most common burial practice in first-century Israel. The latter would require that the shrouded body be placed in a rectangular notch in the soil. But, "whatever explanation one prefers . . . his bones could not have been collected in an ossuary, at least not if we follow the Gospel accounts."[46] The point is not that the Gospels must be followed at all costs but that once again we must utilize our chief sources of information. So if the most common kind of reburial were employed—burial in a trench grave—the bones would not have been reburied a year or so later.

Tabor is undecided as to whether Joseph would have told Jesus' family about the initial reburial in a different tomb.[47] However, how could Joseph, a respected man who attempted to honor Jesus, never have informed anyone of his decision? Surely this would be a private choice within the purview of the deceased individual's family. To neglect to inform Jesus' family of the new location of His body would be indecent and almost unconscionable. Anything else seems so out of place as to be almost ridiculous. Moreover, if Jesus' bones are to show up later in the *family tomb*, with His name scratched on the outside of the ossuary, we can assume that many family members must have been aware of it.

Furthermore, it is unlikely that Joseph moved Jesus' body by himself. Would no one else have witnessed the removal, especially when Joseph was not attempting to act secretively? And assuming that he received some assistance in relocating Jesus' body, perhaps from more than one person, what prevents those assistants from sharing this incredibly newsworthy information? If Joseph and any other helpers or witnesses kept

46 Jodi Magness, "Has the Tomb of Jesus Been Discovered?" *Biblical Archaeology Review* (5 March 2007): 3 [http://bib-arch.org/bswbKCtombmagness.html].
47 Tabor, "Two Burials," 2, which emphasizes his conflict over whether Jesus' family did the reburying, as per his original thesis (*Jesus Dynasty*, 235).

their actions hidden for some reason, especially if they never told Jesus' mother and family, the hypothesis seems to require Joseph and his associates to have been guilty of conspiracy and fraud. It is almost reminiscent of the old Egyptian stories that those who buried the Pharaohs had to be killed so as not to divulge the whereabouts of the tomb.

Due to these and other serious problems, let us suppose that Joseph did tell Jesus' family that he had moved the body. It makes the most sense that Joseph would have informed Jesus' family *before* actually moving the body. In any culture and time, would someone who appears to be virtually unknown to a family (as far as we know) simply move their son's or brother's dead body without informing them ahead of time? Such an imposition would appear to be simply incredible.

Yet this becomes a thorny issue in that the women, *including Jesus' mother Mary*, still went to the vacated tomb on Sunday morning. The women then concluded that it was momentous that Jesus' body was no longer there. And even if Joseph straightened out the matter upon hearing the rumors of their mistake, or at some later time after the Christian preaching began, further serious problems would ensue due to the rise of their initial resurrection faith. We will pursue this further in the next portion of the essay.

So the burial and the empty tomb present major problems for Tabor, in spite of his overall agreement with some of the broad contours of the Gospel narratives. But when he gets to some of the sticky questions, such as those raised here, he simply punts and states that we can go no further due to the theological nature of the Gospels. Not only is this response itself problematic, given the most recent New Testament studies; but by this time in his discussion, Tabor has already borrowed from the Gospels whenever he wants to make the points or implications that favor his thesis. As we have seen, he accepts the general crucifixion and burial scenarios, the existence of Joseph of Arimathea and his role in Jesus' burial, the day of the week as well as the time of day in which Jesus was buried, the hasty nature of Jesus' burial, the nature of the rock tomb, the stone rolled in front, and on and on.[48] But when these *exact same* texts agree against his hypothesis, he opts out of the process.

One major roadblock so far for the Talpiot reburial hypothesis is that the evidence for the empty tomb is both specific and powerful. Indeed,

48 Tabor, "Two Burials," 1–2, 4.

Tabor concedes because of the early date of Paul's tradition and the difficulty of making sense of the data otherwise.[49] But then he reinterprets it and bases his reinterpretation on mere speculation without evidence from ancient sources for doing so. Thus the empty tomb alone plays havoc with the Talpiot thesis.

Many problems need to be solved by those who espouse the likelihood of the Talpiot scenario with virtually no specific data to sort them out. To summarize: (1) There is no known rationale or evidence for either Joseph or Jesus' family to rebury the body within a mere 24 hours or so. (2) If Jesus' body had been reburied in the most common manner employed by the Jews of this time and moved to a trench grave, His bones would not have been placed later in the Talpiot tomb ossuary. Furthermore, there seems to be no reason for simply relocating the body to another tomb that was similar to that in which Jesus was initially buried. (3) If Joseph never told anyone else that he had reburied the body, how would he keep this fact from becoming known? Whether or not he needed help, this course of action would almost certainly attract attention. Even worse, the decision violates every rule of privacy, as well as meaning that the Talpiot tomb could not be Jesus' *family tomb*, for they would not know about it. (4) If Joseph did inform especially the family beforehand, as seems highly likely, then why do Mary the mother of Jesus and others proceed to the now empty tomb on Sunday morning, apparently having no idea where to find Jesus' body? If they are not told until later, then an entirely new set of problems emerge, as we will see next. (5) Over this entire procedure, a methodological pitfall continues to be manifest. By what justification do we accept such a large amount of the Gospel textual substantiation of Jesus' death and burial, except when it clearly opposes our hypotheses?

THE RESURRECTION APPEARANCES OF JESUS

Whether liberal, moderate, or conservative, scholars generally concur on a fair number of historical details from the end of Jesus' life to the beginning of the early church. For instance, virtually all critical scholars

---

49 Ibid., 1.

today think that Jesus' disciples along with others really experienced what they were utterly convinced were appearances of the risen Jesus.[50]

Why are these crucial historical experiences conceded by the vast majority of scholars, including skeptics? Of the many reasons several are especially significant.[51] Scholars often begin with (1) Paul's eyewitness testimony to an experience of the risen Jesus (1 Cor 9:1; 15:8–10), which prompted his conversion from a vigorous persecutor of Christians to a passionate missionary (1 Cor 15:9; Gal 1:13–14; Phil 3:4–6). Equally important is (2) the early creedal material containing the gospel data that Paul had received and passed on to others, including Jesus' appearances to His followers (1 Cor 15:3–7). We have said that most scholars hold that the content of this tradition dates from immediately after Jesus' crucifixion, and that Paul probably received it in the early to mid–30s AD. Most likely Peter and James the brother of Jesus passed it on to Paul during his initial visit to Jerusalem (Gal 1:13–20). Moreover, (3) these gospel data were so crucial to Paul that years later he took great care to establish the message again with Peter, James the brother of Jesus, and John. These key Christian leaders confirmed Paul's view of the gospel, adding nothing (Gal 2:1–10). (4) Paul attests that he knew what the other apostles were teaching regarding their own experiences of the resurrected Jesus, and their message was the same as his (1 Cor 15:11–14).

Additional factors indicate that the other disciples had also seen the risen Jesus. (5) As we will note later, the predominant scholarly view is that James the brother of Jesus was an unbelieving skeptic until he was convinced that he had seen an appearance of the risen Jesus too (1 Cor 15:7). (6) Jesus' disciples were willing to die specifically for their message of the resurrection, and some did, which indicates that they were totally persuaded that it was accurate. (7) Many other creedal texts that date from the earliest period of Christianity also confirm Jesus' resurrection appearances.[52] (8) As addressed above, the empty tomb argues that whatever happened involved Jesus' body, which is another indication in the direction of actual appearances of the risen Jesus.

These eight arguments are also espoused by most scholars, and they all indicate strongly that the earliest disciples were utterly convinced that

---

50 For many details here, see Habermas, "Experiences of the Risen Jesus," 288–97; Habermas, "Resurrection Research from 1975 to the Present," esp. 149–53.
51 See Habermas, *The Risen Jesus and Future Hope*, 15–31.
52 For specific details, see Habermas, *The Risen Jesus and Future Hope*, 22–23.

they had witnessed actual appearances of the risen Jesus. Additionally, most scholars agree that alternative attempts to rule out the resurrection on natural grounds fail to explain the known data.[53] In light of the eight arguments just presented, if natural explanations are inadequate, then the best explanation for what the disciples experienced is actual appearances of the risen Jesus.

In brief, the historical evidence indicates that the disciples thought they had seen appearances of the risen Jesus. If natural events have not explained these experiences, then the resurrection appearances remain as the most probable explanation. Therefore, the experiences of the risen Jesus plus the absence of natural alternatives equals resurrection appearances!

To repeat, we have *not* accepted these facts just because they are reported in the New Testament. If that were the case, then skeptical scholars who reject the inspiration or reliability of Scripture would presumably also discard these data. But virtually all critical scholars think that Jesus' disciples had real experiences that they thought were appearances of their risen Lord. Actually, it is rare to discover scholars who deny this. That is because there are so many credible reasons to accept these facts as historical, such as the eight we just listed. *That* is the reason so many scholars grant these data.

How does the Talpiot hypothesis deal with all this critically accredited historical data? It did not fare well with the burial and empty tomb records. Does it do any better in addressing the nature of the resurrection appearances? My contention is that the Talpiot tomb thesis is pressed even harder on this subject.

I have argued that it makes by far the most sense that if Joseph of Arimathea had reburied Jesus' body, that he would have informed the family *before* he did so. As a fairly obscure follower of Jesus, it is highly unlikely that he would decide privately to move the body without telling the family and friends. Regardless, Jesus' family would necessarily have to know at least at some later time since it was their family tomb and they would have to know where to find Jesus' bones in order to rebury them in the ossuary that would bear His name.

According to every burial scenario that we entertained, Mary the mother of Jesus must have known, sooner or later, that her son Jesus had

53 For both points here, see Habermas, "Experiences of the Risen Jesus," 289–93; Habermas, "Resurrection Research from 1975 to the Present," esp. 140–45.

been reburied from the initial tomb in which His body had been placed. She would also have to know that His bones were placed in an ossuary in the family tomb, perhaps a year later. After all, she was the family matriarch, and preparing bodies for burial was generally a job for the women, as we see in the Gospels.

We have also said that if the women, including Mary and Mary Magdalene, knew of the reburial ahead of time, they would have no reason to go to the initial tomb on Sunday morning to finish the burial, which Joseph would have completed. Plus, they would *expect* to find the tomb empty. But this leads to the next problem—even critical scholars take seriously the claim that the women also had experiences that they thought were appearances of the risen Jesus.[54] Needless to say, their conviction that they had seen the risen Jesus would collide with the knowledge that Jesus' body, at that very moment, lay dead in another tomb.

Though highly unlikely, what if Joseph did move the body but waited until later to inform them? This still does not dissolve the problems of either the initial resurrection appearances that reportedly occurred to the women near the tomb (Matt 28:9–10; John 20:14–18), or the later appearances, where they would assuredly be present in the groups to which Jesus appeared.[55] For instance, the women are specifically mentioned as being present after the ascension (Acts 1:14). Even apart from these texts, it is simply shortsighted to think that Jesus' own mother along with His female disciples would not be in attendance during several of Jesus' appearances.

So there ought to be no question that the relevant texts make it obvious that both Jesus' mother Mary and Mary Magdalene were believers, thought they had also seen the risen Jesus, and supported the efforts of the early church. Yet if within a year or so of His death, Jesus' bones inside the Talpiot tomb now needed to be placed in an ossuary, what would happen to their ongoing faith?

Over the years, each time one of Jesus' family members entered their tomb in order to rebury another relative, they would be confronted by the reality of Jesus' horrible death by crucifixion. From time to time,

---

54 For instance, Funk and the Jesus Seminar, *The Acts of Jesus*, 454; Helmut Koester, *History and Literature of Early Christianity*, vol. 2 of *Introduction to the New Testament* (Philadelphia: Fortress, 1982), 84. Each of these highly critical texts treats the women's experiences of the risen Jesus as probable data.
55 As in 1 Cor 15:5–7; cp. Luke 24:33.

it was perhaps necessary to shift Jesus' own ossuary or at least to step over or around it. Mother Mary could not help but remember. And since the predominant Jewish view at that time was that one's corpse would be raised, with the ossuaries themselves serving as an ongoing pointer to the importance of the human bones, how could the women go on believing that Jesus truly had been raised from the dead? Then what about their firm conviction that He had appeared alive to them after His death?

In the case of James the brother of Jesus, we have a different angle to this problem. As the head of the family after Jesus died, James obviously would be another one who would have to have known where the family tomb was located. He also would know that Jesus' name was displayed on the outside of the ossuary. Like Mary, James also would have to trip almost repeatedly over or at least pass by his brothers' bones as they reburied additional family members during the intervening years prior to his own death.

But this would be highly problematic. Due to the dual source attestation,[56] as well as the extreme example of embarrassment if Jesus had an unbelieving brother who later became the head of the Jerusalem church, the predominant scholarly view[57] is that James had converted from skepticism due to a resurrection appearance of Jesus (1 Cor 15:7).[58] James was transformed from believing Jesus was deranged to experiencing a profound faith change.

However, this generally accepted scholarly view cannot be reconciled with the claim that James knew without a doubt that Jesus' "body" was still interred in the family tomb. As a pious Jew, how could James truly believe that Jesus had been raised from the dead? His brother's bones were plainly safe and sound in the family tomb, awaiting the resurrection at the end of time. But this introduces far more serious problems in James's case that were not present for the two Marys.

Given Jesus' second burial in the family tomb followed by His final interment in the ossuary, what would account for James' conversion from skepticism? If James had not been informed immediately that his brother's corpse had simply been moved, what about Jesus' appear-

---

56 Mark 3:21; John 7:5.

57 In fact, among critical scholars, John Painter acknowledges that he is one of the few dissenters to this view. See Painter, "Who Was James?" in *The Brother of Jesus: James the Just and His Mission,* ed. Bruce Chilton and Jacob Neusner (Louisville: Westminster John Knox, 2001), 24.

58 For details, see Habermas, *The Risen Jesus and Future Hope,* 21–22.

ance to him after he discovered the truth? Beyond his initial conversion because of the resurrection appearance, as held by the majority of scholars, why did he *keep* believing upon learning the truth? A few years after Jesus' death, James is still the leader of the Jerusalem church.[59] And if it is thought that James is the author of the letter that bears his name, written later, he refers to his brother as the "Lord Jesus Christ" (1:1; 2:1), as "glorious" (2:1), waiting to return (5:7), and preparing to serve as the Judge (5:9). Indeed, Bauckham refers to the early date of James' "high Christology."[60]

Another item regarding James should also be mentioned briefly. Although strongly disputed, if the recently discovered James ossuary is authentic, it might actually work *against* the Talpiot scenario. The ossuary designation "James son of Joseph brother of Jesus" would arguably signify that until his death, James continued to be identified with Christianity. This would corroborate the New Testament witness, as well as Josephus's account of James's martyrdom in Jerusalem.[61] Additionally, the ossuary inscription may actually insinuate Jesus' resurrection, for if James doubted that Jesus had been resurrected and if He was therefore less than Lord, it would seem that he would no longer be so identified with Jesus in his death.[62]

This leads us to another devastating problem for the Talpiot thesis. Whenever mother Mary, Mary Magdalene, and James found out about the reburial of Jesus' body, it would have to be within the first year or so after the crucifixion, occasioned by both the reburial in the Talpiot family tomb and the later move to the ossuary. This also would constitute the first year in the life of the Christian Church. But how could this information of the double reburial of Jesus' body and bones possibly remain concealed from Jesus' apostles and other early leaders, especially when the Talpiot tomb has outside decorations that demand attention and contained an ossuary that bears Jesus' name? But the effect on the Christian faith and message would be overwhelmingly devastating.

As soon as the horrible secret leaked out, how would the early proclamation of the gospel—the deity, death, and resurrection of Jesus—ever

---

59 See Gal 1:18–19; 2:1,9; Acts 15:13–21.
60 Richard Bauckham, "James and Jesus," in *The Brother of Jesus*, 135.
61 Josephus, *Ant.* 20:9:1.
62 For details, see Hershel Shanks and Ben Witherington, *The Brother of Jesus* (San Francisco: Harper Collins, 2004).

be the same? The knowledge of Jesus' reburial and the present where-abouts of His bones would hit the movement right between the eyes, indeed, in its very heart. How would it affect Peter? John? Others?

Even further, how can we make sense of Paul's conversion, based on what he likewise thought was a resurrection appearance of Jesus? With both Jesus' body and bones already being reburied by this time, does the Talpiot hypothesis reveal any new insights regarding Paul's conversion? It does not appear that the thesis helps in any way to account for Paul's transformation from a fearsome persecutor to an ardent believer in Jesus Christ. But Paul's conversion must be explained thoroughly, due to the central nature of his experience and his early resurrection report. As a former Pharisee (Phil 3:5–6), it is even more clear that Paul believed in bodily resurrection, as they did. This is further evident in his works.[63]

There is not the slightest sign that Jesus' disciples or Paul thought that Jesus might not have been raised, that His bones were resting in a Talpiot grave, or that they were less than totally committed to the truth of the resurrection. The testimonies of James, Peter, and Paul were sealed by their deaths as martyrs for the gospel they preached, as indicated by first-century sources.[64] This means that they were totally convinced of the central truth of Jesus' resurrection, and they believed this gospel message to the end of their lives. This resurrection belief provides several powerful refutations of the Talpiot hypothesis.

As mentioned above, Tabor holds that James and perhaps even Jesus' disciples did not believe in Jesus' resurrection but saw Him as simply continuing the line of the Jewish prophets and John the Baptist. We cannot repeat our earlier evaluation, but there are multiple reasons why this view fails. The early pre-Pauline creedal formula in 1 Cor 15:3–7 and Paul's visits to Jerusalem (Gal 1:18–2:10) to confirm the gospel message are highly evidential. And these texts pertain not only to Paul himself but to at least the views of James, Peter, and John. As the chief leaders of the church, this was their message too (1 Cor 15:11–15), resulting in a renewed effort to continue their missionary activity with more zeal than ever (Gal 2:9–10).

63 See Wright, *Resurrection of the Son of God,* chaps. 5–8; Gundry, chaps. 5–7, 13; Habermas and Licona, chap. 9, and Michael Licona's essay in this volume.
64 For James' martyrdom, see Josephus, *Ant.* 20:9:1. For Peter's and Paul's martyrdom, see Clement of Rome, *To the Corinthians* 5.

This is why there is minimal scholarly dissent to the assertion that the resurrection of Jesus was absolutely central to Christian origins, contrary to Tabor's thesis. This definitely includes not only the four main leaders—Paul, James, Peter, and John—but also mother Mary and Mary Magdalene, as well as the other disciples.

Tabor also holds that Paul believed in spiritual resurrection appearances. But the problems with this hypothesis are simply immense. From the beginning, the earliest proclamation was the unwavering conviction that Jesus had appeared to His followers. From centuries before Jesus until a couple of centuries after His death, the chief New Testament terms for "resurrection" *(anastasis)* and "raise" *(egeirō)* virtually always referred to the *body*, not to the immaterial portion of persons. And the words were used in this manner by almost everyone in the ancient world—pagans, Jews, and Christians alike.[65] Moreover, in Paul's works, the human body *(sōma)* was corporeal, and the resurrection body of Jesus was "physical in nature."[66] So Paul did *not* claim that Jesus was somehow spiritually alive while His body rotted.

Additionally, in the pre-Pauline creed(s) that we have discussed (1 Cor 15:3–7), both individuals and groups claimed to have seen the risen Jesus, which is hardly even questioned in the critical scholarly literature. But group appearances, like an empty tomb, are much more conducive to substantial, bodily appearances. Once again we must account for what the earliest evidence indicates rather than trying to fit another scenario instead. Michael Licona's chapter in this volume addresses other aspects of this view in much greater detail.

Now we must summarize the issue in this chapter by *adding* to the earlier list of problems related to Jesus' burial, as engendered by the Talpiot hypothesis. This thesis does not adequately explain the critically ascertained historical facts regarding the convictions of the disciples, James the brother of Jesus, and Paul that they had seen the risen Jesus, convictions that seem to be verified by their subsequent transformations and martyrdoms for the gospel message.[67]

---

65 See especially Wright, *The Resurrection of the Son of God,* chaps. 2–11.

66 Gundry, *Sōma in Biblical Theology,* 82. See also chaps. 5–7, and especially chap. 13: "The *Sōma* in Death and Resurrection."

67 This conclusion was derived by critical means, *not* by concluding that the Talpiot position is wrong because the New Testament says so. Thus, the evidence that we have used to support the historical facts indicates that the thesis is repeatedly mistaken. This is why virtually all scholars have reacted so strongly against these ideas.

Some of the chief issues are as follows: (1) That the early Christian view is that of *bodily* resurrection is established by many factors, including a) the predominant Jewish view in the first century AD, b) the almost unanimous use of the relevant terms *anastasis* and *egeirō* in the ancient world, whether by pagans, Jews, or Christians alike, c) Paul's use of the term *sōma*, and d) the ossuary process itself. (2) With such a definition, how could Jesus' mother Mary and Mary Magdalene reconcile their eyewitness experience of appearances of the risen Jesus with their certainty that His body and bones remained in a local tomb? (3) How can we explain the conversion of James, the brother of Jesus, from skepticism, his personal confirmation of the gospel message of the deity, death, and resurrection of Jesus, as well as his lifelong piety and service to the Jerusalem church, when he too, knew that Jesus' bones were in the family tomb? (4) Peter, John, and the other apostles also confirmed this gospel message, including the centrality of the resurrection. To postulate that word of Jesus' reburial by Joseph and His later interment in the ossuary never leaked out to the apostles is simply too much to suppose. (5) The Talpiot hypothesis fails to account for Paul's experience of Jesus' postresurrection appearance and his own conversion, which would most likely have occurred after the ossuary reburial. (6) The zeal of Jesus' chief apostles, followed by their recorded martyrdoms, indicates that they believed to the very end, in spite of their knowledge of the reburials.

CONCLUSION

The Talpiot tomb hypothesis lacks explanatory scope and power, both of which are key ingredients in historical research. It is opposed by the historical evidence at virtually every turn. Thus it stumbles on virtually every one of its major claims. Scarcely has a theory regarding the historical Jesus *ever* been confronted by more major refutations.

Even more seldom has almost the entire scholarly community—skeptical, liberal, moderate, and conservative alike—joined ranks and reacted with almost a single voice against a hypothesis. In fact, a quick survey indicates that critical scholars may be leading the charge even more than their conservative counterparts. "The thesis is clearly refuted by the evidence" could be the clarion cry that has arisen time and again.

In light of virtually all the facts attested by contemporary biblical scholarship, there can be little doubt that the Talpiot hypothesis was tried in the scholarly courts and found wanting.

PAUL ON THE NATURE OF THE RESURRECTION BODY

Michael Licona

INTRODUCTION

Suppose you are watching the evening news and the lead story concerns a team of archaeologists in Jerusalem all of whom are highly respected for their painfully careful work. They have just discovered an interesting ossuary in a tomb that has been sealed since the first century. The ossuary is a box that is approximately 20 inches long, 10 inches wide, and 12 inches tall. They observe an inscription on the side of the ossuary that is uniquely written in Aramaic, Greek, and Latin.

The archaeologists carefully brush and blow the dirt off of the box until they are able to discern the inscription in all three languages: "Jesus of Nazareth, son of Joseph." The lid of the ossuary is carefully removed, and we are all startled by what we see: the skeletal remains of a victim that appears to have been crucified and an ancient document made of papyrus written in Greek.

Two of the archaeologists are skilled at reading the ancient language, and after one minute their voices become noticeably louder and their speech more rapid as they compare their translations of the first page, which contains a single statement in large letters. They look at each other in amazement then share their translations with the news crews present. "This document says, 'We fooled the world until today!' And it is signed by Matthew, Mark, Luke, and John!"

This scenario isn't even close to what occurred in New York City on February 25, 2007 when James Cameron, Simcha Jacobovici, and

Charles Pellegrino announced they had identified the family tomb and skeletal remains of Jesus in Jerusalem. The announcement rightfully received wide coverage. After all, for 2,000 years Christians have proclaimed, "Christ has been raised from the dead." If the resurrection of Jesus actually occurred, then whose bones are we looking at? Or should we instead be asking whether we can still believe Christ is risen if these are the bones of Jesus?

In the book that quickly followed the announcement, Pellegrino wrote, "People who believe in a physical Resurrection would not be affected by the discovery of a Jesus bone box."[1] He also published a correspondence concerning the resurrection of Jesus he had with Father Mervyn Fernando of the Subhodi Institute in Sri Lanka. Fernando wrote that "the risen body of Christ (as understood by the apostle Paul) is a spiritual one, not the material/physical one he had in his lifetime. That physical body would have perished, and if any parts of it (bones) are recovered/identified, it would in no way affect the reality of his Resurrection."[2]

Fernando is not the only one to hold this position. James Tabor of UNC (Charlotte), who is perhaps the only scholar who has supported the Talpiot tomb proposal by Jacobovici, Pellegrino, and Cameron, made a similar statement during the Ted Koppel panel discussion that aired immediately after the documentary's initial showing on the Discovery Channel. Answering New Testament scholar Darrell Bock, he appealed to the writings of Paul in support of his position that the initial claim of Christians is that Jesus was raised *spiritually*.[3] In the documentary itself, John Dominic Crossan of the Jesus Seminar commented that if the bones of Jesus were ever discovered it would not affect his Christian faith.

Should a discovery of Jesus' bones impact the faith of Christians? Would such a discovery reveal that Christianity is a false religion? Why is Paul's understanding of *resurrection* so important in answering these questions? For Paul and the other apostles, the resurrection of Jesus is the divine event that confirms the truth of Christianity. They preached this in their sermons, and the Gospels report that Jesus Himself named His

1 Simcha Jacobovici and Charles Pellegrino, *The Jesus Family Tomb* (San Francisco: HarperSanFrancisco, 2007), 70.
2 Ibid., 74.
3 Also see James D. Tabor, *The Jesus Dynasty: The Hidden History of Jesus, His Royal Family, and the Birth of Christianity* (New York: Simon and Schuster, 2006), 232, 262–64.

resurrection as the event that would confirm His message.[4] Paul asserted, "If Christ has not been raised, your faith is *worthless!* You are still in your sins. Moreover, those who have already died with hope in Christ have perished."[5]

If the claim of the apostles is that Christ was raised in a *spiritual* (meaning immaterial) sense, a discovery of His bones would not falsify Christianity. On the other hand, if the claim of the apostles is that Christ was raised *bodily* leaving behind an empty tomb, a discovery of His bones would indeed falsify Christianity, revealing that its confirming event never occurred. Accordingly, this is not a "splitting of theological hairs" with little impact. A lot hinges on the definition of *resurrection*; more specifically, what the apostles meant when they claimed that Jesus had been raised from the dead.

ANCIENT VIEWS OF THE AFTERLIFE

No differently than today, those who lived in antiquity had numerous views of the afterlife. Some denied it altogether. Others thought of the afterlife in terms of disembodied existence. Still others anticipated embodied existence. Even Jewish views of the afterlife varied. A number of Jews believed that on the final day when God judges the world, the corpses of believers will be restored to life and transformed into immortal bodies.[6] They called this "resurrection."[7]

This provides a little background on at least one meaning of resurrection for Jews in the first century, and it may be the only one. The most recent comprehensive treatment of the subject was done by British scholar N. T. Wright.[8] Wright concluded that when ancient Jews prior to and contemporaneous with Jesus spoke of a future resurrection, they

4 Matthew 12:38–40; 16:1–4; John 2:18–21; Acts 2:23–32; 10:39–43; 13:28–39; 17:2–3, 30–32; Rom 1:4.
5 First Corinthians 15:17–18. In the Greek text, the location of the word translated "worthless" gives it emphasis. All translations provided in this chapter are my own unless indicated otherwise.
6 In the Old Testament, see Exod 37; Isa 26:19; Dan 12:2. Also see 2 Macc. 7:9–42; 12:43–45 in the Intertestamental Period.
7 Two Greek words were usually employed for "resurrection": *anastasis*, a noun that means a "rising up"; *egeirō*, a verb that means "to arise" (sometimes used of those waking from sleep).
8 N. T. Wright, *The Resurrection of the Son of God* (Philadelphia: Fortress, 2003). See especially 32–206 for a treatment of views of the afterlife in the world prior to Jesus. See

always meant by it as something that occurred to corpses. However, I do not wish to belabor this point. For we know that the early Christians, who were Jews, apparently felt freedom to revise long-held Jewish views such as the role of the Jewish Law, the observance of the Sabbath, the role of Messiah, the nature of the kingdom of God, and even the nature of God. If they were willing to modify their view of God to conceive of Him as existing in three Persons, an even radical modification of the meaning of *resurrection* is not out of the question. Moreover, if the first-century Christians did not make such a change, the Gnostics of the second and third centuries did.[9] And thoughts similar to those held by the Gnostics related to the meaning of resurrection may even go as far back as the first century.[10] Whether the early Christians modified the view of resurrection as an event that happens to a corpse is another matter and one to which this chapter seeks to contribute.

PAUL'S VIEW OF THE AFTERLIFE

The New Testament Gospels are clear that the resurrection of Jesus was an event that restored the corpse of Jesus to a new and immortal life. His tomb was empty, and the disciples were able to see Him, hear Him, walk with Him, touch Him, and share a meal with Him. Their view of res-urrection fit well with the Jewish view at the time. But the Gospels may have been written 30–70 years after Jesus' death. The majority of schol-ars believe that they were all written after Paul had carried out his entire ministry, had written all of his letters, and had been martyred. Could they have modified an even earlier Christian view of resurrection?

Virtually all who study first-century Christianity admit that Paul is the earliest known author to comment on the resurrection of Jesus. Accordingly, his views on what happened to Jesus after His crucifixion carry a great amount of weight. What then if Paul—who is certain to have known the apostles and even had the gospel he preached approved by them—taught that the corpse of Jesus was not at all impacted by His resurrection, which was solely *spiritual*, meaning on an *immaterial*

also Wright's response to critics in N. T. Wright, "Resurrecting Old Arguments: Respond-ing to Four Essays," *Journal for the Study of the Historical Jesus* 3 (1985): 209–31.
9 *Apocalypse of Peter* 82–83; *Exeg. Soul* 134.6–12; *Gos. Phil.* 56.15–19; 66.7–22; 73.1–4; *Testim. Truth* 34–37; *Treat. Res.* (a.k.a. *The Epistle to Rheginos*) 45.40–46.1; 48.3–50.1.
10 Second Timothy 2:17–18.

dimension?[11] The atheist New Testament scholar Gerd Lüdemann would be correct when he asserts, "You have to start with Paul and see that the Gospel stories are later developments."[12] If Pellegrino (*a la* Fernando), Tabor, and Crossan are correct, the resurrection narratives in the Gospels would be later developments that do not reflect the earlier teachings of Paul on the resurrection of Jesus nor probably those of the other apostles who first reported that Jesus had been resurrected.

What did Paul mean when he claimed that Christ has been raised? Fortunately, we have several letters written by him, and they are rightly the focal point for a discussion on what the apostles meant when they claimed that Jesus had been raised. Since Paul's letters were written to address specific situations and questions in the particular churches to whom they are addressed, the topic of the nature of Jesus' resurrection apparently was not often part of those situations and questions. However, on five occasions Paul states that the resurrection of Jesus is a model for our own future resurrection at the second coming of Christ.[13] Therefore, when Paul discusses the future resurrection of believers, we may gain insight into his beliefs about the nature of the resurrection of Jesus. There are five major texts in Paul's letters that are important: 1 Cor 15:42–54; 2 Cor 4:16–5:8; Rom 8:11; Phil 3:21; Gal 1:11–19. By far, the first is of greatest importance and is the text appealed to most by those who contend that Jesus' resurrection did not involve His corpse and that He was instead raised in a "spiritual" or immaterial body. Accordingly, given space restraints we will devote the remainder of this chapter to a careful examination of this text.

> So also is the resurrection of the dead. It is sown
> in corruption. It is raised in incorruption. It is sown in
> dishonor. It is raised in glory. It is sown in weakness.
> It is raised in power. It is sown a natural body. It is
> raised a spiritual body. If there is a natural body, there
> is also a spiritual [body]. So also it is written, "The

---

11 See Gal 1:18–19; 2:1–10. Few modern scholars hold that Paul invented Christianity as we know it today. For reasons, see Michael R. Licona, *Paul Meets Muhammad* (Grand Rapids: Baker, 2006), 73–81.

12 Gerd Lüdemann, "First Rebuttal," in Paul Copan and Ronald K. Tacelli, eds., *Jesus' Resurrection: Fact or Figment? A Debate Between William Lane Craig and Gerd Lüdemann* (Downers Grove: InterVarsity, 2000), 55.

13 First Thessalonians 4:14; 1 Cor 6:14; 15:20; 2 Cor 4:14; Rom 8:11.

first man, Adam, became a living soul. The last Adam [became] a life-giving spirit." But the spiritual is not first, but the natural; then the spiritual. The first man is from the dust; the second man is from heaven. As the dust is, such also are the dusty [i.e., earthly] ones. And as the heaven is, such also are the heavenly ones. And just as we have borne the image of dust, we shall also bear the image of the heavenly. Now this I say, brothers: Flesh and blood is not able to inherit the kingdom of God; nor can the corruptible inherit the incorruptible. Behold, I tell you a mystery. All shall not sleep, but all will be changed in a moment, in a blink of an eye, at the last trumpet. For the trumpet will sound and the dead in Christ will be raised incorruptible and we will be changed. For, it is necessary that this corruptible will put on incorruption and this mortal will put on immortality. Now when this corruptible has put on incorruption and this mortal has put on immortality, then the word that was written shall be [fulfilled]: "Death is swallowed up in victory" (1 Cor 15:42–54).

This is Paul's most important passage on resurrection. In it, Paul answered two questions: "How are the dead raised and what will our future bodies be like?" He answered both questions, "So is the resurrection of the dead. It is sown. . . . It is raised" (15:42). At first glance the change from the plural "dead" to the singular "it" in his answer appears slightly awkward. A closer look provides clarity. For in 15:42 Paul answered the questions asked in 15:35: How are the dead (plural) raised and with what kind of body (singular) do they come? In 15:42–44 he wrote, "So also is the resurrection of the dead (plural): It [i.e., the body] (singular) is sown. . . . It is raised." In the text immediately preceding (15:37–38), Paul provided the analogy of a seed: A seed is sown and something different comes up. But there is continuity between the seed and the plant that comes forth from it as indicated by 15:36: "That which you sow is not *made alive* unless it dies." The seed that is *dead* and *sown* (buried) is *made alive* once again. In the same way, there is continuity between the believer's present body (the seed) and the resurrection body. What dies and goes down in burial comes up in resurrection, having been made alive and transformed.[14] This is confirmed by Paul's use of the pronoun "this" in 15:53–54: "*This* perishable will put on the imperishable; *this* mortal will put on immortality"; and so forth.[15] One can almost see Paul grabbing his arm as he emphasizes that *this* body will put on immortality as one puts on a coat. A transformation of the corpse will occur, and it will be clothed with immortality and imperishability. There can be no doubt that what is being sown in 15:42–44 is our present body. There can be little doubt that the third-person singular "it" that is sown is what is raised. Thus, the body that is sown is transformed and raised. There is neither an elimination of a body nor an exchange of the old for the new. Rather, it is the mortal body being transformed into immortality.

This implies a bodily resurrection and an empty tomb. If it is true that Paul is employing the term *resurrection* in a sense that the body that is buried is the same body that is raised, though transformed, one need not ask why the empty tomb is never mentioned in the Pauline corpus. For him, it is so clear that it need not be mentioned. Today, if a child dies of SIDS, the parents would not need to make a point of an empty crib. It is implied. It is therefore interesting to note a number of scholars who assert that Paul was not aware of an empty tomb.[16] Even the skeptical New Testament scholar Marcus Borg writes, "One additional comment as we leave Paul: he does not mention an empty tomb. What to make of this is unclear. Is it without significance? Possibly. Paul may have known

14 Paul Ellingsworth and Howard Hatton, *A Translator's Handbook on Paul's First Letter to the Corinthians* (New York: United Bible Societies, 1993), 317; Gordon D. Fee, *The First Epistle to the Corinthians* (Grand Rapids: Eerdmans, 1987), 777; Simon J. Kistemaker, *Exposition of the First Epistle to the Corinthians* (Grand Rapids: Baker, 1993), 572–73. N. T. Wright, *The Resurrection of the Son of God* (Minneapolis: Fortress, 2003), is correct, however, in writing, "The new resurrected body will be in continuity and discontinuity with the present one" (341). The discontinuity pertains to the corruption/incorruption, etc. (360; cf. 371).

15 William Lane Craig, *Assessing the New Testament Evidence for the Historicity of the Resurrection of Jesus* (New York: Edwin Mellen Press, 1989), 144; Robert H. Gundry, "Trimming the Debate," in *Jesus' Resurrection*, 122; Alan F. Segal, *Life after Death: A History of the Afterlife in Western Religion* (New York: Doubleday, 2004), 433; cf. 439–40.

16 Peter Carnley, *The Structure of Resurrection Belief* (New York: Oxford, 1987), 53; Roy W. Hoover, "A Contest Between Orthodoxy and Veracity," in *Jesus' Resurrection*, 130; Gerd Lüdemann, *The Resurrection of Jesus* (London: SCM, 1995), 46. However, see what may be a reversal in Gerd Lüdemann who now grants that, based largely on 1 Corinthians 15, "it is reasonable to assume that Paul considered Jesus' tomb to have been empty" (Gerd Lüdemann, *The Resurrection of Christ* [Amherst, NY: Prometheus, 2004], 70); Segal, *Life after Death*, 447.

about and believed that the tomb of Jesus was empty but found it unnecessary to mention this in letters written to people whom he had taught in person."[17] We come now to four points of contention in this passage:

"Natural" and "Spiritual" Bodies. In 15:44 Paul stated that the body is sown as a "natural" *(psychikon)* and raised a "spiritual" *(pneumatikon)* body. Members of the Talpiot tomb team and some scholars interpret these words to mean "physical" and "immaterial."[18] Indeed, a few English translations and even a few Greek lexica have adopted these meanings related to this passage.[19] We will need to search the ancient literature carefully in order to obtain a good understanding of what the ancients meant when using these words.

There are 846 occurrences of "natural" *(psychikon)* from the eighth century BC through the third century AD.[20] There were only five occurrences prior to the fourth century BC in extant sources, but usage exploded in the first century BC and continued into the first century AD. Then the number of occurrences in the first century increased by 1,000 percent in the second century. Especially interesting is that "natural" is often contrasted with "body."[21] In fact, "natural" can dwell in the "body."[22] Starting with Pseudo-Galen in the second/third-century AD, "natural" *(psychikon)* is often contrasted with another word for "natural" *(physikon)*, which lays an emphasis on the natural order of things and can even mean "physical."[23] In Pseudo-Plutarch, "demons" are described

17 Marcus J. Borg, *Jesus: Uncovering the Life, Teachings, and Relevance of a Religious Revolutionary* (San Francisco: HarperSanFrancisco, 2006), 279.
18 Pellegrino in Jacobovici and Pellegrino, *Jesus Family Tomb*, 74.
19 See the RSV, NRSV, AMP. For Greek lexica, see Walter Bauer, *A Greek-English Lexicon of the New Testament and Other Early Christian Literature*, 3rd ed. by Frederick W. Danker (Chicago: University of Chicago Press, 2000), 1,100; Timothy Friberg, Barbara Friberg, and Neva F. Miller, *Analytical Lexicon of the Greek New Testament* (Grand Rapids: Baker Books, 2000), 414; Barclay Moon Newman, *Concise Greek-English Dictionary of the New Testament* (New York: United Bible Societies, 1993), 201; Johannes P. Louw and Eugene Albert Nida, *Greek-English Lexicon of the New Testament: Based on Semantic Domains*, electronic ed. of the 2nd edition (New York: United Bible Societies, 1996, © 1989), 1:693.
20 These and the findings for *pneumatikon* are the results of a TLG search (disk E). There were no occurrences of either word in the Oxyrhynchus papyri.
21 *psychikon/sōma.*
22 *psychikon/sōma.*
23 See *Introductio seu medicus* 14.697.7; 14.726.7; Alexander, *De anima libri mantissa* 104.4, mentions a *sōmatos phusikou.*

as "natural."[24] Of even more interest are the combinations "of spiritual nature," "natural spirit," "of natural spirit," and "the natural spirit,"[25] first appearing in the third century BC in Erasistratus[26] and Chrysippus,[27] then Alexander,[28] then Cassius Iatrosophista,[29] and Vettius Valens.[30] Although I did not look at all of the 846 occurrences. I viewed most. I failed to find a single reference where the word natural *(psychikon) possessed a meaning of "physical" or "material."*

There were 1,131 occurrences of "spiritual" *(pneumatikon)* during the same time period.[31] It appeared first in the sixth century BC, with an explosion of occurrences in the first century AD. An almost 400-percent growth occurred in the second century. On numerous occasions the word referred to the immaterial. However, there are a robust number of exceptions. Of particular interest is Zeno's "spiritual ones" who enjoy Stoic teachings.[32] The Corpus Hermeticum (second century AD) mentions the "spiritual man."[33] Chrysippus (third century BC) spoke of our "bodies" having a "spiritual" essence[34] and of a "spiritual and ethereal body."[35] Notice that "spiritual" is distinguished here from "ethereal." A "spiritual body" was mentioned also by Democritus (fifth century BC),[36] Straton (third century BC),[37] Comarius (second century AD),[38] Clement of Alexandria (third century AD),[39] and Pseudo-Plutarch (third/fourth century).[40] With the possible exception of Chrysippus, none of these seem to be referring to immaterial or ethereal bodies. However, Ptolemaeus (second

---

24 *daimonioi/psychikas. Placita philosophorum* 882.B.5. Outside of Christian writings, demons were not necessarily regarded as evil beings.
25 *pneumatos psychikou*; *psychikon pneuma*; *psychikou pneumatos; to pneuma to psychikon.*
26 *Testimonia et fragmenta* 112.2; 147.17; 203.1.
27 *Fragmenta logica et physica* 716.2; 722.2; 781.3; 783.2; 870.2.
28 *Problemata* 2.64.28; 2.67.40.
29 *Quaestiones medicae et problemata physica* 52.3; 72.9.
30 *Anthologiarum libri ix* 109.13.
31 Of these, 610 appear in Origen (third century AD), the majority of which describe the "spirituality" of the Law.
32 *hoi pneumatikoi. Testimonia et fragmenta* 33.2.
33 *pneumatikon anthrōpon. Fragmenta varia* 21.2.
34 *sōmatikōn/pneumatikē. Fragmenta logica et physica* 389.5.
35 *sōma pneumatikon kai aitherōdes. Fragmenta logica et physica* 1054.13.
36 *Testimonia* 140.2.
37 *Fragmenta* 94.2.
38 *De lapide philosophorum* 2.290.18.
39 *Eclogae propheticae* 55.1.1.
40 *Placita philosophorum* 905.B.7.

century AD) appears to think along these lines when he spoke of converting or changing from "bodily" to "spiritual."[41] Philo argued that some prophets and angels changed their former essence from "spiritual" and "natural" to "one of human form."[42] For him, angels have an essence that is "spiritual" and "natural" and neither relate to human form.

I realize this is all quite technical. So, I will summarize our discussion thus far on the two terms in 1 Cor 15:44: "natural" and "spiritual." The term "spiritual" *(pneumatikon)* has numerous meanings throughout the ancient literature and can refer to something as "immaterial," although this is not necessary and there are other meanings for the term. With only one possible exception, when the term "spiritual" is connected to the word "body," it does not refer to an "immaterial body." The word "natural" *(psychikon)* never appears to take a meaning of "physical" or "material." Focusing our attention on early Christian uses of these two words will prove even more helpful.

The term "spiritual" *(pneumatikon)* appears 28 times within the New Testament writings. All but three of these occurrences appear in Paul's letters.[43] "Spiritual" was employed by Paul in 1 Cor 2:15; 3:1; 14:37; and Gal 6:1 in the sense of the spiritually mature. In 1 Cor 2:13–14 (spiritual wisdom); 9:11 (spiritual blessings); 10:3–4 (spiritual food and drink in the wilderness; i.e., physical food provided by God); 12:1 (spiritual gifts); and 14:1 (spiritual gifts), it refers to something that has to do with the Holy Spirit or has the Holy Spirit as its origin or power. Other occurrences in Paul's letters include Rom 1:11 (spiritual gift); 7:14 (the Law is spiritual); 15:27 (spiritual blessings); Eph 1:3 (spiritual blessing); 5:19 (spiritual songs); 6:12 (where "spiritual" forces of evil are contrasted with "flesh and blood"); Col 1:9 (spiritual wisdom and understanding); and 3:16 (spiritual songs). The term appears in two New Testament passages outside of Paul's letters: 1 Pet 2:5 (spiritual sacrifices) and Rev 11:8 (spiritually named). In the latter reference the word may be translated "figuratively" (NIV), "symbolically" (NET), "mystically" (NASB), "allegorically" (RSV), or "prophetically" (NRSV). "Spiritual" *(pneumatikon)* is absent in the ancient Greek translation of the Old Tes-

---

41 *Epistula ad Floram* 6.4.2.

42 *pnematikēs kai psychoeidous; anthrōpomorphon. On Abraham* 113.2; see also *1 Genesis* 1.92.

43 Romans 1:11; 7:14; 15:27; 1 Cor 2:13 (twice), 14,15; 3:1; 9:11; 10:3,4 (twice); 12:1; 14:1, 37; 15:44 (twice), 46 (twice); Gal 6:1; Eph 1:3; 5:19; 6:12; Col 1:9; 3:16; 1 Pet 2:5 (twice); Rev 11:8.

tament called the Septuagint. Therefore, with the possible exception of Eph 6:12, Paul never employs "spiritual" *(pneumatikon)* in a sense that means "immaterial."[44]

"Natural" *(psychikon)* appears only six times in the New Testament, ~~four of which are in Paul's letter of 1 Corinthians (2:14, 15:44 [2x],~~ 15:46). The first reference is of particular interest, since not only is it the lone appearance in Paul outside of 1 Corinthians 15 but also because Paul used the precise contrast of terms he employed in 1 Cor 15:44 and 46. He wrote:

> But the *natural* man does not accept the things
> of the Spirit of God, for they are foolishness to him.
> And he is unable to understand them because they are
> *spiritually* examined.

In the following verse (2:15), Paul spoke of *spiritual* persons in contrast to the *natural* persons: "But the *spiritual* examine all things, but he himself is examined by no one." It is clear here that Paul was not contrasting physical beings with those who are immaterial. Rather, he was contrasting those who are led or animated by their fleshly and sinful desires and who think in accordance with the world's wisdom with those led by holy desires and heavenly wisdom who are centered on God. Richard Hays of Duke put it this way: "The term *psychikoi* is difficult to translate properly; it refers to human beings living in their natural state apart from the Spirit of God and therefore unenlightened and blind to the truth. They just don't 'get it.'"[45] On the other hand, the *spiritual* person "has a privileged understanding of reality."[46] We can imagine Paul handing out T-shirts to the members of the Corinth Community Church. The front of the shirt reads, "The Wisdom of God." The back reads, "You wouldn't understand. It's a spiritual thing." Again, it is crystal clear that Paul was not contrasting material and immaterial things since for him humans can be *natural* or *spiritual*. In other words, when employing

---

44 We will observe below that the term "flesh and blood" refers to "mortals" rather than "physical." Thus, even in Eph 6:12, "spiritual" *(pneumatikos)* probably does not mean "immaterial."

45 Richard B. Hays, *First Corinthians* (Louisville: John Knox, 1997), 46. David A. Ackerman, *Lo, I Tell You a Mystery: Cross, Resurrection, and Paraenesis in the Rhetoric of 1 Corinthians* (Eugene, OR: Pickwick, 2006) renders *psychikos* in 1 Cor 2:15 as "unspiritual" (53) and in 15:44 as "earthbound" or "unspiritual" (94).

46 Hays, *First Corinthians*, 46.

the terms "natural" and "spiritual," Paul was not referring to the substance or composition of the old and new bodies but rather their mode of existence.[47] Later on in 15:44 when Paul employed these same terms, he was saying that our current body is buried with all of its "natural" or "this-worldly" appetites and weaknesses but is raised and transformed into a new body with spiritual appetites and qualities.[48] He may also have been including the power that animates the body.[49] Modern machines are empowered in numerous ways: steam, diesel, nuclear, and such. Our present mortal body is animated or empowered by a heart, lungs, and so forth. Our resurrection body will be empowered by God's Spirit.

Other New Testament occurrences of the term "natural" support an interpretation along these lines. "Natural" appears on two other occasions in the New Testament. In Jas 3:15, it is used to contrast a proper spiritual state of the heart with one that is not from God, which James describes as earthly, *natural*, or even demonic. In Jude 19, the term refers to mockers focused on their ungodly lusts, who cause divisions, are *natural*, and do not have the Holy Spirit. The word appears three times in the Septuagint, all in the Apocrypha. In 2 Macc 4:37 and 14:24, it is employed as an adverb to mean "heartily" in reference to emotions of grief and warmth. In 4 Macc 1:32, being temperate is mastery over the desires of "souls" and the desires of bodies.[50] As examples of the former, the author mentioned overcoming greed, choosing virtue over affection for parents, and a willingness to rebuke one's wife, children, and friends when they act wrongly. It repeals the love of power, vainglory, pride, arrogance, slander, and anger (2:8–20). Thus, with the lone improbable exception of Eph 6:12, neither Paul nor any other New Testament author nor any writer or translator of the Septuagint refers to "natural" *(psychikos)* or "spiritual" *(pneumatikos)* in the senses understood by the Talpiot tomb team and certain scholars.[51] Granted, the terms maintain a

---

47 Alan F. Johnson, *1 Corinthians,* IVP New Testament Commentary, ed. Grant R. Osborne (Downers Grove: InterVarsity, 2004), 304–5; Craig S. Keener, *1–2 Corinthians* (New York: Cambridge, 2005), 132; Kevin Quest, *Reading the Corinthian Correspondence: An Introduction* (New York and Mahwah, NJ: Paulist, 1994), 96; Nigel Watson, *The First Epistle to the Corinthians,* Epworth Commentaries (London: Epworth, 1992), 176.

48 Ackerman, *Lo I Tell You a Mystery,* 96.

49 Hays, *First Corinthians,* 272.

50 *psychika/sōmatikai.*

51 The following modern commentators maintain that Paul's contrast between "natural" *(psychikos)* and "spiritual" *(pneumatikos)* is not a contrast between the "physical" and "immaterial": Ackerman, *Lo, I Tell You a Mystery,* 96; C. K. Barrett, *A Commentary on the*

First Epistle to the Corinthians (New York: Harper and Row, 1968), 373; Gerald Bostock, "Osiris and the Resurrection of Christ," *Expository Times* 112 (2001): 271; Scott Brodeur, *The Holy Spirit's Agency in the Resurrection of the Dead: An Exegetico-Theological Study of 1 Corinthians 15,44b–49 and Romans 8,9–13* (Rome: Gregorian University Press, 1996), 122; Raymond F. Collins, *First Corinthians*, Sacra Pagina 7, ed. Daniel J. Harrington (Collegeville, MN: Liturgical Press, 1999), 567; Hans Conzelmann, *1 Corinthians*, trans. James W. Leitch (Philadelphia: Fortress, 1975), 290; Fee, *The First Epistle to the Corinthians*, 788–89; Robert H. Gundry, *Sōma in Biblical Theology: With Emphasis on Pauline Anthropology* (New York: Cambridge, 1976), 165–66; Murray J. Harris, *Raised Immortal: Resurrection and Immortality in the New Testament* (Grand Rapids: Eerdmans, 1985), 118; Hays, *First Corinthians*, contends that the "NRSV's translation ('physical body') is especially unfortunate, for it reinstates precisely the dualistic dichotomy between physical and spiritual that Paul is struggling to overcome. In any case, *psychikon* certainly does not mean 'physical'" (272); Jean Héring, *The First Epistle of Saint Paul to the Corinthians* (London: Epworth Press, 1962), 176–77; Larry Hurtado, *Lord Jesus Christ: Devotion to Jesus in Earliest Christianity* (Grand Rapids: Eerdmans, 2003): "'Spiritual' here can only mean empowered by the Spirit, as Paul consistently uses the term in this epistle" (170–71n29). Elsewhere he opines that the translation "physical" has "seriously misleading connotations" (Larry W. Hurtado, "Jesus' Resurrection in the Early Christian Texts: An Engagement with N. T. Wright," *JSHJ* 3 [2005]: 200), Alan F. Johnson, *1 Corinthians*, IVP New Testament Commentary, ed. Grant R. Osborne (Downers Grove: InterVarsity, 2004), 304–5; Kistemaker, *Exposition of the First Epistle to the Corinthians*, 573; Gregory J. Lockwood, *1 Corinthians*, Doubleday Bible Commentary (New York: Doubleday, 1998), 584–85, 589, 594–95, 602; D. Michael Martin, *1, 2 Thessalonians*, New American Commentary 3 (Nashville: Broadman & Holman, 1995), 189; Segal, *Life after Death*, like Hays above, refers to "physical body" as "an unfortunate English translation" (429); Graydon F. Snyder, *First Corinthians: A Faith Community Commentary* (Macon, GA: Mercer University Press, 1992), 206; Anthony C. Thiselton, *The First Epistle to the Corinthians: A Commentary on the Greek Text* (Grand Rapids: Eerdmans, 2000), 1275–76, 1278; Ben Witherington III, *Conflict and Community in Corinth: A Socio-Rhetorical Commentary on 1 and 2 Corinthians* (Grand Rapids: Eerdmans, 1995), 309; Wright, *The Resurrection of the Son of God*, 282, 348–55. For a contrary position, see Anthony Baxter, "Historical Judgement, Transcendent Perspective and 'Resurrection Appearances,'" *Heythrop Journal* 40 (1999): 27; John M. G. Barclay, "The Resurrection in Contemporary New Testament Scholarship" in *Resurrection Reconsidered*, ed. Gavin D'Costa (Rockport, MA: Oneworld, 1996), 17; Borg (Marcus J. Borg and N. T. Wright, *The Meaning of Jesus: Two Visions* [San Francisco: HarperSanFrancisco, 1998]) correctly understands what these terms mean before allowing his misunderstanding of the term "flesh and blood" to lead him astray: "the Greek phrase behind 'physical body' means literally 'a body animated by soul,' and the second phrase means 'a body animated by spirit.' Yet the context suggests to me that the contrast 'physical body' and 'spiritual body' does express what Paul means. According to other things Paul says in the immediate context the 'body animated by soul' is 'flesh and blood,' 'perishable,' 'of the earth,' 'of dust.' This is what we typically mean by a physical body. The 'body animated by spirit,' on the other hand, is none of these things" (133); James D. G. Dunn, *1 Corinthians*, New Testament Guides (Sheffield: Sheffield Academic Press, 1995): "It makes better sense to see his distinction between the 'natural (physical) body' of this life and the 'spiritual body' of the resurrection (15.44) as an attempt to re-express Jewish understanding of existence as always an embodied existence in a way which made more sense to those who thought in Greek terms" (40); S. H. Hooke, *The Resurrection of Christ as History and Experience* (London: Darton, Longman and Todd, 1967), 55; Jerome

degree of ambiguity for us modern readers and, perhaps, for Paul's readers as well. Notwithstanding, we can come fairly close to understanding
Paul's meaning, and we may have certainty that this does not include his
comparing a physical/material body with one that is immaterial.

We have covered a lot of ground—eleven centuries worth. Our word
study of "natural" *(psychikon)* and "spiritual" *(pneumatikon)* has taken
us from the eighth century BC through the third century AD. We have
observed that "natural" *(psychikon)* is never employed in a sense that
carries the meaning of "physical" or "material." Of greater importance is
that this conclusion carries throughout the writings of the New Testament.
Of greatest importance is that Paul did not employ "natural" *(psychikon)*
and "spiritual" *(pneumatikon)* to describe a contrast of "physical/mate-
rial" and "ethereal/immaterial" in 1 Corinthians. Moreover, I would like
to add that had Paul desired to communicate this sort of contrast, he had
better words at his disposal, one of which he had used just a few chapters
earlier while using a seed analogy similar to that of 1 Corinthians 15.
In 9:11 he wrote, "If we sowed "spiritual" *(pneumatika)* things in you,
is it too much if we reap "material" *(sarkika)* things from you?"[52] If the
apostles were providing *spiritual* teachings to the Corinthian Christians,
were not they entitled to receive *material* benefits like food, clothing,
and shelter?[53] Since Paul had used both "natural" *(psychikos)* and "mate-
rial/fleshly" *(sarkikos)* earlier, if he had desired to communicate that our
resurrection body would not be physical but rather immaterial in nature,
why use the former term in a sense not employed earlier in his letter or
for that matter anywhere else in his letters, the New Testament, or by any
known author from the eighth century BC through the third century AD,

Murphy-O'Connor, *1 Corinthians,* Doubleday Bible Commentary (New York and Mahwah, NJ: Paulist, 1998), 171; Quest, *Reading the Corinthian Correspondence,* 96, 122–23;
A. J. M. Wedderburn, *Beyond Resurrection* (Peabody: Hendrickson, 1999), 66. Also see
Paul W. Gooch, *Partial Knowledge: Philosophical Studies in Paul* (Notre Dame, IN: University of Notre Dame, 1987), 69–70 and Roy A. Harrisville, *1 Corinthians,* Augsburg
Commentary on the New Testament (Minneapolis: Augsburg, 1987), 274, 281, who understand the resurrection state of believers as one of disembodiment and without continuity
with our present body, although Harrisville contends that "natural" does not mean physical
(276). I found four of 31 English translations that rendered *psychikon* as "physical": RSV,
NRSV, GWN (God's Word to the Nations Bible), and the Amplified Bible.

52 See also Rom 15:27 where Paul writes, "For if the Gentiles shared in their [i.e., Jews]
spiritual things, they ought also in their material things to serve them." Paul employs the
same Greek words for "spiritual" and "material" that he does in 1 Cor 9:11.

53 *Sarkikos* is likewise found in Rom 15:27; 1 Cor 3:3; 2 Cor 1:12; 10:4; 1 Pet 2:11. All
but the Petrine reference are found in Paul's letters.

while ignoring a clearer term used just a few chapters earlier in a similar seed analogy?[54]

"Life-Giving Spirit." We now move to the second point of contention. In 15:45 Paul referred to Adam as a "living soul" *(psychēn zōsan)* and Jesus as a "life-giving spirit" *(pneuma zōopoioun)*. He alluded to Gen 2:7: "And God formed man from the dust of the earth and breathed into his face the breath of life; and man became a living soul." In Gen 2:7 God breathed on Adam the "breath of life" *(pnoēn zōēs)*. As a result he became a "living soul" *(psychēn zōsan)*. In 1 Cor 15:45, Paul changed "breath of life" *(pnoēn zōēs)* to "spirit that is life-producing" *(pneuma zōopoioun)*: "Thus also it is written the first Adam became a living soul. The last Adam a life-giving spirit." Paul was implying that God breathed life into mortal man. Jesus will breathe life into spiritual man. The words Paul used for "soul" *(psychēn)* and "spirit" *(pneuma)* are also the roots for the terms "natural" *(psychikos)* and "spiritual" *(pneumatikos)* just discussed in the previous section. This would seem to provide little support for interpreting Paul as suggesting an immaterial body when he referred to Jesus as a "life-giving spirit." Moreover, the word for "life-giving" *(zōopoioun)* appears eleven times in the New Testament.[55] For most of these, God is said to be the giver of eschatological life and the future tense indicates that this will be a future event, namely the final resurrection of the dead. It was used by Paul in Rom 8:11 where he wrote, "The Spirit who raised Jesus from the dead will also *give life* to your mortal bodies." In this text Paul said the "life-giving Spirit" will give life to the *mortal bodies* of believers and speaks of this as a dual benefit. In 8:10 he asserted that the spirit of the Christian is made alive while the body of the Christian is dead to sin in this life. However, at the Second Coming, the body itself will be redeemed (8:23) and the Spirit that now dwells in us serves as a guarantee of our future resurrection.[56]

54 I would add that had Paul wanted to communicate that our resurrection bodies will be immaterial, he might have used *aoratos*. In Paul, this term is found in Rom 1:20; Col 1:16; 1 Tim 1:17, all in this sense. While many question the Pauline authorship of Colossians and many more reject it for 1 Timothy, a large number agree that these contain Pauline thought. Outside the writings of Paul, *aoratos* appears in Heb 11:27. In the Septuagint, it occurs in Gen 1:2; Isa 45:3; and 2 Macc 9:5.

55 John 5:21 (twice); 6:63; Rom 4:17; 8:11; 1 Cor 15:22,36,45; 2 Cor 3:6; Gal 3:21; 1 Pet 3:18; seven are in the Pauline corpus.

56 Brendan Byrne, *Romans,* Sacra Pagina Series 6, ed. Daniel J. Harrington (Collegeville, MN: The Liturgical Press, 1996), 241; Craig, *Assessing the New Testament,* 146–47; Stephen T. Davis, *Risen Indeed: Making Sense of the Resurrection* (Grand Rapids: Eerdmans,

Since Paul used the same Greek word on the same subject of our future bodies, it seems quite clear that, in 1 Corinthians and Romans, Paul held that a transformation of our present and mortal body will occur. Since Jesus was the "first fruits" of those who have died (1 Cor 15:20), it seems that Paul would likewise have thought Jesus' mortal body was raised as he appears to hint in Rom 8:11.

"Flesh and Blood." The third point of contention in 1 Corinthians 15 is verse 50 in which Paul states that "flesh and blood cannot inherit the kingdom of God, nor does the perishable inherit the imperishable." Some scholars assert that Paul was contradicting Luke, who reported Jesus saying, "A spirit does not have *flesh and bones* as you see I have" (Luke 24:39). A significant minority of today's commentators interprets "flesh and blood" as a synonym for "physical."[57] Most scholars, however, agree that it is a figure of speech—and probably a Semitism—referring to man as a mortal being. Thus Paul meant *"the living* cannot inherit the kingdom of God."[58] It resembles North Ameri-

1993), 76n24; James D. G. Dunn, *Romans 1–8,* Word Biblical Commentary 38a (Dallas: Word, 1988), 445; Joseph A. Fitzmyer, *Romans,* Anchor Bible 33 (New York: Doubleday, 1993), 491; Leon Morris, *1 Corinthians,* Tyndale New Testament Commentaries (Leicester, England: InterVarsity Press, reprint 1976), 227–28; C. F. D. Moule, "St. Paul and Dualism: The Pauline Concept of Resurrection" *NTS* 12 (1965): 106–23, 108; Robert H. Mounce, *Romans,* New American Commentary 27 (Nashville: Broadman & Holman, 1995), 179–80; John Murray, *The Epistle to the Romans,* New International Commentary on the New Testament (Grand Rapids: Eerdmans, 1968), 291–92; Grant R. Osborne, *Romans,* IVP New Testament Commentary, ed. Grant R. Osborne (Downers Grove: Intervarsity, 2004), 201; Thomas R. Schreiner, *Romans,* Baker Exegetical Commentary on the New Testament (Grand Rapids, Baker, 1998), 416; N. T. Wright, *The Resurrection of the Son of God* (Grand Rapids: Fortress, 2003), 256. Contra is C. H. Dodd, *The Epistle of Paul to the Romans,* Moffatt New Testament Commentary (London: Hodder and Stoughton, 1932), 125.

57 For an exception, see Borg, *Jesus: Uncovering the Life,* 289; Donald Wayne Viney, "Grave Doubts about the Resurrection," *Encounter* 50 (1989): 130; Watson, *First Epistle to the Corinthians,* 179.

58 Although a few of the following do not note a figure of speech, they all agree on the meaning of the phrase "flesh and blood": Paul Barnett, "The Apostle Paul, the Bishop of Newark, and the Resurrection of Jesus," *Crux* 30: (1994), 9; D. A. Carson, *Matthew,* Expositor's Bible Commentary on CD-ROM, ed. Frank Gaebelein (Grand Rapids: Zondervan, 1998), comments on Matthew 16:17; Collins, *First Corinthians,* 579; Conzelmann, *1 Corinthians,* 289–90; Craig, *Assessing the New Testament,* 141; Anders Eriksson, *Tradition as Rhetorical Proof: Pauline Argumentation in 1 Corinthians,* Coniectanea Biblica NT 29 (Stockholm: Almqvist & Wiksell, 1998), 273; David E. Garland, *1 Corinthians,* Baker Exegetical Commentary on the New Testament (Grand Rapids: Baker, 2003), 739–41; Gundry, *Sōma in Biblical Theology,* 166; Johnson, *1 Corinthians,* 306; Keener, *1–2 Corinthians,* 133; Kistemaker, *Exposition of the First Epistle,* 580–81; Lockwood,

can idioms that refer to a person as being cold-blooded, hot-blooded, or red-blooded. When referring to a "red-blooded male," North Americans are not contrasting him with one who is green-blooded. The color and temperature of one's blood are not relevant when these figures of speech are used. The term "flesh and blood" appears five times in the New Testament (three of these occurrences are in Paul's letters).[59] It appears twice in the Septuagint[60] and is common in the Rabbinic literature. In all of these instances, the term bears the primary sense of *mortality* rather than physicality.[61] That "flesh and blood" is employed in this sense in 1 Cor 15:50 is confirmed by the fact that, elsewhere in 1 Corinthians 15 where the present body is described, its mortality rather than physicality is the issue.

If "flesh and blood" is understood with the majority of commentators as a figure of speech meaning "mortal," interpreting Paul as claiming in 1 Cor 15:50 that our future bodies will be "immaterial" is exegetically unfounded.[62] He is saying that our mortal bodies in their weak state will not be what we have in the resurrection. They must be transformed. Since "flesh and blood" was a figure of speech and "flesh and bone" apparently was not, Paul is not at all contradicting Luke. Moreover, since Paul strongly hints at a resurrection of our mortal bodies elsewhere (e.g., Rom 8:11,23; 1 Cor 15:42; Phil 3:21), any interpretation of 1 Cor 15:50 that has Paul referring to an immaterial body proposes a Paul who contradicts not only Luke but also himself.

"We will be changed." The fourth and final point of contention is found in 1 Cor 15:51–52, where Paul said that on the day of resurrection "we will be changed":

> All shall not sleep, but all will be changed in a
> moment, in a blink of an eye, at the last trumpet. For

1 Corinthians, 596; William F. Orr and James Arthur Walther, *I Corinthians*, Anchor Bible (New York: Doubleday, 1976), 359; Thiselton, *The First Epistle to the Corinthians*, 1291.
59 Matthew 16:17; 1 Cor 15:50; Gal 1:16; Eph 6:12; Heb 2:14.
60 Sirach 14:18; 17:31.
61 Rudolf Meyer, *TDNT,* 7:116.
62 Ben F. Meyer, "Did Paul's View of the Resurrection of the Dead Undergo Development?" *Theological Studies* 47 (1986): "Jeremias' 1955 essay all but put an end to the idea that 'flesh and blood' (interpreted as the corporeal principle itself) had no part in final salvation. After 1955 that particular reading of the text of 1 Cor 15:50 was largely abandoned, few today being ready to follow Teichmann in suppressing the prima-facie sense of 'change' ('we shall all be changed') in favor of making it mean annihilation and new creation" (110).

the trumpet will sound and the dead in Christ will be
raised incorruptible and we will be changed. For it is
necessary that this corruptible will put on incorruption
and this mortal will put on immortality.

These verses have an earlier parallel in 1 Thess 4:16–17 where Paul
wrote:

For with a shout of command, with the voice of
an archangel, and with the trumpet of God the Lord
Himself will descend from heaven and the dead in
Christ will be raised first. Next, we who are living and
remaining will be taken at the same time with them in
the clouds to meet the Lord in the air. And thus we will
be with the Lord always.

Paul did not believe in a "soul sleep" where believers have no con-
scious existence until the second coming of Christ since, for Paul, to be
absent from the body is to be present with the Lord and this will occur
immediately upon death (2 Cor 5:8; Phil 1:21–24). Paul imagined that
dead believers are with Christ until the Second Coming, at which time
they return to their bodies and experience resurrection. Believers who are
alive at the Second Coming will have their bodies changed to immortality and will be similar to the resurrection bodies of the formerly dead
believers. Paul's thoughts in 1 Cor 15:51–52 and 1 Thess 4:16–17 support a "transformation" of the mortal body.

Some have contended that Paul is not communicating that we will
be changed in the sense of altering but is instead employing a meaning of
mercantile exchange, in other words, of *trading* one thing for another.[63]
While this meaning is possible, it is unlikely. It is difficult to translate
1 Cor 15:51–52 and 1 Thess 4:16–17 to mean an exchange. If the dead
are already with Christ, why are they raised at His second coming: "the
dead in Christ will be raised incorruptible" (1 Cor 15:52); "the dead in
Christ will be raised first" (1 Thess 4:16)?[64]

63 C. K. Barrett, *The Second Epistle to the Corinthians* (New York: Harper and Row,
1973), 153; Carnley (1987), 58; Murray J. Harris, *From Grave to Glory: Resurrection in
the New Testament* (Grand Rapids: Academie Books, 1990), writes that in verse 44 the
discontinuity is so emphasized that "the 'exchange' motif is present," but only alongside a
dominant transformation motif in verses 36–37 and 51–54 (201–2).
64 Word usage elsewhere is not very helpful. Several instances in biblical texts exist where
the meaning of *exchange* is present (Lev 27:10,33; Judg 14:13; 1 Kings 5:28; 2 Kings

Thus far we have discovered that the meaning of "altering" is clearly more at home than "exchanging" in 1 Corinthians 15 through verse 50. Paul has stated that *this* present mortal body will put on immortality, and the few remaining scholars who understand the terms "spiritual" in ~~15:44 and "flesh and blood" in 15:50 to be referring to an immaterial~~ existence are demonstrably mistaken. Indeed, most scholars agree that Paul meant an *altering* of the present mortal body.[65]

For Paul to be thinking of an exchange, he would have to be going against what he had just written earlier in the same chapter of the same letter and what he would later write in Romans and Philippians.[66] Moreover, it would go against what appears to have been a common Jewish view of resurrection as reported in the Jewish literature.[67] Thus, there is no indication that Paul imagines an exchange of one body for another. Everything points to an altering of the mortal body.

We have looked carefully at four points of contention in this passage and discovered that Paul held that resurrection is an event that happens

5:5,22,23; Ps 101 [102]:27; Gen 41:14; Neh 9:26; Isa 24:5; Ps 105 [106]:20; Jer 2:11; 2 Sam 12:20; Jer 52:33.). However, there are also instances, though fewer, where the term is used of *altering*, such as in Gen 31:7 ("your father has cheated me and *changed* my wages ten times"). For other uses in nonbiblical sources more contemporary with 1 Corinthians 15, see Josephus's *Ant.* 2:97, where Joseph's face had *changed* over the years due to aging so that his brothers did not recognize him, and the *Shephard of Hermas* Parable 9, 4:5, 8, which tells of stones that change or alter their colors. A few other texts could adopt either meaning: 3 Macc 1:29; Barnabas 10:7; 15:5. The only biblical references contemporary with 1 Corinthians 15 are likewise found in Paul, who only employs it twice (Rom 1:23; Gal 4:20), and Heb 1:12. In Rom 1:23 the meaning of "exchanging" is clear, but in Gal 4:20 the meaning of "altering" is clear. In Heb 1:12 the word refers to an exchange.

65 Brodeur, *The Holy Spirit's Agency*, 31, 83, 96; Fee, *The First Epistle to the Corinthians*, 800; Garland, *1 Corinthians*, 743; Harris, *Raised Immortal*, 216; Héring, *The First Epistle of Saint Paul*, 180; Richard A. Horsley, *1 Corinthians,* Abingdon New Testament Commentaries (Nashville: Abingdon Press, 1998), 214; Kistemaker, *Exposition of the First Epistle to the Corinthians*, 582; Leon Morris, *1 Corinthians,* Tyndale New Testament Commentaries (Leicester, England: InterVarsity, reprint 1976), 233; C. F. C. Moule, "St. Paul and Dualism: The Pauline Concept of Resurrection," *NTS* 12 (1965):106–23, 120; Richard E. Oster, Jr., *1 Corinthians,* College Press NIV Commentary (Joplin: College Press, 1995), 407; Wolfhart Pannenberg, "History and the Reality of the Resurrection," in *Resurrection Reconsidered*, 67; Charles H. Talbert, *Reading Corinthians: A Literary and Theological Commentary on 1 and 2 Corinthians* (New York: Crossroad, 1987), 103; Thiselton, *The First Epistle to the Corinthians*, 1294–95.

66 I believe that an exchange is likewise contrary to what Paul taught in the difficult text of 2 Cor 4:16–5:8. However, a discussion on that passage would take us beyond what space permits.

67 In the Old Testament, see Ezekiel 37; Isa 26:19; Dan 12:2. Also see 2 Macc 7:9–42; 12:43–45; 14:41–46 in the Intertestamental period. For an extensive discussion, see Wright, *Resurrection of the Son of God*, 85–206.

to a corpse. Since on five occasions he asserts that the resurrection of Jesus is the model for our future resurrection, Paul must have believed that the resurrection of Jesus meant a transformed corpse resulting in His empty tomb.[68]

We have worked our way carefully through an important text. The path has become clear. We can definitely see light ahead and are getting fresh air. It is time to emerge and look at our findings.

CONCLUSION

We have worked carefully through the primary text in all of Paul's letters pertaining to resurrection and have discovered a few exegetical diamonds that are clear and valuable. In 1 Corinthians 15 we observed that Paul contends that the mortal bodies of believers will be changed by being transformed into immortal bodies. He imagines a new body in heaven being placed over the earthly one which in turn will consume it so that there is some continuity between the old creation and the new. Two portions of 1 Corinthians 15 have led a number of scholars as well as the Talpiot tomb team to conclude that Paul was thinking of resurrection in terms of an immaterial body. This understanding is based on the comparison of "natural" and "spiritual" in 15:44, which is understood as "physical" and "immaterial," and the phrase "flesh and blood," which is understood as our physical/material body. We searched carefully through eleven centuries of ancient writings and discovered that *the term "natural" was never employed to describe something as "physical."* While the term "spiritual" could mean "immaterial," it had other meanings as well. And *with only a single unlikely exception, Paul never used the term "spiritual" to refer to something as "immaterial."* Without the possibility that "natural" means "physical," there is no chance that in 1 Cor 15:44 Paul is stating that our present body is physical/material while our resurrection body is immaterial—none. Moreover, we observed that *the phrase "flesh and blood" was probably an ancient figure of speech that simply referred to the mortal body with all of its weaknesses and is not to be associated with Luke's description of Jesus' resurrection body as*

---

68 Romans 8:11; 1 Cor 6:14; 15:20; 2 Cor 4:14; 1 Thess 4:14. Accordingly, Borg, *The Meaning of Jesus: Two Visions,* seems to me seriously mistaken when he asserts that 1 Corinthians 15 is "a chapter that strongly suggests that the resurrection body is not a physical body" (134).

"flesh and bone" any more than we associate the term "cold-blooded" with "O-positive blood." These results are devastating to those who propose that the apostle Paul thought of Jesus' resurrection body as being immaterial.

In short, we have observed that, contrary to the Talpiot tomb team and a number of scholars, the most important Pauline text on resurrection cannot be employed legitimately to assert that his view of resurrection in general and Jesus' resurrection in particular differed fundamentally from the resurrection narratives in the canonical Gospels. In this text Paul never regarded the final post-mortem state of believers to be one of disembodiment. Indeed I would argue for a similar conclusion in all five of the most important Pauline texts on the subject. Like the authors of the Gospels, when Paul claimed that Jesus had risen from the dead, he intended to communicate that the corpse of Jesus had returned to life and that no bones of His remain on earth to be discovered.

Recently I watched the popular television news program *20/20*. The first news item concerned kidnapped children and featured Jessyca Mullenberg, who was abducted just days after her thirteenth birthday and kept for three and a half months at a hotel.[69] Her kidnapper repeatedly molested her until an alert hotel maid reported her suspicion to the FBI, who in turn rescued her. Jessyca informed authorities that the man told her every day that her new name was Cindy Johnson. After hearing this for months, when the FBI rescued her, she was asked if she was Jessyca Mullenberg. Because she had been drilled into thinking she was Cindy Johnson, she told them no.[70] The point to be made here is that for decades we have heard from a number of scholars that "resurrection" as defined by Paul in 1 Corinthians 15 was not something involving the corpse. We have heard this interpretation so often that a few of these scholars appear to maintain it as though it is an assured conclusion. I do not for a moment want to suggest that, like Mullenberg's abductor, mal-intent is present on their part. We draw conclusions hopefully on what we believe is supported most strongly by the available data and all conclusions must be held with the provision that future finds may overturn our present conviction. Whether we were adamant in the past that 1 Cor

69 The story is posted at http://abcnews.go.com/2020/story?id=2954522&page=1 (accessed 21 March 2007).
70 This part of the story does not appear in the article but was on the television program aired 16 March 2007.

15:42–54 pointed to the conclusion that Paul rejected a resurrection of the corpse is irrelevant. We have now seen that this interpretation is no longer sustainable.

CONCLUSIONS ON THE TALPIOT TOMB AND OBSERVATIONS ON RECENT CLAIMS ABOUT CHRISTIANITY

Darrell L. Bock

My relationship with the claims about the Talpiot tomb predates the public announcement and broadcast of this special. The Discovery Channel asked me to look at this special before it was released, after it had been scheduled to air. It was the type of assignment I had had before, and I was glad to take a look. I sat down and wrote an e-mail report as I watched a prerelease version. My initial report was made on the evening of February 10, 2007, 16 days before the press conference in New York announced the find. My first sentence in my e-mailed report told a great deal: "I am halfway through. This is a mess." It was the first of two reports I wrote that night. In my second report I made this observation: "I find it interesting that the most expert of those interviewed (Cross, the curator, Ilan of Berlin, and even Bovon) do not speak to the main thesis; and when they do, it is with a negative." My last sentence in the report was, "Yes, I think this will tar the Discovery Channel for many without some access to rebuttal." It was my way of saying that they had no idea what they were in for, given what was being claimed. To the Discovery Channel's credit, when they received this report, they began quickly to make sure both sides of the story were aired as Ted Koppel was brought in to offer a critical evaluation of the special right after it aired.

The essays you have read explain calmly and directly why the claims associated with Jesus of Nazareth and the Talpiot tomb deserve a negative evaluation. My responsibility is to summarize these essays, add my own observations, and then make a few additional points about how information about Jesus is coming to the public in this new digital age and how people should process the new manner in which such claims are being made.

SUMMARIZING THE ESSAYS

ORTIZ AND ARCHAEOLOGICAL METHOD

The initial essay by Steven M. Ortiz discusses what is involved in an archaeological find and how interpretation of such evidence requires a full appreciation of the context of such a find. The essay correctly complains about the "Indiana Jones" feel of many such specials that really do not reflect the real story of how archaeology works, where the goal is not to find the glitzy artifact but to gain understanding about a period and the manner in which people lived. According to Ortiz, the 10-point script of popularly driven archaeology goes like this:

1. The prevailing hypothesis affirmed by the consensus of the scholarly community is wrong.
2. The "discoverer" is not a trained archaeologist but is self-taught, and he knows the "true story" that all others have overlooked.
3. An expedition is planned for one season, and (lo and behold) at the first attempt they find exactly what they are looking for.
4. This is all documented while a camera crew happens to be filming the discovery.
5. The process is "detective work" that has been missed by the academic community, and they (amateur archaeologists) are the ones who are able to unravel the mystery or solve the problem that has perplexed the experts.
6. No new data is presented, only a reworking of previously published data. A corollary is that not all the data is consulted.
7. Upon the presentation of the discovery, the scholarly community scoffs at the find, and it is claimed that there is a secret monopoly by those in power to suppress the information.

200

8. The amateurs sensationalize the "discovery" by claiming that it is so revolutionary that it will change our way of thinking and our lifestyle.

9. The old "discovery" is presented to the media as a "brand-new" discovery.

10. Usually a book or movie comes out within a week of the "new" discovery.

Ironically, the presentation of *The Lost Tomb of Jesus* follows the above script.

People develop expertise for a reason. This does not mean they are always right or that it is wrong to challenge widely held views. Advances in the study of history take place that way all the time. However, it usually is because someone has been more careful than usual or more precise, not by simply walking in with a new idea and then trying only to look for that which *might* confirm it. Ortiz said it well when he wrote:

> Most archaeologists go to school for several years in order to earn a PhD in archaeology or a related field and receive years of field training. Archaeology is not treasure-hunting—digging holes and robbing tombs of special finds. Granted, the basic unit of study of an archaeologist is the artifact—but it is not studied in isolation. An artifact is part of a larger cultural system. Archaeologists study the artifacts in their cultural context, while treasure hunters focus on the artifact itself. The removal of an artifact from its archaeological context removes it from its historical and cultural context. This is why the antiquities market is so detrimental to archaeological research. . . . Archaeology requires a systematic research design, knowledge of the historical context of the region and area of study, a theoretical basis for the reconstruction of ancient society based on the material correlates, and years of study of various artifacts and material culture. The archaeological enterprise consists of many specialists from auxiliary disciplines who aid the archaeologist in the interpretation and excavation of artifacts. While some artifacts have significant value in terms of information

that is provided to the scholar (such as inscriptions),
it is not the single artifact, but the patterning of many
artifacts within the archaeological record that is used
to interpret the past. The Talpiot tomb is an example of
an isolated discovery taken out of context to interpret
a larger historical picture.

Within a week of the airing of the special, I happened to be in Israel
for a lectureship. There I was able to interview the supervisor of the
excavation of the Talpiot tomb, Amos Kloner. He is a delightful man,
who despite having faced the pressure of dozens of interviews at the
time, hosted a colleague (Stephen Bremar) and myself one evening at his
house and showed me his original notes. He told us the story of how the
tomb had been discovered as digging to build a set of apartment houses
had started, how the time to examine the site was compressed because
of this circumstance, and yet how notes were made. His summary was
that the special had a major error just about every five minutes. It was his
report the Discovery Channel Web site posted as it presented what had
been said about the tomb previously. It is important to note that whereas
most archaeological work that is professionally done and supervised
might be like a CSI investigation, this site was examined fairly hastily
by archaeological standards, but it is the Israelis who have experience at
this. They managed to catalog the finds and explain them all, even post-
ing the dimensions of the ossuaries found and the nature of the inscriptions, something that also was posted on the Discovery Channel site.

What was found is also well summarized by Ortiz when he says:

> The Talpiot tomb is one of a hundred tombs exca-
> vated in the environs of Jerusalem. Even today, the
> casual tourist hiking around the hills of Jerusalem will
> discover many exposed tombs. As the modern city of
> Jerusalem has expanded and several suburbs have been
> developed, it is very common that many construction
> crews have come upon the necropolis of Jerusalem
> during the Hellenistic and early Roman period. The
> Jerusalem necropolis (ancient cemetery) stretches as
> far south as the Arab village of Sur Bahir and as far
> north as Mt. Scopus and Sanhedria. All suburbs and
> even most housing complexes have a tomb within the

boundaries of the community. For the modern Jerusalemite, the discovery of another tomb is commonplace, part of the urban landscape of parks, apartment
complexes, and parking lots.

He went on to summarize how "urban archaeology" often takes
place:

> The Israel Antiquities Authority (formerly the
> Department of Antiquities) is responsible for all
> archaeological sites of cultural and historical value.
> The IAA has several teams led by archaeologists who
> are available to conduct an excavation at a moment's
> notice. In addition, there are several districts and sub-
> districts supervised by archaeologists who are respon-
> sible to protect and identify the archaeological heri-
> tage. These district archaeologists oversee excavations
> in their assigned area, help the police stop any illegal
> activity such as antiquities smuggling and/or robbing,
> serve as liaisons between the state and the various
> communities and businesses that have property con-
> taining cultural and historical heritage.
>
> Although salvage excavations, as the name
> implies, usually salvage the cultural remains of an
> archaeological site—they are conducted using proper
> excavation methodology and excavation techniques.
> Usually someone reports to the Israel Antiquities
> Authority or police when there is an archaeological
> site that might get damaged or destroyed. An inspector
> is quickly dispatched to determine if any action needs
> to be taken. Construction work immediately stops as
> plans are quickly negotiated to coordinate the construc-
> tion work and the salvage excavation. The excavation
> is conducted by archaeologists and workers of the IAA
> and is usually funded by the construction company or
> property owner. Due to time constraints the excava-
> tion is usually intense. While the excavations are com-
> pleted rapidly the work is not done haphazardly.

As of 1993 about 800 tombs had been found. Kloner was one of the most important people on these IAA teams. Kloner will release an English edition of his study of the Jerusalem necropolis in the next year that will update these figures. If anyone knows about such tombs, it is Amos Kloner. The original Talpiot tomb was discussed without fanfare both in 1980 and in his 1996 published report because it was a typical find that had a collection of common names. As Ortiz again said:

> The East Talpiot tomb was a typical first-century AD burial that was one of hundreds of tombs excavated throughout the modern suburbs of Jerusalem. The excavation of the tomb was done properly and the results have been available to the academic community and the general public for decades. Contrary to the docudrama, nothing was mishandled in the excavation or publication. The tomb and inscriptions were known to the academic community and no one proposed that the Jesus in the Talpiot tomb should be associated with the Jesus found in the Gospel accounts. There is no evidence or tradition of this tomb being the tomb of Jesus of Nazareth nor as a site of sacredness to the early Christian community in Jerusalem.

Later Ortiz concluded about the Talpiot tomb, "All that the archaeological data can tell us is that the Talpiot tomb contained a person whose name was Jesus." As my interview with him indicates, Amos Kloner would agree with such a summary.

It is instructive to see how the report on the tomb appeared in a reviewed journal, in contrast to the special, which went directly to the public without any careful scrutiny by a team of professional peers. This is one of the differences in how material is coming to the public these days. I do not think this trend can be reversed. Pandora cannot be put back into her box. So when we conclude our review, we shall have to note how new times and processes require new ways to respond for all of us, even the public to whom such direct reports are made.

EVANS—THE EAST TALPIOT TOMB IN CONTEXT

Well-known New Testament scholar Craig Evans weighed in next by giving us a context for Jewish burial in the first century. In particular, he treated the custom of secondary burial, known as *ossilegium*. Noting that tombs like Talpiot reflect an affluent background, he then described how there was a burial almost immediately with mourning lasting a week. Next, after a year the bones were collected and placed in an ossuary, a limestone bone box. What is significant is that this practice was limited for the most part to Jerusalem and only took place in a period that covered the first century BC to the fall of Jerusalem. This allows us instantly to date such finds in this area.

Evans described the practice this way:

> Secondary burial takes place about one year after death (*b. Qiddushin* 31b "twelve months"). During this time the flesh has decomposed and the bones may be gathered and placed in an ossuary. Mourning at the time of secondary burial is only for one day. Sometimes the bones were anointed with oil or wine. It was believed, moreover, that the decomposition of the flesh atoned for what sins may have remained.

Evans also treated the fascinating find of a collection of ossuaries at *Dominus Flevit*, the traditional place where the Lord is said to have wept over Jerusalem (Luke 19:41–44). The Latin phrase means "the Lord wept." He mentioned an ossuary worded "Simon bar Jonah" and how Bagatti, the archaeologist who wrote about this find, argued this could be a fragment of Peter's ossuary. However, this seems unlikely given the seemingly solid tradition that Peter was martyred in Rome. Evans then walked us through a solid treatment of the Jesus burial tradition.

How did burial take place for those executed as Jesus was? Evans explained:

> There is no evidence that Roman authorities, during peacetime, denied burial to criminals. Besides the aforementioned evidence of the crucified Yehohanan, whose body was properly buried, we have literary evidence that the Romans respected Jewish sensitivities in this regard. The primary motivation for burying the dead before nightfall was to avoid defiling the land, as commanded in Scripture (cp. Deut 21:22–23). Both Philo and Josephus claim that the Romans honored

Jewish law and customs (Philo, *Leg. ad Gaium* 300;
Flaccus 83; Josephus, *Ag. Apion* 2.73). Even Roman
law allowed the bodies of the crucified to be taken
down and be buried (*Digesta* 48.24.1, 3).[1]

Wherever Jesus was buried, and the locale at the church of the Holy
Sepulchre is the best attested locale, He got there courtesy of Joseph of
Arimathea's request and provision.

For the current discussion, the key part of Evans's essay looks at
three key claims of the Talpiot tomb theory that Evans claims are wrong.
We look at them one at a time.

Claim 1. The claim that the X-mark at the beginning of the inscription, "Yeshua, son of Yehosef," signifies a cross and as such is a Christian
symbol is unlikely in light of ancient evidence. There also are difficulties
with the incision of the name Yeshua.

Evans surveyed the ancient evidence that indicates "the typical
function of the X-mark was to align the lid with the ossuary." He also
explored the debate surrounding the inscription of Jesus' name, which is
written so sloppily that it is even hard to confirm. My own observation
about this phenomenon is that although it is the case that such inscriptions are not for public reading but merely for internal family indexing of
the ossuary and that often such inscriptions are sloppily written, it is hard
to accept that an inscription for a revered Jesus would be done so sloppily. I asked Amos Kloner about the sloppy nature of this inscription in
my interview with him, and he agreed with my observation. The inscription on High Priest Caiaphas's tomb is also sloppy, despite all the other
elaborate decorations on it, yet each letter of his name is still clearly
distinct, something that is not the case on the Talpiot tomb.

Claim 2. The claim that the gable and circle above the tomb's
entrance is a Jewish-Christian symbol is also incorrect. As Evans said,
again after noting several ancient examples,

> The gable over a circle (or rosette) is not mys-
> terious, and it is not Christian. It is Jewish and it is
> pre-Christian.

---

1 For these reasons and others the novel proposal that the body of Jesus was not buried but
either was left hanging on the cross or was cast into a ditch where it was eaten by animals
must be rejected without reservation. For this proposal, see J. D. Crossan, *Who Killed
Jesus? Exposing the Roots of Anti-Semitism in the Gospel Story of the Death of Jesus* (San
Francisco: HarperCollins, 1995).

. . . The evidence is overwhelming. The pointed
gable and circle over the entrance to the East Talpiot
tomb is Jewish and has nothing to do with Jesus and
early Christians. The symbol is probably in refer-

~~ence to the temple. Given the fact that aristocratic and~~

high priestly families were buried in the greater Talpiot area and the fact that every single name in the
East Talpiot tomb is Hasmonean, it is probable that
this tomb belonged to a wealthy, aristocratic Jerusalem family with ties to the temple. Indeed, some of the
members of the family buried in the East Talpiot tomb
may have been ruling priests. The suggestion that the
gable and circle constituted an early Christian symbol
has no foundation and ignores a mountain of contrary
evidence.

Claim 3. The idea that the James ossuary, which was brought to public attention in 2002, is the tenth, so-called "missing" ossuary of the East
Talpiot tomb is also to be rejected. Here Evans is very direct: "This claim,
however, is utterly gratuitous and contradicts the published accounts of
archaeologists Yosef Gat and Amos Kloner. Kloner described the [tenth]
ossuary as 'plain,' lacking adornment and an inscription. In the wake
of the recent controversy, he has publicly stated that the tenth ossuary
is not the James ossuary."[2] In my interview with Kloner, he showed me
his notes on the dimensions and makeup of this tenth ossuary as a plain,
uninscribed ossuary. Evans went on to make one more point:

Moreover, the dimensions of the tenth ossuary do
not exactly match the dimensions of the James ossuary. Kloner reported the tenth ossuary as 60 cm in
length, 26 cm wide, and 30 cm deep. The James ossuary, however, is some 50 cm in length (at the base),
lengthening to about 56 cm at the top, some 30 cm
wide at one end and 26 cm wide at the other end, and
about 30 cm deep. Admittedly, the width and depth of

2 Amos Kloner, David Mevorah (curator, Israel Museum), and others have stated that plain
ossuaries (i.e., ossuaries that are uninscribed and unadorned) are sometimes not stored in
the museum warehouse but are placed outside. Accordingly, there is nothing mysterious
about not finding ossuary 80.509 on a shelf in the warehouse.

the two ossuaries approximate one another, but there is
a significant discrepancy in their respective lengths.

I knew this fact when I interviewed Kloner and asked him specifically if measurements can differ as greatly as the differences here. I
asked the question because I had had a conversation with James Tabor,
the historical consultant on the special, in which he claimed that such
differences could take place. Kloner said that differences can emerge but
not differences that cover four centimeters. I might add that these differences are 4 cm on a couple of the dimensions as well.

Evans concluded his study by noting one other problem with the
tenth ossuary=the James ossuary theory. Again I quote him: "There is
also a serious chronological problem with the argument that these ossuaries are and the same. The East Talpiot tomb was discovered in 1980.
There is dated photographic evidence that the James ossuary was in circulation years earlier." Of course, even the point Evans made assumes
that the James ossuary is authentic, something that itself is debated with
the jury still being out on that question.

In sum, Evans showed and my interview with Kloner confirmed the
strong likelihood that all three of these claims are highly problematic and
almost certainly false.

Bauckham—The Names on the Ossuaries

In one of the most technical of these essays, Richard Bauckham of
St. Andrews worked through the issue of the six names that were contained in the Talpiot inscriptions found on the 10 ossuaries (four had
no names). The claim was that this collection of names was unusual,
so unusual that the odds were great that this was Jesus' family tomb.
This claim stands behind the numbers generated for the statistics in the
special that the tomb had a great chance of containing Jesus' family.
Anything said about the statistics depends on this part of the argument
being accurate. Here is where the experts most challenged the claims, by
noting just how common these names were. Bauckham's article works
through this point in careful detail, one name at a time based on what we
know today about the use of those names. In my interviews in Israel, I
got to meet with Tal Ilan, who is the world's expert on the topic of Jewish names in this period, who was interviewed for this special, and who

commented on all of this for me. Her work is the source that Bauckham uses most, along with his own analysis.

She told me these names are far too common to make as much of them as the special claimed. In fact, she said as much on the special in the one quote in the entire two hours that let an expert directly address this issue. More than that, she said she was upset with how she was interviewed, feeling she was a "hostile witness on behalf of a murderer." Ilan is an Israeli scholar with no axe to grind on the fate of Jesus. She noted how they continually asked her variations of the same question making it more hypothetical until they could get her to say that something was at least possible. She was not pleased with how she was used by the special. Bauckham's article explains why the claim about the combination of names is off the mark.

Bauckham's article starts off by noting how names in general were engraved on ossuaries and what their purpose was:

> Though some inscriptions are in ink or charcoal, most, like those in the Talpiot tomb, were incised with a chisel or nail. They are not integrated into the decorations of the decorated ossuaries and are "carelessly executed, clumsily spaced, and, often, contain spelling mistakes . . . even in cases of renowned families, including those of high-priestly rank." They were usually made by relatives of the dead and often in the darkness of the tombs. It is not surprising that some of the inscriptions on the ossuaries from the Talpiot tomb are very difficult to read.
>
> The inscriptions are not like those on modern tombstones, set in a public place and intended to identify and describe the dead for anyone reading them. They would not normally have been seen by anyone except members of the family that used the tomb.

In other words, these inscriptions were for identification purposes for the family. My own view is that it is still unusual that an inscription for a supposedly revered Jesus would be done so sloppily. This observation points to the fact that the Jesus mentioned is not Jesus of Nazareth. I asked Tal Ilan and Amos Kloner about this separately. They both agreed that the likelihood is that the Jesus inscription, had it been the respected figure of the family, would have been done with more care than the graffiti-like inscription we have on the Jesus ossuary.

Bauckham first reviewed what we know about Jesus' family and how we know what we do about ancient names in Israel. He summarized the commonality of the names this way:

> We can be pretty sure that Simon (243 occurrences) and Joseph (218 occurrences) were the most popular male names, but we cannot really be sure that, say, Hillel (11 occurrences) was more popular than Zebedee (5 occurrences). But in the case of the names on the ossuaries from the Talpiot tomb we are in luck because they are all among the most common names, as are the names of Jesus and His close family (parents and siblings).[3] Moreover, the accuracy of the calculations of relative popularity among the most common names can be checked by observing the breakdown of the total figures for certain identifiable sources of the data: the New Testament, Josephus, ossuaries, and the texts from the Judean desert. (These four sources complement one another in being of different kinds: literary, epigraphic, and documentary.)

As for the names on the Talpiot ossuaries, he said this: "It is striking that the matches between the two categories (names that occur in both cases) are confined to some of the most common names of all: the second, fourth, and sixth most popular male names, and the most common female name." He then examined each name one at a time.

Fortunately for us, Bauckham pulled all his most technical data together in one grand summary, having paid special attention to claims made about the name that the special tied to Mary Magdalene, including the issue of the evidence for Mary Magdalene and Jesus being married, something for which there is no historical evidence at all.

Here are Bauckham's fourteen conclusions, which speak for themselves in light of the data in the essay:

---

3 Clopas, the name of his uncle, is rare.

1. There is no reason to think a person called Matia (cp. ossuary 703) belonged to the family of Jesus.
2. In the light of parallel examples, it is not at all unlikely that the Yeshuaᶜ bar Yehosef of ossuary 704 (and 702) was a different indi-vidual from Jesus of Nazareth.
3. Yose (ossuary 705), as a short form of the name Yehosef, was not unusual.
4. Yose (ossuary 705) could have been the same person as Yehosef (ossuary 704).
5. Maria (ossuary 706) was a common form of the name Mary among first-century Jews, both in Greek and in Hebrew.
6. There is no reason to think that the mother of Jesus was known as Maria rather than Mariam.
7. The inscription on ossuary 701 should probably be read as 'Mari-ame and Mara' (with 'and Mara' as a later addition).
8. Mara is here a name, not a title, and may refer to a man (perhaps Mariame's husband) or to a woman.
9. In Christian literature up to the middle of the second century, Mary Magdalene is always called either Maria or Mariam, never Mari-am*m*e or Mariam*n*e.
10. Only in some Christian Gnostic circles in the second and third centuries was Mary Magdalene known as Mariamme.
11. The form Mariamne, found only in Hippolytus (early third cen-tury) and the Acts of Philip (late fourth century), is probably not connected with Mariamenon (even if this is the correct reading of ossuary 701), but is a late Christian variation of Mariamme.
12. We cannot be sure that the samples from ossuaries 701 and 704 that were DNA tested were of Mariamenon/Mariame and Yeshuaᶜ, rather than of other individuals interred in the same ossuaries.
13. The DNA results are compatible with a wide variety of family relationships between the persons tested.
14. Jesus of Nazareth was almost certainly celibate, and so the Yeshuaᶜ of ossuary 702 (Yehuda bar Yeshuaᶜ) is unlikely to be He.

In sum, the names do not point to Jesus of Nazareth having ever occupied the Talpiot tomb.

DEMBSKI AND MARKS—THE JESUS TOMB MATH

Perhaps the most compelling argument in defense of the identification of the Talpiot tomb as the tomb of Jesus of Nazareth is the statistical argument. When Andrey Feuerverger finished crunching the numbers for the Discovery Channel special, he claimed that the odds were only 1 in 600 that the tomb belonged to someone other than the Jesus of the Gospels. However, William Dembski and Robert Marks vigorously challenged Feuerverger at a number of points.

First, they argued that Feuerverger's work was not properly evaluated by peers in his field before it was presented to the public. They objected:

> Andrey Feuerverger, on whose probability calculations their case rests, admits that this work has yet to be properly done and vetted. On his academic Web site, addressed to "Dear Statistical Colleagues," he writes: "A detailed paper is being prepared and hopefully will undergo timely peer review; if successful in the refereeing process, it will be made available." Such an admission hardly inspires confidence given the extravagant claims being made on the basis of Feuerverger's work. Not only has the rigorous statistical work not been properly vetted; it is still in the process of preparation.

More importantly, Dembski and Roberts also challenged the so-called Jesus equation, the formula that resulted in Feuerverger's claim that the Talpiot tomb was likely the tomb of Jesus of Nazareth. Their first correction actually tipped the scales in favor of identifying the Talpiot tomb as the tomb of Jesus of Nazareth. Dembski and Roberts pointed out that all of the name statistics were conditioned on the gender of the individual and needed to be multiplied by one-half to reflect the roughly equal proportion of men and women in first-century Palestine. Their willingness to make this adjustment demonstrates that they are playing honestly with the numbers and are not manipulating them to arrive at a desired probability.

Second, the authors argued that Feuerverger's analysis was guilty of the fallacy of overspecification. Calculations should be based on the generic forms of names rather than particular forms.

Third, Feuerverger's correction factors appear to be capriciously formulated or, in the words of Dembski and Roberts, "taken out of a hat." The scholars argued that one of the correction factors should be formulated with Fisherian and the other with Bayesian probabilistic reasoning.

Fourth, the authors claimed that Feuerverger's analysis was based on an incorrect reference population. He examined the likelihood of the names appearing in one of the one thousand tombs of Jerusalem rather than the frequency with which this pool of names appeared in Jewish Palestinian families during the ossuary period. Dembski and Roberts saw this aspect of Feuerverger's calculation as problematic for two reasons:

> (1) In determining whether some family or other around Jerusalem might by chance exhibit some pattern of names, what's crucial is how many such families there were and not how many of them could additionally have afforded a tomb with ossuaries. The correction factor c_3 therefore should not have been set to the maximum number of actual tombs in the Jerusalem area around the time of Jesus but to the total number of relevant families in the area—regardless of whether they had the financial resources to own a tomb. Most families in the time of Jesus were too poor to afford such tombs. In particular, because Joseph, Jesus' legal father, was a carpenter and because carpentry was not a lucrative profession, Jesus' family seems not to have been an ideal candidate for having a family tomb. Accordingly, what's crucial in assessing the probability that the Talpiot tomb was the family tomb of Jesus is not the actual number of family tombs but the actual number of families living at that time and in that area. (2) The second problem is that Feuerverger focuses unduly on Jerusalem and its immediate surroundings. Yes, the Talpiot tomb is just a few miles from Jerusalem; and, yes, Jesus' brother James was active in Jerusalem. If we knew nothing else, we might therefore think it likely that James should be buried in the immediate vicinity of Jerusalem (though the evidence

is against his having an ossuary in the Talpiot tomb). But we know a lot more. We know that Jesus and His family throughout His life was based 65 miles north of Jerusalem in the town of Nazareth—in fact He is often called "Jesus of Nazareth." Moreover, Magdala, the town from which Mary Magdalene hails, is 15 miles still further north. Thus the number of families in the immediate vicinity of Jerusalem in the period of ossuary use underestimates the number of relevant families to deciding whether the Talpiot tomb is, on probabilistic grounds, the tomb of Jesus. In calculating this number of families, we need to consider a radius of at least 80 miles around Jerusalem. In other words, we need to consider all Jewish families living in ancient Palestine during the time that ossuaries were popular.

Dembski and Roberts used a conservative estimate that some 100,000 Jewish families lived in Palestine during the period of ossuary use. They sought to determine merely the probability of the pool of names from Talpiot appearing in a Jewish family from the period and not the probability of these names showing up in an excavated tomb in Jerusalem.

Based on these corrections, Demski and Roberts developed a new and improved Jesus equation. When they crunched the numbers, they arrived at significantly different conclusions from those reached by Feuerverger.

> Given realistic naming probabilities, we find that for small families of size 10 we would expect to see 30 of them exhibit the Talpiot pattern of New Testament of names and for medium families of size 20 we would expect to see 154 of them exhibit this pattern of names. Even in case 2, taking family size at 20, we are more likely to see two rather than one family with the more restrictive name set and lowered probabilities promoted by *The Jesus Family Tomb* people.

> Bottom line: when the math is done correctly, probabilities that might be cited in evidence for the Talpiot tomb being the final resting place of the New

Testament Jesus are not impressive and would not even achieve a minimal level of significance as gauged by conventional statistical theory.

The authors then argued that even this probability analysis needed to be updated in light of Bayes's theorem, which allowed one to account for data that seemed inconsistent with the occurrence of a particular event. Feuerverger's analysis did not incorporate considerations that decrease the likelihood that the Talpiot tomb belonged to Jesus of Nazareth. These include:

- The New Testament evidence that Jesus and His family were of modest means and therefore would be unlikely to be able to afford a tomb.
- The fact that Jesus and His family hailed from Nazareth, which was 65 miles north of Jerusalem, and that His supposed wife, as conjectured by *The Jesus Family Tomb* people (i.e., Mary Magdalene), was from the town of Magdala even further north of Jerusalem.
- The uniform witness of the best attested historical sources that Jesus was unmarried, to say nothing of His not being married to Mary Magdalene.
- The widespread perception shortly after Jesus' crucifixion that He had been resurrected (Paul, writing in Galatians, which both liberal and conservative scholars date around AD 50, demonstrates a clearly developed understanding of Jesus' resurrection). Regardless of whether Jesus actually did resurrect, the perception early on among His followers that He did and the interest of His followers in denying that there was any tomb that housed His bones would have tended to preclude any tomb that purported to hold His remains.

After incorporating these observations into their probability model, Dembski and Roberts concluded: "That additional information removes all reasonable doubt that the Talpiot tomb might, after all, be the family tomb of the New Testament Jesus. The statistical evidence rules decisively against this hypothesis."

This analysis has clearly dealt the death blow to the Talpiot hypothesis. I suspect that *The Jesus Family Tomb* group will vigorously defend aspects of their calculation against this new and improved model. Peer review of the Dembski-Roberts model will likely be far more favorable than peer review of the Feuerverger model.

HABERMAS—THE RESURRECTION OF JESUS

Habermas reviewed the Tabor thesis after making an important note about how he will proceed. Nothing that he claimed was presupposed simply because of information in the New Testament. He made his point this way: "Conversely, we will rely almost exclusively on the established information that the vast majority of scholars who study this topic take to be historical. Whenever such scholarly agreement is present concerning particular historical data, it is usually because strong reasons exist to establish such a consensus. This is especially intriguing when specialists of different theological persuasions still share similar views on historical issues that are crucial to the Christian faith."[4]

As was the case with the other essays, Habermas selected some key points to consider. They are "the best historiographical use of the Gospels and Paul, Tabor's response to Jesus' burial and the empty tomb, and Tabor's response to the appearances of the risen Jesus. I hold that not only does the Talpiot hypothesis fare poorly in its overall attempt to establish this tomb as the burial place for Jesus' family[5] but that, at each of these three critical junctures, it especially misses the mark by a wide margin."

On Tabor's Use of the Gospels. On Tabor's use of the New Testament, Habermas made this observation: "When Tabor repeatedly seems to use the New Testament when it favors his viewpoint while parting from it when it does not support his view, even though there are good scholarly reasons for affirming the authenticity of the New Testament material [at such points], this provides cause for concern. Yet I am afraid that this tendency manifests itself too often."[6]

Concerning Tabor on the Resurrection. Tabor's response to Jesus' burial and resurrection ignored a key historical feature of the tradition. Tabor "dismisses the widely held view affirmed by the majority of schol-

---

4 It is crucial to distinguish that scholars often agree about particular facts while still disagreeing about either additional specifics or their applications.

5 The overall thesis is the purview of the rest of this volume. Also, Habermas is writing a brief book on the Talpiot tomb hypothesis titled, *The Secret of the Talpiot Tomb* (Nashville: B&H Publishing Group, 2007).

6 The clarification in brackets is mine.

ars that Paul checked out his gospel message with the chief apostles, James the brother of Jesus, Peter, and later John and received their affirmation (Gal. 1:18–2:10)."

Habermas went on to observe that Tabor's thesis places a great deal of distance between Jesus' teaching and that of Paul. When it comes to resurrection, this distancing runs headlong into 1 Cor 15:1–8, which is a creedal statement expressing the church's tradition about Jesus that Paul recorded in the mid to late 50s of the first century but is actually rooted much earlier. Habermas correctly noted it is a pre-Pauline creedal statement, whose roots are much earlier, stretching back into the same decade as the events tied to Jesus. Habermas dated this in the early to mid-30s.

His argument is so important it needs to be cited in full[7]:

> The material in 1 Cor 15:3–7 is more strongly supported on all counts [than the sources Tabor prefers: James, Q, and *Didache*]: a much earlier date, probable authorship, strong pedigree, and scholarly approval.
>
> Additionally, most scholars conclude that Paul received this material or at least its general content from the apostle Peter and James the brother of Jesus during Paul's first visit to Jerusalem (Gal 1:18–20). Most scholars also concur that during Paul's second trip to Jerusalem (Gal. 2:1–10) he subjected his gospel message to the apostolic scrutiny not only of Peter and James but also of John, lest he be mistaken (2:2). However, the most influential leaders in the early church added nothing to Paul's gospel presentation (2:6) and welcomed his witness to its truth (2:9). Paul likewise attests that he knew the details of their message about the death, burial, and resurrection appearances of Jesus, and that they all taught the same thing (1 Cor 15:11–15).
>
> These data are so well attested and affirmed by contemporary critical scholars that it is difficult to understand how a critique could dislodge these central conclusions. . . .

7 Clarifications in brackets are mine.

In order to sidestep the force of Gal 1:18–2:10, one must somehow challenge Paul's credibility. Yet Paul is both the earliest and most accredited source that we have in the early church as is attested by the vast majority of contemporary critical scholars. What source that contradicts Paul is both earlier and more reliable?

This strong argument can be tightened even more in my view. Paul's conversion as a result of his encounter with Jesus is a corroborated event, being doubly attested in distinct sources (Gal 1; Acts 9). That event is dated to the middle 30s at the latest. Paul needs to have enough theology in place to "process" that experience. Where did the theology come from for him to process that event as he did? It had to come from the preaching of the church, a message about resurrection that 1 Corinthians 15 affirms. In other words, we have solid historical grounding for the idea that the teaching of 1 Corinthians 15 belongs to the very period of the events being described. This is an important observation because it means that the core claim of the church about Jesus' resurrection goes back at the latest to this extremely early period. The same is true for claims about Jesus' having appeared to others in a raised form *like that which Paul preached* in 1 Corinthians 15, that is, not as merely a raised spirit but as a raised, glorified, spiritual body. The tradition of resurrection in a glorified form is more than simply a raising of the soul without a body. Such a view has deep and solid historical roots. That message is one the intimate followers of Jesus shared.

On Tabor's Take on the Appearances. Teaching on the empty tomb and the appearances tied to it are just as solid in terms of its roots. Habermas in particular highlights one key feature, that women are the first witnesses:

> Surprisingly, the scholarly literature lists more than 20 reasons for the historicity of the empty tomb. Most frequently championed is the unanimous agreement that women were the initial witnesses. In the patriarchal culture of Palestine in the first century AD, women were unlikely to be asked to provide important testimony. Although there were exceptions, there was generally an inverse relation between the magnitude

of the subject and whether women would be allowed to testify in court.

Why are the women enumerated by each Gospel as the initial witnesses to the empty tomb, unless they actually were the first witnesses? Moreover, why would we be told also that Jesus' male disciples reacted to the report by belittling the women and accusing them of spreading tales—basically gossip (see Luke 24:11)? Here we have two examples of the principle of embarrassment since it is unlikely that the New Testament authors would embarrass their heroes without good reasons.

Several strange items are operating here. If the authors wanted the greatest impact in evidencing the crucial report of the empty tomb, and are as uncritical as some contemporary scholars think, why not simply invent the story that the men found the empty tomb? Their testimony would certainly be received more readily. Even if female testimony was used, by all means avoid criticizing the later leaders of the church, the male disciples. After all, it is counterproductive to make the early church leaders, who were taught by Jesus, look so badly mistaken. This is a horrible way to establish a case for the empty tomb unless the Evangelists were committed to reporting the events precisely as they occurred.

Once again this argument can be affirmed from yet another angle on the premise that such a story is an early church invention. In such a scenario, those creating the story get to make up the rules. Now the question is, why would one make up a story to sell a difficult idea to a skeptical culture (remember resurrection was not an acceptable idea to Greeks and was debated among Jews) and then pick as your front line witnesses women who do not have standing in courts as witnesses? Such a scenario makes no cultural sense, *if the story is made up.* The best explanation for the story of the empty tomb being as it is, is because that is the way it was. The account was not created with women at the hub; it was recounted because that is how it took place. In other words, the women are there because the women were there. All of this challenges Tabor's take on these events. In making this point, we do not even mention the incongruity of the family reburying Jesus and yet putting their life on the line in proclaiming a raised Jesus, while knowing He is not raised.

Habermas summarizes with five conclusions:

> (1) There is no known rationale or evidence for either Joseph's or Jesus' family to rebury the body within a mere 24 hours or so. (2) If Jesus' body had been reburied in the most common manner employed by the Jews of this time and moved to a trench grave, His bones would not have been placed later in the Talpiot tomb ossuary. Furthermore, there seems to be no reason for simply relocating the body to another tomb that was similar to that in which Jesus was initially buried. (3) If Joseph never told anyone else that he had moved and reburied the body, how would he keep this fact from becoming known? Whether or not he needed help, this course of action would almost certainly attract attention. . . . (4) If Joseph did inform especially the family beforehand, as seems highly likely, then why do Mary the mother of Jesus and others proceed to the now empty tomb on Sunday morning, apparently having no idea where to find Jesus' body? If they are not told until later, then an entirely new set of problems emerge, as we will see next. (5) Over this entire procedure, a methodological pitfall continues to be manifest. By what justification do we accept such a large amount of the Gospel textual substantiation of Jesus' death and burial, except when it clearly opposes our hypotheses?

Habermas closed with eight summary arguments concerning the appearances:

> (1) Paul's eyewitness testimony to the appearance of the risen Jesus (1 Cor 9:1; 15:8–10), which prompted his conversion from a vigorous persecutor

of Christians to a passionate missionary (1 Cor 15:9; Gal 1:13–14; Phil 3:4–6). Equally important is (2) the early creedal material containing the gospel data that Paul had received and passed on to others . . . (1 Cor 15:3–7). We have said that most scholars hold that the content of this tradition dates from immediately after Jesus' crucifixion, and that Paul probably received it in the early to mid–30s AD. Most likely Peter and James the brother of Jesus passed it on to Paul during his initial visit to Jerusalem (Gal 1:13–20). Moreover, (3) these gospel data were so crucial to Paul that years later he took great care to confirm the message again with Peter, James the brother of Jesus, and also with John. These key Christian leaders confirmed Paul's view of the gospel, adding nothing (Gal 2:1–10). (4) Paul attests that he knew what the other apostles were teaching regarding their own experiences of the resurrected Jesus, and their message was the same as his (1 Cor 15:11–14).

Additional factors indicate the other disciples had also seen the risen Jesus. (5) As we will point out below, the predominant scholarly view is that James the brother of Jesus was an unbelieving skeptic until he was convinced that he had seen an appearance of the risen Jesus too (1 Cor 15:7). (6) Jesus' disciples were willing to die specifically for their message of the resurrection, and some did, which indicates that they were totally persuaded that it was accurate. (7) Many other creedal texts that date from the earliest period of Christianity also confirm Jesus' resurrection appearances.[8] (8) As addressed above, the empty tomb argues that whatever happened involved Jesus' body, which is another indication in the direction of actual appearances of the risen Jesus.

8 For specific details, see Habermas, *The Risen Jesus and Future Hope*, 22–23.

This is a solid summary of the reasons many take seriously the historical testimony that comes from our earliest Christian sources. Again I would add one point, since some, including James Tabor, like to make Paul's faith distinct from that of those who followed Jesus. It is that in the same book where Paul acknowledges some tension between himself and the other church leaders when it comes to how the gospel impacts relationships with Gentiles (Gal 1–2), he is clear that both those leaders and he preached the same gospel and gave each other the "right hand of fellowship" (Gal. 2:6–10). When Paul confronts Peter later in Gal 2:11–14, it is not because they disagree on the gospel, but because Paul sees Peter's behavior as inconsistent with their earlier agreement about how to relate that gospel to Gentiles. So efforts to sever Paul from the earliest apostles on the resurrection and how it was preached represent a failure to come to grips with the historical sources.

Habermas makes one final key point. Again in making this argument, he assumes for a moment the hypothesis of the special. Here is his observation, assuming the theory of a double burial stretched across a year is true:

> This leads us to a devastating problem for the Talpiot thesis. Whenever mother Mary, Mary Magdalene, and James found out about the reburial of Jesus' body, it would have to be within the first year or so after the crucifixion, occasioned by both the reburial in the Talpiot family tomb and the later move to the ossuary. This also would constitute the first year in the life of the Christian church. But how could this information of the double reburial of Jesus' body and bones possibly remain concealed from Jesus' apostles and other early leaders, especially when the Talpiot tomb has outside decorations [according to the theory] that demand attention and contained an ossuary that bears Jesus' name? . . . . As soon as the horrible secret leaked out, how would the early proclamation of the gospel—the deity, death, and resurrection of Jesus—ever be the same? The knowledge of Jesus' reburial and the present whereabouts of His bones would hit the movement

right between the eyes, indeed, in its very heart. How would it affect Peter? John? Others?[9]

So Habermas concluded that the Talpiot thesis lacks "explanatory scope and power, both of which are key ingredients in historical research. It is opposed by the historical evidence at virtually every turn. Thus it stumbles on virtually every one of its major claims. Scarcely has a theory regarding the historical Jesus *ever* been confronted by more major refutations."

This point also can be driven home. Rarely has a thesis garnered so much unanimous condemnation from scholars ranging from conservative to liberal, from Christian to Jewish to secular. This theory has managed to accomplish something that is rare in historical claims about Jesus, to generate near unanimity that the theory's claims are false.

LICONA—PAUL'S VIEW OF THE NATURE OF THE RESURRECTION BODY

This summary survey of the essays has already laid much ground for what is to be said in Mike Licona's study. We will major on the fresh points. The issue here is whether it is of significance for the Christian faith whether Jesus was raised bodily or not. Is this splitting theological hairs, and is the claim of the special really true that discovering Jesus' bones does not impact the Christian faith? Licona summarizes the point well: "If the claim of the apostles is that Christ was raised in a *spiritual* (meaning immaterial) sense, a discovery of His bones would not falsify Christianity. On the other hand, if the claim of the apostles is that Christ was raised *bodily* leaving behind an empty tomb, a discovery of His bones would indeed falsify Christianity, revealing that its confirming event never occurred. Accordingly, this is not a 'splitting of theological hairs' with little impact."

When it comes to views on the afterlife, it is important to remember that the Greeks had no view of resurrection, and for many Greeks death meant death. Other Greeks might entertain the idea of the immortality of the soul. All of this is detailed in a book titled *The Resurrection of the Son of God* by N.T. Wright. He works through the variety of views on the afterlife in some detail with a myriad of citations. Jews had a few basic views as well. Some, like the Sadducees, denied a resurrection (Sir 38:16–23; Acts 23:8). A few Jews appear to have held to a form of res-

9 Bracket clarification is mine.

urrection of the soul. At least this is possible according to *Jubilees* and *1 Enoch* (1 En. 22:3,9, although here it may be souls waiting for the final resurrection; Jub. 23:30–31). However, this view was a minority position and fell out of favor. The belief in resurrection among at least the Pharisees is shown vividly in 2 Maccabees 7. Here seven sons are being put to death, actually mutilated to death, one at a time before their mother for refusing to eat pork, during the time of Antiochus Ephiphanes. When the third son's turn comes, he sticks out his tongue and hands saying that they can take these because one day the Lord will give them back. Licona's work in this section is not all it should be, and he moves past the point too quickly.

It is important to recall that (1) Paul was a Pharisee and (2) we have texts where Jesus defends the resurrection in such a way that Pharisees present compliment him for his views. This indicates that the view Christians held about resurrection paralleled the views of Pharisees. The point is crucial because it is this kind of afterlife that is being debated.[10]

This background means that when we get to Paul and 1 Corinthians 15 we already know what kind of resurrection he has in mind because of this background. If he had meant something different, a clear differentiation would have been made. The Habermas essay had already made clear that Paul agreed with Jesus' disciples about resurrection, whose view would parallel the accounts where Jesus defends a resurrection from the Torah (Mark 12:18–23=Matt 22:23–33=Luke 20:27–36). So Paul's view is very much rooted in Jewish views that also touch on the Old Testament (see the picture in Ezek 37–39 and the text in Dan 12:1–2), not to mention the traditions about resurrection tied to Jesus that Licona notes.

The key Pauline text is 1 Corinthians 15, especially verses 42–54 as Licona observes. The other Pauline texts are worth noting. The passage in 2 Cor 4:16–5:8 is also important for here the "tent" of carnal flesh will be replaced with a "heavenly dwelling," which surely alludes to far more than a disembodied soul, which is the other afterlife alternative on the table. There is no "nakedness" for our soul/spirit in heaven according to this text. Romans 8:11 makes clear that our resurrection is like the one Jesus' experienced, meaning that a physical element belongs to the

---

10 Licona's remark about the possibility of Gnosticism in the first century also may concede too much on that point. See my *The Missing Gospels* (Nashville: Thomas Nelson, 2006), which argues that Christian Gnosticism is likely a second-century phenomenon. The best we can get to in the late first century is a proto-Gnosticism.

belief, a point also affirmed in Phil 3:21 where our glorious body will be like his. Galatians 1:11–19 alludes briefly to Jesus' appearance to Paul, which is detailed three times in Acts (Acts 9; 22; 26). The Acts text indicates what Paul saw was not an internal vision of Jesus, but an event about which those around him also had a limited awareness. Thus, these texts corroborate what Licona focuses on in 1 Corinthians 15, that there is a physical element to resurrection as Paul affirms it in this text.

One of the most important observations Licona makes comes from 1 Cor 15:36–44. It is a point I made to Jim Tabor on the Ted Koppel special that the introductory essay of this volume described, namely that the same elements went into our physical body that resurrection treats when the body becomes a spiritual body as a result of resurrection. The seed that becomes a plant is dealing with the same matter. Licona said it this way:

> But there is continuity between the seed and the plant that comes forth from it as indicated by 15:36: "That which you sow is not *made alive* unless it dies." The seed that is *dead* and *sown* (buried) is *made alive* once again. In the same way there is continuity between the believer's present body (the seed) and the resurrection body. What dies and goes down in burial comes up in resurrection, having been made alive and transformed.[11] This is confirmed by Paul's use of the pronoun "this" in 15:53–54: "*This* perishable will put on the imperishable; *this* mortal will put on immortality"; and so forth.[12] One can almost see Paul grabbing his arm as he emphasizes that *this* body will put on immortality as one puts on a coat. A transfor-

11 Paul Ellingsworth and Howard Hatton, *A Translator's Handbook on Paul's First Letter to the Corinthians* (New York: United Bible Societies, 1993), 317; Gordon D. Fee, *The First Epistle to the Corinthians* (Grand Rapids: Eerdmans, 1987), 777; Simon J. Kistemaker, *Exposition of the First Epistle to the Corinthians* (Grand Rapids: Baker, 1993), 572–73. N. T. Wright, *The Resurrection of the Son of God* (Minneapolis: Fortress, 2003) is correct, however, in writing, "The new resurrected body will be in continuity and discontinuity with the present one" (341). The discontinuity pertains to the corruption/incorruption, etc. (360; cf. 371).

12 William Lane Craig, *Assessing the New Testament Evidence for the Historicity of the Resurrection of Jesus* (New York: Edwin Mellen Press, 1989), 144; Robert H. Gundry, "Trimming the Debate," in *Jesus' Resurrection,* 122; Alan F. Segal, *Life after Death: A History of the Afterlife in Western Religion* (New York: Doubleday, 2004), 433; cf. 439–40.

mation of the corpse will occur, and it will be clothed
with immortality and imperishability. There can be no
doubt that what is being sown in 15:42–44 is our present body. There can be little doubt that the third-person
singular "it" that is sown is what is raised. Thus, the
body that is sown is transformed and raised. There is
neither an elimination of a body nor an exchange of
the old for the new. Rather, it is the mortal body being
transformed into immortality.

Licona went into great detail to show that a "spiritual" body has a
physical dimension. It is important to understand that this body is not
"carnal" exactly like flesh, but it is a transformed, glorified form of that
flesh. After a thorough and detailed treatment of the key terms Licona
summarized, "Our present mortal body is animated or empowered by a
heart, lungs, and so forth. Our resurrection body will be empowered by
God's Spirit." The body is a spiritual one because it is the eternal Spirit
of God that gives it never-ending life.

When Licona treated 1 Cor 15:50 and the teaching that flesh and
blood do not inherit the kingdom, it is this conception of Spirit animation
that is in the background. Licona said it well:

He is saying that our mortal bodies in their weak
state will not be what we have in the resurrection.
They must be transformed. Since "flesh and blood"
was a figure of speech and "flesh and bone" apparently was not, Paul is not at all contradicting Luke
[24:39]. Moreover, since Paul strongly hints at a resurrection of our mortal bodies elsewhere (e.g., Rom
8:11,23; 1 Cor 15:42; Phil 3:21), any interpretation of
1 Cor 15:50 that has Paul referring to an immaterial
body proposes a Paul who contradicts not only Luke
but also himself.[13]

Paul would not teach a view against himself.

Licona summarized his treatment: "The most important Pauline text
on resurrection cannot be employed legitimately to assert that his view
of resurrection in general and Jesus' resurrection in particular differed

13 Brackets for clarification are mine.

fundamentally from the resurrection narratives in the canonical Gospels. In this text Paul never regarded the final post-mortem state of believers to be one of disembodiment."

The emerging point is clear. In line with Jewish resurrection expectation and with what the church knew and taught about Jesus' resurrection, Paul taught that the glorified resurrection body had a physical dimension that was not merely flesh but was not merely a disembodied spirit.

We have now surveyed the essays, but one issue remains. How is religious information coming to us in the digital age, and how should the public react to their new "direct" access to such claims?

RELIGIOUS CLAIMS IN THE DIGITAL AGE

As I write, archaeologists in Egypt have just announced directly to the public that a mummy long discovered has been confirmed by forensic tests as belonging to the "queen of the Nile" Hatshepsut. The announcement came with a huge press conference and notes on the national news. Some of the work was underwritten by the Discovery Channel. This direct access to the public versus presenting material and vetting it among scholars has become big business with money and prestige at stake. In sum, archaeological work has become a glitzy industry. Now some scholars can and do complain about this development, but nothing is going to take us back to the days when work was done and vetted in scholarly contexts and then published for public consumption after such a process. Those days are now gone, long gone. The many outlets of information in the digital age and the need for funding to perform the most complex digs are the causes for this way of doing things (not to mention the fame that can come from a truly historical find).

This direct access to the public is the way such historical information is being presented to the public. It means that the public needs to be patient with this new process.

I do not know if this newest Egyptian discovery is in fact true. Initial reports look promising. However, the same has been said at the early stages of other such announcements (the Talpiot tomb was an exception in this regard, as it never really got off the ground as plausible). Time will tell about Hatshepsut. The vetting that used to take place in private now takes place in public in real time, often on blogs. Only after some time does the vetting mimic the old way of doing things with the production of scholarly papers and books weighing in on their take. In fact, this book in many ways represents an effort to vet the Talpiot find after its announcement. That is the new pattern. A public claim is announced, then comes the careful vetting of that claim. That vetting takes place in real time over the Net, just as the initial news spreads through digital media as well as through the support of cable channels.

What this requires of the public is simply patience to let the new process play itself out. Sometimes the hype of a new announcement will be on target if the subsequent vetting shows it to be so. Sometimes the debate will linger and the vetting will show that. In other cases the vetting will show that the original claims were oversold as was the case with Talpiot.

So the most important piece of advice about such claims and finds is that when they are first made enjoy the glitz, take note, and then take a deep breath. Experts will weigh in, often on the Net before they publish more formal pieces. The verdict will not be in the initial press conference but in the reflection it generates. As the saying goes, "Only time [and a little give and take] will tell." Be patient. Let the new process play out. In some cases we may well find the initial hype was worth the attention. Or, as was the case with the Talpiot tomb, we may find that the only thing that emerged was an important reminder that not everything is initially what it was cracked up to be.

Name Index

Ackerman, D. A. 187, 188
Alföldy, G. 57
Alsup, J. 161
Amsler, F. 96, 98
Arav, R. 42
Avi-Yonah, M. 51
Aviam, M. 52
Avigad, N. 58, 64, 65
Avni, G. 54, 66

Bagatti, B. 14, 56, 63, 205
Baigent, M. 89
Barclay, J. M. G. 184, 189
Barkat, A. 68
Barkay, G. 42
Barnett, P. 192
Barrett, C. K. 188, 194
Bauckham, R. viii, 24, 47, 49, 69,
    69–112, 71, 72, 73, 80, 92,
    129, 159, 160, 161, 172, 208,
    208–211, 209, 210
Bauer, W. 184
Baxter, A. 189
Betz, H. D. 161
Bloedhorn, H. 86

Bock, D. 19, 20, 26, 178, 199
Borg, M. J. 183, 184, 189, 192,
    196
Bostock, G. 189
Bourvier, B. 96, 98
Bovon, F. 13, 18, 21, 86, 96, 98,
    99, 127, 199
Bremar, S. 202
Brent, A. 18
Brock, A. G. 97, 98
Brodeur, S. 189, 195
Brown, D. 13, 14, 26, 89
Brown, R. E. 79
Byrne, B. 191

Cameron, J. 1, 2, 3, 4, 7, 39, 113,
    177, 178
von Campenhausen, H. 160
Carnley, P. 183, 194
Carson, D. A. 192
Chadwick, H. 96
Charlesworth, C. H. 59
Chen, L. 6
Cohen, J. 102
Collins, R. F. 189, 192

229

Subject Index

Scripture Index

John

Acts

Apocrypha Index

M000018905

Don't "Should" On Your Kids

Build their mental toughness

Dr. Rob Bell & Bill Parisi

© 2015 Dr. Rob Bell & Bill Parisi. All rights reserved.

No part of this book may be reproduced in any form without written permission of both copyright owners.

ISBN 978-0-9899184-1-1 (Hardback)
ISBN 978-0-9899184-2-8 (Paperback)
ISBN 978-0-9899184-3-5 (E-book)

Book Design: Fresh Design, Inc.

Published by
DRB Press

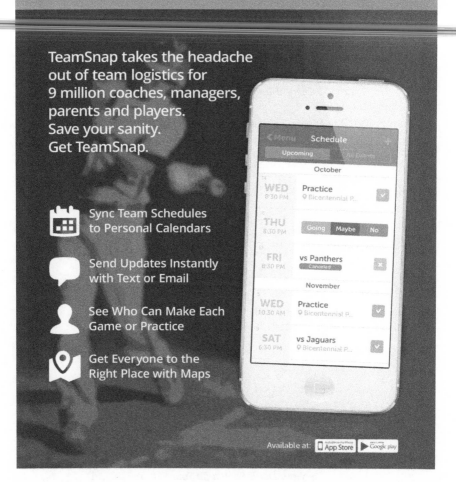

Save Time With Your Team!
You'll Be Cheering Long After The Game Is Over.

TeamSnap takes the headache out of team logistics for 9 million coaches, managers, parents and players. Save your sanity. Get TeamSnap.

Sync Team Schedules to Personal Calendars

Send Updates Instantly with Text or Email

See Who Can Make Each Game or Practice

Get Everyone to the Right Place with Maps

Available at:

Sign up at TeamSnap.com
Free and Paid Plans Available

teamSNAP

ALSO BY DR. ROB BELL

Mental Toughness Training for Golf

The Hinge: The Importance of Mental Toughness

NO FEAR: A Simple Guide to Mental Toughness

Follow *Don't Should on Your Kids* at

 The-Hinge-The-Importance-of-Mental-Toughness

 @parisispeed   www.parisischool.com
@drrobbell   www.drrobbell.com
#DontShould

Advance Praise

"As a NFL head coach, when a bad play occurs, we need to move on and focus on the next one. As parents, the best focus means enjoying the process of our kids' journey and being supportive along the way. This book helps with our kids and our own mental toughness."

— CHUCK PAGANO, NFL HEAD COACH

....

"Read this book and I'll send you a participation trophy."

— JOHN BRUBAKER, AWARD-WINNING AUTHOR, COACH & PARENT

....

*"Just like in **The Hinge**, this book provides both parents and coaches with simple, actionable steps to help their athletes develop mental toughness. I highly recommend it."*

— JOHN O'SULLIVAN, AUTHOR OF **CHANGING THE GAME.**

....

"Rob Bell and Bill Parisi have contributed an important distinction between 'supportive parents and vicarious parents.' Don't Should on Your Kids includes many practical thoughts for parents including one of my favorites, 'Great parents ask their kid, How was your day?' not just 'How was your practice?'"

— JIM THOMPSON, POSITIVE COACHING ALLIANCE FOUNDER AND AUTHOR OF **ELEVATING YOUR GAME: BECOMING A TRIPLE-IMPACT COMPETITOR**

....

The Contributors

*Thank you to the 105 coaches, parents and leaders
who contributed to this book.*

Contributor	Website
Adam Ritz	www.adamritz.com
Adam Schaechterle	www.und.com
Adam Spencer	
Adam Wiginton	www.twitter.com/coachwig
Alan Edwards	www.lamarcardinals.com
Alan Jaeger	www.jaegersports.com
Alexa Dvorak	www.twitter.com/alexajodvorak
Andy Dorrell	www.culver.org/athletics-page
Andy Pedersen	www.southeasternswim.org
Angus Mugford	www.imgacademy.com
Ann Buck	www.twitter.com/AnnBuck10
Armstrong Family	
Anthony Boone	
Bill Parisi	www.parisischool.com
Bill Van Valer	www.stonycreekgolfclub.com
Boo Rigsbee	
Brandon Dhue	www.ontariobluejays.com
Brandon Gray	
Brett Hawke	www.auburntigers.com
Brian Griffits	www.spartaindy.com
Brian Hofman	www.onusports.com
Brian Satterfield	www.twitter.com/hseboysbball
Bryan & Jeff Smith	www.tennisprogram.com
Chad Odaffer	www.alteredphysique.com
Charles Rodgers	
Conrad Ray	www.gostanford.com
Corey Smallwood	www.goperformance.com
Correct2Compete Staff	www.correct2compete.com
Craig Haworth	www.winningyouthcoaching.com
Cris James	www.und.com
Dan Gould	www.educ.msu.edu
Daniel Jackson	
Darcy Rahjes	www.wlavikings.org
Dave Sickelsteel	www.rdsoffice.com
David Roux	www.davidrouxcoaching.com
Deeana Gumpf	www.und.com
Dennis Papadatos	www.gohofstra.com
Derrick Williams	www.menofthefamily.weebly.com
Doc O'Neal	www.prairieviewgc.com
Dr. Bernice Sorenson	www.onlychild.org.uk
Dr. Mark Robinson	www.amazon.com/Mark-Robinson
Dr. Robert A. Weil	www.sportsdoctorradio.com

Contributor	Website
Dr. Scotty Hamilton	www.elitesportspsychology.com
Duane Weber	www.thetrustpointe.com
Eddie Gill	www.allout-eddiegill.com
Emily Cohen	www.teamsnap.com
Frank Agin	www.frankagin.com
Floyd Keith	www.ppaservices.org
Greg Liberto	www.mymentalgamecoach.com
Hamilton Family	
Jake Gilbert	www.twitter.com/coachgilbert10
James Leath	www.jamesleath.com
Janis Meredith	www.jbmthinks.com
Jenn Bryden	www.fastpitchfit.com
Jenna Abraham	www.twitter.com/jennanicole33
Jennie Hebermehl Van Allen	
Jill Kramer	www.gofrogs.com
Jim Anthony	www.so-mark.com
Jim Thompson	www.positivecoach.org
Joe Jones	www.goterriers.com
Joe Skovron	www.twitter.com/skovy14
John Brubaker	www.coachbru.com
John Groce	www.fightingillini.com
John O'Sullivan	www.changingthegameproject.com
John Wingfield	www.ripfest.net
Jon Stutz	www.purgatorygolf.com
Justin Dehmer	www.1pitchwarrior.com
KC Woods	
Kelly Johnson	www.gopeacepacers.com
Kelsey Steuer	www.rugbyindiana.com
Kent Kinnear	www.usta.com
Kevin DeShazo	www.fieldhousemedia.net
Kevin Kennedy	
Kirk Mango	www.becomingatruechampion.com
Kristi O'Brien	www.brigadoonfitness.com
Kurt Schier	www.southerndunesgolfcourse.com
Kyle Lynn Veltri	www.und.com
Larry Lauer	www.usta.com
Levar Johnson	www.twitter.com/ljohnson26qbnwr
Marcus Amos	www.marcusamos.com
Mark James	
Marvin Cornish Jr.	www.linkedin.com/in/mbcornish1911
Maurice Hart	www.cortlandreddragons.com
Michael Mann	
Michelle Morton	
Mike Fleck	www.ballstatesports.com
Mike Christman	www.fitnessgarageindy.com
Mike Lingenfelter	www.munciana.com
Nicole Weller	www.nicoleweller.com

Contributor	Website
P.K. Gaeger	www.twitter.com/CoachGaegerRMU
Prairie View Academy	www.prairieviewgc.com
Quinn Barham	www.gopack.com
Renard Woodmore	
Rick & Julie Allen	www.informedathlete.com
Robert Taylor	www.smarterteamtraining.com
Rusty Kennedy	www.leavener.com
Ryan Sachire	www.und.com
Scott Haynes	
Scott Lien	
Scott McNealy	
Sean Bartram	www.corepilatesandfitness.com
Shaun Wines	
Shawn Jezek	www.linkedin.com/pub/shawn-jezek
Stephanie Hazlett	www.tennisprogram.com
Stu Singer	www.wellperformancecoach.com
Sue Poeschi	www.athletics.uwsp.edu
Susan Holt	www.und.com
Tim Roberts	www.thetrustpointe.com
Tariq Sbiet	www.northpolehoops.com
Tobais Palmer	
Tom Burchill	www.lawrenceswimteam.org
Tom Evangelista	www.sewaneetigers.com
Tommy Laurendine	www.sewaneetigers.com
Tony Monteleone	
Tony Pancake	www.crookedstick.org
Tyler Miller	www.forcebarbell.com
Tyler Russell	
Virgil Herring	www.virgilherring.com
Weslye Saunders	

Acknowledgments

Dr. Rob Bell:

First, thank you to Bill Parisi, who brought an incredible wealth of experience and perspective to this book. A special thank you to Will Drumright, an incredible person who goes above and beyond. He will become a cannon in the field of Sport Psychology. The interns—Hayden Reece, Bryanna Brugar, and Megan Melchiorre. Thank you to my amazing book designer, Teri Capron. Thank you to Derek Tow of South 40 media My family, Nicole, Ryan, and Porter, who live through it. I simply could not have done it without you. Love you! Thank you to God and Jesus Christ who made me redeemed, sanctified, and worthy.

Bill Parisi:

I would like to thank my partner on this project Dr. Rob Bell. His perseverance and tenacity to get this book done was the driving force to completing this manuscript. I have learned a great deal from him throughout this project.

To my wife Jennifer, and my two sons, William and Daniel. You have taught me, and continue to teach me, how to be a great sports parent. I have made my share of mistakes, like every parent, and I will probably make a few more. However every time I erred, you all were always there to accept and forgive. Life is about learning new strategies, and trial and error are a part of learning. My family is my rock and I love you more than anything in the world. Thank you for being a part of helping me deliver such important information.

To my parents, Mary and Nick. You have given me the most important thing any parent can give their child — unconditional love. You are always there for me and I aspire to be just like you with my own children.

To the entire Parisi Speed School network...all my fellow co-workers, strategic partners, facility owners, program directors, coaches, parents and most important, the athletes. If it were not for all of you, I would never be in the position to help Dr. Bell deliver these strategies. Your willingness to constantly improve motivates me everyday. I am blessed to be around and interact with so many great people.

Most important, I want to thank God. The Creator who has proven time and time again that with a strong faith, things always work out in the end...and realizing that if they don't, it's not the end.

Contents

Foreword

We all want the best for our children, but what does that mean when it comes to their sports and activities?

As an Olympic coach of the USA diving national training center for 15 years I have worked with many families and athletes from the talent identification process through Olympic games.

Our motto "from lessons to Olympians" puts us in a unique position of working with children from pre-adolescence through young adulthood. My experience has shown that the most well-rounded and best developed athletes come from families that are supportive and engaged but not vicarious in their approach to their child's sport.

With all of my background as an elite level coach for the United States, when it comes to your own child it is interesting how difficult it is sometimes to balance your wants for their success. I have often found myself reflecting and even biting my tongue on occasion as I parent my state champion daughter.

Dr. Rob Bell & Bill Parisi's approach towards this topic is positive, insightful, and inherently relative to our role as an athlete's parent. Don't Should On Your Kids brings to light many of the attributes that are necessary to assist your child in their athletic endeavors.

—JOHN V. WINGFIELD
2008 UNITED STATES OLYMPIC HEAD DIVING COACH

Introduction

Those who criticize this generation forget who raised it.

Somewhere, at some point, a change occurred in society. Some call it a perversion.

Youth athletics became professionalized. It became trophies over toughness, product over process, talent over tenacity, and winning over development. The death of backyard basketball and the slow fade of true open gyms gave way to structure, organization, and over-parented involvement.

The level of investment has increased and the expectations of the return of investment have followed suit. Maybe it is because no one has an ugly child or the emergence of elite under-ten travel teams. Perhaps it was the specialization of year-round athletes or tourney-cations instead of family vacations. Sprinkle in the absurd rising cost of tuition across universities and it makes sense—the talent and pressure have increased, and more is seemingly at stake. There is a systemic and malignant issue—the allure of the Division I scholarship.

- We have young athletes today who look like Greek gods in the batting cage, but can't effectively run the bases.

- There are more collegiate scholarships than ever offered to girls before they have driven a car.[1]

- We rank the number one 7th grade basketball player in the nation.

- Almost 45 million kids play at least one organized sport, but more than 85 percent quit before age fifteen.[2]

- Nearly half of all sport-related injuries at the high-school age are due to chronic overuse.[3]

- Parents will spend between $4,000 and $10,000 on athletics per year.[4,5]

- Young athletes will spend so much time invested in their sport that by the time they are sophomores in college, they won't understand why they are so tired all the time.

- Forty percent of male Division I basketball players will depart their initial school by the end of their sophomore year.[6]

At some point, the system created an attitude of What's in it for me? more than it did about the skills and life-lessons that sport can teach. We miniaturized long-term growth and development and maximized a short-term focus on winning or losing.

Unfortunately, a schism occurred in sports. Somewhere, the journey became more about the parents and the results than it did about the athletes and their growth. Like Jim Thompson, founder of the Positive Coaching Alliance stated, it created "perversion of potential."

Our kids became our trophies. We polished them off to show others and boasted proudly of their accomplishments. In doing so, kids became perfectionists and played safe. At some point, these athletes were not allowed to fail. They were judged too harshly on their mistakes—so much that they quickly discerned to just "not mess up." What fun!

This book is not intended to solve the issues around sports. It took a long time getting us into that mess and it would take a lot more to get us out. No, this book is to help build your child's mental toughness—a skill that will transfer into real life and go beyond their playing days.

Parents, we play a huge role in this area of development with our kids. As life becomes more complex and inundated with distractions, mental toughness becomes more important, yet also more complex. We may believe that back in the day was the 70's, 80's or even the 90's, but back in the day was ten years ago. Think about the vast differences our society has gone through since just ten years ago. How could we have adapted our parenting skills to the changes?

For most of us, our goal has been clear: We want our children to be happy, well adjusted and successful, for them to lead productive roles in society and make it a better place. When it is time for them to leave the nest—and leave they will (hopefully)—will they be ready? Our role is two-sided—we must enjoy each moment of them growing up and prepare them for eventual departure. That is our job.

Sadly, more parents are not allowing their kids to leave home. A new trend is when they leave for college; parents are following them to school, buying a place nearby. 6b This style of parenting unfortunately builds dependence, not independence. These actions display a lack of belief in their child's abilities to cope, deal, or handle adversity.

When our children were born, the clock grew legs. We turned around, and they were all grown up. That means we need to get serious about the business of shaping our kids and preparing them for their lives. Parents, we need to be their greatest supportive coach. It is our job to be the coach that we always wanted. Our actions shape their beliefs. We are the greatest influence on our children's lives and in their development, stability, attitudes, likes, and dislikes. Children watch everything we do and learn by modeling behaviors and beliefs about ourselves. Everything a parent does either reinforces a child's confidence or discredits their self-esteem. We shape their identities. Let's do it right.

This book will help.

Mental Toughness

Simple, but not easy.

One of the biggest misnomers is that sports are 90 percent mental. When we watch or play any sport, except for a few, it is something physical. Shooting a basket, throwing a pitch, sprinting, swimming, and so on, are physical. It's just that the remaining 10 percent is mental. It unhinges the other 90 percent, so if the 10 percent is not strong the other 90 percent is in vain.

Mental toughness is simple; it's just not easy. It's how we handle, cope, and deal with the setbacks and adversity. Mental toughness also involves how we perform under pressure; these "have to" moments. And it's only a matter of when, not if, these moments will occur.

We share with players and coaches that mental toughness will not win anyone a championship, but not having mental toughness will lose it. We are preparing for that one moment, and when our opportunity hits, it's too late to prepare.

Let's start with the end in mind. What is the goal of having our kids participate in sports? If the reason for playing is externally driven (such as a college scholarship,) then building mental toughness will be extremely difficult. Outcomes and external factors need to be the byproduct of sports, not the driver.

If the goal of playing is having fun and learning the skills needed in life, you're reading the right book. Having our youth and children become confident and resilient is the goal. We like to think that mental toughness is a result of sports, however it often just reveals it.

Mental toughness is not all or nothing. All or nothing is either/or thinking, black and white. All or nothing thinking means I'm either the best or I'm the worst. You're either first or you're last. We are the shark or the minnow, the Viking or the victim, the ulcer giver or the ulcer getter.

Addicts and perfectionists view life in all or nothing terms.

The difficulty with all or nothing thinking is that it is inherent in sports. We enjoy this part of athletics because it is unambiguous—there is a winner and a loser. Life isn't that way because there isn't a finish line, and there is much uncertainty. However, sport ONLY wants us to focus on the results. That's why "Did you win?" is the first question asked after any competition. We won or lost, got a hit or didn't, the best time or not, scored or didn't. All or nothing.

Mental toughness is getting away from all or nothing thinking and being able to focus on the process. It's about progress, not perfection.

Mental toughness is a continuum. It's not either I have it or I don't. Mental toughness is how much. How much mental toughness do I have left after making mistakes or after a bad performance? The skills that will translate into life are guts, resilience, and the willpower to fight and never give up.

Most people talk about mental toughness rather than instructing it. Coaches and programs that specifically address mental skills, character, and leadership are the ways that mental toughness is built.

Mental toughness, grit, or resilience is two-fold. The first part is how we handle, deal, and cope with adversity and setbacks. The second part is how well we perform under pressure. We are all going to face times of hardship, adversity, and struggle. These are inevitable. There will also be "have to" pressure moments. It is a matter of when, not if.

Mental toughness will be the deciding factor in one way or another for long-term success. Sure, some people may be inherently more mentally tough, just as some people are faster or better looking, but it still can be learned.

Don't "Should" On Your Kids

We take an adult view and impose it on our kids.

—*Dr. Angus Mumford*

An interesting thing occurs in every profession whether an ICU nurse, a grade school teacher, attorney or professor. When they are excellent at their job and possess talent, they are promoted. A nurse becomes an administrator, a grade school teacher becomes an assistant principal, an attorney makes partner, a professor becomes department head or dean, etc.

See, people get *should* on, even as adults. A nurse "*should* be an administrator." Maybe it is the right progression for them. However, a nurse's true passion may be working with patients, and becoming an administrator took her away from it. She realized later where her true passion resides, but she spent years doing what other people expected of her.

Our entire lives we have been *should* on. You should join the advanced program, you should double major, play the piano, play Division I, go into finance, become a president.

All of these positive "*shoulds*" are noble and well intentioned. It is great when people believe in you to have such high expectations. However, *shoulding* can get messy—and stink. It creates expectations to meet other's expectations. And these are just the positive types of *shoulds*.

As adults, we can hopefully recognize that, in most cases, people were just trying to provide advice and be helpful. However, when does *should* cross the line between helpful and hurtful?

Then there are the negative shoulds: You "*shouldn't*" wear that. You "*should*" call your mother more often. You "*shouldn't*" feel that way. You "*shouldn't*" make these mistakes. You "*should*" be more like your friend.

Does everyone know what's best for you? When others *should* on us, they are imposing their beliefs and experiences into our world. Making us feel like our experience, feelings, and beliefs don't matter that much. In reality, when people *should* on us, it's all about them and how they will somehow be affected by our actions or non-actions.

Parents who constantly *should* on their kids produce kids who *should* on themselves. If we were *should* on long enough and severe enough as a youth, the voice of should becomes internalized and we started *shoulding* on ourselves.

I "*should*" not have eaten that huge piece of cake last night. Maybe I *shouldn't* have said that. No, I definitely *shouldn't* have written that, etc.

When we conjure up feelings of "*should*," it doesn't motivate us. It does the opposite. A pile of *should* just reinforce the negative and reminds us that we are not good enough. See, I told you—you *shouldn't* have those negative thoughts!

Pain is temporary, but soreness lasts. We forget how full that one piece of cake made us feel. But, when reminded that we *shouldn't* have eaten it, it conjures up other feelings of how we *should* do better in other areas as well. The *shoulds* pile up. Directive statements about your child's past performances do little to inspire, instead creating fear. Condemnation, guilt, and shame are the result.

It's best to realize and be aware that a child will do almost anything to please his parents and his coach. When we *should* on our kids, we are establishing expectations, brutally reminding them of negatives, mistakes, and that they aren't good enough. When kids fail to reach your expectations, they can suffer and feel like a failure. *Shoulding* on them creates expectations that that they may or not be able to reach.

*Alex, you **shouldn't** be nervous.*

Kristen, you have to play well today.

John, you must perform better if you want to go further.

Callie, you need to practice.

*Dwayne, you **shouldn't** make so many mistakes.*

Billy, whatever you do, don't make the last out.

The title of this book reflects one of the strategies for building your child's mental toughness instead of tearing it down. The following pages will expand on and provide many more techniques. In this book, we don't demand that as a parent, you *should*, must, or have to execute these strategies. These recommended strategies are based on research and applied experience—it's up to you. However, you want to parent and coach, you've gotten this book for a reason, and athletics needs to remain about your son or daughter.

What do Wes Welker, Kurt Warner, Rod Smith, John Starkes, Warren Moon, London Fletcher, and Adam Vinatieri all have in common?

They will be hall of famers at some level, and all went undrafted. Why?

Speculation—it's the mother of all evil. Professional scouts are paid to evaluate talent and pick only the winners. It is such an inaccurate discipline that it has out of necessity become a combination of art and science. Scouts admit that they aren't always trying to hit home runs; they are interested in singles and doubles. However, scouts and organizations often still miss the mark on selecting the best. It's surface judgments based only on stats and performance, which are not a real predictor of success.

Likewise, trying to predict the eventual outcome of our son or daughter is futile. When immersed in the journey of sports development and success, try to start with the end in mind. But honestly, does the end you have in your mind mean a collegiate Division I scholarship? Beginning with the end in mind means visualizing the type of person we want our son or daughter to become.

The most important skill to learn from sport is mental toughness, grit, and resilience. The mental toughness of your son or daughter is largely due to how you parent, model your life, and surround them with a healthy environment. The arena of sport can provide the skills, ethic, ethos that we desire, and the life lessons that will transfer and permeate long after their career is over.

The foundations of this book are passion and confidence. However, drive, intrinsic motivation, perseverance, and persistence must come from your child. They must want it. They must be in touch with their own "why." It cannot come from us because it's hard to be driven when you're being driven.

Passion and confidence are the most important attributes in our children's development of mental toughness because it will become difficult at times. If they only play to please their parents or coach, for a scholarship or for pats on the back, it won't be enough. They will instead become "at-least," the subject of the next chapter.

Winners, Losers, and At-Leasters

The best coaching job is the head coach of an orphanage.

Wade was a very talented 12-year-old hockey player, but he was a coach's nightmare. He would only play hard when he felt like it, which was, unfortunately, only about a quarter of the time.

Not surprisingly, Wade's father also worked whenever he felt like it. He had Dilbert comic strips up in his office and often bragged about how little he worked.

Children will become in many ways what we as parents are, and we shape their belief systems. Most of us want our children to be better than ourselves and to have it better than we did. However, we cannot give away what we do not possess ourselves.

Let's oversimplify and say there are three types of people: winners, losers, and at-leasters. These are not only three types of people, but three distinct beliefs or mindsets that we form as children. They shape who we eventually become.

We love winners. For example, when anyone discusses athletes in life, no one talks about the 20th or 40th best athlete in that sport. They reference just a select few, the very best, the top 1/10 of 1 percent. Tiger Woods, Serena Williams, Tom Brady, Peyton Manning, LeBron James, and Missy Franklin, to name a few. They are referencing winners, athletic geniuses blessed to excel. These people will be successful in any situation.

Those perceived as losers, on the other hand, are born from a combination of poor circumstances and choices and a belief that everything turns out poorly for them. These are the victims of life. It never is about them; it's someone else's fault. Again, this represents a very small percentage of the population.

Most, however, are the at-leasters. At-leasters are not losers, far from it. They are involved, active, and in it. But, they lack the ingredients at becoming a winner. They believe that at-least we showed up, at-least we weren't last, at-least we weren't as bad as the other team. It's a defense mechanism that protects them from the pain of not being winners. It is a struggle for at-leasters to get out of their comfort zones. We have all been there, but we don't have to live there.

At-leasters go through the motions. Settling is okay. Playing it safe is good enough. Our comfort zone is too comfortable. We would rather be a maybe than a no. Be good, but not great. If we happened to be really good for one day, we dismiss it, saying, "Yeah, but I'm not *that* good."

The at-least mentality is toxic and systemic. The environment of youth sport has perpetuated at-leasters.

Youth sport that gives everyone a trophy has created an at-least mentality. At least we got a trophy... We don't create winners by making everyone **not** losers.

Youth sport often stresses winning so much over development that it has also created a culture of at-leasters. The short-term is magnified, and the long-term is miniaturized. The long-term is viewed through a telescope and the short-term through a microscope.

No one wants to lose, but when we only value winning over development, it causes us to self-protect. One way or another, "at least we weren't last" creeps into our mentality. We rarely create winners by only treasuring winning.

Athletes seek comfort and will do everything they can to please both coaches and parents. Athletes learn that the way to please coach and parents is to just not lose.

As a parent, we can inadvertently drive a child into the at-least mentality when we make it all about us. If this is one of your parenting techniques, remember—it's about them. We can't make it about us, and it cannot become about us. We fail when it becomes about us. The best sports parents seem to be behind the scenes, providing encouragement and a supportive environment. Appreciate the long-term, and depreciate the short-term.

No One Has an Ugly Child

It's tough to make predictions even about the future.

—*Yogi Berra*

No one has an ugly baby. It is tough to admit, but parents often lack the perspective and emotion to assess our own child's ability level accurately. We form an all or nothing mentality. We think they're either the best or that they are the worst.

It doesn't matter what you think of your child's ability level. We as parents over-estimate their ability and talent level. You're Mom and Dad—your role is to be supportive, not vicarious. Few scouts or recruiting directors will be calling you to ask how good you think your son or daughter is. Coaches will most likely observe the interactions among family members and how your son or daughter handles setbacks. What we value most, as a family, is on what we focus. Our role is to stress effort, accountability, character, and create a supportive environment—not measure their vertical leap, bat speed, or split times.

> *Mrs. Riggs was a walking scorer at a PGA event, one of those who keep track of each shot a player hits. After the round, she made it a point to call this PGA player's father and tell him what a mature, class act his son was. She didn't have to call, but what greater compliment could a father receive than unsolicited praise about his son's character. And this was from one afternoon of interactions during a round of professional golf.*

Do not hesitate to share with others the positives about someone else. By the same token, resist the urge to tell others how talented your child is. Allow others close to your child to boast about him or her. Hopefully, they describe an aspect of your child's character, rather than just their talent. We often forget that youth sports are intended to build character and serve as a metaphor for life.

Vicarious vs. Supportive

Do you live through your child or with your child?

Your child is having a great season as the post-season approaches. He is worried. He asks you the question, "What if I lose?"

What is your response?

A *vicarious parent* would reply along the lines of, "That's not going to happen, you're so good" or "You shouldn't think that way." If you're a parent who responds this way, you're likely living directly through your child's success or failure. You still mean well and love your kid, but you've just become too emotionally invested in the results.

These types of parents, unfortunately, lack the perspective to make rational decisions. They live and die with every play and game. Their child is the best when he or she wins, and they are the worst when they lose. All or nothing.

- Vicarious parents are as close as physically possible to every practice.

- Vicarious parents often blame others when the important outcomes do not go well.

- Vicarious parents are the ones comparing their son or daughter to others.

- Vicarious parents stress out quickly and easily.

- Vicarious parents are usually the ones at the games shouting instructions.

- Vicarious parents feel their child's success is a reflection of themselves.

- Vicarious parents don't realize they are living through their child.

A *supportive parent*, on the other hand, answers the "What if I lose?" question a different way. They approach along the lines of, "Why do you think that?" or "Let's talk it through…what if you lose?" Supportive parents provide an environment that remains safe. They don't try to solve their kids concerns. They encourage their children to think for themselves, come up with their solutions and handle their outcomes. Home is not a fan base. Athletes can rest assured that in the home, no matter how they perform, their identity is not just as an athlete. They have unconditional love and support. Lastly, these children aren't nagged about their preparation or whether they are nervous before important performances.

- Supportive parents attend from a distance and may even miss a practice.

- Supportive parents ensure their son or daughter assumes responsibility, not blaming coaches or situations.

- Supportive parents stress effort over results.

- Supportive parents know their son or daughter's performance is just a shadow of them, not a reflection.

- Supportive parents make sure they aren't over the top.

- Supportive parents are aware of the long-term development.

- Supportive parents don't *should* on their kids.

Both types of parents make sacrifices and difficult decisions for their child along the journey. No one questions whether the love and support are there. Unfortunately, these vicarious or supportive labels are not mutually exclusive. We may sometimes be one type of parent with one child and another type with another. It's possible for the pendulum to swing to both extremes and even for us to live in the middle. This is about progress, not perfection. We are going to make mistakes, but that is the point. How can we help our child build mental toughness? How can we become better, more self-aware parents in the process?

When you think about parents of famous athletes, who comes to mind? Was it a parent that stayed behind the scenes or one that sparked controversy?

Archie and Olivia Manning are examples of successful sports parents. The couple produced two number-one overall NFL draft picks, two Super Bowl winning quarterbacks, and two Super Bowl MVPs. Archie Manning said it best, *"We just tried to raise good kids and have a good family. I don't like the perception that it (having the boys play pro football) was a plan."[7]*

On the opposite end of the spectrum, a mother of a collegiate basketball player uttered these words to the head coach when asked about her son's goals, *"My goals are his goals."* Okay, then.

Three Types of Parents

Most parents build dependency, great parents build capacity.

All parents want the absolute best for their child. The easy tell of a parent's confidence is to watch them during their child's competition. The most confident parents are relaxed and not stressing at all. Those who lack self-confidence are uptight, pacing, and even providing instructions.

Parents who are comfortable in who they are, their identity, and their roles in life produce children who are comfortable, confident, and relaxed. However, parents who are truly insecure reflect that insecurity at home to their kids. They should on their kid, because they need them to be successful to make somehow up for their feelings of insecurity.

The Simple Parent

The first type of parent knows very little about their kid's sport. And these are often the best types of parents. They were never gymnasts or tennis players, so they are unable to provide any knowledgeable feedback.

Of course, there are also those who never played, so they think it is different and easier than it is. It is funny and sad to watch a parent who knows jack donuts about the sport they are trying to teach when they can't even do it themselves.

The Assistant Coach

The second type of parent is the one who played sports. They achieved some success, but may not have achieved what they thought to be their full potential. They are knowledgeable on how they approached and played the game. Since they know the answers, these are often the most vicarious type of parent because they are smart enough to be very dangerous. These parents criticize more than they commend and point out the one mistake rather than the many positives.

The Success

A third type of parent is the former elite athlete. They can be very hands-off, knowing full well the sacrifices that need to be made for success. If the typical parent knew what it took to be a professional athlete, they wouldn't sign up—for their kids or themselves. These former athletes are aware that it must be about their child and helping them develop their own passion. They do allow their son or daughter to experience failure because they know how instructive it can be. However, they can also place high expectations on their child because of their own past successes.

If you recognize yourself in the above descriptions, take some advice: Allow coaches to do the tough coaching. That's not your role. Coaches are the ones who can and should provide the appropriate feedback. Too often, athletes receive one message from the coach on a technique or strategy, only to have parents provide their interpretation and feedback that contradicts the coach. This is confusing for the child, who may feel torn over what to do.

Three Types of Athletes

Show me an athlete afraid to look bad, and I'll show you an athlete you can beat every time.

—Unknown

The Safe Perfectionist

The first type of athlete is the safe perfectionist. This type of athlete has become the new normal. Playing it safe is the way to maintain the appearance of perfectionism. However, perfectionism is another word for insanity.

> *The point guard at this university was a good player, made few mistakes, and played consistently. However, he often held back and never took over a game. As a result, the team bowed out early during the postseason. This player never reached his potential.*

Athletic directors and coaches stress one huge change in recent years. More and more athletes have become perfectionists, safe, and afraid to make mistakes. They struggle with handling adversity and being able to make adjustments.

From helmets used in soccer, face-masks for fielding, and mouth guards galore, we have become overly concerned about an athletes safety. In some cases, this is justified. However, when it comes to reaching our potential, safe doesn't cut it. Playing it safe is risky. The safe perfectionist plays not to lose, rather than to win.

The safe perfectionist is afraid of messing up. She knows she can play it safe and not get judged too harshly nor risk defeat through her play. Playing it safe means she will not be called out, and she can't be the one who is blamed if a loss occurs. The motivation to put yourself *out there* simply does not outweigh the risk of defeat.

At some point, these athletes became afraid to fail! They were judged too harshly on their mistakes or put way too much pressure on themselves. The athlete quickly discerned to do their best not to mess up.

Vicarious parents often unconsciously contribute to the safe perfectionist athlete, as we only pointing out the negative or comparing their performance to someone else. Vicarious parents struggle with praise and feel pushing their child is the only way to long-term success.

Building mental toughness in your child means helping them to play their best when it matters the most. There is a saying that "if it bleeds, it leads." Sport is the arena where our kids should learn how to put themselves out there, go for it, lead from the front, and play with whatever passion is in their hearts. Nervousness, excitement, and risk exist when you're putting everything on the line. As Billy Jean King stated, "pressure is a privilege."

Mental toughness is also how we all learn to deal and cope with adversity. These are the skills to emphasize in youth sports. Mental toughness is paramount beyond the field of play, assuming the goal is to build skills that transfer into life. When we face pressure moments, will we play it safe or have the confidence to take the risk?

> The first female billionaire and inventor of Spanx, Sara Blakely, reported her secret to success was the influence of her father. She was encouraged by failing, because failing means you are trying, and she learned from her dad that true failure meant not trying at all. She credits what she learned from her father to her success because she wasn't intimidated later in life, taking a risk in the massive field of retail—and pushing through to become a success.[8]

Game Day or Practice Day Athlete

Watch this or don't miss?

Two other types of athletes are the game day athlete and the practice day athlete.

Game day athletes are the ones who don't particularly practice that hard, but they show up on game day. What frustrates coaches is their true potential is never realized. These are the athletes with talent. The issue is that we have no idea that athlete is going to show up on game day—it could be Taylor Swift or Lady Gaga, Tom Cruise or Adam Sandler. There is little consistency in their performance. Game day athletes can be great at times, but they *could* be the very best. Depending on their ability level the next level is often a huge awakener for them because everyone is good, yet they may lack the dedication that it takes to get there and stay there.

Practice day athletes, on the other hand, are the ones who practice the best and usually work the hardest. They are ones who complete every pass in practice, shoot the lowest scores before the tournament, and have killer pick-up games.

But when the lights turn on, for some reason, their confidence fizzles. Practice day athletes shrink and morph into the type of player who goes from "watch this" to "I hope I don't miss."

From a parent's perspective, these types will wear you out and can be frustrating. You've seen their best and you're aware of their potential, but they don't always play that way.

Vicarious parents do much harm with either of these athletes. They want consistent and progressive results and stress out and blame others when playing levels off. The *shoulds* often occur during these times.

Supportive parents do their best parenting with these types. They can notice when their son or daughter is not doing as well as hoped. They want to help, and remain objective and empathize rather than judge or question their effort level. Supportive parents point out success, no matter how small.

The path may be troublesome and setbacks will occur, many of which are inevitable. It is a curvy path toward mastery, not a straight line. Allow the coaches to do their craft, and remain supportive. This isn't a snap your fingers kind of revelation, but a process that evolves sometimes quickly, sometimes slowly.

Confidence—Prepare Them for the Hinge Moment

Every door has a hinge; if it doesn't, it's just a wall.

The pilot of an AirBus A320 took off from La Guardia airport on a flight to Charlotte. Less than three minutes into the flight, the plane with 155 passengers aboard struck a flock of geese and immediately lost both engines and all power to the airplane. The pilot immediately knew that he couldn't get back to the airport and needed to find a place to land the plane in the most populated area in the entire world. The incident became known as the miracle on the Hudson, as Captain Chelsey "Sully" Sullenberger successfully landed the plane on the Hudson River.

Throughout Captain Sully's more than forty years of flying and 20,000 hours of airtime, he had achieved his goal of never crashing an airplane. What he didn't and couldn't realize is that his entire life had been in preparation for that one moment. Who else would you have wanted piloting that airplane?[9]

The Hinge: The Importance of Mental Toughness was written because in every one's life there are significant moments. In every important game, the outcome is usually decided by one play. At the highest level, an entire season is dictated by one game. The hinge is that one play, game, event or person that makes all the difference in our lives. We do not know when it will happen or who it will be, except in retrospect.

The importance of mental toughness is that it only takes one. It doesn't matter how poorly we played last season, how we messed up last game or even the last play. It only takes one play or game to turn everything around! We need to be mentally tough because when our opportunity hits, it's too late to prepare. We need to be ready.

The hinge connects who we are with who we become. Although it only takes one, there will be many possible hinge moments in our lives.

An interesting aspect of hinge moments is that we are not aware of them until after they occur, which may be days, weeks, months, or even years after they occur. We can't connect the dots looking ahead; we can only connect them looking backward.

Unfortunately, a lack of mental toughness can keep the hinge from connecting. If we lack the ability to refocus, play with confidence, or handle adversity, then we will likely miss the most important play, the next one. We prepare for the few moments that decide the outcome of the game.

We can't predict the future, we can only prepare for the unpredictable. Since we have no idea which moments or games or people will make all the difference, we need to treat every game and moment as a possible hinge moment.

Parenting Hinge Moments

It only takes one.

John Starks played only one year of high school basketball and went undrafted out of college. He played in the independent leagues of basketball and even played a season in the NBA for the Golden State Warriors. However, no one could have predicted that he would become a NBA all-star and the New York Knicks all-time leader in three-pointers. It was an injury that led him to Knicks stardom.

He received a try-out with the Knicks but wasn't expected to make the team. Fortune favors the bold and Starks had plenty of that intangible skill. During try-outs, his 6'3" frame attempted a dunk over 7'0" Patrick Ewing. The hall of fame center rejected the dunk and slammed Starks to the ground, causing Starks to injure his knee. NBA rules state that a player cannot be cut from a roster if they are injured, so he remained on the team. It was after he returned that the Knicks began to value his work ethic so much that he garnered playing time. His injury became a hinge moment.[10]

It doesn't matter where your children are on the depth chart, or how bad things seem. We need to stay ready because it only takes one! For our hinge to connect, we must have confidence.

People think that most hinge moments are only in big games. It's true, games hold important moments; however many occur in practice, in normal games or even on the ride home. Once an athlete makes the connection with their true confidence or they figure something out, these serve as hinge moments. These are the events that transcend the world of sports and into everyday life skills.

Can the ride home be a hinge moment? Remember the old rhyme, *"Sticks and stones may break my bones, but words will never hurt me?"* That lie ranks right alongside with, *"Don't worry, that ball won't hurt."*

What hurts worse than someone criticizing us, especially someone close to us? Words can cause emotional scarring. We have to be careful about what we say to our loved ones because they are listening. If we continually criticize and mention only the negatives from a performance and how they need to get better, then that is what they will hear and focus on.

A golf instructor mentioned how a father of a player told him that he was playing great, but "pulled a Sara, I choked on the last hole." Sara, his daughter, directly heard it, and the instructor said that you could see the confidence leak out of her. How many times had she heard that label, and what kind of self-concept did she have?

We cannot build up certain moments or games because this only makes athletes tight and try to force things to happen. We need to stress that effort is everything. Our effort in practice and in games where we are behind or the season is going poorly. These are hinge moments as well. Unfortunately, tragedies are immediate and powerful hinges. From that moment on, everything is changed. It doesn't mean that it has to remain bad, but things have changed.

The death of a loved one, cancer, accidents, and natural disasters are examples of tragedies. Making an error, missing a shot, or messing up are not any fun at all and will hurt, but they are still just challenging experiences in comparison.

There is an important difference between tragedies and challenging experiences. This may be difficult, but no matter how bad an outcome is in sports, even at the highest level, it is a challenging experience—it is not a tragedy. Failure is never fatal. It may feel like it for a while, but it is only a challenge. Keeping athletics in the proper perspective for our children helps them keep their problems in perspective.

And as your son or daughter reflects back and connects the dots on these challenging experiences, it will be their mental toughness that defines their success. Sometimes the biggest setbacks in life can be setups for the biggest comebacks. Overcoming challenging experiences is what helps our children grow.

Ann was a dancer who started at a young age and had goals of becoming the prima ballerina for a ballet company. As a young girl, her coach also had a daughter who danced and competed. Sadly, this coach favored her own daughter a bit more over Ann and began to slowly chip away at Ann's self-confidence throughout the years. Anyone who has been on the opposite end of being a coach's favorite understands what this feels like.

Ann's parents were of course empathetic. It pained them to watch their daughter struggle with her chosen passion. They listened and supported her but they also built Ann's mental toughness. Ann's parents refused to directly intervene. They allowed Ann to work out the issues on her own. Her parents had a rule that once Ann chose to commit to a season she could not quit. They remained supportive, but not vicarious.

It was extremely painful experience for Ann at the time, but the lessons would prove to be fruitful. Her mental toughness garnered from overcoming challenges in her sport had effectively prepared for her professional career.

Confidence is King, Focus is Queen

This is chess—this isn't checkers.

In the movie *Training Day*, Denzel Washington has a great line where he says, "This is chess—this isn't checkers." Sport and life are the same way. There are no grand masters in checkers. However, I'm sure there are a lot of ties. We quit playing checkers because it's no longer a challenge. In chess, however, there are a lot of moving parts and no ceiling.

Confidence is king because the lack of confidence is how games are lost. When the king dies the game is over. Once we lose confidence or trust in coaches, our parents or ourselves it is difficult to get it back. If confidence is lost at the elite levels of the sport, the game is over.

The king in chess does not win the game. The king only moves one space at a time. Likewise, confidence is a fragile commodity. It can take weeks and months to build it up, but only one poor choice of words on our part as a parent to tear it down.

Focus is queen. The game is won by moving our queen. We gain confidence by addressing our focus. Whatever we focus on grows. When we play and practice, where and what do we focus on?

If athletes focus on messing up, try **not** to make a mistake or playing it safe, then their lack of confidence will grow. If they label themselves as a slow starter, poor finisher or an at-leaster, then this focus becomes their reality. On the other hand, if athletes are focused on the next play in front of them, making a play, and staying aggressive, confidence grows and success is the result.

Confidence is a Feeling

*Pressure can burst a pipe, but we think
it only produces diamonds.*

If you ask any athlete what they're thinking about when they're playing at their best, the answer is always the same: "Nothing." Athletes that achieve mind-blowing streaks in any sport when asked how they did it also say: "I don't know."

Elite performers all stress that when they are playing their best, the event slows down. They feel in complete control. Have you ever finished a workout or a run, looked at yourself in the mirror and thought, "Hey, I look good." Honestly, you look no different from when you began, except you now feel different. Depending on our perspective on spirituality, our prayers may not be automatically answered, but we feel better after praying or even meditating. We feel at peace.

When an athlete loses confidence that feeling now turns into thoughts. They just begin to think too much. They no longer trust their instincts, their gut. Instead, they get stuck inside their head and try to think their way into right acting. The first thing that goes when an athlete begins performing poorly is the lack of feeling. Their play or technique may look fine, but if they don't feel confident, they will begin to search.

Confidence eventually becomes the most important part of mental toughness because it affects all other skills. Our children will attempt and continue to participate in activities where they feel successful. Confidence extends to include our children's belief and trust in those around them, coaches, and parents.

Confidence is not only a feeling, however. Mental toughness means being able to play well when our feeling is off. There will be days and weeks that are tough, and due to many different circumstances, the athlete doesn't feel confident. They lose that trust and belief. Hopefully at that time, your child's confidence is plugged into something greater than their performance.

Research has shown that there are various sources of confidence. Sport psychology coaches teach ways to become confident by changing our physiology, our body language, and how we feel. If confidence wasn't a feeling, then why stress focused breathing or becoming centered?

Build Confidence Through Their GPS

We do not know the results from our action,
but if we take no action, there will be no results.

—*GANDHI*

How many of us have been driving in an unfamiliar place, following our GPS, and we suddenly felt that we were not quite in the right spot? So, we turned a corner or drove straight ahead disregarding the map.

Our confidence is our built-in GPS system. Trust is our gut, our intuition, and the belief and ability to trust in our decisions. Confidence is the ability to re-focus, to let go of mistakes, and to listen to our gut, our inborn GPS. Our GPS points us in the direction we are supposed to go. It's our decision whether or not to trust our gut.

Here's what our GPS does not do, however. I've never had the GPS ask me, How did you get here? Why are you in this part of town? Are you going to be late? Our GPS merely redirects us if we miss a turn or take a different route.

Confidence doesn't judge. It never asks questions like, How did you get in this situation? This should be over, why are you even here? Are you really good enough?

Parent Strategy: Program their GPS

Has your child ever asked, "don't you trust me?" One of the myths of trust is like mental toughness; it's not all or nothing. The myth is that we have it, or we don't. Trust is a continuum. Does it become a question of *how much do I trust*? For example, we may trust our kids to drive the car, but not across the country.

Trust is a process... How much do we trust our kids? Trust affects everything because the more we trust and have confidence, the better focused, relaxed, and honest we become. If we give someone a task and know that it will be done, it frees us up to focus on something else.

One of the best traits that we can share with our kids is trust. How much do we trust our gut and our instincts?

Build your son or daughter's GPS by allowing them the choice to listen to it or not. Allow them to make mistakes and learn from it to problem solve and find a way. It's not easy. However, we fail to be a GPS ourselves when we start judging their performance, overly questioning their effort or always fixing it for them.

We confuse our inborn GPS when we become unable to let go of mistakes and bring up past errors. It is difficult, if not impossible, to remain confident if we can't redirect ourselves on the destination and how to get there.

We need to build up and learn to trust our inborn GPS so we can be the steady guide for our children. Listening to our gut is a skill and requires that we remain in the moment and take action.

> There was a parent who no matter what her daughter suggested would offer up the worst possible outcome. The girl was in college and had been hearing this negativity her entire life! It's not a shock that she became unable to trust any decision she made on or off the field. She was very talented but had low detrimental confidence. When things would go wrong in sport, she could not make adjustments.

Bad outcomes, bad breaks, and inconveniences will happen. These are inevitable. The way we build mental toughness in our kids is by allowing them to go through these tough periods and find a way.

However, if we do not take any action there will be no results. If we don't first trust our GPS then we can't give it away.

Confident people can do this skill.

Nothing Bothers You

Body language doesn't talk, it screams.

October 14th, 2003, Game six of the National League Championship Series between the Chicago Cubs and the Florida Marlins. This was supposed to be the year that ended the 95-year World Series drought for the Cubs. There was uneasiness in the crowd even though Mark Prior was pitching great that day, having allowed only three hits going into the eighth inning. The Cubs were leading 3-0 in the game and one win away from taking the series. In many ways, Cubs fans were waiting for it to take a turn for the worse.

What happened in the eighth inning became known as "the Steve Bartman incident." Moises Alou had a chance to catch Louis Castillo's foul ball, in which Cubs fan Bartman tried to catch it as well, denying Alou and the Cubs the second out of the inning. All the fans in the stadium and even the players didn't pay much attention to the actual play, until seconds later, when Moises Alou had a mini-tantrum, lost his cool, slammed his glove, and yelled at the fan. The reaction by Alou communicated to everyone, PANIC. Only then did the entire crowd know and the air completely left the stadium.

It was his reaction to the event that led to a horrible response.

Mark Prior next threw a wild pitch and then shortstop Alex Gonzalez made an error to load the bases. At the end of the inning, it was 8-3 in favor of the Marlins, who won the series the following game.[11]

Body language doesn't talk, it screams. Sometimes it swears.

Now what-if never happened, but had Alou not reacted, the team might have kept their cool and the Marlins may not have been so inspired and relentless.

Think about how real confidence looks and acts? Chances are we mostly think of someone playing well and dominating the sport. Confidence comes naturally at these moments.

The truth is that everyone faces adversity, struggles, and goes through dry spells. This can come in the form of struggle during a game or adversity throughout a season. Can we have confidence during these times as well?

Confidence is the most important part of mental toughness and a true indicator of how an athlete handles the struggle. It's how we handle the struggle and how our children interact with us during these times of stress.

Confidence is simply the belief that it will work out. Fear is the biggest barrier to confidence because we don't believe that it is going to work out like we want it. Playing time, scholarships or failing can all put stress on the confidence level of our children.

The best let nothing bother them. They keep their head in the game when others are losing theirs. They believe in their process so much that they refuse to let setbacks affect their mindset or their team. It's amazing to see, but the best athletes manage their poise and focus. Nothing bothers them. It is the major impact of confidence and the true test of one's level of confidence and mental toughness.

It is common for the major changes or setbacks to bother us. However, ever notice when we get stressed that everything seems to bother us like the person next to us in traffic or our family? When we are confident, these things don't bother us at all but they become the first thing to annoy us when we lose our belief that things will work out.

When we criticize others outside of our family our children hear this. When we become stressed out and we struggle to control our language or behavior, our children witness it. As coach John Brubaker states, "Parenting is contagious." We can't give away what we don't have and if we get uncomfortable our kids will follow suit.

During games most of the poor behavior by parents is because they feel everything must go their way—meaning no bad calls, all the playing time, no drama on the team, and certainly no mistakes. If the goal is to have nothing bad happen during the game, then have your son or daughter play for the Globetrotters, because they're the only team that never loses.

When we lose our cool during a game or criticize after the game, we show our children that we don't believe things will work out. If we did, then we wouldn't let it bother us so much. We still may get upset, but we can refocus, not let it bother us, and certainly not reflect this behavior to our kids.

We can make this mantra a goal to be achieved rather than just an outcome of confidence. The only way we can achieve our goal of "nothing bothers me" is if we are confident. What we agree to is the belief that "I don't need everything to go my way to be successful. I believe it will work out, and I am just going to act as if."

Pre-Season

Pre-season is a time to help build a child's mental toughness. Parents should be saluted during this time of the year because it is not easy. We often contribute the most amount of sacrifice during these times. You have contributed to the cause financially, through car rides, and through multiple conversations about how to make everything work.

The theme of mental toughness during this time of the year is MOTIVATION.

The goal is for them to want it more than you. How do you achieve that? Our job is to allow them to take ownership in their development. Encourage their efforts and compliment them on improving. Most importantly, keep the pre-season in perspective. Don't focus on rankings, predictions or the "what if's" of a season. Instead, focus on the process and having fun. But beware, because the *shoulds* often start to emerge during this time of the season. You *should* have a great season. You *should* work on your weaknesses. Or, this is an important year; you *should* have a good one. These statements put emphasis on the wrong goal. Keep it about the process and keep it positive.

It's Not Who Can Get There First — It's Who Can Get There And Stay There

Have you ever drank wine before it's ready?

—MIKE LINGENFELTER

Let's compare the journeys of two youth athletes. Remember the player as a youth who somehow had a beard? Typically the best athletes at younger ages are the biggest and the most physically developed. But golf is a sport where physical development is less important and occurs much later. It's such a mental game, so this kid had a proverbial mental beard. He played beyond his years, didn't make mistakes, and won—a lot.

He was not only the number-one 12-year-old golfer in California, but he was so good that at one international tournament he shot 73-70 and won it by 16 shots. When he finished 6th at the Junior World Golf Championships that same year, the best field in the world, he was disappointed. At that time in California future PGA champion Rickie Fowler looked up to this kid.

As a freshman in high school, every collegiate program wanted this golfer and everyone approached him. The expectations for this young man were tremendous and he admitted that when he began to struggle he thought he was letting everyone down. When growth occurred his golf swing changed, he became confused with mechanics, started enjoying other sports, and soon lost confidence. Remember, confidence is king.

Luckily, his stellar grades buffered him from finding his complete identity in being only a golfer. He still managed to play in college but at a much lower level. This golfer's name, Joe Skovron, would actually later become Rickie Fowler's caddy on the PGA Tour.

In comparison, the other youth athlete played all different competitive sports at a younger age, including football, baseball, and basketball. Everyone in the state of Indiana played basketball and his dad played basketball in college struggling somewhat when he stopped playing.

The expectation was never for this kid to play professional golf. He didn't start playing competitive golf until 12 years old, much later than other professional golfers. The expectations from every round of golf were to have fun, learn something, have a positive experience, and make a friend. In an 8th grade tournament, he shot an 89 in the first round. In the car ride, they didn't discuss the round at all—only the excellent par on the last hole. He responded by shooting a 71 the next day.

Patrick Rodgers' development and passion for golf took off in high school. His dad and mom always allowed golf to be their son's passion. Patrick ended up playing golf at Stanford, tied Tiger Woods' record with eleven wins, became the number-one ranked collegiate golfer, won the Ben Hogan award, and turned professional after his junior season.

> The Super Bowl features the best two teams and many of
> the best players in the NFL. Super Bowl XLIX between the
> New England Patriots and the Seattle Seahawks was epic.
> An interesting fact about that Super Bowl was that not one
> starter on either team was a five-star recruit.[12]
> As golf professional Virgil Herring said, "It's not who gets
> there first; it's who can get there and stay there."

For smaller schools participating in basketball, making the NCAA tournament is a successful season even though the sport provides the most upsets in major collegiate sports. In 1999, Weber State University in Utah won the Big Sky Conference and was awarded a 14-seed and a 3rd seed opponent powerhouse, University of North Carolina (UNC). North Carolina was making its 25th consecutive tournament and hadn't lost a first round game since 1978.

A star was introduced to the country that day. Harold Arceneaux led Weber State with 36 points and with two free throws in the closing seconds, beat 3rd seeded UNC. It remains as one of the biggest upsets in tournament history, and the last time Weber State won an NCAA tournament game.

Although Weber State lost their next game to the University of Florida in overtime, Harold Arceneaux scored 32 points. He declared for the NBA draft, but instead returned to Weber State for his senior season, against the recommendations of many NBA scouts.

Due to Harold Arceneux returning for his senior season, NBA scouts were at most games, and they began to notice his teammate, Eddie Gill. Eddie was also a senior and by all accounts, was the 2nd best player on the Weber State team. Arceneaux was awarded Big Sky player of the year, whereas Gill was 1st team all-Big Sky Conference.

Both players were heavily scouted and received invitations to the many select pre-NBA draft camps. However, due to the bizarre nature of scouting neither player was drafted. Arceneaux never played one NBA game but Gill went on to have an 8-year NBA career. The difference wasn't talent, it was something else. It's not who gets there first; it's who can get there and stay there.

We are only as good as our practice and our passion toward it. The passion of a player translates into their dedication, work ethic, and overall mentality. These are the intangibles of a player that cannot be measured effectively. The story of Gill is one of persistence that is often manifested throughout all sports at all levels.

Can't Want It More Than Them

It all works out in the end. If it hasn't, it's just not the end.

Dale Earnhardt, the hall of fame race car driver was once in a terrible accident. It was so bad that he could not finish his next race at Indianapolis Motor Speedway. He started the race but they had to remove him from the car. Here was the greatest race car driver, basically crying because they had to take him out of the car. He said, *"Nobody loves anything more than my driving a race car."*

The best love to play.

They possess an unquenchable thirst to see how good they can become, and they enjoy the process of it. I'm not certain when exactly this passion, tenacity, and drive are born. I think mental toughness is something that's caught more than it's taught.

Herschel Walker was made fun of at school and never went out to recess because he was afraid of getting beat up. His teacher used to put him in the corner of the room because he had a speech impediment and called him "special." His father used to give him a quarter to buy a snack at school. Herschel would instead give it to another kid, so they could buy a snack as long as they would talk to him. After the kid had finished his snack, he would go back to making fun of him.

The last day of school in 8th grade, he went out to recess and got beat up, bad. He said to himself, *"never again. When your name is called, you have to stand up."*

From that hinge moment in school, he didn't train to become a great athlete, he trained to become a superhero. How did he do it?

Herschel did about 5,000 sit-ups and 5,000 push-ups every day. He also ran on a dirt track every day with a rope tied around his waist dragging a tire. He transformed himself from one of the slowest guys in the school to one of the fastest in the state of Georgia by the 9th grade.[13]

Consider this example: Imagine if a parent told their child they had to do Herschel's workout.

Most champion athletes did not start out in the sport with the aspirations of being an elite champion athlete. They played a variety of sports and only after they fell in love with the sport and showed potential did they develop champion athlete aspirations.

As parents, there is a fine line between wanting to show our kids the path and wanting to clear the path. Mental toughness means helping equip them to encounter the struggles, adapt, and persevere. Their path can only be accomplished in pursuits that we love.

The idea of arranged marriages in the United States is unthinkable. But, we now seem to approach sports this way. We bought into the idea that kids need to pick a sport and stay with it.

Dating is a risk, but matrimony is a bigger risk. We love romance because it involves dating, courtship, talking, and sharing. However, is the first person you fall in love with the same person you're with today? Allowing younger children to experiment and sample a variety of sports is healthy and encourages them to choose eventually the one they love.

The systems in place may try to steer you toward year-round sport, which involves little off-season and no time for any other sport. The lines may even come across as "if they want to play at the next level, then…" The organizations in place are also tiered for longer and longer seasons. If they do well at a tournament, they are invited to another and so on. Tournaments are a multi-billion dollar industry so it's in their best interests for your son or daughter to pick their sport.

Specializing any time before the age of 12 is a gamble. Yes, it occurs, and a few of these athletes are successful; however, this is a major outlier. We honestly don't know the precise age where specialization should or should not occur. Different governing bodies set various standards. Of course there are exceptions, but the point is to allow them to discover their true passion.

We receive calls every week from parents wanting our mental coaching for their son or daughter. We discuss the goals and struggles. We also discuss ways parents can get better as a sports parent (hence, this book). Near the end of these introductory calls is the screening of each parent, with one question, *"Is this something your child wants?"*

If the child initiates the possibility of mental training, then we have a good chance of success. If the parent hasn't even asked their son or daughter about mental training—forget about it. It won't work.

Whatever the situation, they have to want it—period. No matter the sport, the best athletes have to possess **passion**. They don't have to be asked to work at it, nagged to do something or coerced into it. And that's the way it should be. Wait, did we just *should* on you?

What's Your Why?

~~Our why must make us cry.~~ If it doesn't, it's not our why.

The first question we ask athletes working on their mental game is, "Why do you play?" It is a powerful question and we receive a variety of answers. They commonly answer with *the competition, the fun,* and *the camaraderie* or *the friendships.* Delving deep into someone's "why" for playing, one thing gets revealed: The reason they began playing is often not the same reason they are playing now.

The why uncovers someone's real desire for playing and can unlock some of the small performance issues. I have only come across one kiss of death for someone's why and that is, "I'm good at it." Being good at something can increase the enjoyment for certain, but it's not a powerful enough reason because at some point everyone is good. Eventually their why catches up with them.

They play because they are good at it, and they win. Along with the winning brings the pats on the back, the cheers, and an athletic identity of "This is who I am." It's not a powerful enough why, at some point they are no longer the best, they don't win all the time, and many times they didn't work on their weaknesses while they were dominating. If they don't have a deeper reason for playing and it is no longer fun, they can become stagnant in their development. The worst is the collegiate athlete who is good, but no longer enjoys their sport and now feels trapped.

Parent Strategy: Know Your Own Why

Whatever you value the most in life is how you'll parent. You will make decisions based on these values. For instance, if your values in life are family and money, then the balance between career and travel will be a factor in your decision. Whatever you decide will reveal which priority is number one. It's not realistic to have both.

Why do you want your child involved in the sport? What do you value most from having your kids play youth sports? If it is the benefits that sport, coaching, and the lessons it can provide, then tough decisions will follow your values. If you value achievement, opportunities for your child, and playing at the *next level*, then most decisions will be based on these values. It's difficult to have both of these as the motivation because we either focus on the process or the product. One of these "why's" becomes the driver, while the other "why" sits in the backseat.

Scholarship as the Byproduct

Wake up [parents], we've got the dreamer's disease.

—*New Radicals*

An important study interviewed U.S. Olympic champions with over 28 combined gold medals. The results showed that the parents and coaches played a critical role in the development of the athlete. Most importantly, there was little outside pressure to win and an increased emphasis on the psychological development. The emphasis was on the process, not the outcome. Parents stressed the ability to focus, manage their emotions, and remain confident.[14]

However, the goal for many today is for their son or daughter to play at the next level and obtain a college scholarship. More specifically, a Division I full scholarship. If that's the goal, the "why" is skewed.

Professional athletics is not addressed in this book for a reason. These athletes need a ridiculous amount of talent and persistence to play professional sports that few can relate. However, the insanity is that an inordinate amount of parents think professional athletics is achievable and realistic. Recent research reported that twenty-six percent of parents with high-school-age children think that they will play professional sports.[14B] What?! The saddest part of this statistic is someone at some point voiced to these parents that professional athletics was possible. If this is the belief related to professional athletes, what is the impression of receiving a Division I scholarship?

First, the likelihood of playing Division I athletics is slim. The average is between three and six percent of high school athletes will play NCAA athletics, not to mention earn a scholarship. Unless you have a daughter or your son plays either basketball or football, a partial Division I scholarship is likely all that they could procure. The financial commitment to the next level of play may or may not yield a return.[15]

Second, if a scholarship is the motivation for playing there is an expectation for this to be fulfilled. The expectations can lead to overall greater stress, pressure, and more issues such as early specialization, burnout, less creativity, and increased chance of over-use injuries. Once the sacrifice and pressure become greater than the rewards and the enjoyment, athletes begin to quit or switch to another endeavor.

- *Cordell Broadus might be a name you've heard. He was a four-star player recruited by several high-profile Division I schools. He also happened to be rapper Snoop Dogg's son and his journey of playing football was well documented on the television show of A Dad's Dream. Cordell accepted a scholarship to UCLA to play football but quit before his freshman season began.*[16]

- *Becky Dionne was a swimmer since the age of six, and three-time swimmer of the year in New Hampshire. She accepted a scholarship to swim at Savannah College of Art and Design, one of the top schools in the nation for fashion design. After one season, she left the team. She said, "The words 'your scholarship will be pulled' were some of the best I've heard in my life."*[17]

- *Zach McRoberts was a good high school basketball player who committed to the University of Vermont. As a 6'7" forward, he saw action his freshman year and even averaged 7 points and 4 rebounds a game during post-season play. He dropped basketball and transferred after his freshman year because "his heart wasn't in it anymore."*[18]

- *Maggie Teets competed year round in gymnastics since the age of three. After her sophomore year at Stanford University, she made the difficult decision to stop competing. "But coming in and starting, I think I cried every day for months. It was a lot to take in."*[19]

These examples are not necessarily the norm, but they are more common than you might think.

Third, parents often only see the bright shiny diamond of Division I athletics. In some cases, that is the accurate way to go, but Division I athletics are exceptionally demanding. An NCAA survey revealed that a typical athlete in-season spent 39 hours a week on academics and 33 hours per week on their chosen sport. For instance, in Division I basketball alone, approximately forty percent depart their initial school by the end of their sophomore year. Transfers have become an entire recruiting class essentially.[20]

Parents can get caught up in only the route of Division I that they don't even look for good opportunities at other levels with great educations such as NAIA or Division II schools. Other levels of play can provide athletic-based financial aid, often augmented with academic scholarships.

We've seen parents blind-sided because their son or daughter received a recruiting letter from a Division I university, thinking it was only a matter of time before a scholarship offer would follow. Reality is not best served on a plate of expectations of a Division I scholarship. Vicarious parents ride the wave of recruiting and often use their child's talents as a surfboard, showing them off as their own accomplishments. These actions by parents add to the pressure kids experience.

We see too often individuals with necessary athletic ability to play at the Division I level, but due to poor grades that option was unavailable. Athletics should remain a privilege, not a right. Academics are the true indicator of the options that will remain open for athletes. Academics can also make the biggest difference over an entire lifespan well beyond playing athletics.

If a scholarship is the byproduct and not the driver, then parents can emphasize and reinforce all of the benefits that sport can provide: confidence, motivation, mental toughness, teamwork, communication, and leadership. If a scholarship is a byproduct, then options remain open. These decisions can range from no longer playing in college to examining other avenues of collegiate participation.

The goal is for our child to benefit as a person from the lessons that sport and coaching can provide. There are so many talented athletes at the collegiate level that participating in college needs to be a good fit. There is not a one size fits all. They may be talented enough for a larger program, so is that what your child wants? Some schools are simply better suited for different types of individuals.

A few questions to assess the proper fit of a college:

1. How much do they value winning compared to playing?

2. Can your child earn playing time?

3. How important is a balance between academics and athletics?

4. What is the level of commitment between academics and athletics? *(Every school varies.)*

5. Did they enjoy the feel of the program and underclass members of the team, not just the seniors?

6. How important is proximity to home?

7. If they were injured, would they still want to attend this school for the education?

8. Do they know and understand the communication style of the coach?

Tenacity is More Important Than Talent

Work for a cause, not an applause.

If you watch any collegiate event in basically any sport, you'll witness talent. Talent is through the roof. Bigger, stronger, faster is the proof.[21,22]

- More players than ever before are throwing faster than 90 mph.

- The men's marathon record currently sits at 2:03, which is an average of 4:42 per mile.

- The average lineman in Division I college football is 6'3" and weighs 302 pounds.

- College team golf scores have gotten better by ten strokes per round between the best team and the 60th best team.

All of these improvements are not due solely to God-given genetics. Technology and improvement in training methods have also made a big difference.

David Epstein, the author of *The Sports Gene*, points out that 2012 Usain Bolt's world record-setting the pace in the 100-meter dash bested 1936 winner and world record holder Jesse Owens by 14 feet. However, he goes on to show the technological differences. Jesse Owens ran on cinders and had to use a towel to help dig his feet in at the start. Today's sprinters run on specifically made surfaces with optimal starting blocks. If no technology differences existed, the difference between the two would have only been one stride.[23]

Everyone at the next level has talent. So talent is not the deciding variable. The difference eventually becomes mental toughness: how one responds to adversity and the will to improve. College basketball coach Bobby Knight said, "The will to prepare has to be greater than the will to win."

Coaching motivation is like pushing a rope; it is difficult. Our kids have to want it, they have to initiate, and they need to drive themselves from within.

Our role is to help them foster the tenacity and drive. Tenacity will eventually win out over education and talent. More importantly, tenacity is a skill that transfers outside of sport into life. That's the goal of sport.

Parent Strategy: End Practice Early

There are a few secrets to success: courage, goal setting, and focus. However, one secret that seems to hold true is the ability of "one more." When we are tired and fatigued, the key is to be able to endure just one more. Doing one more rep, writing one more page, making one more sales call, and taking one more step. Just one more. Often, it is effective. There is a prerequisite to implementing this strategy—first we must have the passion and the will or coaching to do one more.

As parents, we have heard and proclaimed this just one more technique. We push, just a little bit (some, unfortunately, push a lot) for our son or daughter to give more effort. Add up the number of practices and seasons of one more and that is a lot of externally driven passion in the form of nagging or strong-arming our son or daughter into practice.

Hall of fame tennis coach Jeff Smith used a different strategy to help build the passion in his son Bryan Smith; he would end practice early. First he would tell Bryan how long they were going to hit tennis balls on the court. It would be either 30 minutes, 45 minutes, or an hour. So, if they were going to hit for 45 minutes, after 20 or 25 minutes he would end the practice and tell Bryan they were ending.

Bryan, having fun, didn't want to end early. So, he would ask his dad to continue. The seed of passion was growing slowly without the nagging, pleading or coercion of "one more." Try out this technique to build motivation. It works.

Reward Effort, Not Rankings or Winnings

Great parents ask their kid, "How was your day?"
not just "How was your practice?"

A father once told us a cute story of how his young 4-year-old daughter began playing golf. As she would ride along in the cart, she noticed people became happy when the ball went in the cup. So, on the next hole, she ran out of the cart, picked up the ball and put it into the cup, raising her hands and waiting for the cheer.

There is nothing wrong with winning—just the emphasis on winning. The applause, pats on the back, and the recognition from winning are infectious. They feel really good. The recognition feels so good that an interesting change occurs. Children actually start to play for the cheers and the recognition that winning brings. Our identity becomes engrossed in the belief that this is how people show appreciation.

Winning, rankings, and trophies cannot be the main emphasis. It's best to stress development, mastery, and effort over other goals. Parents have expressed that their kid at age 13 or 14 is at a crossroads. How can a child be at a crossroad at such a young age unless we are emphasizing the wrong things?

An emphasis only on winning brings pressure to win. The number one reason children quit playing is because it is no longer fun, due to the pressure to win. Sports are fun, allow it to be fun.

The funny thing about sports and life is that we lose more than we win. We will miss more shots, putts, and matches than we will ever connect on. Tiger Woods at his most dominant stretch during the early 2000s won only 25 percent of his tournaments. The top 100 women professional tennis players have a win/loss ratio of only 1.5/1—meaning the best in the world win only a half of a match more than they lose.[24]

Are we concerned mostly with winning, or the lessons that setbacks, adversity, and losing can convey? How do we respond when these occur? Winning doesn't need much of a teacher except how to win with respect. The outside pressure to win is evident. We must avoid the emphasis and discussion with our child.

How many points did you score? What did you shoot? Did you win? Are all questions based on outcome and raise the flag of the importance of winning. Instead, address questions that emphasize effort. *Did you give all of your total effort, and what did you learn?* Ask questions that emphasize the values that matter the most to you.

Ownership, Not Buy-In

Supportive parents build capacity, not dependence.

One of the coolest stories in Mark Twain's *The Adventures of Tom Sawyer* is about the fence. Aunt Polly tasked Tom Sawyer on a sunny day to whitewash the entire fence. What took place is that Tom conveyed to every other kid that came along that he was having fun. He wouldn't let anyone else join in the fun. Only after the kids started pleading and begging did he "allow" others to join in the "fun" and help whitewash the entire fence. He made each person who joined take ownership that it was something they wanted to do.

Some of the first jobs we had were most likely working for someone. A good boss had conversations with us about the company vision, our roles, and possible goals. He or she had us buy in. If things went wrong with the company, we could find another job. Ownership, on the other hand, is much deeper. It means we have a total vested interest in the bottom line, who we hire, and our customers. A good owner must be all in.

Often parents and coaches think of getting athletes to buy in instead of taking ownership. When athletes take ownership of their development, it means that they have skin in the game and stock in the company.

UCLA basketball coach John Wooden stated that the worst punishment he could give would be to withhold practice. The worst punishment was for him to announce, "Gentleman, practice is over." His players took ownership that playing and practicing at UCLA was a privilege and it could be taken away.

Allow your child to take ownership. Ownership builds mental toughness. Let them fail and learn from that failure. Don't try to save the day by not letting them experience the setbacks or the mistakes. Working through the setbacks is a part of learning and growing mentally tough.

Dara Torres, who won twelve Olympic medals in five Olympic Games in swimming, has a strategy for building ownership—she drops her daughter off at practice. It keeps her from getting too involved and allows the coaches to do their job. Athletics can teach whatever we want it to teach, so try allowing the practice to go on without your involvement. Coaches coach, parents parent.

Parent Strategy: I Pack, We Pack, You Pack...

When and if your son or daughter forgets a piece of equipment at home *(glove, Gatorade, jersey, goggles, putter)*, DO NOT PICK IT UP FOR THEM. They will assume ownership in their development and equipment, and they won't forget it again. Interesting how they never seem to forget their hair gel though.

Parents often comment how they get worn out nagging their kids to pack their things and to practice. Who would have thought the task of packing up would become its own sport?

Dan Gould, head of the Institute for the Study of Youth Sports, provides an ownership strategy for athletes. They take ownership of their equipment bag. It's called, *"I pack, we pack, you pack."*

1. I pack the bag first, and you watch how it's done and observe everything that's needed.

2. Next, we pack the bag together, taking turns, quizzing each other, and making it collaborative.

3. Finally, you pack the bag, and I'll supervise and integrate when and if needed, again, making it fun.

After the last packing, it is completely up to them from that moment on.

It seems such a simple concept so many tasks can be completed with this method. Lastly, allow them ownership to carry their own packed bag.

Don't You Think I'm Trying?

How good do you want to be?

Finding Forrester is a great movie. Jamal Wallace, the main character, is a brilliant mind and a great basketball player. In one of the last scenes of the movie, Jamal (who made 50 consecutive free-throws earlier in the movie) misses two free throws and loses the championship game. What is crucial is the implication that he missed both free throws on purpose.

Parents, I can assure you that your child does not hit a drive out of bounds, miss a shot, throw an interception or race poorly ON PURPOSE!

Yes, they may not always put forth their best effort or their preparation may not be up to the standard it takes, but their mistakes are not punitive at you. Remember, it is not about you.

It's risky to overly question their mistakes as a lack of effort because that line will get old fast. They'll perceive the questions you ask really as accusations: "Why did you, "How could you" and "Are you" type questions. Remember, don't should on your kid. Once they perceive you as constantly accusing them of not giving their best effort, two things can happen:

1. They will shut down and withdraw from you.

2. They will play worse because they become afraid of making mistakes.

There is a solution to this issue. There is an easier, softer way to keep the relationship strong and help them build mental toughness at the same time.

Effort is a non-negotiable when it comes to preparation. Shouldn't we expect that our son or daughter give total effort? This skill will transfer into real life and beyond.

Talk to your children about how good they want to become. Parents often lack the knowledge of what is required for elite status and most

8-year-olds do not have the awareness of what it actually takes to be elite. Allow them to set realistic expectations for the season and receive permission to hold them accountable.

Parent Strategy: I Notice

Parents sometimes struggle with not being able to get through to their kids. Instead of *shoulding* on your kids or asking questions they perceive as challenging their effort or attitude, try a different strategy.

Use the phrase "I notice" instead. James Altucher devised this strategy of "I notice" as a means to look at the situation from a different perspective. For example, instead of "I'm anxious," James says, "I notice I'm feeling anxious." It separates himself from the anxiety.

Instead of saying, "I shouldn't have eaten that piece of cake," try, "I notice I ate the piece of cake." Practicing non-judgmental behavior is better than shaming others or ourselves.

Which of the following statements do you think is better to use?

- You shouldn't be so passive out there; you need to hustle more.

OR

- I noticed you looked a little laid back out there. You seemed like you didn't have much energy.

Make statements of observations instead of pointed commands. Allow them a voice in how they explain themselves and what transpired. The communication stays open and they can internalize the feedback much easier and effectively. When we *should* on our kids, we are making it about our feelings and not their experience. Our role is to be supportive, not vicarious. We aren't supposed to solve their issues or coach, merely provide them opportunities to become mentally tough.

When the Student is Ready, the Teacher Will Appear

Teacher Will Appear

*I felt like if I pushed these kids into sports,
I thought that'd backfire on me.*

—Archie Manning

On some of the mini tours in golf, we've heard a similar story from several players who just played a bad round. They'd say, "I hit thirteen greens today [great], hit twelve fairways [great], and thirty-six putts [not good]." After processing, they'd say, "I need to work on my driver." Every outside golf professional and statistician would have had the same question we did. "Thirty-six putts, and it's your *driver?*"

We desire to improve our situation but are unwilling to improve ourselves. If someone has not experienced enough negative outcomes from their actions, then they won't see the need or have the desire to improve. At some point as an athlete, you realize you need to improve. When a child can humbly come to terms with that moment, hopefully, they will address the issue.

When the student is ready, the teacher will appear...

The worst type of advice is unsolicited advice. Just like we would never go up to someone cold and say, "You know what your problem is," we cannot assume an aggressive position when trying to help our own child. They must invite it. The desire must come from them.

As teenagers, Peyton and Eli Manning would go to the football field with their dad to throw and practice. They would watch their 40-year-old father doing 350-yard sprints on the track. As Mr. Manning illustrates, be the model you want your son or daughter to witness.

Asking your son or daughter to practice *with* you is different than telling them to practice for you. It's a difference between a vicarious and supportive parent. Have fun with them; enjoy the times at practice and spending time with one another. Some kids will remain more coachable than others and some will be more iron-willed. Our role is to have them ready to receive the information—even soliciting it themselves.

The skill is to offer feedback, not force feedback. Ask them if they want to discuss their game or strategy. "Just let me know" is a more open and safe approach to creating the atmosphere for growth and confidence building.

Parent Strategy: Permission, Please

Often the best lessons and feedback are ones we don't know we are receiving. Having a discussion about expectations for the upcoming season is healthy, as long it is a conversation and not a mandate.

Ask and gain permission to discuss how your son or daughter will prepare this upcoming season. What kind of goals do they want to set? Encourage them to think about a plan they're comfortable with. Will it be three days a week of making 10 free throws in a row, or maybe one day a week of extra batting practice?

We can operate much better as parents when we know what it is that they want. Then we can ask, "Permission to hold you accountable and support your commitment?"

We want the drive to come from them and they have to want it. When they commit and we've gained their permission, then we can hold them accountable.

We must be able to accept the alternative, however. They may just want to play with their friends recreationally as opposed to tournament play. If this is the case, pulling the plug and shutting down the lessons will be difficult (for you) but necessary. Their passion needs to be present. It may hurt, but we need to scale back our wants and be ready to jump back in and support them, when and if they become ready.

The fear is often that if they don't play at ages 8-10, then they won't be able to play later on at ages 13-15. The solution is to keep active with them and ensuring development still takes place. That way, their options can remain open.

Pre-Game

The pre-game season is also the pre-game period of mental toughness. The theme of pre-game mental toughness is CONFIDENCE.

Less is more during these times. Too often, we err on the complex, heavy side. We try to do too much. We question if our children are prepared or nervous. We nag them about their routine or make it more important than it really is. This section is devoted simply to a few key roles that we can implement to help build their confidence.

Don't Build It Up

Life is a daring adventure or not at all.

—*Helen Keller*

Olympic diving coach John Wingfield, coach of 2012 gold medalist David Boudia, says there are two types of game-day athletes. He calls them "plus or minus athletes." His theory is based on the research from George Miller. The principle that the average number of information bits we retain in our short-term memory is seven. For example, the length of our phone number.[25]

Plus-two athletes can comprehend more information and perform better when they are aware of all the necessary information. These individuals need the information, yet can be over-thinkers at times.

Minus-two athletes perform worse with added information. These are the "wash and wear" type of competitors. They can handle only three pieces of information at any one time. This type plays better when told very little.

The closer we get to competition and during days of competition, stress levels and cognitive processes automatically increase and the amount of information we can process drops. Some information bits, for example, are what and when to eat, where to park, and is everything packed.

As important competitions get closer, general stress levels increase around the whole family. Athletes start to narrow their focus and small issues can become larger than life.

As parents, we help those around us by not adding undue pressure. However, we tend to want to talk about strategy, competition or other things going on around the team or event.

Pressure mounts the more we discuss and analyze the event and the occasion. It is here you need to comprehend the seven bits principle.

Discuss anything but the upcoming competition. We must understand that this is the process of competing and we can't solve anything for them. Our role is to provide a safe environment free from added pressure.

Recognize that your child's stress level will be high as well. Be aware not to acknowledge any disagreements, squabbles or skirmishes. It doesn't mean to ignore these issues, but merely assign a better time to discuss them.

Information and logistics that need to be discussed prior to the event should take place at least three to five days beforehand. It can then be followed up—but not introduced the day before.

Words of encouragement the day before and on game day are awesome, and again these words spoken should address the process, not the product.

Nervous or Excited?

Know so you can show.

*Claire Eccles, 16-year-old rookie pitcher for Canadian Women's
National Team, got her start at the Women's Baseball World Cup.
She said, "I wasn't [nervous] this time, just extremely excited."[26]*

What's the difference between being nervous or excited? It is such a
sought-after answer that the question became a huge part of the book,
NO FEAR: A Simple Guide to Mental Toughness.

Our reaction to stress and pressure physiologically is the same. Our heart
races, our minds are full of thoughts, our breathing gets shallow, palms
get sweaty, and we even feel the urge to urinate. Back in caveman days,
our reaction was a defense mechanism to escape from a predator. Our
ancestors responded to this feeling or died.

The difference between getting nervous and excited is our perception and
response to our perception. If we perceive events with the expectation
that something bad can happen, (I could lose or I don't want to be in the
situation), then we will get nervous. On the other hand, if we perceive
situations with the expectation that something good could happen, (I could
win or I want to be here), then we get excited.

That's the difference!

Parent Strategy: Get Excited

Aren't we actually excited for the tournament rather than anxious?
Remove the word nervous from your vocabulary and replace it with
excited instead. When the time is close to important events do not
ask your child if they are nervous. This doesn't help. Should they be
nervous? Not if you don't tell them they should. Avoid even introducing
the thought.

Likewise, remember the feeling you have as a parent means you're excited as well, not nervous. Anticipate good things. If you're relaxed, then your child will be more relaxed.

In sports and life, things can go wrong. The game and situation itself will provide enough excitement, so be excited, not nervous. Your role is not to live vicariously through their performance.

Focus on the Process, Not the Product

*An emphasis on winning does not lead
to winning—a focus on the process does.*

A disgusting thing occurs after every national championship in professional sports. After the celebration and speeches, the media ends with an odd question. They ask, "Do you think they will repeat?" This is immediately after a team has won the greatest prize!

Fear emerges from focusing only on the outcome. *Will they make it? Will they earn a partial scholarship? Will they win?* All are rhetorical questions based on the result, the outcome, and the product. There is an unknown to these questions, which brings fear. If fear were a person, it would tell us only to focus on things we cannot control.

Too often, we focus only on winning or losing. To change the atmosphere to positive, focus on and address the process and what they did well, not the outcome of the competition.

It's not what we get from winning; it's who we become. A focus on the process means noticing how we compete, what we do when we play our best, and knowing our own recipe for success. The process is also about who we are becoming, what we excel at, and learn from. The process means addressing effort, teammates, other people excelling, how we handle bad calls, referees, and coaches. These are the lessons and skills that show us how to be successful and that transfer into life.

If we were to dig deeper into this and have the courage to uncover what is bothering us, it is a lack of confidence that the product will turn out how and when we want. We feel anxious and try to put more emphasis on the outcome, only creating more pressure.

Championships are not given away. Not one person would accept a trophy if they did nothing for it. The best athletes shed tears after such championships because they realize how much sacrifice and struggle it took to achieve their goal. It's the journey and the sacrifice that makes it actually mean something.

Call Them This. . .

Don't let the noise of others' opinions drown out your own inner voice.

—STEVE JOBS

A study in 2002 from the *Journal of Attitudes and Social Cognition* examined people's names and the impact on careers they chose. The researchers found that people named Dennis were statistically more likely to become dentists. They contended that a phenomenon existed called "implicit egotism." The words that we associate with our names can actually shape our decisions and identity. It doesn't mean that every Lauren becomes a lawyer or every Dennis becomes a dentist, but merely that we gravitate toward the things and names that we associate most with.[28]

"Perfect little Rachel." That's how her parents described and introduced their child, a high-school second baseman. Perfection is a pretty high expectation and I was curious how long they had been calling her that. Unfortunately, she was not mentally tough, and it had little to do with her and more to do with expectations placed on her.

How do you introduce and describe your kids? *"There goes our little winner"* or *"Here comes Johnny, our star goalie."* Be careful about using descriptors that emphasize only part of your child's identity. No one is always a winner and we certainly don't always lose. We are also only an athlete at certain times. These are just things we do—not who we are.

Parent Strategy: Call Them a Competitor!

We can compete in everything we do. We can compete in grades, paying attention, and playing sports. However, too much of competition involves beating or besting someone else. To define it in a healthy way for your child, emphasize that competition means against yourself, not anyone else. In this way you will be teaching your child not to compare themselves to others, which often results in low self-esteem. Teach them to have an audience of one and that is the only one that matters.

In The Game

In-game is where it all comes out. Everything that's been going on behind the scenes is now up front for everyone to see. During the game is when so many parents are criticized. Coaches remark that the kids haven't changed as much as the parents have throughout the years. Frankly, we have no idea what happens behind closed doors inside of someone's home. We don't know if they push their kid or if they criticize effort. However, we can and do witness their behavior at the games and on the field. Parental behavior on the field not only affects your own children but anyone else in earshot.

To create in-game mental toughness, our focus should be on modeling. Our goal is to model the behavior that we want to see in our own children. If an outsider were to watch only the parents' behavior during competition, they would be able to tell from that which athletes are relaxed and which ones are stressed. Parents model the behavior and kids follow it. Parents that are relaxed and not stressed during games produce athletes of like mind.

We can do more harm than good during these times. The toughest part is that we want it so bad for them, but it is out of our control; we can't do anything about their performance. It is at this crucial time during the game that our behavior is most influential—and where the most harm can be done.

The Lion's Den

Did you think the lion was sleeping because he didn't roar?

—*Friedrich Schiller*

There is an energy to sports. One of the coolest feelings is that electricity of an important game or match. Electricity can cause shocks, however, and it only takes one charge for the current to get started.

The lion's den is the area where all the parents congregate during the game.

This area is usually the bleachers, but it varies depending on the sport. The lion's den can be a very happy or downright scary place. During the happy times, the lions are playful with one another. Everyone is cheering, joking around, and discussing the local culture.

However, it takes only one negative play or person for the lion's den to roar. It's like the pack spotted a gazelle and they start to froth at the mouth.

Here's how it often transpires: One person yells at their kid to grab a rebound or hustle or jeers the team for running a certain play or not executing. Once a ref makes a questionable call, all of the parents are now in complete unison. The electricity is now directed as a collective unit toward a ref or an opposing player. Once the cheering turns into shouting, the lion's den is complete. They are ready to devour anyone that crosses them.

It's almost impossible to control emotions in the lion's den because the energy and environment are so emotionally charged. Many of the transgressions and ill-fated reactions throughout history from negative parents have occurred directly within the lion's den. You would be wise to check yourself in this situation that you do not get caught up in the mob mentality and pounce on anyone.

Parent Strategy: The Blow Pop

Umpires possess the toughest position on the field and are discussed only when something bad happens. However, one little league umpire came up with a genius way to settle down the lion's den of parents. He was finished with all of the loud parents who would criticize their son and daughter when they played. Since umpires are not a favorite type of person, anytime this guy approached the crowd to settle down boisterous parents, it rarely went well. So, he devised a strategy with an action that spoke louder than any words.

He started taking Charms Blow Pops with him to the game and told the coaches at every game what he was going to do. When a parent would become too loud and criticize their son or daughter, he would have the Blow Pop delivered to the parent with no explanation. No words were spoken. Many of the parents would just enjoy the Blow Pop. Immediately they quieted down, and they got the message quickly. Blow Pops meant shut it up. It worked!

You Can Communicate Too Much

You "can't" communicate too much with your team.

—Coach John Groce

During a youth hockey game, a 12-year-old crossed the blue line with the puck. From the stands, his dad yelled, "Shoot it!" The 12-year-old froze! That voice was stuck inside his head for the entire season. He was a great passer at that age but had not yet developed a strong slap shot. One critical shout from his dad and he now began to have doubts and think instead of just play.

There are good opportunities to talk about their performance—and some not good ones. During the game is NOT a good time to bring it up. However, we constantly see parents communicating with their son or daughter while they are playing.

A strange thing occurs when a parent regularly provides instructions or feedback while a young athlete plays—the athlete hears it! There can be hundreds of people in the stands and a young athlete will single out a parent's voice. Since your voice is the one they've heard their whole life, they can't block it out.

The above quote by John Groce seems contradictory to the section title, but there is a difference between a coach and a parent. Sport requires focus and the one voice they should be listening to is the coach. Athletes at all levels mention that when they feel they have conflicting coaches, they are less likely to play well. They want to do what the coach demands, but also please their parents at the same time.

Cheer and be positive during games and especially for other teammates, but avoid feedback or coaching while your son or daughter is playing the game. There may be a time and place for that—but it's not here and not now.

Parent Strategy: Have a Plan

We didn't plan to fail; we just failed to plan. Often we didn't mean to yell or scream or lose it in the stands. We just allowed our emotions to take over. The game cannot turn into an occasion for that. As parents, we must have a plan as to how we will conduct ourselves and how we will cheer.

Make an agreement with yourself and son or daughter about how you'll act and cheer. This agreement with ourselves must take place before we arrive. Again, root for others on the team, not just your child.

Body Language Doesn't Talk, It Screams

Sometimes it swears.

Question: In which sport do you think body language is the most crucial?

Yes, all of them, but more so in gymnastics. They not only have incredible athleticism, but they must always smile at the end of their performance. Smiling to the judges is crucial even after a poor routine or dismount, although it might be the last thing they want to do. A gymnast's smile is either extremely genuine or extremely fake.

In all sports, we see positive and negative body language on the field. As parents, our body language off the field speaks so loud your son or daughter doesn't need to hear a word you're saying. They can see you slump, get upset or throw your hands up in disgust. I repeat—they can see your negative body language.

This is not easy, but it is essential—your own body language must remain confident and supportive. That means your head is always up, you are clapping or cheering, and giving thumbs up.

When things are not going as well as we'd like, we must immediately focus on our own body language and what it is communicating. Why?

Negative body language doesn't show that you care or are passionate; it reveals a lack of confidence. Things are going to go wrong, our kids will face adversity, and people will make mistakes. If we lose our cool and show horrible reactions to events, then what are we really saying?

When our body language is negative, we are demonstrating and showing that we don't think the result is going to turn out like we'd hoped. We don't have confidence or faith in our child.

I am not an advocate of faking it until we make it, because then we are just faking it. I merely say act as if. Act as if they will turn it around and finish strong.

Great parents demonstrate confident body language.

Respond, Don't React

"Do you have the patience to wait till the mud
settles and the water is clear?"

—Lao Tzu

In the book, *NO FEAR: A Simple Guide to Mental Toughness*, the concept of respond, don't react was a huge component of mental toughness.[27]

Think of a reactor and you get a vision of a nuclear power plant or a chemical bond. A reactor is someone who can't keep his or her cool under pressure. Picture a responder on the other hand, and you get a first responder, someone who has been trained to handle adversity.

We need to be a responder with our athletes, not a reactor. When we respond, it is devoid of emotion and we usually make good decisions. It is operating from a place of calmness and reason. When we react, however, it is full of emotion and knee-jerk behaviors. Many careers and mistakes have occurred due to a bad reaction.

Parent Strategy: What Your Kid Really Wants to Hear

Baseball coach Adam Wiginton from Kansas implemented a new strategy. Before the first parent meeting of the season, he asked his players to anonymously write out how they wanted their parents to act at the game. He felt that having his players' voices heard was key to changing the behavior of parents.

Some of the responses by his players included:

"Don't talk to me on the mound."

"Don't talk to me in the on-deck circle."

"Don't yell at umps; it's just embarrassing."

"Don't criticize coach's decision or tell me what he should have done."

At the parent meeting, Wiginton shared all of the responses and made the parents aware that this is their son speaking directly to them. I'm sure it stung a bit, but as a result of the proactive approach, the result was the best year ever.

Post-Game

Some text messages a coach or player receives after a national championship win can range in the hundreds to the thousands, not to mention the number of mentions on Twitter. How many messages does a coach or player receive after a similar loss? Depending on how the game was lost, not many.

Winning is usually not as difficult to deal with unless we are that parent who manages to criticize why they weren't perfect. Losing is where the pain resides. Not just losing the game—this can be over losing playing time, a bad play or the big loss. We should see the bigger picture that we are all going to lose more than we are ever going to win. Developing a plan on how to handle losing and keeping it in perspective is an important life skill.

The post-game and even post-practice can be raw. After the game is when players question their "why." Why am I out here? Why do I keep playing? Why are others getting more praise?

Mental toughness can be greatly enhanced when the post-game is handled correctly. Conversely, mental toughness can take a big hit if post-games are not handled correctly.

Ride the Carousel, Not the Roller Coaster

Success has a thousand fathers. Failure is an orphan.

A caddy on the PGA tour is the closest experience to being a sideline coach. Besides walking with and helping them, you're the only person who can give them advice during the round.

On the PGA tour, the golfer's name is on the bag for a reason—they are the one hitting the shots. However, there is a common saying among caddies. When their golfer plays well, they say, "*We* shot sixty-seven." If their golfer does not play well, they say, "*He* shot seventy-four."

It is difficult being a caddy, though, when your player makes a mistake, bogies or misses a cut. The margin between success and failure is so slim and a caddie's income depends on how the player performs. One can easily get fixed up in the emotion and disappointment that a player feels when playing poorly. Great caddies have that bond and rapport down pat. They simply know what their player thinks before he or she says anything.

Great caddies remain emotionally unattached from poor outcomes. Parenting is the same way. As a caddy and parent, we cannot ride the emotional roller coaster that our competitor will feel during a game or season. When we do, it means that we've become vicarious parents and are living and dying on every play.

Our role is to be supportive. That means we must stay emotionally stable and available. When players struggle, they need a supportive, non-judgmental environment. Also, if and when they ask us for advice or suggestions, we need to be there for them.

If we have been riding the roller coaster of ups and downs, then we cannot be unbiased and level-headed like we should be. The carousel is not as fun to ride, but as for how we parent, it's the best ride we can take.

The Car Ride

Great caddying is all about timing.

—*Joe Skovron*

During his junior season in college, this discus and hammer thrower was having a good season. However, during NCAA regionals, he had his worst meet of the season and did not qualify for nationals. His parents were at the meet and he decided to spend a few minutes after his poor performance talking with them. Even though the season was over his coach wanted to discuss what he did wrong at that exact moment, interrupting his family time. Let's just say, that the interaction between coach and athlete went less than favorable.

Coaching is all about timing.

We have all been there: Our son or daughter not only played poorly, but played with little energy, couldn't let go of mistakes, and they may even have looked like they didn't want to be there.

Since we value effort and it wasn't there, we took mental notes on what we were going to say and how to best get our point across. We wanted to make sure that history does not repeat itself.

Parenting is all about timing.

There are good times to talk with your son or daughter about the game, and then there are bad times. *On the ride home from the game and practice is a bad time.*

Worth repeating: The worst time to discuss" performance is on the ride home. We may want to talk so bad that it is like acid in our mouth—they need to know what we think. We have great points, and they need to know how they can improve. All true, but we just cannot share them on the ride home.

Even if we commend and not criticize, we may get in the habit of making the car ride *the time* and *place* to discuss. They are trapped in the confines and have to listen. When athletes play poorly, the last thing they want to hear is someone trying to make them feel better. In fact, it doesn't help build their mental toughness because they need to feel the pain of not getting what they want.

Parent Strategy: The Talk

Sadly, many parents have an over-reliance of using text messaging to communicate important thoughts and sensitive subjects. Communicating the game or practice via text is not the best medium because too much gets lost in translation. It's impossible to effectively listen to or share personal thoughts. Remember, it's not what you say; it's what they hear. Sending a 300-word text may be perceived as shouting or *shoulding* on them, and in return, you'll receive a one-word reply. If you find yourself upset because "we don't talk anymore," evaluate your use of text messaging. Set the example of how effective in-person communication should take place. For in-depth conversations, one text is too many and a thousand is never enough.

Try setting up an agreed-upon time for an in-person discussion about the game or practice. This might be after dinner or after cleaning up or even the next day—whatever you agree upon as a family. Your child will appreciate the time to decompress and not dread the car ride home like their friends who get grilled every time.

So much can be accomplished after we are cool, calm, and collected. And especially after your child is calm and given time to process.

Resist the urge to talk more than listen. Allow them to provide the feedback about what they did well and what they learned from their play. They take much more ownership when they are doing the talking.

Lastly, as coach Brett Hawke said, "catch them doing it right."

Cover Your Answers

Let them figure it out.

We were in the office of a Division I basketball team during a pre-season meeting. The outstanding group of staff and coaches approach the game the right way. On this particular morning, the head coach and his two assistants were going over the "pick and roll" offensive play at length.

After five minutes, it was like learning Spanish and then trying to follow a conversation between three very fluent speakers. No one understood what was going on. Here's the key—as coaches, sports are our profession and we are compensated very well to know the intricacies of all sports. However, this level of explanation and description between the three coaches went six levels deep, and fast!

A successful collegiate coach recently said, "I wish they wouldn't keep asking, 'What am I doing wrong?' all the time! I want them to find a way, battle, and make adjustments."

If we want to know why kids feel entitled to playing time, winning, and success, then you may particularly enjoy the following. What's changed is that kids no longer have to "figure it out." They don't have to remain uncomfortable or find a way. Nowadays, when athletes struggle, someone else provides the answer sheet. We take care of it and taking care of it doesn't build mental toughness, it builds entitlement.

On a micro-level, when players are struggling for answers, they can just look it up on the Internet or ask someone to fix it. "Fix my technique" often becomes a battle cry. The answers are very accessible and affordable. If they don't like the answer, then they can ask someone else. Also, they don't have to wait for anything; the patience of having to figure things out only adds stress.

A recent study revealed that we utilize the Internet for so much information that we think we are smarter than we really are. Participants in the study were asked a series of questions in which one group had to think of the answer and the other group was allowed to use Google to find the answer. The research showed that people who merely searched the Internet had an inflated sense of intelligence. The authors concluded that there is a distinct line between what we know and what we think we know.[29]

We are unaware of what takes place in our mind if we are in a social gathering and someone asks the question, "Where was Woodstock held?" or "Who has the Super Bowl single game rushing record?" It actually rarely happens because we don't ask—we just look it up so we won't look silly.

It's like we have morphed into Alex Trebek on Jeopardy! We appear that we have it all together and know the answer. Yes, Mr. Trebek is intelligent, but if we had every answer in front of us, we would appear to be the smartest person on the planet as well.

Personally, searching our own mind and getting uncomfortable with not knowing the answer is a good thing. It causes us to figure it out, find a way, and utilize our mind. That's mental toughness. Isn't it more satisfying when we suddenly realize that Woodstock was at Yasgur's farm or the Super Bowl rushing record was Timmy Smith?

It seems every profession allows us to retake the test as many times as we want: the BAR exam, MCAT, SAT, ACT, and even a driver's test. We don't have an issue with this approach, because it does reward persistence. However, it has become the norm, not the exception and the entitlement spreads. Yes, the person who finishes last in their class is still an M.D., but I don't want that surgeon. There's little accountability or even incentive to handle adversity. Instead, we remove the struggle.

The system has perpetuated the issue. Since we've been providing the answers, why are we shocked when our children expect entitlement? It occurred every step along the path because we removed the learning experience of failing.

Not knowing the solution is painful and uncomfortable. However, the only way to build mental toughness and improve is to find a way, figure it out, and make adjustments. Athletics is one of the last bastions of having to find a way and figure it out, because unlike the test examples above, an athlete's test is the game. Unfortunately, many parents have tried to remove those painful experiences of failing as well.

Don't Should on Your Kids

Let Them Fail

People have no idea how many times you have to finish second, in order to finish first.

— *JACK NICKLAUS*

It really hurts when we lose and fail. It is no fun at all. There is major discomfort. Even though it hurts, losing is never fatal. But most of us have to go through that experience to figure that part out. Mental toughness is often caught rather than taught.

The big loss is the most difficult. We've unfortunately been in the locker room after the big loss that ended a season—teams and athletes that were confident, yet lost. Anger and sadness accompany the big loss, but the main feeling inside is numbness, the lack of any feeling. If you're in sport and life long enough, you'll experience it.

These losses camouflage as learning lessons. Learning experiences hurt. When we don't win, we learn. That's the path to growth and success.

Losing and failing is challenging, not a tragedy. The pain eventually subsides, but many have removed the setbacks, adversity, and ownership of failing. As a result, we have cheapened the joy of success and winning. We cannot truly appreciate winning and improvement if we have never lost. When we eliminate the pain of losing, we also eliminate the lesson.

Parents remove the pain of teachable moments by blaming coaches, other players or changing teams. If parents do this, they are trying to save the day, but in reality they are not teaching the right lesson. Instead of working on improving our weaknesses and shortcomings, we teach that mom or dad will take care of it.

We must allow our athletes to experience the natural setbacks and struggles, and learn how to overcome these obstacles. They cannot improve if we remove the obstacles. Worse yet, they don't learn how to effectively deal and cope with losing. We cannot remove the natural setbacks and teachable moments that occur at this level.

When our children lose, it's important to let them take ownership and not allow them to blame others. Losing isn't fatal—it just stings a lot. Proper perspective is important. At the right time, ask good questions: What did they learn from it? What do they need to improve upon?

Losing is tough, so allowing them to take ownership does not mean piling on with criticism or critique. We are all vulnerable to a loss, so they still need encouragement, love, and support. As we can't let a win go to our head, we can't allow a loss to go to our heart. They need reassurance after losing that they are still great.

We cannot give away something that we don't have. To provide proper perspective, we must have perspective ourselves. Losing does not make you a bad parent, and winning does not make you a great parent. This experience is about them; it's not about you.

We emphasize winning over development way too much. Kids are focused on having fun, the way they should be. Winning should be the byproduct and its internal reward. Did we just *should* on you again?

We Don't Keep Score, But We Are Up 8-4

"They don't give trophies away...wait, yes, they do."

Trophies by themselves are not bad. Trophies actually don't mean anything. Many Olympians have their gold medals in a sock drawer. We give meaning to the trophy and what it represents. The belief behind trophies is that kids be recognized for participating and showing up. Every participant is awarded a trophy. We've implemented our adult viewpoint on youth sports.

Olympians didn't participate for a medal; it was not the driver. They wanted to test themselves against the best. Their mental toughness and talent are the reasons for their success. I doubt if even one kid ever began to play sports because they thought, "Hey, I get a trophy at the end." They play for the fun and the Capri Sun. When we give kids trophies for participating, it is more about the adults than it is the kids.

The belief of participation trophies is that it will help inspire, motivate, and keep kids coming back. Or perhaps later on our kids can look at their dresser and get a sense of accomplishment from their participation trophy?

However, awarding participation trophies may do more harm than good. We think that providing an external reward for hard work will build motivation, but the opposite may be the case. It may diminish their motivation.

Yale researcher Amy Wrzesniewski examined the motives of over 11,000 West Point cadets across the span of 14 years. They wanted to assess the impact of cadets reason for entering the academy. Cadets that had internal motivators were more likely to graduate, receive promotions, commissions, and stay in the military. Cadets that entered with both strong internal and external motivators (*such as get a good job later in life*) revealed drastically less success. Amazingly, external factors such as get a better job and make more money had a negative impact on overall success.[30]

We all have different internal motivators and are more likely to accomplish a task when we tap into our own "why" rather than a carrot or stick approach. (*Such as returning a wallet because it's the right thing to do, rather than the possible reward I could get.*)

Adults don't need to give trophies to kids for participating; they just need to praise their effort and allow them to have fun and also fail. Have a year-end banquet and provide everyone a ribbon or certificate but just realize that we don't create motivation or make everyone a winner by making everyone not a loser. It may even create more losers.

There is a line of demarcation in athletics when winning eventually trumps development. We are not exactly sure when this occurs, but it's usually when coaches are hired and fired based on performance. When we value winning we stop giving trophies away, and they start earning them.

Don't Go Back to the Cook

A coach is somebody who takes you somewhere you want to go.

—MARTIN ROONEY

A head football coach said, *"I've eaten out at restaurants my entire life and never have I once gone back to the kitchen to tell the cook, this is how you should prepare the meal."* In sports, however, we seem to think that because we can visibly see what takes place on the field, it makes us somewhat of an expert. Coaches devote their time, energy, and expertise to the passion. It's their livelihood to know the nuances and personnel of preparation and execution. Frankly, it's their job to know more than you! Even at the recreational level, they have devoted time.

As parents, we must accept that our perception is skewed because of our emotional investment. To illustrate, imagine you are at a youth football game and the quarterback just throws his second consecutive interception. Do you boo and criticize the kid who threw the ball? Probably not, because this is youth football. So after our initial reaction, we don't boo. But, we are still upset and the anger has to go somewhere. So we say something like, *"Why does coach keep calling so many pass plays?"*

Simply put, there are going to be good and not so good coaches. And our kids learn from both. They learn the healthy way to treat others, and how to communicate, and also, unfortunately, the unhealthy ways. But, kids need to be free to form their own opinions and experience situations without our coloring their perceptions.

Criticizing coaches' play calling, schemes or playing time does much harm to a situation. Coaching from the stands is horrendous.[31] A youth coach once stated that he knows when parents are talking about him behind his back. "The kids won't look me in the eye." Sad.

The lessons learned in sport can transfer out of sport. There are going to be good bosses and not so good bosses. If we wouldn't call up our child's boss ourselves, then why would we call the coach? If there is an issue that your son or daughter needs to communicate with coach, they should be the one communicating.

Mike Lingenfelter is director of Munciana volleyball, a nationally ranked program. He knows coaching. One of his young daughters had a particularly rough season with a basketball coach. At the end of the season, Mike met with the coach. He simply thanked the coach for his time that he devoted to the team. His wife, a bit confused, asked how he could actually thank the coach when they felt he did a poor job?

Lingenfelter understood that coaches make a sacrifice of time away from their own family, no matter the quality of their craft. He thanked the coach for his time, not for his coaching style, and that was all that needed to be said.

Coaches are an important part of our society. Anyone can count shots, laps or drills, but as coach Robert Taylor states, "we don't count reps, we coach reps." We can remember the coach who made an impact in our lives and became a hinge. The great coach that either made a deep and profound impact in our life or even the bad coach that showed us how not to operate or communicate.

Everyone can use a coach.

Unfortunately, coaches at large have stopped receiving their due appreciation. The opposite has occurred; they have become a lightning rod for parents. Parents complain, yell, and even write anonymous emails to the coaches themselves, administration or other parents. Coaches are pestered with questions focused on playing time such as "why didn't my kid start, or play more." Worse, coaches are questioned about other kids performance or strategy, for instance, "why is he/she playing," and "why did you do that play?"

Coaches at all levels sacrifice their time. If you don't coach, then you are awarded more freedom to finish your own business without having to show up early and leave late. It's your choice, we don't judge. But, if you do not step up to coach, you have forfeited your right to sit down and coach.

Parent Strategy: Thank the Cook

Coaches Mark James and Brian Satterfield end practice the same way, they shake each player's hand. Simple, yet powerful. No matter the type of practice or outcome of game, the ending is the same. It was created as a way to put a type of positive closure on a poor day, a way to end it positively. It takes more mental toughness to lift up one's head than it does to raise a trophy.

Players even started looking forward to the handshake. The worst punishment coach could ever deliver is telling one of their players, "I don't want to see you after practice." They would get it together pretty quick.

A positive ending is essential because we can't know the last time we are ever going to see someone. Travis Smith was a freshman golfer in college and we never had another chance to say goodbye after practice. He died in a car accident that weekend. His parents would have given anything to spend just a few more moments with him.

Money isn't the most precious resource, its time. End everything with a handshake and a thank you.

True Success

True success means rooting for everyone.

Duke Basketball fans have one of the most indelible student sections in all of the sports: the Cameron Crazies. They are beyond passionate camping out in Krzyzewskiville for three months prior to games. They are organized and witty, handing out cheat sheets for the student cheers and even coined the now famous "air-ball" chant.

Can you imagine that they once actually cheered for an opposing rival's player? During one game in 1995, Joe Smith of Maryland was unstoppable. He scored forty points against them, had eighteen rebounds, and had a tip-in basket as time expired to beat Duke, 94-92.[32] At the end of the game, after Duke lost, they applauded Joe Smith.

RFK Stadium in Washington, D.C. was considered one of the toughest places in the NFL for away teams to play. The stadium swayed with excitement from the crowd and the Washington fans were some of the most spirited. During a game in 1986 against the New York Giants, Coach Bill Parcells approached his quarterback Phil Simms and told him, *"They hate us so much that they like us."*

True success is being able to root for everyone.

It doesn't mean that we cheer or root for our direct competition. When I post this philosophy on-line, I'll get questions like, "Even the Yankees?"

When we root for others, it means that we are confident. Rooting for everyone means wanting to beat people at their best. It is honoring them for their talent and respecting them as fellow athletes. We should want them to play well, but just for us to play a little bit better. It doesn't take away from our drive or our hating to lose, but we need others to succeed so we know what we have to do to improve.

During the 2015 NBA Finals between the Cleveland Cavaliers and the Golden State Warriors, Kyrie Irving of the Cavaliers re-injured his knee. Steve Kerr, the head coach of the Warriors said, "I hope he can play the rest of the series. You probably don't believe me, but I mean that."[33]

Usually, though, we do the opposite. When others are successful, we are often threatened. Success reminds us of our shortcomings or as Bette Midler said, "the toughest part of success is trying to find others who are happy for you." Conflict between team members is based on the belief that success is limited. Therefore, not only do I need to be the best that I can be, but remove any obstacle in that path, including teammates vying for my position or record.

Parents, unfortunately, perpetuate this notion and encourage this culture as well. Whenever we call out or put down a coach or another child on the team, we are doing so based out of fear and insecurity. The child internalizes these discussions toward other players or coaches, and it teaches them the wrong thing—that it's okay to put others down.

The imaginary lines between towns and teams are witness to these conflicts as well. We spend so much time hating on the success of others that we lose all proportion and focus of improving our own game.

Great sports parents are confident enough in themselves to root for others and show the strength in lifting others up.

Off-Season

This time of the year has significantly been reduced because many fear any off-season. "No off-season" has also been romanticized in today's culture as a badge of honor. Frankly, an off-season is needed from a primary sport. Back when everyone still played multiple sports, there were other sports to play and the transition and break happened naturally. However, now the pressure to play only one sport does not allow for other sports at all.

Kids need rest and disengagement from their sport. The physical side is a huge part of the recovery, but more so is the need for emotional and psychological rest. Competing is stressful and going through mini-slumps and struggle is stressful. The main reason kids stop playing sports is because it is no longer fun. How much mental energy does it take to play five tournaments in a row?

The off-season is the time of year for honest reflection and assessment and time to de-stress and decompress. Encourage your child to stay active and participate in average kid activities. As Dr. Bernice Sorensen said, "a lost childhood is one of the greatest difficulties anyone has to overcome in adulthood."

I Love My Multi-Sport Athletes

Be the coach you wish you had.

—Martin Rooney

Bison once roamed North America and met the food needs of an entire population of indigenous people. Eventually, it was hunted merely for its hide and almost became extinct. Once as many as 60 million bison roamed the plains but in the 1900s that number was reduced to only 300. Thankfully, the numbers have returned to over 400,000.[34]

Like the bison, the multi-sport athlete has slowly been killed off. Playing multiple sports was once revered for the benefits it offered: fun, teamwork, creativity, self-governing, motivation, fitness, and confidence. However, lost somewhere between adolescence and puberty is the specialist, an athlete whose sole purpose is to try and excel at one sport.

The difference between the bison and the multi-sport athlete, however, is that humans could never domesticate the American Bison. We've been able to contain the multi-sport athlete under the guise of falling behind or getting hurt if they don't stick with it.

The latter, "You'll get hurt," is a major misnomer that has been shown to have the opposite effect. *Athletes who specialize have a greater rate of injury compared to non-specialized athletes.* John Smoltz was the first pitcher drafted in the hall of fame who had Tommy John surgery, a surgical procedure commonly prescribed due to overuse injury. Now, almost as many adolescents as professionals are having Tommy John surgery.[35]

"You'll get left out" is the true bison in the room.

The sports skills transfer. Eighty-seven percent of the draft picks in the 2015 NFL draft were multi-sport athletes. This isn't a one-year anomaly either. The average hovers around *70 percent*. All athletic movements transfer—quickness, running, jumping, agility, throwing. For example, the athletic movement of jumping for a basketball is similar and builds the same muscles needed to push off the blocks in swimming and have a good kick.[36]

Indian Wells Tennis Garden in California holds some of the best tennis tournaments every year. Next to the tennis stadium is a massive soccer field. You'll often see many European professional tennis players also playing soccer during tournament downtime. They are multi-sport athletes.

Multi-sport athletes have a greater sport I.Q. They develop a feel for any game they are playing. They are more creative and less mechanical in their approach. They look and move athletically. Conversely, a recent phenomenon in volleyball is that some players in college have never served a ball in competition, ever. There are now specialists inside of specialized athletes.

Multi-sport athletes learn to compete. Each sport is different and requires different levels of focus and resiliency. To become mentally tough, they need to be in different sports situations that test their resilience and ability to make a comeback. If they learn to compete early on, that skill will transfer into other areas as well. They'll be able to compete in anything.

Another benefit—burnout becomes less frequent in multi-sport athletes. How long do you think going to five showcase events and traveling each weekend in the summer to play remains fun? Trust me, once every single tournament becomes a *must do*, the fewer tournaments are. Keep your child's passion and fun alive by allowing breaks and time off.

- Elena Delle Donne was the top basketball recruit in the nation. However, she suffered from burnout and played volleyball her first year in college.

- Marcelo Chierighini was SEC swimmer of the year at Auburn University, a national champion, and Olympian; he didn't start swimming until age 16.

- Andy Roddick played high-school basketball for four years along with tennis.

- Dara Torres, the only U.S. swimmer to swim in five Olympic games, lettered in volleyball during her fifth year of eligibility at the University of Florida.

- Steve Nash played soccer, rugby, and basketball in high school.

- Pat McAfee, the punter in the NFL, played soccer at West Virginia University.

- Maverick McNealy, the top-ranked amateur golfer in the United States while at Stanford University, played hockey, soccer, and golf into his senior year at high school.

- NBA Hall of Famer Tim Duncan was a competitive swimmer who had goals of making the Olympic team.

Multi-sport athletes are better teammates. For example, if your son or daughter plays an individual sport as their primary, they can still garner all the benefits of teamwork in a team sport.

In college, all sports in one way or another are team sports. However, parents and even coaches tend to stress the opposite, coercing kids to specialize too early so they can improve, thereby bypassing the entire team concept in sports. High school sports in general are also going the way of the bison. If your son or daughter plays an individual sport as their primary, they can still garner all the benefits of teamwork in a team sport. Don't discount team play but instead encourage it. As Notre Dame Softball Head Coach Deanna Gumpf says when recruiting, "I love my multi-sport athletes."

What can be learned from playing different sports can be applied to the primary sport. The grit, tenacity, and will to compete are the traits that transfer across all sports.

A final point: The single-sport athlete isn't the worst culprit. It's the multi-sport specialist, the individual who plays on three or four teams for one sport. They specialize early for exposure, meaning they bounce around several different elite travel teams every year. This is the new wave of overlapping specialized sports, where an athlete spreads himself thin but keeps it within the single game.

Where is the time to play unorganized games? Remember fun?

Are You Quitting or Switching?

Persistence means you get one percent better every day,
~~no matter how you add it up.~~

—JAMES ALTUCHER

At the end of the Cold War the United States remained the lone superpower, but somewhere along the way adopted the old East German approach to sporting development. The best athletes were selected and sent to athletic boarding schools to develop their sporting skills. In China, children are tested on athletic qualities from ages 8 to 13. Flexible children are sent to diving and gymnastics camps, quick reflexes are sent to Ping-Pong, short-arms are guided to weight-lifting and so on.

Currently, systems are in place where if a child shows any level of talent, they are celebrated and elevated. They are encouraged to year-round training and playing. The *next level* verbiage gets tossed around.

Now, if they have a passion for it, by all means, go for it. However, if a child falls out of love or does not enjoy a sport, we must allow them an out. It's best to know the difference between switching sports and quitting.

Speaking with parents of elite U.S. divers, the question was asked, "Should we allow them to quit?" Our answer was YES! Now, we did cringe a little bit even as we said it, and the parent seemed disgusted at our response. Her daughter was probably in the room. Our response was based on the premise that the passion and love must be there, and no child can be forced to love a sport. It's challenging to get better at something if it is no longer fun. Many athletes have taken breaks from their sport to rediscover their passion and their why later on. Mental toughness is more often caught than it is taught.

One of the backbones to success is that to never give up. It was the first point in the book, *NO FEAR: A Simple Guide to Mental Toughness.*

The switching or quitting choice that many athletes face does not fall into the category of never giving up vs. giving up. Quitting and blaming have become more common in today's culture rather than perseverance and responsibility. That is also one of the goals that sport can provide. However, there is a lot more gray area to this situation, so it's best not to be so black and white.

Quitting involves dropping out and not wanting to go through the struggle that is inherent in the sport though the love is still there. Our role is to remain supportive and provide perspective to help see them through.

Switching involves taking a break from a bad situation. It's important to see the distinction and to know which your child is going through so that you can help them work through the decision to their best advantage.

The difference between switching and quitting may even take place in college. Blair Socci played volleyball at UCLA, became a starter, and made the elite eight her freshman year. Unfortunately, Blair hurt her knee at the beginning of her sophomore season. She didn't travel that season and quit the team after Christmas break after the team made the Final Four.

Or did she switch?

Blair wrote that she had "The newfound freedom to reinvent myself...I was invigorated and strangely at peace." She switched from playing volleyball at the highest level to channeling her focus into other things that she never had time before, including writing. When those around her tried to talk her out of it, she never regretted the decision and didn't look back. If it weren't for her injury and switching away from sport, she wouldn't have become a successful comedian and writer.[37]

Mentioning Money and Time

Commend, don't criticize.

"We are paying how much for lessons, and you play this way?"

"We've invested too much time to have you quit."

"This has to pay off."

"Boy, we sure have been doing this a long time."

"You'll take care of your momma one day."

Are these comments intended to increase motivation or pull rank as a parent?

Not all sports are created equal. You are probably already aware of the costs of participating. Depending on where you live, what sport your child plays, and what summer camps they attend, you may pay upwards of $4,000 to $10,000 each year, maybe more. These don't include costs incurred to attend tournaments.[38]

Research on scholarships of Division I athletes shows that behavior of a coach is most important for motivation. Motivation increased or decreased on how the scholarship was communicated to them. If a coach communicated the scholarship as informational (*you're good enough*), then motivation increased. However, if a coach used the scholarship as controlling (*you'll do this because you're on scholarship*), motivation decreased.[39]

The perception of money and time is what is crucial. If it is seen as a tool of information, it will increase motivation. If it is viewed as controlling, then motivation can wane.

As a parent, the role is to be supportive, not controlling. When money or time or the amount of sacrifice that you have made is brought up, it adds pressure. Students and athletes today are in the know; they are aware of cost and sacrifices. Due to the sacrifices made by parents, they often internalize their play and struggle as letting others down.

Discuss all pressure and uncomfortable topics in non-pressure and comfortable environments. Discussing money, time, and financial independence are essential. There is a place to discuss money and time. Communicating and planning from both ends are best discussed before and after every season, certainly not during the season or after bad outcomes.

The financial commitment can be expensive. If college is the goal, then the optimal situation is that money and resources have been invested wisely. Outside of the sports investment that may or may not pay off, financial security in terms of 529 savings or other investment options are advisable. Visit your financial planner or fiduciary to account for a plan B to pay for college rather than relying solely on athletic scholarships.

Parent Strategy: Soft Questions vs. Hard Questions

Basketball coach Jeff Van Gundy once stated, "talk about all pressure decisions and moments in non-pressure environments." His team and staff needed to communicate and be on the same page way before the game began. There needed to be no ambiguity on what play or who was going to take shots in certain situations. He couldn't call a time-out in a pressure-packed NBA game with 6 seconds left and then begin to discuss which play to implement. These were already discussed.

Communication is key and how we approach the two-way conversations can make a huge difference. Timing is vital and these discussions are best at the end of the season, not during when emotions are high and athletes are competing. How you approach these conversations can make incredible strides towards being either a vicarious or supportive parent.

Co-author, Bill Parisi has worked with tens of thousands of athletes and parents. He contends asking soft questions is preferable to asking hard questions. Consider the one-on-one environment when having this discussion as well as a safe environment, such as over breakfast or lunch. Soft questions are non-confrontational and seek to understand experience. Hard questions are more focused on facts and knowledge than on understanding.

Delve deeper into understanding their perspective without becoming defensive. A hard question: "Isn't that why we paid for lessons?" A soft question: "Tell me about what you learned from this season?"

Hard questions also often turn into statements that attempt to fix the struggle: " we will need to talk to coach earlier." As opposed to soft questions that don't try to solve the problem. "Wow, that sounds like it was tough." A hard question creates an ultimatum about the immediate future: "Do you want to play sports?" A soft question addresses possibilities: "What do you think about taking some time off?"

Kids want to impress their coaches and parents. They want your approval! We must allow them an out, the emotional space to make their choices, and ensure that this is a path they want to continue.

It is important to know your child because one approach for a child may not work for another. The communication style can vary, and we must coach ourselves. The hardest thing to do for some parents is to not over communicate. It is having the same discipline as a parent that we want for our kids. If we expect our child to control their emotions and effort on the athletic field, then we need to prove we can control our emotions when mentoring them through sports and life.

The Gateway Drug to Specialization

Sport teaches what we want it to teach

—JON AMAECHI

National Baseball Director Keith Madison showed tongue-in-cheek that kids in the Dominican Republic exclusively play travel ball. They travel to the field by walking and they compete. No trophies at these games. He commented that these kids are "excited to get a bottle of water, and elated to get a used ball, cap or glove."

Traveling too early is the gateway drug to sports specialization. Kids should not participate in extended travel before late middle school. A few tournaments during the summer are great fun and important for experience, but today these showcases and tournaments are scheduled every single weekend. They are scheduled for exposure, not experience. Hanging over the head of parents is *if they want to play at the next level.* We applaud yet wince when parents have two kids in different sports around the same age. Their lives are centered and split between the sports and travel.

There is a cost of traveling too early. It becomes expensive once they start traveling, but the larger cost is a cognitive bias. It becomes too easy to buy the *idea* that they now have to pick one sport and stay with it.

Once dollars are shoveled into a sport too soon, it may be too late. Two seasons of early travel and you've invested a lot of money. The cognitive bias is that it can't go to waste and the kid *should* now stay involved at the highest level, which means year-round, early specialization to improve rapidly. This process occurring before age 13 or 14 means it is a huge risk of taking over the child's life.

Later on, traveling to a set number of showcases or large tournaments is wonderful. It is a great experience. However, we've seen the number explode to sometimes a dozen or more per year. Every large showcase or tournament does not need to be attended; make sure to limit the number attending. Have a plan in place of when and how much to travel and trust your plan.[40]

Parent Strategy: Take Time OFF

Robert Taylor Jr., owner of Smarter Team Training, is one of the best in the sports performance industry. He labels time-off for athletes as a time to "de-stress and decompress."

Parents often question why their son or daughter plays awful after five straight weekends on the road in the summer. Sophomores in college athletics ponder why they are tired all of the time. Simply put, never-ending competition does not allow for peak performance.

Competing is stressful. Training is tough. Winning and losing both take their toll on an athlete's psyche. There is now more attention surrounding everyone's record and statistics that it can add to the stress of poor play. Mix in some poor sleep habits, tough classes, and a rigorous training schedule, and there is a recipe for poor play. It may seem oversimplified, but so often overlooked: take some time off. Your child may not, so you need to be the one leading this effort to rest.

Quality sleep is paramount for good health and optimal performance. Too many people are going to bed late and getting up early as a badge of honor. Again, they wonder why they get sick? Under-sleeping is a curse in disguise because sleep repairs the mind and body, especially when we are young and in college. Lack of sleep is like working out and never taking time off.

Bring Back Sandlot

Creativity can be taught.

Professor Matt Bowers from the University of Texas examined the link between adult creativity and youth sport. His team assessed adult levels of creativity and youth sports experiences. Results were revealing.[41]

Time spent playing informal sports showed a positive and significant correlation with creativity. On the other hand, time devoted only to formal sports participation revealed a negative relationship with creativity. Organized sports hurt a child's creativity.

A recent IBM study of 1,500 CEO's showed that creativity was the primary "leadership competency" of the future. There is a creativity crisis. In society, intelligence scores have progressed upwards on a linear plane. Each generation shows scores increasing by 10 points. Creativity scores, however, have reversed and plummeted.

Early childhood development stresses free-play as the catalyst for creativity. Watch any young kids making forts, becoming Superman or pretending to be dinosaurs. Soon, free-play and creativity is no longer revered. Schools no longer have time for it, and video games at home have trumped free time.

The professionalization of youth sports has led to the elimination of unorganized, unstructured free-play (*Remember The Sandlot?*). Practice and play are parent-run. An adult viewpoint toward play is imposed on kids.

Sports have morphed into a mutated version where parents dictate, call the shots, and hand out the trophies. This doesn't draw the fun out of the sport; it merely sucks out the creativity. All kids have to do is show up and parents get the kids to buy in. The ownership is missing. Everything is structured for them. Kids are much more creative when given the freedom. There are no more bottle caps as the touchdown line or cars as the out of bounds. Fewer teams are being decided by shooting for sides.

It is also important not to surround our athletes with a constant cheering section and fan club. We develop best with no crowds, no one to play for, and no pats on the back. Athletes need a chance to figure things out for themselves, but instead coaches are doing all the thinking for them. Even open gym has become structured.

When young kids run the show, they figure it out on their own. Pick-up and street games are self-governed, self-policed, and encourage problem-solving. Kids take ownership. What develops is mental toughness—the willpower to fight, stand-up for oneself, and to find a way.

Head coach Andy Dorrel at Culver Academy pointed out that before the advent of text messaging, we actually had to walk over to the others to set up a game. Remember that? If no one was there, we were still outside. Another outside activity was bound to happen. Now, if no one answers the text, we are still on the couch.

The message is clear: Allow time for unstructured, unsupervised play. Encourage your kids to get together with friends or play with them. The off-season isn't meant to be spent on the couch—it is merely free from the pressure of competing in front of crowds. The problem solving and creativity they develop will last longer than any trophy from the league.

Injured—Now What?

Injuries change the way you approach the game.

—BRETT FAVRE

Hall of fame athletic trainer Jenny Moshak worked alongside Pat Summit at the University of Tennessee for over 17 years. She treated injuries from nagging to the career-ending type. During one of her lectures she said, "An athlete who is injured goes through some depression."

She didn't mean clinical depression necessarily, although in some cases it's true. However, athletes go through feeling down, getting the blues, and can experience the negative thoughts and emotions that accompany depression.

Athletes deal with life through their sport and how they play. If they are playing well, a part of the team, and enjoying it, then all of life's problems fall into line. However, once an athlete becomes injured, every little problem becomes larger than life. Their coping mechanism has been removed and so they struggle and cannot deal. They may behave completely different, because their identity as an athlete is shaken.

Injuries are a catalyst for larger issues.

Often, athletes return to play too soon after an injury. They want to return and often will do whatever it takes. In the athlete's mind, they're feeling close to how they felt before the injury; however, after returning too fast, they soon discover they are off. They may feel fine for nine out of ten plays, but that one play where they can't cut, accelerate or move like before causes doubt.

Physically, it causes them to muscle guard and protect the injured area. Doubt, which has never been there before, is suddenly present. Doubt causes slight hesitations, over thinking or even trying to do too much. As a result of the doubt and less than stellar play, they lose confidence. It occurs at all levels and especially to the better players. Once an athlete loses confidence, it is extremely difficult to get it back.

Parent Strategy: The Injured Athlete

The role of the caregiver and coach is two-fold for injured athletes. First, ensure the athlete remains part of the team; stay included in travel, team functions, and especially practice. Second, stay in contact with the athlete and stay supportive, but relieve the pressure to return. Too often, injured athletes isolate themselves and start to internalize their struggle and don't reach out. Negative thoughts and feeling down can have a dramatic effect.

Sports Illustrated covered a story in 2015 involving injured athletes, however the authors addressed how the use of painkillers has transitioned into full-blown heroin abuse. Sadly, there is an epidemic in the United States involving prescription drug abuse and athletes are a sub-set.[42]

No athlete who gets injured says to themselves "I want to become an addict," their only goal at the time is to return to play. After a serious injury, they'll receive a prescription for an opioid painkiller such as Oxycontin, Percocet, or Vicodin. The athletes who take painkillers immediately become at-risk. Research revealed that high school male athletes are four times more likely to misuse painkillers than non-male athletes. The negative progression can spiral down fast because once their pills are no longer available an athlete will seek out other pills or cheaper means to maintain the painkiller high. The transition to heroin is actually fairly seamless since the molecular make-up of opioids is almost identical. They begin by smoking it and later injecting it.

Unfortunately, we've seen the progression. Prevention is key because there is no fast track or executive course to recovery. Opiate dependency is an on-going addiction that affects the entire family and community. Unfortunately if the community at large has an issue, it is safe to assume that the athletes themselves are part of it. You know your kids patterns so trust your gut when it comes to recognizing signs and behaviors. For example, do they complain about hurting but suddenly are no longer in pain? Has your own medicine cabinet been depleted? Are they sometimes sleeping in their same clothes? As advocate Marcus Amos states, "you can't prevent it, but you can prevent from participating in it." Further information on prescription dependency can be accessed through Centers for Disease Control and Prevention at www.cdc.gov.

Next Season

Life is not a dress rehearsal.

—Herm Edwards

At some point, all athletic careers end. It used to be the end of high school when this took place, but more recently, 85 percent drop out of sports by the age of 14. When they drop out from the sport so early, the long-term benefits haven't had a chance to take hold.

The saddest part, however, is that they simply stop playing. Think about it: How often in your life do you currently play? Hopefully, we do but often life gets in the way. They have their entire lives to grow up, but only one childhood to play and develop the love of playing. An adult viewpoint on youth athletics causes the fun to diminish and why would they pursue something that isn't really about having fun, but more about the external reward of playing at the next level?

This section is devoted to our IDENTITY—who are we and what our values, our real contributions are.

Who You I is Not Who You R

What do you want to BE is different
~~than what do you want to DO.~~

Curious why many high-profile athletes return to sport even after they retire? It's the same reason many professional athletes struggle with life issues when their career is over.

Elite athletes spend such a considerable amount of time on achieving their goals and these years include sacrifices both in and out of the sport. When they leave the sport, there is the immediate void that practicing and competition once filled. Being an athlete was their identity.

Then there are others who do not take on the athlete as their identity but rather, it is a role they are playing for a season in their life— something they do. These are the ones who successfully and easily transition out of the sport.

There is a huge difference between our identity and role. When we confuse these two, a struggle occurs. Athletes are the largest section of society that struggles with confusing one's identity with their roles. Our identity (I) is who we are, whereas our role (R) is what we do. Who you I is not who you R. Although important, the role of an athlete is just part of their identity. The family identity becomes wrapped up in the athletic success as well.

Dr. Mark Robinson's book *Athletic Identity* states that athletes not only play sports for the competition, but also for the entitlement and social aspect, including rewards, gifts, and social interactions. The entitlement factor shapes the athlete's world-view and their identity. When young athletes are treated like the cat's meow for their role, their identity can become skewed. And this is only the positive aspects we are considering in shaping our athletic role.[43]

We rarely look at how the negative features of being an athlete can affect our identity. For instance, specializing as a youth athlete closes off growth alternatives to one's identity. Johnny's identity as a star second-baseman is great until he is no longer the star second-baseman. Now he must struggle to find multiple identities, many which have been closed off because all he was known for is being a star second baseman. At some point, ceasing to play will occur for *every* athlete.

Social Media and Technology

The web has scaled everything down.

Kevin DeShazo, the founder of Fieldhouse Media, teaches social media best practices to collegiate and high school students. To illustrate the importance of social media, he tells a story that when Facebook was created, his first profile picture was actually of him picking his nose. And social media education is his profession.

Social media has completely changed the face of athletics, especially in the last ten years. Emojis, memes, GIF's, and vines, for example, have become part of the culture in just the past few years. Social media has scaled everything down so that what people were previously ignorant to is now widely known in a matter of minutes.[44]

Pat Welch won New Hampshire basketball player of the year. But after the state title game, which his team won, he lost the award. What never could have existed 10 years ago has changed the game. Pat made a poor decision: a bad tweet directed toward the team they had just beat. The tweet was only on-line for 15 minutes before he removed it however, the damage had been done. The basketball coaches retracted his award.[46]

On the positive side, a highlight film of an athletic performance shared on social media can delight millions of people in mere moments. On the flip side, an ill-advised post can now dampen a kid's future in a matter of seconds, with no way to take it back. It's amazing how much power each on-line post can have—and almost instantaneously—whether positive or negative. Once it is out there, it is influencing. College coaches follow possible recruits long before they can speak to them. Penn State assistant football coach Herb Hand tweeted out: *Dropped another prospect this AM due to his social media presence ... Glad I got to see the "real" person before we offered him.*[45]

This area of social media and technology is but one facet of how life has changed for our athletes. What is perhaps more important is the impact social media has created on our children's identity. Before, an athlete would have to search diligently for another player's talent level and performance. However, now, since the web has scaled everything down, comparison amongst athletes and parents is rampant. Comparison is the thief of all joy. The constant evaluation of others across many time zones can cause increased stress.

Your son or daughter will have a complete on-line profile before the time they are teenagers. Social media allows us to create a perception of how we want others to view us. To the average social media viewer, it would appear that everyone else is happy, beautiful, and successful leading the perfect life. We are often guilty of this misrepresentation too. How many of us post bad photos of ourselves?

If everyone else is perfect, and we are feeling sad or not good enough, this perception creates enhanced feelings of anxiety and perfectionism. Social media has exacerbated this level of comparison.

Madison Holleran was a beautiful, successful 19-year-old track athlete at the University of Pennsylvania. She was also a perfectionist who struggled with depression. Sadly, she took her own life during her freshman year. What is interesting about this occurrence is the role that she portrayed via social media. On Instagram, she would post pictures often that communicated the life she wanted others to see. Few could have been able to see the signs of a struggle.[47]

Social media has created another avenue to have difficult conversations. As parents, we are in charge of shaping our kid's identity and helping them differentiate it from their role.

Parent Strategy: Remove the Distraction

Communication is key to any successful relationship, whether it is between a player-coach, administrator-coach, spouse-spouse, or player-player. Sports like volleyball and basketball require constant communication. Teammates cannot text to one another on the court or field that they are open.

The volleyball team at Ohio Northern University had a strategy to increase communication among the team. They removed the biggest distraction to effective interactions. Before every road trip, every player put their phone in a basket for coaches to collect and the coaches returned their phones when they arrived back at campus. Some of us may cringe just thinking about giving up our phone.

The coaches realized that on the road trips, phones caused everyone to have their head down and in their own world, they would not talk with one another, they would text to their teammate behind them. The bus was often silent.

When coaches removed the phones, they talked with one another, joked around, and interacted. Communication improved. It made a vast difference not only off the court but on the court as well.

When the coaches returned the phones, it became a funny contest about how many hundreds of text messages each received. They also reverted quickly back the solo version of communication.

Phones and social media were an issue that coaches or parents 10 or more years ago did not have to encounter. Nonetheless, the coaches made an executive decision that was not popular at the time but was best for the team.

Scott McNealy, the father of top-ranked Stanford University golfer Maverick McNealy, placed specific guidelines on electronic device usage inside of the home. No phones or any electronics inside of the bedroom. The reasoning was that the bedroom was meant for sleeping and anything else was a distraction. Even studying was done outside of the bedroom.[48]

It was suggested to another parent seeking advice for his son's disrespectful behavior to remove his son's phone as a punishment. He dismissed the idea as foreign and exclaimed, "I could never do that!" This same father also refused to remove his son's activity of basketball. He viewed both as rights rather than privileges.

This is a more advanced time with more distractions than before. Technology has made most everything accessible and anonymous, which means free reign. As NFL coach Dick Vermeil stated, "Teams respond to discipline and attention to detail." We must not be afraid to make difficult decisions and set parameters about phones and electronics.

Our families should have guidelines in place of no phones at the dinner table. When you value the precious time that families spend together, phones simply interrupt.

Conclusion

Be the change you want to see in the world.

—GANDHI

In basketball, a popular move is the head fake, which gets the defender going one way while the dribbler goes the other way. So, here's the head fake. Hopefully, we think about how we can help our son or daughter with their mental toughness. But we need to start with ourselves. Our kids are not a reflection of our parenting, just a shadow.

We can't parent our kids to be more relaxed or mentally tough if we don't possess that quality. Our daughter won't listen to mom about her body image if mom doesn't value her body. If we are not patient or react badly when we lose our keys, then our kids will mirror this behavior. If we lose trust in others around us and blame and criticize, then our kids will serve as our shadow.

Being a supportive parent is difficult. Mental toughness is needed. It certainly hasn't gotten easier in today's culture, because there are so many more distractions. We are going to mess up and make mistakes. Remember, it's not about the setback; it's about the comeback. What's important is that we do the next right thing. When we do a poor job, own up to it. The key is to know that we can make adjustments and to show these adjustments. We can auto-correct when we notice that we've started talking about being nervous, discussing the game on the ride home, or putting more emphasis on winning rather than effort.

Our role as a parent is just part of our identity. It is a positive thing if we are not too wrapped up in our kid's lives. Some vicarious parents feel that their child's performance completely represents them. It can cause us as parents to stress out and lose perspective on the overall goal.

As we come to the close of this book, hopefully, you have gained a better understanding of how not to should on your kids. As you consider what you have just read, it is my hope you will have seen yourself in these words, or a vision of yourself you wish not to become.

Parenting Strategy: Ask the Right Questions

There is a saying—there's a good reason, and then there is the real reason. With that in mind, we want you to consider some of these important questions to ask yourself. Talk them over with your significant other. The way you answer these questions may give you a glimpse into whether you have been *shoulding* on your kid, and perhaps require an adjustment of direction.

- Why do you want your son or daughter to participate in sports?

- What do you want your child to become outside of sport?

- How much value do you place on academics?

- How often do we discuss winning and expectations as opposed to the effort?

The team that makes the fewest mistakes will win.

–GENERAL NEYLAND

The above is the first maxim created in the 1930's still used in football circles. Most games are lost more than they are won. This is true not only in sports and life but also in parenting.

There is not a one size fits all mentality to building mental toughness. Much of it depends on situations and experiences. For example, an injured athlete recovers better if they have been injured before because they cope with it better. We are going to make mistakes; that's not the goal. The objective is to become better ourselves so we can help our children become better.

One sharp word of criticism after a game or practice will do more harm than ten positive affirmations. It only takes one. We all can recall the incident when we felt shamed by a coach, family member or friend. There was so much emotion with the occurrence that it left a huge impression. With some of us, it became damaging.

Parenting out of anger or fear simply does not work. We need to be strategic and have a plan of helping our child build mental toughness. If our presence and feedback do not help our children, it will be difficult to handle, but that is the objective of not allowing it to be about us. It is sometimes better not to say anything than it is to make a mistake that loses the game.

Commend, don't criticize. Everyone has different shortcomings and weaknesses, and these are what cause us to lose games. Remember the goal.

References

1. Popper, N. (2014, January 26). Committing to Play for a College, Then Starting 9th Grade. New York Times.

2. Atkinson, J. (2014, May 4). How parents are ruining youth sports - The Boston Globe

3. Valovich McLeod, T. C., Decoster, L. C., Loud, K. J., Micheli, L. J., Parker, J. T., Sandrey, M. A., & White, C. (2011). National Athletic Trainers' Association Position Statement: Prevention of Pediatric Overuse Injuries. *Journal of Athletic Training*, 46(2), 206–220

4. Butler, S. (2011, April 29). $4,000 for Youth Baseball: Kids' Sports Costs Are Out of Control. *CBSNEWS*.

5. Calonia, J. (2014, August 3). These Are the 5 Most Expensive Sports for Kids | GOBankingRates.

6. Osterman, Z., & Neddenriep, K. (2014, April 25). Number of college basketball transfers escalating for various reasons. *Indy Star*.

6b. Hoyt, E. (2015, February 3). New Trend: Parents Moving to College with Their Students. *Fastweb*.

7. Karpf, R. (Director). (2013). *The Book of Manning* [Motion picture]. ESPN Home Entertainment.

8. Frank, R. (2013, October 16). Spanx billionaire's secret to success: Failure. *CNBC*.

9. Couric, K. (2009, Feb 8). Flight 1549: A Routine Takeoff Turns Ugly CBS: *60 Minutes*

10. Akelson, M. (2010, May 9). Super Starks: The Story and Legacy of John Starks. *Bleacher Report*.

11. Gibney, A. (Director). (2011). *Catching hell* [Motion picture]. ESPN Home Entertainment.

12. Mello, I. (2015, January 30). Super Bowl 49: Not one starter was a 5-star recruit out of high school. *CBS Sports*.

13. Peebles, M. (Director). (2011). *Herschel* [Motion picture]. ESPN Home Entertainment.

14. Gould, D., Dieffenbach, K., & Moffett, A. (2002) Psychological Characteristics and Their Development in Olympic Champions, *Journal of Applied Sport Psychology*, 14:3, 172-204.

14b.   Dell'antonia, K.J. (2015, September 8). Odds are, Your sport playing child isn't going pro. Now what? *The New York Times*.

15.   College Athletic Scholarship Limits - Scholarship Stats.com. (2013).

16.   Daniels, T. (2015, August 14). Cordell Broadus, Snoop Dogg's son gives up football. *Bleacher Report.*

17.   Holland, K & Schoen, J. (2014 October 14). Think athletic scholarships are the 'holy grail'? Think again. *ETNBC.com*

18.   Abrami, A. (2015, July 7). McRoberts leaves University of Vermont men's basketball. *Burlington Free Press*.

19.   Westham, A. (2014, February 27). Cardinal athletes weigh decisions to quit. *The Stanford Daily.*

20.   Tracking Transfer in Division I Men's Basketball. (2014, November 1). *NCAA.org*

21.   Nadeau, R. (2014, June 27). Size Matters: College Football's Biggest Offensive Linemen. *SportsNOLA.*

22.   Ringler, L. (2015, May 7). Deeper field, new format could create an NCAA postseason for the books. *GOLFWEEK.*

23.   Epstein, D. (2013). *The sports gene: Inside the science of extraordinary athletic performance.* London: Penguin Books

24.   Bell, R. (2012). *Mental Toughness Training for Golf.* Authorhouse.

25.   Miller, G. (1956). The magical number seven, plus or minus two: Some limits on our capacity for processing information. *Psychological Review* 63 (2): 81–97.

26.   (September 6, 2014). Stellar rookie performance overshadowed by Women's National Team's extra-inning loss. *Baseball Canada.*

27.   Pelham, B., Mirenberg, M., & Jones, J., (2002). Why Susie sells seashells by the seashore: Implicit egotism and major life decisions. *Journal of Personality and Social Psychology*, 82(4) 469-487.

28.   Bell, R. (2015). *NO FEAR: A Simple Guide to Mental Toughness.* DRB Press.

29.   Gregiore, C. (2015, April 1). Google makes you think you're smarter than you actually are. T*he Huffington Post.*

30.   Wrzeniewski, A., & Schwartz, B. (2014, July 4). The Secret of Effective Motivation. *The New York Times.*

31.   Moor, B. (2015, May 17). Cheering Parents May Be Too Abundant. *South Bend Tribune.*

32. Markus, D. (1995, March 2). Smith put-back helps Maryland put down Duke. *The Baltimore Sun*.

33. ASAP Sports Transcripts (2015, June 4). NBA Finals- Cavaliers vs. Warriors Steve Kerr.

34. Shaw, J. (1995). How many bison originally populated western rangelands?. *Rangelands*, 148-150.

35. Loyola University Health System. (2013, April 19). Intense, specialized training in young athletes linked to serious overuse injuries. *ScienceDaily*.

36. Cook, B. (2015, May 8). What It Means To Youth Sports That Multi-Sport Athletes Dominated NFL Draft. *Forbes*.

37. Socci, B. (2013, December 5). IT HAPPENED TO ME: I Worked My Entire Life To Play Division I College Volleyball And Then Quit When I Got There. *Xojane.com*

38. Koba, M. (2014, January 13). Spending big on kids' sports? You're not alone. *CNBC.com*

39. Medic, N., Mack, D., Wilson, P., & Starkes, J. (2007). The Effects of Athletic Scholarships on Motivation in Sport. *Journal of Sport Behavior*, 30(3), 292-306.

40. Martinez, V. (2015, May 21). Being a great sports parent. *El Paso Times*.

41. Bowers, M., Green, B., Hemme, F., & Chalip, L. (2014). Assessing the Relationship Between Youth Sport Participation Settings and Creativity in Adulthood. *Creativity Research Journal*, 314-327.

42. Wertheim, J. L., & Rodriquez, K. (2015, June 22). Smack Epidemic: How painkillers are turning young athletes into heroin addicts. *Sports Illustrated*.

43. Robinson, M. (2014). *Athletic identity: Invincible and invisible, the personal development of the athlete*. First edition design publishing.

44. Patsko, S. (2015, February 3). How social media behavior of high school athletes can negatively impact NCAA recruiting: Photos, polls National Signing Day 2015.

45. Newport, K. (2014, March 28). New Hampshire HS Basketball player of the year loses award after obscene tweet. *Bleacher Report*.

46. Boren, C. (2014, July 30). Penn State assistant says football recruit was dropped over 'social media presence.' *The Washington Post*.

47. Fagan, K. (2015, May 7). Split Image. *ESPNW*.

48. Newport, J. (2015, May 8). The Golf Upstart of Silicon Valley. *The Wall Street Journal*.

CPSIA information can be obtained
at www.ICGtesting.com
Printed in the USA
BVHW032041050619
549930BV00014B/387/P